WHEN THEY COME FOR YOU

ALSO BY DAVID KIRBY

Death at SeaWorld

Animal Factory

Evidence of Harm

CONTENTS

AUTHOR'S NOTE ix

PREFACE xiii

1. WHEN COPS BURST THROUGH YOUR DOOR:
WARRANTLESS HOME RAIDS 1

2. L'ENFANT C'EST MOI—CHILD PROTECTIVE SERVICES
AND STATE-SPONSORED KIDNAPPING 32

3. YOUR MONEY OR YOUR FREEDOM 73

4. WHEN POLICING PAYS FOR ITSELF 96

5. FREE SPEECH AND THE INDIVIDUAL AMERICAN 131

6. PROTESTORS, THE PRESS, AND AN EMBATTLED FIRST AMENDMENT 203

7. STATE POWER RUN AMOK 261

8. COPS, COURTS, AND JAILS 308

AFTERWORD 333

ACKNOWLEDGMENTS 339

NOTES 343

INDEX 369

First published in the United States by St. Martin's Press, an imprint
of St. Martin's Publishing Group

www.stmartins.com

Designed by Steven Seighman

The Library of Congress Cataloging-in-Publication Data is available upon request.

ISBN 978-1-250-06436-3 (hardcover)
ISBN 978-1-4668-7005-5 (e-book)

First Edition: October 2019

10 9 8 7 6 5 4 3 2 1

WHEN THEY COME FOR YOU

HOW
POLICE AND GOVERNMENT
ARE TRAMPLING OUR LIBERTIES—
AND HOW TO TAKE
THEM BACK

David Kirby

ST. MARTIN'S PRESS ✹ NEW YORK

For Todd Shuster and George Witte, the best agent and editor
that any writer could ever have

Americans who have had their guns taken away without probable cause or due process. I support rational gun reform laws, and I personally dislike firearms, but I also support Second Amendment rights to gun ownership. And, as Justice Antonin Scalia argued in the landmark *Heller v. District of Columbia* case, the amendment does not preclude limits on certain types of weapons or the manner in which they are sold. If I truly believed that the right to keep and bear arms was under attack in today's America, I would have explored the controversy amid these pages.

What follows are the stories of individuals who have felt the brunt of the government's power. I have told these stories from the victims' perspectives, based on their allegations in legal documents, in media reports, and, in many cases, interviews with me. It should be understood that the government actors often dispute these depictions and that some continue to believe that they were acting within the law and in the best interests of their communities. In a few of the circumstances I relate in this book, the courts have agreed. However, in many cases, the victims have sought relief from the courts, won settlements, and effected real change.

AUTHOR'S NOTE

Of the four investigative books that I have written, this was by far the most challenging. Choosing what to include, and how to do justice to hundreds of individual stories, was less difficult than deciding what *not* to include. Each chapter, with its extensive legal backstory, offered material rich enough to warrant an individual book on its own. Space limitations did not allow me to include much of the research and interviews I had conducted to illuminate the stories.

And what of the material that did not make the final draft? Over my five years of research, I considered other trends that fall under the rubric of government overreach. Such crucial matters included reproductive rights, perennially under assault in courts and statehouses; treatment of undocumented immigrants, and their small children, who are entitled to the same Bill-of-Rights protections against government abuse guaranteed to all people on American soil; the federal crackdown on medical and recreational marijuana, especially in the Obama years; and the horrendous treatment of Muslim Americans at ports of entry to the United States.

The omission that I regret the most, perhaps, is the threat to voting rights in the United States. Indeed, an entire book could, and should, be written about the 2018 midterm elections, when active voter suppression and voter-roll purging, aimed largely at African Americans, Native Americans, students, and other populations, were carried out with varying degrees of success in states like Georgia, Florida, North Dakota, Texas, New Hampshire, and elsewhere.[1]

One final hot-button issue that I chose to omit was the battle over the Second Amendment. Why? Because I could find few stories of law-abiding

*The Constitution is not an instrument for the government to restrain the people;
it is an instrument for the people to restrain the government.*
—PATRICK HENRY

*I believe every individual is naturally entitled to do as he pleases
with himself and the fruits of his labor, so far as it in
no way interferes with any other men's rights.*
—ABRAHAM LINCOLN

PREFACE

October 4, 2018—The people profiled in the pages that follow no doubt believed in the statements at the opening of this book. They believed that if you obeyed the letter of the law, then you had nothing to worry about. But their belief in a just government—and in justice itself—was forever shattered the day that federal, state, or local authorities came for them.

This book, then, is for everyone else—for those hundreds of millions of Americans who remain skeptical that their lives could ever be upended by overzealous or trigger-happy police, unethical investigators, corrupt prosecutors, indifferent or malevolent judges, and power-hungry bureaucrats at all levels of government. These people—all representing the government—have aggressively threatened the safety, peace of mind, and civil rights of everyday citizens who were simply—and in most cases legally—going about their daily lives.

When I first began researching this book, nearly five years ago, many people I knew regarded it as an earnest civics project. Today, they tell me the subject is of the utmost urgency. I hear it from many people I know—from Far Left friends to those who voted for Donald Trump and still support him, if somewhat less enthusiastically than they once did. Perhaps their fading allegiance stems from Trump's documented record of assaulting the civil and constitutional rights of millions in this country.

But it remains critical to state: The steady erosion of liberties that we witness daily, and the corresponding uptick in state-sanctioned abuse of citizens, did not begin with the Trump administration. (Although matters have, I would argue, grown considerably worse since January 20, 2017.) As we shall see in these pages, the Obama years were also marked by dark patterns of official abuse: spying on the media; prosecuting state leakers; monitoring and sometimes repressing political activists; aggressively seizing the civil assets of innocent Americans; viciously prosecuting legal cannabis growers, distributors, and consumers—and much more. Given Obama's progressive public rhetoric, I was taken aback to discover the Obama administration's shameful record on legal and judicial matters.

It is my sincere hope that people of all political stripes will find the lessons in this book not only compelling but politically universal. Everyone should be unsettled by the stories that I have curated here as they come to realize that something similar *could* happen to them or to someone they love. Indeed, this book is neither liberal nor conservative in scope. To paraphrase the noted libertarian expression: When the state's boot is on your throat, it doesn't matter if it's a left boot or a right boot.

I consider myself a leftist libertarian—or "leftitarian," as some people have dubbed the concept. It may sound ideologically oxymoronic, but it is not. As a progressive who grew up in California and spent most of my adulthood in New York City, I am hardly anti-government. In fact, I worked in New York City government for a number of years and witnessed firsthand how dedicated public servants can accomplish miracles for ordinary citizens. I still maintain that taxpayer money should fund quality schools, clean parks, safe streets, solid infrastructure, protection of our fragile environment, and access to affordable food and medicine that will not kill us because it was not tested properly by authorities. On the other hand, I have *always* cast a jaundiced eye upon the powers exerted by government authorities—no matter who is in office, no matter how beguiling their promises. As much as I admire good government, I don't always trust it. I have seen the damage done when its powers grow unchecked, out of control.

In short, leftitarians neither hate government nor love government. We see it as necessary, but we never forget that the potential for abuse of power is always lurking behind the walls of buildings of the state.

When I was coming of age in 1970s California, dislike and distrust of nearly all things governmental was widespread, especially among the young. Consider the evidence of the era: Vietnam, Watergate, and the Pentagon Papers dominated the headlines. We hated Nixon. We hated the draft. We hated the National Guard, local police, and antidrug agents. Our generation's guiding motto was omnipresent. You saw it on T-shirts, on buttons, on the bumpers of Volkswagen vans rumbling up and down the coast. It was simple, stark, and eloquent: QUESTION AUTHORITY.

That motto of my youth endures. I still do not want any government, no matter how well-meaning, to proscribe what I can eat, drink, and inhale, whom I can and cannot marry, and what I can and cannot do with my words, beliefs, property, or person, as long as it inflicts no injury upon others.

In gathering and analyzing the stories of these people whose rights—and lives—were unjustly assaulted, I have arrived at two pressing questions for the authorities responsible for these miscarriages of justice: Just because you have the power to do something, does that mean you have the legal and moral right? And even if you *do* have the right, does that give you justification to carelessly and rashly exercise it?

My book documents many real-life stories in today's America—shocking, terrifying, deeply depressing, and heartbreaking sagas of the human costs of government overreach. But you should also consider this book to be a call to action, a beacon of hope and inspiration. As you will read, victims of state crimes who mustered their wits, resources, and—often—outside help challenged the abuse of power inflicted upon them and, in many cases, prevailed.

This book is about the threat of losing our rights. But it's even more about taking back—and preserving—those rights. In the face of overreaching government, it is up to us, the American people, to protect and defend the Constitution of the United States. The Bill of Rights has largely (though not entirely) shielded us from domestic tyranny for nearly 230 years. As the inheritors and stewards of this extraordinary document, we have no choice but to guard its protections jealously, rather than wrongly—and fatally—take them for granted. Fighting back, standing up, being counted—that is America at its best. And those are the best ways to prevent having our most fundamental rights yanked from beneath us. Vigilance matters.

One of the most eloquent landmark decisions of the U.S. Supreme Court came in the 1943 case *West Virginia v. Barnette,* in which the court ruled 6–3 that students cannot be compelled to say the Pledge of Allegiance in class. In his majority opinion, Justice Robert H. Jackson wrote that "one's right to life, liberty and property, to free speech, free press, freedom of worship and assembly and other fundamental rights may not be submitted to vote."[1]

In other words, these, our most basic and cherished liberties, are not sub-ject to the outcome of any election, political whim, or ideological trend. No elected official, nor their appointed deputies, can strip us of our natural-born rights without the severest of consequences.

That is, of course, unless we let them.

WHEN THEY COME FOR YOU

1

WHEN COPS BURST THROUGH YOUR DOOR: WARRANTLESS HOME RAIDS

You are relaxing with your family at home one evening when a band of armed thugs crashes through the door and invades your house. Their shouting is terrifying. Glass breaks, walls are smashed, and your children scream. When the men grab you, you resist, so they beat you and use a stun gun—or maybe even a real gun—against you. You are now battered and bloody, frightened and confused. The home invaders wrench you and your loved ones from your sanctuary and, in the dark of night, whisk you away in a car.

Now imagine these hooligans are wearing uniforms and badges.

Your home is your castle, impervious to entry by any agent of the state unless you grant them permission, or if they show up with a warrant signed by a judge—with the exception of certain emergency situations.

But some cops don't see it that way. They all but ignore the Fourth Amendment and its protections against "unreasonable search and seizure."

You may think you are safe in the security and privacy of your four walls. So did the people profiled here. As with so many issues concerning abridgment of civil liberties, you never know it can happen until it happens to you.

The nation's founders wisely created the Fourth Amendment to act as a personal firewall against overzealous policing:

The right of the people to be secure in their persons, houses, papers, and effects, against unreasonable searches and seizures, shall not be violated, and no Warrants shall issue, but upon probable cause, supported by Oath or affirmation, and particularly describing the place to be searched, and the persons or things to be seized.

The amendment protects us against warrantless searches and raids of places where we have a "legitimate expectation of privacy"—legally defined as an expectation that is generally accepted by society as being "reasonable."

But what is reasonable and what is not? That question has been rigorously litigated in U.S. courts for decades. In making a determination, courts must strike a balance between protecting privacy rights and maintaining the legitimate interests of the state, such as upholding public safety. Unfortunately, in recent decades marked by violent crime and the growing threat of terrorism, the needle seems to be gradually shifting away from privacy concerns and toward government interests.

In certain cases, police can search "persons, houses, papers, and effects" without a warrant. Chief among them is an "exigent circumstance"—an emergency situation where delaying action in order to obtain a warrant is not feasible, including when someone's life or safety is at stake, when a suspect is about to escape, or when evidence is about to be removed or destroyed. Police also don't need a warrant to search a person or property when the search is related to a lawful arrest or if the suspected illegal items to be seized are in plain sight.

But citizens still have the ability to demand that their Fourth Amendment rights be upheld when their expectation of privacy is being violated—and to seek redress from the courts when in fact it has been.

Consider the Magas family. When the police showed up at their Maryland home one night during a birthday party to investigate allegations of underage drinking, the family had every right to refuse the cops' demand for entry. The officers, who had no warrant, had already entered onto their property, peered into the backyard area, and spotted young people drinking from plastic cups. In that rear space, protected from street view, the family had a reasonable expectation of privacy.

But the cops didn't see it that way.

The Magases' hometown of Damascus, Maryland, rests in a bucolic corner of Montgomery County, about forty miles northwest of Washington. On the outskirts rise some large custom-built houses, well spaced across towering trees and clipped lawns, including the Magas family home, a three-story, 5,900-square-foot residence with three acres, a pool, and a five-car garage, set far back from Damascus Road.

George Magas, a long-established member of the community with a successful at-home CPA practice, moved there in 2002 with his wife, Cathy, and their four sons, star football players at high school in the mostly white, mostly upper-middle-class town of eleven thousand.

The close-knit family spent a lot of time together, and George and Cathy were active in the community, supporting several youth groups with time and money. George had coached the high school football, baseball, and basketball teams, and Cathy kept busy with the football team's booster club and served as team mother.

Life was good. But that all changed on one Saturday evening, January 4, 2014.

It was a punishing winter night, with plummeting temperatures and snow on the ground from a recent storm. But that didn't deter about forty-five people from attending their son Nicholas's twenty-first birthday party. The younger guests gathered downstairs in the large finished basement, where cold beer in cases and a half keg awaited them, even though some were under twenty-one.

Upstairs, George, Cathy, and about five friends—including Tom Stack, a seasoned detective for the Montgomery County Police Department—were watching football and enjoying pizza delivered from the local Papa John's. This being a small town, they knew the delivery guy; he'd gone to school with their kids, and his father was an acquaintance. Just before midnight, they brought a cake downstairs, and everyone sang "Happy Birthday."

George and Cathy had no idea that, as they headed down to the basement, a text was being delivered to the Montgomery County Police Department's Alcohol Initiatives Section:

> Hey man, not sure if your working but if your not busy there I just de-
> livered a pizza to a party at [xxxx] Damascus rd and saw some young
> looking people with beer.

Yes, the pizza guy turned in his own customers.

The police department forwarded the tip to Officer Jeremy Smalley and Montgomery County sheriff's deputy John Durham, who were both working on the Alcohol Initiatives Section's Holiday Task Force.

No one saw Smalley and Durham as they pulled up in an unmarked black van and parked next door at Saint Paul's Catholic Church. They quietly crossed onto the Magases' property and moved toward the rear of the house, where an outdoor stairwell leads to the basement. The police could hear the sounds of a party. Through binoculars, Durham spotted young people laughing and drinking from red plastic cups. One young man was urinating in the bushes. Based solely on those observations, Smalley and Durham determined there was probable cause to suspect underage drinking.

The persistent lawmen made their way past the detached garage to the rear corner of the house. There they saw another young man urinating who, to them, appeared to be under twenty-one.

Durham walked to the top of the stairwell and peered down, spotting three individuals at the bottom, "appearing to be underage with half a keg and all holding solo cups with Amber beverage," his partner Smalley wrote in the police report.[1] "And they're taking a selfie." Durham demanded ID and determined all three were under twenty-one. He seized their smartphone as evidence.

They called in backup from the Alcohol Initiatives Section to cordon off the property, lest anyone tried to flee.

What happened after that is deeply disputed.

The Magases' version of events differs wildly from the police report. George said that he and his wife, Cathy, had gone back upstairs when they saw a flashlight streaming through the windows. George walked into the kitchen and spotted two uniformed officers peering through the window. He opened the door, stepped outside, and asked what they were doing.

"They said they had a suspicion of an underage drinking party here and were very adamant about smelling marijuana," George recalled.[2] "And I said, 'Well, there's no marijuana, I can't smell any here. And I don't think any underage drinking's going on, either.'"

To George, the men seemed to be itching for a confrontation. "I felt like I was in a boxing ring, and I started getting a little scared because they were rocking back and forth and trying to egg me on," he said.

George had no stomach for a fight with the cops. Instead, he offered to fetch his driver's license to identify himself. Walking back into the kitchen, he saw Nicholas and told him to lock the door. "I really don't trust them. I'm scared," he said. He got the license and rejoined the cops waiting out front.

The police, according to George, were not in the mood for cordiality. "One officer told me, 'You guys in your fucking big houses think you can do anything you want,'" George said.

Magas began to feel threatened and denied them permission several times to enter the home. But the officers kept demanding entry, each time with a rising underscore of menace. George, now actually frightened, turned and went back inside. Cathy, meanwhile, had returned to the basement, where she found her oldest son, Marc, speaking calmly with Officer Smalley and Deputy Durham. They were soon joined by George, who closed the basement door behind him.

"I talked to you guys out front," George told the cops in his backyard, whom he had mistaken for the same police at the door. "There's just no reason for you to come in right now." But the officers were adamant, even threatening, George said. Fearing some kind of physical confrontation, he asked Cathy and Marc to go back inside. He told the police once again that they were not entering his house. "That's final. We're not talking about it, and I'd really appreciate you guys just leaving," he said before shutting the stairwell door and heading back upstairs.

The next thing that George knew, people downstairs were screaming and yelling that the cops were coming in. He rushed down to find an officer trying to push the basement door open as two young men struggled to keep it closed.

George approached the officer. "I wasn't threatening at all, or anything like that," he told me. "All I said to him was, 'I thought we talked about this.'"

At that, the deputy grabbed George's arm and yanked him outside. "One officer held my one arm, and the other held the other arm," George said. One of them began pummeling him in the face. Eric ran over, pulled the deputy off his father, and pushed him up against a wall. When George struggled to his feet, he saw a policeman grab Eric by the neck and zap him with a Taser.

Eric fell to the ground, screaming and writhing in pain. Cathy tried to help their son but was pushed violently away. George took a step toward Eric to help him. Two cops grabbed George and slammed him back on the ground, beating him yet again. They put him in handcuffs. "Once I tried to stand up, the deputy that was beating me in the face grabbed the Taser from the other police officer and tased me. I went back down, and then they were just completely on top of me," George said. He was tased three times within ninety seconds.

The temperature had plummeted to a bone-crunching seven degrees, with a north wind gusting up to twenty miles per hour. George was led down the driveway to a waiting patrol car. There he saw Eric, also in handcuffs. George was in shorts and a T-shirt, and Eric was shoeless. "It's a miracle we didn't get frostbite," he told me.

George had no idea what had become of his wife, who was up near the house, being placed under arrest.

According to the Magas family, as George and his son quivered in the cold, Deputy Durham approached George and said, "You tried to grab my gun."

George was staggered. "There's no way I'd try to grab your gun! I couldn't do it. It would be impossible to try," he protested. "You guys had my arms the whole time. Besides, I've never fired or touched a firearm in my life. I wouldn't know what to do with it if I did try." But Durham insisted it was true. George felt like he had tumbled down a spider hole.

The cops kept the father and son outside for so long, they both had to be taken, under custody, to Shady Grove Hospital for treatment of hypothermia. George also had cuts on his face and a black eye.

"At the hospital, the police told Eric that if he did anything funny, they would knock him so hard he wouldn't remember anything," George told me. He said Eric was given a drug test, which came back negative.

But according to the official charging document, members of the Magas family were the aggressors, accusing Nicholas Magas of growing violent when the cops tried to remove a beer keg from the home, and George Magas of striking officers, as well as grabbing one officer's gun. Cathy Magas was also charged with striking an officer in the face—with her elbow.

The police report alleged that George was "visibly intoxicated and was slurring his speech . . . he became belligerent and put his finger in Deputy Durham's face while shouting at the officers."[3]

George had then yanked the door open, allegedly punching an officer in the face and striking Durham in the chest, the report said.

"During the struggle, George Magas placed his hand onto the grip of Dep. Durham's weapon and tried to remove it from its holster," it claimed. Durham then struck George several times "in an attempt to achieve a change of behavior."

As the melee continued, the noise level from inside the house rose. Several individuals were banging on the glass, shouting profanities, and recording the incident. "All the officers at the house were concerned for their safety due to the rising tension and the fact that they were severely outnumbered," the report said. "An emergency call for officers in trouble was placed."

George called the police report "bullshit." He was not drunk, he did not try to grab Durham's gun, and neither he nor his family members assaulted any officer, he told me. A smartphone video shot by one of the guests seemed to back him up. It depicted the father "offering little or no resistance to police," reported *The Sentinel* newspaper, which reviewed the video.[4]

After the arrests, more young people exited the house and surrendered peacefully. Minors were issued citations for "possession of alcohol by a person under 21." But other guests were still inside.

That's when the police decided, finally, they needed a search warrant. It was granted by local judge Patricia Mitchell. Incredibly, the warrant application made no mention of the alleged assaults against the officers described in the charging document. Instead, it sought to search the home for possession of marijuana and provision of alcohol to minors. The list of particular items to search for was extensive. Much of the warrant talked about drug traffickers and how they store evidence on computers, in books, and elsewhere.

The cops returned to the home nearly five hours later, warrant in hand. It was now six in the morning. Durham used a battering ram to get through the basement door. The remaining guests were found throughout the house. Some turned themselves in, and the rest were "collected," as the police put it. A glass pipe assumed to be for marijuana was found in a basement drawer.

Everyone had their cell phones seized. Three days later, the police obtained warrants to search the contents of each phone. (This time, however, they did mention an incident between the Magases and officers when seeking permission.)

Twenty-two people were issued citations for underage drinking—fourteen of them were age twenty, and the others were eighteen and nineteen. Nicholas Magas was arrested for underage drinking, even though he had turned twenty-one at midnight.

During the raid, the police rifled through the premises, emptying closets and throwing clothes all over the floor. They raided George's home office and pulled plugs from his computer network. "They ruined our basement door with the battering ram and chipped our closet doors when they kicked them in, and they put a hole in our ceiling to the attic and scattered insulation all over," he said. A ceramic sign outside the door saying "Happy Birthday" was broken in half. House repairs would eventually cost about $4,000.

During their investigation, cops used the Magases' propane and wood to build a fire outside to keep themselves warm.

The four members of the Magas family were hit with a total of 108 charges, many of them serious enough to carry prison sentences.[5] George was charged with resisting arrest, second-degree assault, obstructing police, attempting to disarm a police officer, and twenty-one counts of knowingly allowing underage possession of alcohol.

Cathy was charged with second-degree assault, obstructing and hindering a police officer, and twenty-one counts of furnishing alcohol to a minor; Nicholas was charged with obstructing and hindering a police officer and twenty-one counts of furnishing alcohol to a minor; and Eric was charged with second-degree assault, obstructing and hindering a police officer, twenty-one counts of furnishing alcohol to a minor, and possession of a fake ID. (George Magas admitted only one legitimate charge: that his son possessed a fake ID.)

All four posted bail and returned home, hoping to quietly recover from the ordeal. But the raid had become a scandal in Damascus, and it sullied the Magas family's standing in the community.

On Monday, Officer Tom Didone of the Montgomery County Police held a press conference to brag about the raid. Local media portrayed the Magases as barbarians who encouraged juvenile delinquency, obstructed justice, and assaulted law enforcement officials. The NBC affiliate in Washington ran a news story that included Damascus residents expressing contempt for their neighbors.

"It really hurt," George recalled. "It was hell having to explain to clients what happened. Even going to Safeway was tough because people looked at us like we were very, very bad people." The student newspaper at Damascus High School, where the youngest Magas boy still attended, ran a damning article about the family.

"It went on and on and on," George said. "You try to hold your head up, but it's not easy. This is a close-knit community, and everyone kind of knows everyone. But we stuck together as a family. It made us even closer than we were before."

The Magases nervously awaited their day in court.

The state of Maryland does not look kindly on people who host underage parties, with a $2,500 fine for the first underage drinker and $5,000 for each additional drinker—or slightly more than $100,000 in the Magas case. Homeowners can also be sued for any damages or harm that underage drinkers cause.

George Magas says he did not know that minors were drinking in his basement, though that is certainly no excuse. Still, one wonders how many homeowners in similar situations would demand ID of every party guest on their property. Moreover, not all the people under twenty-one were drinking that night, according to the family's attorney, Rene Sandler.

"Many of them were required to submit to a breath test—which of course you're not required to, but they scare you, and they make you do it," Sandler told me.[6] "Many of these kids blew a 0.0, meaning no alcohol in their body. But they were charged anyway. With possession of alcohol," she said, adding that they all had to enter an alcohol diversion program for their cases to be dropped.

But can you be charged with possession of alcohol if you're just in a house where it is served?

Under something called "constructive possession," if you're a minor who is in, near, or around a place where alcohol is being consumed, you can be charged, Sandler said. "Even if it's not in your body. So, if you're at a bar mitzvah and they serve alcohol and you're under twenty-one, you're near or around alcohol, can you be charged? It's ludicrous."

Constructive possession is used in drug and alcohol arrests all over the country. Sandler said, "I've researched this into the ground, and I've never seen another state charge it the way these cops here in Montgomery County charge it."

Then, of course, there are the far more serious felony offenses the family members allegedly committed, especially assaulting the police and reaching for an officer's gun. But the Magases said the cops had trumped up the allegations in order to justify their violent outbursts that night. There is evidence to back that up, including the video showing police pummeling a passive George. When Sandler interviewed most party invitees, none of the eyewitnesses corroborated the police account. Then there is the curious fact that the police did not include any mention of assault when they sought the initial warrant, nor did they allege in it that George tried to grab an officer's gun.

Whatever happened that night, and however one feels about the Magas family, what the officers did raises serious questions about constitutional protections that are supposed to be granted to every citizen under the Fourth Amendment.

George and his family girded for prosecution—and an enormous fine and possible prison time. They knew what they were up against. The police made it clear they were prepared to come down hard on the defendants—not only in repeated media appearances but in not-so-subtle messages to the family, including following Cathy around when she left home, George said.

In July 2014, prosecutors offered the defendants a deal: no jail time if they pleaded guilty and paid a fine. Their attorney at the time said they should grab the offer.

"I looked at him, like, are you crazy?" George told me. "I said, 'We didn't do anything wrong!' Our whole family was in agreement with this. We were not saying, 'Yeah, we did this,' when we didn't do anything."

The Magases quickly hired a new legal team, headed by Sandler, a powerhouse attorney and constitutional crusader well known in D.C. circles as a tenacious thorn in the side of law enforcement, even though she herself is a former prosecutor.

The new team moved to suppress the evidence and observations gathered by the police during the raid, and thus force a dismissal of the charges. Although the officers had not entered the house until they had a warrant, Sandler said they had nonetheless invaded what is called the property's "curtilage."

The word, from the Old French *courtillage,* or "small court," describes the area immediately surrounding the home "to which extends the intimate activity associated with the 'sanctity of a man's home and the privacies of life,' and therefore has been considered part of the home itself for Fourth Amendment purposes," the U.S. Supreme Court wrote in a pivotal 1984 case.[7]

The question of exactly where the police may enter private property without a warrant or exigent circumstances is often debated in court cases. So, which parts of your home's exterior are protected, and which parts aren't? It largely comes down to what can be seen in public.

What you do on your front porch, driveway, or front yard, or even in front of an open window (assuming the view is not blocked), can usually be observed from the street. In those places, you have no reasonable expectation of privacy and no Fourth Amendment protections. That's why the police can enter your property and knock on your front door without a warrant or even probable cause. They can also approach your property from open fields.

But any area close to your home that is blocked from public view, where you can demonstrate an expectation of privacy that society would consider "reasonable," is considered curtilage. That even includes places that are accessible to the public.

The Supreme Court, in a 1987 decision, established four factors that must be considered when determining if an area "is so intimately tied to the home" that it is protected curtilage.[8] They are: "the proximity of the area to the home; whether the area is within an enclosure surrounding the home; the nature and uses to which the area is put; and the steps taken by the resident to protect the area from observation by passersby."

In the Magas case, Sandler was convinced that the area behind the house and detached garage, where the basement stairwell is located, clearly met all four criteria. The cops had no right to be there. They made the decision to search the area based solely on flimsy evidence and subjective observations, she said, most of it gathered in violation of the Fourth Amendment.

Curtilage aside, it is unsettling to think that the whole incident began with an employee of a private company notifying the police to report a possible crime inside someone's home. That kind of underhanded behavior seems to skirt the spirit, if not the letter, of the Fourth Amendment.

"It's beyond disturbing," Sandler said. "To use a pizza delivery person to intrude upon a person's right to privacy inside their home violates the core of one's protection in their home from any unlawful intrusion by law enforcement without a warrant." She said the young man was known around town as someone who aspired to a career in law enforcement, with close ties to the cops. His text message, which began with "Hey man, not sure if your working but if your not busy there," seemed to imply that he knew the officer quite well and had been in contact with him in the past, presumably to alert the police to other possible crimes going on *inside* people's homes. Encouraging the young man to do this would be a clever but insidious way to skirt the Fourth Amendment.

At the hearing for the Magases' motions to suppress evidence and dismiss the charges, Sandler and her cocounsel, Terrell Roberts, focused on the home's curtilage—and whether the evidence and observations gathered by the police resulted from unreasonable search and seizure. The questions were critical: If the police were shown to have violated the Fourth Amendment through their actions, their evidence and testimony would not be allowed at trial, including evidence gathered *even* after a search warrant was issued.

Such an argument is known in law as the "fruits of the poisonous tree" doctrine. If successful, the Magases' challenge would make it almost impossible to prosecute them.

The hearing took place on November 6, 2014, at the circuit court for Montgomery County in Rockville, Maryland, with Judge Steven G. Salant presiding.

It lasted all day.

The Magas team argued that there had been no exigency—nor even probable cause—for the police to trespass without a warrant into a clearly protected area of the home.

Prosecutors conceded that there was no exigency that night and that police had conducted a warrantless entry into the curtilage. But they argued that the Magases had no reasonable expectation of privacy in the stairwell area because partygoers were seen coming and going through the back door.

Officer Smalley and Deputy Durham testified that they moved toward the back of the house because the front was dark. The rear was where people were leaving the home to go outside, and they assumed they could make contact with the owner there.

Durham said the operation's main objective at that point was to ensure that nobody left the premises—for their own safety. Young people fleeing underage drinking parties have been known to injure or kill themselves by, say, hiding outside in freezing weather or driving home drunk.

Durham said he could tell from a considerable distance, and just by looking, that the individuals were minors drinking alcohol.

How? Defense attorney Charlie Roberts wanted to know. "The way they were moving with exaggerated movements," Durham testified, "the loudness, just the way they presented themselves was consistent with people who are under the age of twenty-one who have been consuming alcohol. A lot of the kids, they flail their arms and, you know, do more stumbling."

Roberts knew the statement was absurd on its face. He pounced.

"If you saw a twenty-year-old and a twenty-one-year-old who had been consuming alcohol, you would be able to tell the difference, because the twenty-year-old would have more exaggerated movements?" he asked.

"On a general basis," Durham said. "It's not hundred percent."

"No, it isn't," Roberts replied.

When George Magas took the stand, he testified that it would have been impossible for the officers to see what was going on in the stairwell area before they crossed onto his property, which is lined with thick brush and a dense row of pines he planted in 2002, for extra privacy and protection.

"You cannot see the area around the stairwell," he said on the stand. "You can't see anything. The only way you can is to have come on my property."

Roberts then lobbed a question at George that would be central to their case for curtilage.

"Just to put a fine point on this, is the back stairwell of this house a normal entrance for members of the public?" he asked.

"No. No," George replied. "Nobody goes down the stairwell."

It was a "straight-up" Fourth Amendment case, as Sandler put it. It was clear that the Magas raid rose to the standards set down by the Supreme Court for determining what is or is not curtilage.

During the hearing, George's credibility got a significant boost—at the expense of the police—from his good friend Tom Stack, the twenty-six-year veteran detective from the Montgomery County Police Department who was at the Magas home that night and left shortly before the police arrived. Stack, who had since retired from the force, was well known in town as one tough but honest cop.

The brief time Detective Stack spent on the stand was a sucker punch to the prosecution, and it impressed the judge.

Prosecutors said the police went to the rear area of the house because they presumed that the back door was being used as the main point of entry. They cited a similar case, *Alvarez v. Montgomery County,* involving underage drinking where someone had posted a sign out front that read "Party around back."

The defense in that case had argued that the officers' warrantless entry into the backyard violated the Fourth Amendment. "We disagree," a federal appeals court ruled. "The Fourth Amendment does not prohibit police, attempting to speak with a homeowner, from entering the backyard when circumstances indicate they might find him there."[9]

In other words, the owners did not have a reasonable expectation of privacy in that area. "Around back," at least on that night, was not protected curtilage. (Ironically, Sandler, a former state's attorney, successfully argued against the Alvarez family in court.)

Stack, however, testified that everyone at the Magas party knocked on and entered through the front door, which refuted the cops' under-oath testimony that everybody was entering from the rear.

In another setback to his former colleagues' credibility, Stack said there was no smell of marijuana in the home and that neither the Magases nor any of the adults upstairs were intoxicated.

Just four days later, on November 10, Judge Salant was ready to rule on the motions to dismiss the case and suppress all evidence from the police investigation. The trial was to begin in exactly one week and was expected to last about a week. The Magases arrived together in court, still rattled and nervous, to receive the judge's ruling.

"We thought the attorneys did a decent job, and it was good to get off our chest what had happened," George said. "But we still had a very sick feeling."

It did not begin well.

"With respect to the defendants' motion to dismiss," Salant began, "the Court finds [these] indictments are sufficient indictments . . . therefore the motion to dismiss the indictments is denied."[10]

The Magases would be going to trial on felony assault charges.

George was dumbfounded. "I looked back at Cathy and shook my head, like, 'Sorry, we tried,'" he said. "We felt like the very worst was going to happen. I was very nervous."

But then Salant proceeded to shred the police's conflicting and at times untruthful accounts of what happened on that violent January night.

The judge noted that Durham and Smalley saw the lit back of the house where people were making noises consistent with a party. "And that's all they have, at this point," he said. "Nothing else."

Magas sat up in his seat, suddenly reassured.

The judge went on to say the guests were not entering or leaving the party through the rear stairwell but through the front door of the house.

Strike two for the prosecution. And the judge was just warming up.

"The Court finds that the defendants were entitled to, and there was an expectation of privacy in the area," Salant announced. "There is no way that this is open to the public."

Salant said the Alvarez case, where the owners posted the "Party around back" sign, did not apply here because no public "path" had been created to the stairwell. There were not even footsteps in the snow leading to the back.

Instead, the police had entered onto the property "without a warrant and essentially violated that expectation of privacy."

The judge moved on to the search warrant. Although an "incident" occurred between the Magases and police, he said, they failed to mention any altercations in the warrant application.

And then Salant dropped the bomb that the Magas side was praying for.

Evidence used to substantiate the warrant was "unlawfully" seized, the judge declared. Therefore, any evidence or observations obtained before—or *after*—the warrant would be barred at trial. The motion to suppress had prevailed.

Outside the courthouse, the family exchanged hugs, but attorney Sandler's reaction was tempered.

"Be careful, because you still have an *X* on your back," she cautioned.

Sandler was justified; prosecutors had many cards left to play.

"The state may appeal the judge's ruling, or look at dropping some charges against the defendants or may proceed against the defendants despite the setback," *The Montgomery County Sentinel* reported. State's Attorney spokesman Ramon Korionoff told the paper, "We are keeping all options open and will determine how to proceed in the case for Monday's trial date."[11]

But there would be no trial. On the same day it was slated to begin, November 17, the state dropped the charges against the Magases—all 118 of them.

"We would have virtually no evidence to present in the case," Korionoff said. "Respecting and upholding the citizen's constitutional rights can sometimes be difficult for those men and women on the front lines."[12]

It might "sometimes be difficult" for police to uphold constitutional rights, but, as Judge Salant ruled, that was immaterial. And it was certainly no excuse for their actions that night.

Speaking with reporters after the ruling, Sandler had her mind on future policy instead of recent victory.

"It's the hope of the Magas family that the police and the State's Attorney's Office use this case to change their policies and procedures and to educate the police about the rights of individuals in their homes and elsewhere so that no other family will experience what the Magas family did," she told *The Sentinel*.

In the end, however, the Magas case did little to change police tactics and attitudes in Montgomery County—and the family finally opted not to file a civil rights suit against the county or police.

George favored the decision not to sue. "I kind of felt like, you know, I was just done with it. It had been eleven months. I have a business," he said. "I just didn't think it was very healthy for all of this to go on and on for the next year or two, when you get your names posted in the paper and all that."

The Magases were hardly alone. Few Montgomery County homeowners pursue legal action in similar Fourth Amendment cases, Sandler said.

Most lawyers are wary of confronting the criminal justice system for clients in underage-drinking cases, according to Sandler. "They worry about what the judge will think of them. It's a challenge to take on an unpopular cause," she said. "Many are worried about their next case, or what a police officer will think about them."

And so, little changes.

"Every weekend, this alcohol unit goes and scares the living hell out of residents of Montgomery County," Sandler said. "It's very, very troubling how the law is disregarded." But she remains unbowed. A defense attorney for nearly two decades, she has handled "dozens and dozens" of similar cases. "Homeowners, parents, teachers, doctors, lawyers, you name it." Sandler won dismissals or acquittals in every case, she said.

Montgomery County Police spokesman Captain Paul Starks told me that the incident "gave us another opportunity to retrain and review our practices." But he defended the use of a pizza delivery man as a voluntary police informant. "That's not new," he said. "Every police department wants community members to call them if they witness, or know, or suspect criminal activity."

Meanwhile, Sandler told me she felt the prospects of any disciplinary action against the offending officers in the Magas case were slim to none.

But not for lack of trying, Sandler said. "I have some strong contacts on the city council. I went pretty high up to talk about this case," she said. "But I can't really get anybody interested in the legalities of the tactics of this unit."

SEARCH AND SEIZURE—THEN AND NOW

"The poorest man may in his cottage bid defiance to all the forces of the crown," British prime minister William Pitt declared in 1763. "It may be frail—its roof may shake—the wind may blow through it—the storm may enter—the rain may enter—but the King of England cannot enter."

The idea that a person's home is his or her castle has been held for centuries. But it was not always stated law. The British government claimed the right to issue what was euphemistically called "writs of assistance," also known as general warrants. A general warrant provided law enforcement with almost unchecked authority to search and seize any unnamed places, persons, or possessions.

General warrants were banned by the British Parliament in 1766, but the English continued to issue them in the American colonies, mostly against suspected smugglers. They allowed customhouse officials to enter any private home or business—without prior notice or probable cause—to search for evidence of a crime and to seize any incriminating property they came across. Under a general warrant, officials were not required to name the person or place to be searched, nor what items they were specifically looking for. General warrants never expired, and they were transferable among officers. In the colonies, the British considered them just as valid as specific search warrants.

But the colonists despised them, making the writs a battle cry of the American Revolution.

Perhaps the best-known foe of general warrants was James Otis, a lawyer and onetime advocate general of Massachusetts, who coined the timeless phrase "Taxation without representation is tyranny." Boston merchants retained him, pro bono, to argue against the writs before the colony's superior court. In February 1761, he delivered a nearly five-hour speech, railing against the practice as contrary to the British constitution and the rights granted under English common law.

"It appears to me the worst instrument of arbitrary power, the most destructive of English liberty and the fundamental principles of law," he argued.

Otis lost the case, but his impassioned rhetoric inspired budding American revolutionaries opposed to such unchecked power of the Crown, including a young Massachusetts lawyer named John Adams, who was in the audience.

After the war, intense hatred of general warrants was the main catalyst for the Fourth Amendment, which mandates that government agents must always describe *the place to be searched and the persons or things to be seized.*

Without that, there would be no "exclusionary rule" (blocking evidence that was illegally searched for and seized). Or fruit of the poisonous tree. The rule, highly relevant in the Magas case, is considered essential for giving the amendment's Search-and-Seizure Clause its teeth. After all, if the police cannot offer illegally obtained evidence at trial, there is really no point in seizing it.

Today, it's fair to say, Otis, Adams, and other revolutionaries would be mortified by the abuse of Fourth Amendment rights in twenty-first-century America. It certainly is a grave concern for John Wesley Hall, an attorney in Little Rock, Arkansas, and former president of the National Association of Criminal Defense Lawyers. Hall, who publishes the comprehensive website FourthAmendment.com, is widely regarded as one of the nation's leading authorities on the abuse of search-and-seizure protections.

I spoke with Hall about the Magas raid.[13] He was appalled but not surprised.

Raiding an underage drinking party "is just excessive," he said. And while the police can come on the property if they see, for example, an assault happening through the window, "a minor drinking is a much lower level of crime." Public duty is laudable, he said, but doesn't include committing trespass.

Once the police have ignored your Fourth Amendment rights by invading someone's property, things can get out of hand with frightening speed, Hall told me. "If they did *that*, then there's no telling what the hell they'll do once inside," he said. "When they get there, they're going to pull guns on people, they're going to handcuff people and take them away. That's what cops do. Cops are yahoos no matter what department they're from, whenever they choose to get carried away like that."

Any police force is capable of it, Hall said. "Look at Irving, Texas, arresting and handcuffing just a little kid?" he gave as an example, referring to the September 2015 arrest of fourteen-year-old Ahmed Mohamed, who brought a digital clock he'd made from a pencil case to school to show to his teacher. The cops thought he had built a bomb and arrested the youth.

Does Hall think that warrantless searches and seizures are increasing nationally? The truth is, no one really knows, he said, because there is no national database of such incidents. But they are not hard to find. A simple Google news search for "warrantless raids" indicates that cases like the Magases' are not uncommon.

"Cops never really had much respect for the Fourth Amendment that I could see nationwide," Hall said, adding that warrantless raids are hardly new. "But with the advent of everybody having a video recorder on their cell phone, things now are becoming public that never did before. And that's a good thing, because it's always been the cop's word against the citizens', and the cop always gets the benefit of the doubt."

Not surprisingly, people who feel they have been victimized by the police often lose faith in the justice system and develop a chronic fear and distrust of officers. George Magas discovered this the hard way; police injustice could and *did* happen to him and his family.

To George, it is "terrifying" that somebody can break into your house, "and yet you're the one who gets arrested and has to pay all these legal fees and take all his time to defend yourself, and they get off scot-free. Nothing happened to these police officers, and they're the ones who violated the law; they're the ones who violated our Fourth Amendment rights. I think that's very scary."

Yes, there was a low-level crime being committed at the Magas household that evening, and police have the right and the duty to investigate allegations of underage drinking. But what about people who were doing nothing wrong at all when armed officers burst through their door, subjecting them to violence, terror, and, too often, false accusations of assaulting officers and committing other crimes? That happens, too.

STATEN ISLAND, NEW YORK: VIOLENT POLICE RAID OVER A TRAFFIC CONE

A Labor Day weekend barbecue in New York City ended in police brutality and alleged wrongful arrest. On September 2, 2012, fifty-seven-year-old Evelyn Lugo, a mother of ten, had relatives over to her home in the Tompkinsville section of Staten Island for an informal holiday gathering. What happened that day, according to the family, their attorney, media accounts, and a federal civil rights suit they later filed, is as follows.[14]

According to the suit, originally filed in November 2013, Evelyn's son Edwin Avellanet, twenty-six, walked out of his house to toss out a bag of garbage at about 11:00 p.m. He had placed an orange traffic cone outside the home to reserve a parking place for a friend who was expected to arrive shortly. Two NYPD officers passing by on the street ordered the cone removed. Edwin complied. Then they asked for his ID.

Avellanet insisted he had done nothing wrong and refused to hand over his identification, which was within his rights. As he walked back to the house, the officers raced up toward him. Avellanet had one foot in the front door when a cop grabbed his arm. He managed to pull away and close the door behind him.

At least eleven more officers quickly appeared on the scene. They began smashing in the front windows. Evelyn Lugo, though terrified by the noise, opened the front door. Officers dragged her outside, she said in court documents, and threw her to the ground. One of them reportedly shouted, "Shut up, bitch!"

"All they did is curse and treat me like a piece of garbage," Lugo told *The New York Daily News*.[15]

She was detained outside for thirty minutes. Inside, cops flooded through the house, where they found Avellanet. One officer pummeled his head two or three times with a flashlight or a baton and dragged him outside, the family alleged.

From the rear of the house, family friend Luis Ortega heard the commotion and moved toward the front door, where officers grabbed him, threw him to the floor, and struck him multiple times in the face with a baton, then kicked him in the ribs and arrested him, according to the legal complaint. The deep gashes in his face required seventeen stitches.

In the downstairs hallway, one cop grabbed Lugo's daughter Ana Gregorio and slammed her into a dresser. The impact toppled a birdcage containing the family's parakeet, Tito, who tumbled onto the floor.

"The bird! The bird!" Gregorio cried out.

"Fuck the bird," a cop snarled back.

"He just stomped on it," Gregorio told *The New York Daily News*.

Gregorio was acutely afraid for her own safety, but especially that of her children, who were upstairs. The police allowed her to go check on them. What she found was sheer havoc.

In the upstairs hallway, Evelyn's son George Lugo, thirty-five, daughter Alba Cuevas, forty, and grandniece Crystal Cruz, twenty-four, huddled with a number of frightened children. According to the lawsuit, the cops used pepper spray in the room, traumatizing the kids.

One officer began pummeling George Lugo with a baton, throwing him to the floor, where he was pinned down by other cops and repeatedly hit. The assault left deep gashes in his face that would require fourteen staples to close. Cruz cried out, begging the cops to stop beating her uncle. In response, another officer struck her three times in the head with a baton. They cuffed George Lugo and took him out of the house.

Alba Cuevas, who has asthma, ran into a nearby bedroom and closed the door to escape the suffocating pepper spray. Officers broke through the door, leaving a gaping hole. They twisted her arm behind her back, slapped her into painfully tight cuffs, and arrested her.

Eventually, Evelyn Lugo, her daughter Ana, granddaughter Crystal, and, ironically, her son Edwin—whose refusal to show his ID on demand launched the ugly events—were let go without criminal charges.

But George Lugo, Alba Cuevas, and Luis Ortega were taken in squad cars to Staten Island University Hospital, where Lugo and Ortega were treated for multiple lacerations to the face and head. Alba was treated for an asthma attack triggered by pepper spray and tenderness in her left hand, caused by the tight cuffs.

The three "suspects" spent two days in a police precinct awaiting arraignment. George and Luis spent a few more nights on New York's notorious Rikers Island, awaiting bail. After multiple appearances in court, charges against all three were dropped and the records sealed.

In November of 2013, Luis Ortega, Evelyn, and five members of her family sued the City of New York and at least thirteen named NYPD police in U.S. District Court in Brooklyn. They since amended their complaint twice, most recently in August of 2015.

The plaintiffs sued for physical injuries, emotional distress, embarrassment, humiliation, and deprivation of their constitutional rights, including the deployment of needless and excessive force. The cops displayed conduct that was "extreme and outrageous, and exceeded all reasonable bounds of decency." And the brutality was intentional, "for the sole purpose of causing severe emotional distress." The suit further accused the officers of false arrest, unlawful imprisonment, falsification of evidence, and malicious prosecution without probable cause.

Finally, the plaintiffs, all of whom are Hispanic, also alleged that the police violated their civil rights based on national origin and/or race, as granted under the Equal Protection Clause of the Fourteenth Amendment.

For Evelyn Lugo and her son Edwin, their right to be "free from an unlawful entry via the Fourth Amendment" was violated, the suit further alleged. In short, NYPD officers invaded the constitutional sanctity of their home without a warrant, probable cause, exigent circumstances, or any other legal justification.

What's more, George Lugo, Alba Cuevas, and Luis Ortega had been placed under arrest "with malice," the lawsuit said, and then hit with baseless charges filed under false allegations by officers wanting to avoid discipline for their "acts of brutality."

Such "malicious" prosecution and manufacture of false evidence resulted directly from the unconstitutional policies and practices of New York City, the lawsuit went on, including inadequate screening and supervision of police—and a long history of excessive force, falsification of evidence, and gross neglect of civil rights by the NYPD.

It's difficult to fathom the terror, injustice, humiliation, and emotional and physical pain the family endured, all over a traffic cone.

Eventually, New York City agreed to settle the case, the family's attorney, Jason Leventhal, told me. Plaintiffs were awarded a collective total of $450,000, he said.

If the city and the police had prevailed in this case it would have signaled a frightening portent for the rest of us. If you are not safe from illegal police activity in your own home, when you yourself have done nothing illegal, you are not safe anywhere.

"This is so much more serious than a dead parakeet. This is the violation of someone's home. They really came in like cowboys," the family's attorney, Jason Leventhal, told *The Daily News*. "It was completely uncalled for. There was no excuse for going into the house without a warrant."

Evelyn Lugo remained deeply shaken. "The police don't care about us as humans," she said; "they're going to care about the bird?"

HENDERSON, NEVADA: POLICE COMMANDEER HOMES FOR SURVEILLANCE OPERATION

Among the more bizarre warrantless home-invasion stories is one that took place on the edge of the desert outside Las Vegas. In this case, the victims of Fourth Amendment abuses were not the subject of any criminal activity, investigation, or even suspicion. The target was their neighbor.

The botched raid also raises questions about the Constitution's least celebrated amendment, the Third, which states: *No Soldier shall, in time of peace be quartered in any house, without the consent of the Owner.*

At about 9:00 on a hot morning in July 2011, Michael and Linda Mitchell were at their stucco house in Henderson, Nevada, a city of nearly three hundred thousand people about ten miles southeast of Las Vegas, when officers from the Henderson and North Las Vegas Police Departments pulled up outside.

Michael Mitchell's phone rang. It was his neighbor across the street, Phillip White. Police officers were outside his house. White's wife had called in a domestic violence complaint against him, he said, and he was refusing to go outside to speak with them because he had a one-month-old child asleep at home. Instead, he opened the door and sat on the couch, unarmed, inviting the police to come in, according to police records.[16]

The cops, who later said they thought White had barricaded himself and a child in his home, called in a SWAT team. Soon, the blaring of sirens and bullhorns filled the quiet neighborhood. In their zeal to surround the house, the police tore a tree from the ground in White's front yard. They also cut off access to all exits and entrances to the neighborhood.

Michael went outside to get the morning paper. Officers screamed at him to return to his house. Michael was indignant and shouted back at the cops to turn off the sirens. He went back in the house, alarmed by the overwhelming police presence. Michael and Linda began taking photos of the operation through their front windows, telling the police they would turn the images over to local news outlets.

That's when at least ten officers pointed guns at the couple in the window and at several other homes on the street, a lawsuit later filed by the Mitchell family alleged.[17]

One of those homes belonged to Anthony Mitchell, Michael and Linda's son. At about 10:45 a.m., Anthony got a call from a Henderson police officer, asking him to allow the squad to enter Anthony's house and use it to gain a "tactical advantage" over White. Anthony refused. The request deeply disturbed him.

Anthony was frightened for his life and feared that the police would invade his house without a warrant. The officers continued to point weapons at his windows. Anthony put on the protective ballistic vest he used at his job as a bail-enforcement agent.

Now it was Anthony who tried to contact the local news, walking back and forth in front of his window as he made calls. One cop followed Anthony's movements through his gunsight. Anthony snapped a picture of the officer and flipped him off.

"At this point [officers] conspired to remove Anthony from his residence and occupy it for their own use," the legal complaint alleged.

The lawsuit alleged that the officers had predetermined, no matter what, that they would enter and appropriate the home of Anthony, who, like his parents, had committed no crimes.

According to one officer's official report, "It was determined to move to 367 Eveningside and attempt to contact [Anthony] Mitchell. If Mitchell answered the door he would be asked to leave. If he refused to leave he would be arrested for obstructing a police officer. If Mitchell refused to answer the door, forced entry would be made and Mitchell would be arrested."

Did that amount to a police conspiracy? That question would have to wait for a federal jury.

Just before noon, about ten officers approached Anthony's house and began banging loudly on the door. "Resident 367, come to the door!" one of them shouted.

Instead, he called his mother to tell her what was happening. There was a tremendous crash. The officers had deployed a metal ram to enter Anthony's house with neither permission nor a warrant. Pointing their guns at Anthony, he alleged, they ordered him to the floor, still yelling, and now calling him "asshole."

One officer shouted "conflicting orders" at Anthony, commanding him simultaneously to shut off his phone, which was on the floor, and to crawl toward the officer. "Confused and terrified, [he] remained curled on the floor of his living room, with his hands over his face, and made no movement," the lawsuit said.

That's when the police got out the PepperBalls—pepper-spray projectiles that explode on contact—and fired. The Mitchells' lawsuit alleged that Anthony was lying motionless on the ground "and posed no threat." Despite that, the officers fired multiple PepperBall rounds. At first, Anthony thought he had been shot with bullets. He was struck at least three times by balls fired at close range, causing "extreme and prolonged pain" in his eyes, nose, throat, and lungs, and on his skin.

The cops also fired a PepperBall at Anthony's terrorized dog, Sam, who howled in panic and ran from the house, ending up trapped in the backyard without water for the rest of the one-hundred-degree day.

Linda was still on the phone, listening to the chain of events unfolding in her son's home. She screamed his name over and over until a cop grabbed Anthony's phone and hung up. Linda feared her son had been wounded or killed.

The police grabbed Anthony, cuffed him, lifted him up, and yanked him outside. There they shoved him against a wall, slamming his face into the coarse stucco. They held him "in this painful and humiliating configuration for several minutes," the suit alleged. Anthony begged to be released. He was a threat to no one, he said. The officer did not relent. He continued to press Anthony's face against the wall, yelling that he should have come out of his house as commanded.

Anthony was arrested for "obstructing a police officer" and hauled off to the mobile command center that was set up a quarter mile away for the raid on White's house.

At least a dozen police then swarmed through Anthony's home. They searched his rooms and belongings, moving around furniture to get a better view of White's house. Then they settled in to occupy it and deploy it as an observation post.

Meanwhile, across the street, about ten officers poured into Michael and Linda Mitchell's backyard—again without a warrant or permission. They pleaded with Michael to come to the mobile command center, telling him they needed his help on the phone to negotiate a surrender with White. Reluctantly, Michael agreed.

It was a ruse. White was not taking any calls from the police, who refused to let Michael use his own phone to make contact. Michael quickly realized that the police had duped him into coming. The cops told him he could not return home. Michael waited ten minutes, then got up and walked out. Shortly after that, a squad car pulled up beside him as he headed home. The police said Linda was waiting for him back at the command center.

Michael returned to find his wife not there. Exasperated, he called another son, James, to pick him up. This time, when he tried to leave, he was handcuffed, arrested, and put in the back of a police car.

After Michael had left his home, several officers returned and pounded on the back door, demanding that Linda open it. She did and informed them they were not coming into the house without a warrant.

"The officers ignored her, entered through the back door, and began searching the home," the lawsuit said. One officer, a female, forcibly grabbed Linda, seized her purse, and began rummaging through it.

Linda, frightened and protesting, was dragged from her home and hauled to the command center, where her son and husband were being held. A physically frail woman, she had trouble breathing the furnace-like air and keeping up with the cop who forced her into a trot. The officer ignored her pleas to slow down. He also refused to tell her why she was being taken in or, for that matter, why her house had been raided.

The police commandeered their home, also as an observation post. But they did far more than peer next door. They rifled through cabinets and closets and helped themselves to water from the dispenser. They left a sliding glass door open and the refrigerator door ajar and spilled condiments on the kitchen floor. They also opened and searched, without a warrant, two trucks parked in the parents' driveway—one belonging to Anthony, the other to Michael.

Anthony and Michael were jailed overnight at the Henderson Detention Center on charges of obstructing an officer. They spent more than nine hours behind bars before making bail. During that time, police withhold Anthony's seizure medication. He submitted a form asking for it. The request was ignored. That afternoon, his brother delivered the pills to the jail.

Later that day, three of the officers prepared a police report that, the lawsuit alleged, contained "knowingly false statements."

The report portrayed the Mitchells as unstable and rash. It says Michael tried to call his neighbor White three times to disclose law enforcement positions to him. They said he set off his car alarms to "distract, annoy, and obstruct the emergency response" and defied their commands to stay inside his home. When the police called Michael, he "went off on tangents that included the North and South in the Civil War," they wrote.

The police reported that Anthony was also trying to alert White to their whereabouts, that he extended his middle finger toward an officer, and took photos of the police. They said they shot Anthony with PepperBalls because he refused to drop his phone and show his hands. Guns and bullets were found in his house.

Four months later, all charges against Michael and Anthony were dropped "with prejudice," meaning they could never be brought up again.

Two years after the incident, in July 2013, the Mitchells filed suit against the Cities of Henderson and North Las Vegas and the officers involved in the incident. It made twenty-two claims, including retaliation in violation of the Freedom of Speech Clause of the First Amendment; unlawful arrest; unlawful search of homes and vehicles in violation of the Fourth Amendment; excessive force against Anthony in violation of the Fourth Amendment; unlawful punishment of Anthony and "deliberate indifference" to his medical needs, in violation of the Eighth Amendment (against cruel and unusual punishment); municipal liability against the Cities of Henderson and North Las Vegas; as well as conspiracy and neglect to prevent conspiracy.

But the most striking claim was alleged violation of the Third Amendment, which commands that *"No Soldier shall, in time of peace be quartered in any house, without the consent of the Owner, nor in time of war, but in a manner to be prescribed by law."*

It was one of the rare times in U.S. judicial history that the largely forgotten amendment has been evoked. Out of pure coincidence, on the day the lawsuit was filed, *The American Bar Association Journal* ran an essay saying the amendment was so obscure, so archaic, it could be nicknamed the "runt piglet" of the Bill of Rights, because it is "short, overlooked, sometimes the butt of jokes."

Jokes aside, the Mitchells' lawsuit contended that police officers should be considered "soldiers" and that their occupancy of a house, in peacetime, even for less than twenty-four hours, constitutes "quartering" as described in the amendment. (In the Mitchells' case, the occupancy lasted about nine hours.)

Henderson city attorney Josh Reid called the claim a "red herring" and accused the Mitchells of raising the issue for publicity reasons only.

The two cities and their officers moved to dismiss all the claims entirely. In February of 2015, U.S. district judge Andrew P. Gordon refused, and instead returned a mixed bag of rulings on what claims could and could not proceed to trial.

Gordon said the claim of First Amendment Retaliation could be made, writing that the Mitchells' actions—taking photos, yelling at cops to turn off their sirens, flipping off an officer—were all constitutionally protected. And, he added, having police pointing weapons at the Mitchells and entering their homes without a warrant "would chill a person of ordinary firmness from ceasing to engage in protected activity."

The judge also refused to dismiss any of the Fourth Amendment claims against individual officers. The Mitchells had sufficiently pleaded that police violated their Fourth Amendment rights by entering and searching their homes and vehicles without consent or a warrant, forcibly removing Linda from her home, and seizing Anthony without a warrant.

Gordon also allowed the claim of excessive use of force against Anthony to move forward, saying that "it appears that the officers violated clearly established rights."

But many other claims were dismissed. The Mitchells, who are white, could not allege a "conspiracy" to deprive them of their rights because they do not belong to a class of society that the government has determined requires special federal protection. Gordon also dismissed the claims of Negligent Infliction of Emotional Distress, and Abuse of Process.

The long-shot Third Amendment claim was likewise thrown out.

"The relevant questions are thus whether municipal police should be considered soldiers, and whether the time they spent in the house could be considered quartering. To both questions, the answer must be no," Gordon ruled. "This was not a military intrusion into a private home, and thus the intrusion is more effectively protected by the Fourth Amendment."

One can understand why the court would not consider the officers to be "soldiers." The federal Posse Comitatus Act limits the federal government's power in using military personnel for domestic law enforcement—and peace officers do not typically fight in wars.

But there is still something troubling about the ruling. The line between cop and soldier was somewhat vague during the nation's founding, when the Third Amendment was written. So how do we know the founders didn't intend for it to apply to both military and peace officers? The amendment specifically states *in time of peace.*

Today, police departments are again blurring that line as they become ever more militaristic in their tactics, training, equipment, and attitude. Ilya Somin, a professor of law at George Mason University, made some interesting arguments along those lines in a *Washington Post* blog about why the Third Amendment matters, even today.

"When the Amendment was enacted in 1791, there were virtually no professional police of the sort we have today. The distinction between military and law enforcement officials was far less clear than in the world of 2015," he wrote.[18]

And given today's increasingly militarized law enforcement tactics, Somin questioned whether there was an actual difference between quartering a SWAT team in a home, or a National Guard unit.

Judge Gordon may have ruled correctly, but it's conceivable there will be more Third Amendment cases in the future. According to Somin, the judge was "too quick to conclude that no 'municipal police officer could ever qualify' as soldiers."

Somin did offer a novel idea for future cases. In cities and towns where police militarization is the norm—a practice newly bolstered by the Trump administration's October 2017 order to restore the provision of surplus military hardware and vehicles to local police departments—Somin suggested the courts should treat those officers as soldiers "for Third Amendment purposes."

Eventually, the plaintiffs settled their case against the City of Henderson, leaving the City of North Las Vegas and five of its officers, who filed a motion to dismiss, at the U.S. District Court of Nevada. In July 2017, Judge Andrew P. Gordon denied the motion almost in its entirety. Just one city employee was granted dismissal on two counts. Otherwise, the city and the other employees, he ruled, could now be sued for unlawful arrest, excessive force, assault, battery, false arrest and imprisonment, intentional infliction of emotional distress, civil conspiracy, and municipal liability. As of October 2018, the case had not yet gone to trial.

As for Phillip White, the neighbor accused of domestic violence who set off the entire chain of atrocities that day: He was arrested for domestic battery (first offense) and coercion. He was not accused of hurting his child. In November 2011, both charges were dismissed with prejudice. With no clear evidence to convict White, the whole episode, billed to taxpayers, was all for naught.

Meanwhile, the North Las Vegas officers were never subjected to any kind of disciplinary action, plaintiff attorney Benjamin Durham told me. "As I recall, the Henderson officers were subject to disciplinary proceedings, but that information was subject to a protective order," he said.[19]

IF THEY COME FOR YOU

Most citizens presume that the Constitution fully protects their home, family, and possessions—but those protections are eroding. "The overreaching of the police, and I'm going to say the militarization of the police, their tactics and the manner in which they go about their cases, has reached really an all-time high in terms of violating personal rights of homeowners and individuals," Maryland attorney Rene Sandler told me.

It's very hard to say no to a police officers when they're at your door, even if you have done nothing wrong. The right thing to do, Sandler advised, is to "assess the situation, see what's going on, and know that you absolutely do have the right to deny them access. Of course, the police—you have to understand—are not going to be happy with that."

Despite being beaten, tased, and terrorized, the Magases did everything by the book, Sandler said. "They did everything right that a person is supposed to do to deny access to the home absent probable cause."

What rights do you have when cops trespass on your property and violently confront you? Can you physically defend yourself against the police when they shoot, tase, or beat you for no justifiable reason?

"It depends on state law," Fourth Amendment lawyer John Wesley Hall told me. "But the whole point is that you want to make sure that disputes are settled in a civil manner and not just going off on self-help, as it's sometimes called, because it can lead to dangerous confrontations."[20]

The cops, after all, are usually the only ones with guns.

"Let them do what they're going to do, because they're screwing up," he said. "I don't want to counsel anybody to cause a confrontation on the property where somebody gets shot. And cops are trigger-happy; they sometimes show up with a SWAT team when it's completely unnecessary. And you sure as hell don't want that."

It's hard to win, he said, when they have the guns, Tasers, handcuffs, and the means to take you away. "So, just be calm and deal with it in court."

Still, some people do try to physically resist the police when their property is invaded. "State law may very well say you have that right," Hall cautioned, "but do you really want to get into a shoot-out over it?"

Finally, had they gone to trial for assaulting an officer, any of the defendants in this chapter could have invoked something called the Castle Defense, a time-honored legal concept derived from English common law. Also known as the "Make My Day Law," the doctrine generally permits people to use force—even deadly force—when an intruder enters their home and poses a reasonable threat of imminent death or serious harm to them or anyone else inside.

That should, in theory at least, apply to officers, Hall said. "It's part of the model penal code definitions of justifiable use of force. Potentially even against a cop. Which is why cops ought to think twice before they do stupid shit like that." But, he added, if a gun is pulled on the police, "then they've also got a defense."

"People are getting tired of cops beating the shit out of people for no apparent reason," Hall said.

I asked Hall if there was any movement, any effort to address this disturbing problem, either at the state or federal level. He couldn't think of any. But, he added, the need is critical.

"Cops who do that kind of crap run the risk of getting shot. And I don't think they appreciate the significance of that," Hall said. "The reason why we have a knock-and-announce rule is so the cops won't just willy-nilly come charging into somebody's house and run the risk of getting shot themselves by the homeowner that doesn't know what the hell they're doing there."

One of these days, he predicted, some property owner is going to be acquitted for injuring or killing a cop who trespassed on his property.

2

L'ENFANT C'EST MOI—CHILD PROTECTIVE SERVICES AND STATE-SPONSORED KIDNAPPING

Let's say you are a loving parent raising your children in a safe and supportive home—even if it is a bit chaotic and disheveled. You're preparing dinner one evening when there's an urgent rapping at your door. It's the cops, along with a social worker from the county's Child Protective Services (CPS). They want to speak with you about a report they received concerning one of the kids. You are sure there's some sort of mistake, the wrong house probably. Maybe this has something to do with that troubled, sometimes violent family down the street.

No. They want to speak with you and your spouse. You have been accused of abusing your child. The news comes like a sick joke, a sucker punch to the groin. Riddled with confusion, you're not sure what to do. The officials want to come inside, inspect the house, interrogate you and your children. The police do not have a warrant. Certain it will lead to your instant exoneration, you let everybody in.

The police say that someone has tipped them off, though they can't tell you who it was.

There might be any number of allegations they throw at you: Your child has an unexplained scrape or bruise; you feed your kids too much; you feed your kids too little; you discipline them too harshly; you don't discipline them at all; someone heard them screaming and crying as if being beaten; you failed to properly treat them for an illness; you overtreated them or treated them for the wrong illness; you don't vaccinate according to the recommended federal schedule; you let them walk home from the park alone; you smoke pot; you drink too much; you fight too much; you beat your kids; you molest your kids; you're a Satan worshipper.

The agents of the state peer in your fridge. They go on to inspect the children's rooms, rifle through belongings, and begin interrogating everyone in the house. They lift your terrified kids' shirts and look for bruises. They bark questions at you in rapid succession. You grow anxious. You come to realize that these people actually think you are some sort of irredeemable monster.

Two hours later, the CPS worker announces that *all* your children are being taken away—"for their own safety"—even if the allegations involve just one of them. You have few rights, such as due process and equal protection, and little recourse; if you resist, you will be arrested. You will have your day in court, they tell you, in about seventy-two hours, unless it's a weekend, in which case your anguish will be prolonged. There, you can argue why your kids should be returned.

Your wailing children cling to you as you gather up their favorite sweaters and teddy bears, fighting back your own tears, trying to be strong. And then your loved ones are gone, whisked away into the night to an undisclosed facility or a private foster home, in the care of strangers.

You sleep fitfully in the suddenly silent house. But you will need your sleep. You're about to descend into a soul-crushing world you never dreamed existed, a world where parents are presumed guilty until proven otherwise, where mustering that proof is often stymied at every step by a web of social workers fearful for their jobs, indifferent or dishonest agency supervisors, self-interested court-appointed attorneys who'd rather settle than fight, prosecutors who will shred your reputation in court, government psychological experts paid to testify why you are an unfit parent and why your kids need certain psychiatric and/or invasive medical interventions, and judges who are all too often willing to believe their word against yours.

The nightmare about to befall you could end up costing you your savings, your marriage, your sanity. And it could be months, or even years, before you get your kids back—if you get them back at all.

THE STATE, THE CHILD, AND THE LAW OF "PROTECTION"

The government has a right, and a duty, to intervene when children are being harmed or placed in imminent danger. Sadly, many kids fall into that category.

There are some despicable parents and guardians who beat, burn, bruise, or sexually or psychologically abuse children in their care, who are too inebriated or mentally unstable to look after themselves, let alone dependent minors, who lock their kids up, leave them alone at home for hours on end, withhold food, or place them in dangerous situations such as being around drugs and loaded firearms. We as a society owe it to these children to intervene. Many of them, sadly, should leave home forever, to spare their lives.

In many CPS cases, dedicated social workers employ due diligence before deciding to remove children from their homes. Parents are afforded their constitutional right to due process and fighting for their kids' return, especially when reunification—if safe and feasible—is supposed to be the top priority.

Having researched the breadth of the problem, and heard so many stories of innocent parents claiming to have been terrorized by CPS agencies, I came to view much of the system as broken.

The issue has reached crisis proportions and desperately needs nationwide reform. Too many families are still reeling from the protracted legal and emotional hardships they endured, the spurious accusations levied against parents and the extended detention of their children based on falsehoods, fabrication of records, and suppression of evidence that would exonerate them.

Sadly, it appears that too many child protection agencies are fixated on removing kids from their homes as expeditiously as possible and keeping them away for as long as possible. A system designed to protect families has ended up destroying them—trampling their rights in the rush to feed an insatiable machine—namely, CPS.

It was not easy trying to decide which stories to highlight in this chapter—there was no shortage of sagas that reveal the perversion of justice that is unfolding in counties across the country.

THE FORT FAMILY SAGA

The story of the Fort family of California provides a striking example of what I believe to be the corruption and injustice perpetrated against innocent Americans in violation of the letter and spirit of the Bill of Rights. What follows is largely based on allegations made in connection with a federal civil rights complaint filed by the family, media accounts, and interviews with Nathan Fort, the father, and the family's attorney. Local social service officials declined to comment.

Molly and Nathan Fort were a young couple living in Hollister, California, in the largely agricultural region of San Benito County, east of Monterey Bay. They had met in 1995, when they were both seventeen, at a Christian skating party. They began dating steadily. Nathan was preparing for Bible college to become a Christian youth counselor, while Molly worked at a local hospital as a switchboard operator. The following May, they were engaged. Together, they would raise Molly's child, Madison. Madison's biological father left his family when she was born in June 1995, and Madison eventually came to consider Nathan Fort to be her dad.

But there were troubles brewing within the extended family. Before she married, Molly and her daughter had been living at the home of Molly's father, Michael Mewborn, in nearby Prunedale in Monterey County, where Mewborn was a pastor at a Church of God ministry. Coincidentally, Nathan's parents were also ordained ministers and experienced counselors.

Despite his religious orientation, Michael Mewborn was prone to irrational outbursts, according to Nathan, newspaper accounts, and legal documents that would be filed later. "There was a lot of verbal abuse against Molly. It's one reason why I ended up marrying her," Nathan told me. "I didn't know what else to do to help get her and the baby out of that house."[1]

One day after fighting with her dad, Molly had called Nathan and told him she had been kicked out of the house. Nathan tried to smooth things over between Molly and her father, but his efforts went nowhere. As Nathan led his fiancée and Madison out to his '84 Thunderbird, he said Michael Mewborn began shouting at Molly.

"You are Satan's child!" he allegedly yelled repeatedly. "I release you to Satan." According to the complaint, Mewborn warned his daughter that he would take her to court to win custody of Madison and referred to the little girl as "my child."

They fled to the home of Nathan's parents, Robert and Esther Fort, where Nathan was living.

The Forts offered to conduct a mediation session between Mewborn and Molly. Mewborn and his wife, Pamela, drove over to the house, and the meeting began with group prayer. Mewborn quickly became agitated, lashing out at his daughter.

"Molly said, 'Dad, sometimes when you say things like that, it really hurts me,'" Nathan recalled. "He flipped out, stood up, and drove away, leaving his wife there at our house. She called him after that. It all failed miserably."

Pamela begged Robert Fort to get on the phone with Mewborn. It did not go well. "If you don't give me my baby right now, I'm going to call the police and accuse Nathan of being a child molester!" Mewborn yelled, according to Nathan.

The situation deteriorated from there. Mewborn's anger and bizarre behavior grew increasingly more menacing. On several occasions, he told his daughter he would come over and take Madison away.

Two weeks after the failed mediation meeting, Mewborn asked Molly if Madison could spend the weekend with him. She refused.

Soon after that, Molly's mother called to alert her that Mewborn, now enraged, was heading over to the Forts' home. Molly and Nathan grabbed Madison and left to hide out at the home of some friends. When Mewborn showed up at the Forts' door, he demanded that they hand over "my child," meaning Madison.

Mewborn refused to believe that Molly and Madison were not in the house. He demanded to search the premises. Robert Fort agreed and let the raging grandfather come in.

After a fruitless search and several physical threats against Robert, Mewborn called the county sheriff's office demanding that a social worker and an officer be sent to take the child away. Then Mewborn dropped a bomb: He told the officer he had witnessed Nathan fondling Madison, who was thirteen months old at the time. It was a lie. Mewborn had not seen his granddaughter since Molly and Madison moved out of the house.

Mewborn hung up and turned to Robert. "My daddy taught me how to fight," he said, "and I know how to fight dirty." Before the police arrived, Mewborn's wife called the Forts' house to see what was happening. Mewborn told her about his accusation of molestation against Nathan. She was mortified. She begged her husband to retract the allegation.

Mewborn relented and called the sheriff's office to recant, shortly before two deputies arrived at the Fort home. He told them, too, that he had fabricated the accusation out of sheer rage. Mewborn drove away, and Molly, Madison, and Nathan returned home. Molly even allowed Madison to visit her grandfather from time to time. In November of 1996, Molly and Nathan were married at Mewborn's church, with Nathan's father performing the ceremony.

But, as Nathan told me, Molly struggled to adjust to married life. The following year, from August of 1997 to January of 1998, the couple were separated. But the last week of January, despite Molly's pregnancy by another man, Nathan and Molly reunited.

About six months later, Mewborn called Molly and said something disturbing. "Madison tried to hump me," he told his daughter. He always played horsey with her, bouncing her on his legs. "He was saying she tried to have sex with him," Nathan told me. "There's no way that's what she was trying to do."

Deeply disturbed, Molly told her father he could no longer take Madison for overnight or unsupervised visits. This enraged Mewborn, who threatened to drive over to the Forts' house and "kick the door in if I have to" in order to take away Madison, whom he again called "my daughter."

Nathan and Molly called the sheriff. Two deputies arrived and were waiting outside when Mewborn showed up. They attempted to calm him down and prevent him from reaching the home. Mewborn tried to push his way past them. When that failed, he headed for his van. The cops, worried that he might have a gun in his vehicle, ordered him to stop. Mewborn refused and was promptly arrested.

Shortly after the arrest, Molly obtained a restraining order against her father, barring him from any kind of contact with Madison or herself.

But Mewborn wasn't finished. Soon after posting bail, he contacted the district attorney's office, called the victim witness program, and reached out to Donna Elmhurst, a CPS supervisor at the county's Health and Human Services Agency, who also happened to be a friend and a parishioner at his church. Elmhurst had been married at the church, with Mewborn presiding.

Only Elmhurst responded. Representatives of the other two offices, after receiving the calls from Mewborn, described him as being "loud and possibly drunk," according to the federal lawsuit that Molly and Nathan would eventually file against the county and its CPS agency.[2]

On several occasions, Mewborn had threatened to use his parishioner, Donna Elmhurst, to have Molly removed from her home. The two of them allegedly conspired to concoct a bogus story, yet again, that Nathan had molested his stepdaughter, which they hoped would drive Madison out of the Fort house and place the girl with her grandfather.

In late April of 1998, county CPS social worker Rebecca Ochoa-Perez arrived at the Forts' house, unannounced. Only Nathan's mother, Esther, was home. "Someone has made an accusation against Nathan," she said to Esther. "I'd like to interview Madison about it."

Esther explained that Madison was not at home, but she invited Ochoa-Perez inside, showing her the clean, orderly house and its various rooms and contents. When Ochoa-Perez left, Molly, Nathan, and Madison returned home. Esther told them what had happened. Outraged that Mewborn had once again manufactured a molestation charge against Nathan, the couple called Ochoa-Perez. Nathan said they would be happy to bring Madison down to the CPS office for an interview.

Molly was worried about going, but not Nathan. "In my mind, we were going in there to explain to these people what was happening," he said. Surely they would believe their side of the story, he thought. Instead, he told me, "I really had no idea what we were in for. I was really naive. I was thinking, this is America, and we have not done anything wrong. It's going to be real obvious what's going on."

Before they left for the county office, Madison said she was hungry. Molly and Nathan, believing the visit would be brief, promised to take her to McDonald's when it was over. Molly bent down and spoke softly to Madison. "We're taking you to talk to a nice lady who would like to ask you some questions," she said. "You should tell the lady whatever she wants to know."

When they arrived, Ochoa-Perez informed them that her boss, Mewborn's friend and parishioner Donna Elmhurst, had decided that Lucy Perez, an employee with no college degree and little experience or training in child sexual abuse cases, would conduct the interview.

The switch to Perez, according to the legal complaint that would be filed, was "orchestrated by Elmhurst for the very reason that Perez was a young and inexperienced social worker that would do exactly what Elmhurst wanted."

And that is exactly what happened.

Although Molly had the right to sit in on the interview, Perez never informed her of that right. Perez simply demanded that Molly and Nathan hand Madison over at once. She refused to shake Nathan's hand and ordered Nathan and Molly into separate rooms. The couple sensed that Perez had already decided that Nathan had molested Molly.

Madison, who was not yet three, was interrogated for two hours and forty-five minutes, without any food or water. When it was over, Perez confronted the parents.

"Madison has made a disclosure of a sexual nature," Perez announced. "She told me that Nathan touched her on her pee-pee. Molly, do you believe that happened?"

Molly was dumbfounded. There was no way that Nathan would do anything like that, she said.

Later, Perez would state that Madison had made the disclosure within the first ten minutes of the interview. Federal law requires social workers in child abuse cases to halt the interview immediately after any serious disclosure and make arrangements to videotape the questioning, something Perez failed to do, although she did leave the room for a moment to tell Elmhurst what the little girl had said.

According to Perez's account, the little girl made the disclosure when asked how her "Daddy" bathes her.

"But Nathan has never given Madison a bath!" Molly protested. "Clearly, my child was confused."

Molly was then allowed into the interrogation room to speak privately with her daughter.

"Did you tell the lady that Daddy touches your pee-pee?" she asked.

"Yes," Madison said.

"Is that true? Does Daddy touch your pee-pee?"

"No."

"Then why did you say that to the lady?" The little girl shrugged. "Madison, it's very important you tell Mommy the truth. If Daddy did something to you, I want you to tell me."

"He didn't!"

"Madison, it's very important that you tell the truth because if Daddy touches your pee-pee, he could go to jail."

"But he doesn't, Mommy."

"Then why did you say that?"

"Because I was hungry."

"Then you need to tell the lady that."

When Perez came back in the room, a distraught Madison cried, "I don't want Daddy to go to jail!"

It infuriated Perez. She commanded Molly never to speak with Madison about the disclosure again. Molly and Madison, moreover, were barred from returning home to the Forts' house until her investigation was completed. Molly begged the social worker to reconsider. When that failed, she asked if she and Madison could go stay with friends. Perez rejected that request as well. Instead, she made arrangements for mother and daughter to stay at a seedy local motel.

As this was going on, Nathan was waiting impatiently in a separate room, where he had been sitting for three hours. He had no idea what was transpiring until Ochoa-Perez came in to speak with him.

"Madison has made a molestation disclosure against you," she told him, without mentioning that Madison supposedly made the disclosure while talking about Nathan bathing her. Ochoa-Perez failed to ask Nathan if he had ever bathed his stepdaughter.

"That's not true!" Nathan protested. "Please, take me down to the police station and give me a polygraph test, right now."

Ochoa-Perez refused. She turned and walked out the door, having spent just two or three minutes with Nathan. She never asked him for his version of events. Indeed, despite the serious allegations against him, Nathan was never arrested, fingerprinted, or ever legally accused in a manner that would allow him to defend himself against any charges of wrongdoing.

Nathan believes that this case was never about punishing him. It was about getting the little girl out of the house and back with her grandfather.

"It was just her saying that Madison had said something, which didn't make any sense. It was very frustrating," Nathan said.

Molly and Madison were driven to the Fort home to collect some clothes. Esther Fort begged Ochoa-Perez to let them stay at a nicer place at the Forts' own expense. When that was denied, she asked if she could stay with the visibly distraught Molly, who was now seven months pregnant. Ochoa-Perez agreed.

While they were there, Nathan arrived at the home. Lucy Perez was standing outside. Nathan asked what was going on. She told him that Molly and Madison would be staying at a motel pending the investigation.

"But we have rights!" Nathan protested. "What are our rights here?"

"I don't know," Perez responded flatly.

"Is this Nazi Germany?" Nathan asked incredulously. "You get to tell us where we can stay and who we can talk to but you won't give us any information and we have no rights?"

"You'd better watch your attitude, young man," she told him. "When you talk to us, it's 'Yes, ma'am' and 'No, ma'am.'"

It was the last time that Nathan would see Madison for more than four years.

That night at the motel, Madison put down her toys and walked over to Molly and Esther, telling them that another family member had once gotten in the bathtub with her and "touched my pee-pee, and it hurt real bad."

Molly was stunned. "Is that true? Did that really happen?" she asked. Madison said, "Nope," in a nonchalant manner and went back to her playing. Molly and Esther, while deeply unsettled, did not question the girl further because Ochoa-Perez had instructed her not to do so.

The next day, Lucy Perez showed up at the motel to bring Madison to the Hollister Police Department for yet another interview, this one videotaped by a sexual abuse response team.

On the drive there, Molly told Ochoa-Perez what Madison had said about the other family member. The CPS worker dismissed the claim out of hand. "That doesn't matter, because Madison is specifically naming Nathan," she replied. Agency officials never questioned Madison or the family member about the alleged incident.

During the interview, "Madison said absolutely none of the things that Perez claimed she had said the day prior, nor did she make any of the specific hand motions that Perez claimed she had made," the lawsuit said. "The child did not 'pass' the simple qualifying questions Perez asked her, which are designed to determine if the child has the capacity to separate reality from fantasy, understand right from wrong, or the truth from a lie."

That's when the sheriff's department interviewer got up and walked out of the room, mumbling, "This is ludicrous" as he left, Molly and Nathan would later learn. The session was over. But Molly and Esther, who had been sitting in a waiting room, were not made aware of the interviewer's disgust.

California law requires that all evidence favorable to parents in a sexual abuse investigation be turned over to the parents and their legal counsel. It never happened. When asked, years later, where the video was, CPS officials said it "went missing."

Ochoa-Perez drove the three miles back to the motel. She said nothing to Molly about what had happened in the videotaping. Molly and Esther were frantic. The social workers were making things up, they told Ochoa-Perez. Her only response was to tell Molly to cut it out or she would have the restraining order against Michael Mewborn lifted and would have the grandfather visiting Madison "tomorrow." She informed Molly that CPS would be discussing the matter and would call her by 5:00 that evening.

Molly waited nervously by the phone, trying to keep Madison occupied so her daughter wouldn't sense her deep anxiety. Five o'clock came and went. Nothing. Finally, after two hours, there was a knock at the door.

It was Lucy Perez, accompanied by a uniformed police officer.

"We're here to take Madison," Perez said matter-of-factly. She did not have a warrant to search the premises, arrest Molly, or remove Madison to protective custody. The girl, sensing that something terrible was about to transpire, began to tremble and cry. Perez moved toward Madison. Her cries turned into screams of terror. Molly was hysterical, begging Perez not to do it.

"We want to know our rights!" Esther cried. "We want to talk to a lawyer and find out what the law is."

Perez stared coldly at the shaking step-grandmother.

"We *are* the law," she said.

Perez snatched up Madison and carried the screaming child out to the patrol car.

It was the last time Molly was allowed to be alone with her child for years. Molly and Nathan had no idea where the police were taking their little girl.

The next day, Robert Fort called the office of state assemblyman Peter Frusetta and explained to an aide, Jennifer Abundiz, what had happened. She promised to look into the matter. That evening, Abundiz met in person with the CPS director for San Benito County, Lee Collins. Collins said he could not discuss any details about the case, and then he did just that.

"Madison's disclosure was like something out of an X-rated movie," he told Abundiz.

With that, the assemblyman declined to pursue any allegations of conspiracy against the Forts.

A court hearing was set for the following week to determine if there was enough evidence to keep Madison away from her parents. Molly wrote a letter to the judge, telling him about her father's anger issues, threats, and previous false accusations. She pleaded with the judge to require some accountability from CPS. She never heard back.

At the hearing, Molly was not represented by an attorney and was not told of her right to counsel by CPS officials or the court. Much of the legalese used during the hearing was indecipherable to her. Nathan was there, and, despite the fact that he qualified for "de facto parent" status, CPS attorneys requested that he be barred from the courtroom. The judge agreed.

It did not go well for the young mother. The petition presented against her charged Molly with "failure to protect" Madison and accused Molly and Esther Fort of "coaching and coercing" Madison to change her testimony. Making matters worse, Ochoa-Perez testified under oath that she had never given Esther permission to stay with Molly at the hotel, where they allegedly hatched their plan to deceive.

Of course it was not true. "She knew Esther was staying with them at the motel and never told her to leave," Nathan said. "She said that to show that Molly was a liar and unwilling to follow orders."

After the appearance, Ochoa-Perez ordered Molly to be evaluated by a psychologist, *appointed by CPS,* that same day. She said it was mandatory, which was false. "It was made abundantly clear to Molly on several occasions, that her cooperation/submission to anything that Ochoa-Perez asked her to do was a prerequisite to seeing her daughter again," the Forts' lawsuit said. "This was also false." Molly still had no legal representation and no idea what her rights were.

Molly attended one or two sessions with the psychologist, Gloria Lee, but quickly realized that the purpose of the meetings was solely to convince Molly that Nathan had indeed molested her daughter. When Molly protested, Lee told her she was in deep denial.

At around that time, yet another CPS caseworker, Paul Peterlin, who had just been assigned to manage the case, appeared at the Fort home and met for about an hour with Robert, Esther, and Molly. They told him about Mewborn's erratic behavior, threats to take Madison away, and false (and recanted) accusations he had made against Nathan. They explained how those things could be corroborated. Nathan's parents testified to their son's good moral character.

Peterlin was unmoved. "Nathan molested Madison," he said.

But did the case manager really believe that? Much later, Peterlin would play a key role in the federal lawsuit that Nathan and Molly would file against San Benito County and CPS.

The Fort family, now despondent, requested a meeting with CPS director Collins. He agreed. The Forts unleashed their frustration. Donna Elmhurst was a friend and parishioner of Mewborn, they protested, who had already admitted to making false accusations against Nathan. Ochoa-Perez had lied about not authorizing Esther to be with Molly at the motel and had threatened to have the restraining order on Molly's father lifted if Molly continued to accuse CPS workers of lying.

Collins listened before asking, "Has Madison ever seen X-rated movies?" The family was dumbfounded. Of course she hadn't, they said. Finally, Collins blurted out, "We believe Nathan is a child molester."

Even though CPS had refused to give Nathan a polygraph test, Collins advised him that it would be a good idea. Nathan, at his own expense, had the test administered by an expert who conducted polygraphs for local police departments. He was found to be telling the truth when he said he had never touched Madison at any time in a sexual manner.

But, as with so many CPS cases, Nathan would never get his day in court to present those findings.

Meanwhile, Madison was being shunted among a string of foster homes, more than was allowed under state law. Molly was granted just two hours a week of supervised time with her daughter, while Nathan and his parents were banned from seeing the child altogether. Molly was even ordered to remove photos of her husband when Madison came over and to never mention his name to the child, his own stepdaughter.

During the prolonged investigation that followed, no one from CPS ever tried to question Nathan about what Madison had said, nor did they look into his background, friends, or anyone who could supply a character referral. Nobody spoke with Madison's friends, preschool teachers, or family members to see if she had told them about any molestation.

"Nobody was telling her that we missed and loved her," Nathan said. "She just got yanked away. Molly was never allowed to be alone with Madison, who kept asking, 'Where's my daddy?' But Molly could not say anything; she couldn't even mention my name. And Madison would ask, over and over, 'If I'm good today, can I please come home?' It was heartbreaking."

Nathan was growing increasingly depressed. His church asked him to leave the congregation. His weight ballooned to three hundred pounds. He felt Madison would be better off if he and Molly simply dropped dead.

In May of 1998, as the trial to determine whether the county would take jurisdiction over Madison was about to get under way, the court appointed an attorney, Karen Hamilton, to represent Molly. According to Molly and Nathan, the lawyer made it abundantly clear from their first meeting that it would be counterproductive for Molly to speak out in favor of her husband. Hamilton emphasized that her job was not to protect Nathan.

"Molly's lawyer, who worked for the county, told her she would look bad, like a lady that doesn't want to protect her child," he said. "Her own attorney said, 'Do not say he didn't do it.'"

Nathan begged the lawyer to obtain the videotape of Madison's second interview at the sheriff's department. It was the only piece of hard evidence that existed in the case. But Hamilton refused to even try, he said. "CPS already admits there's nothing on it," she told Molly and Nathan.

Nathan was outraged. "Well, isn't that why we should be looking at it?" he demanded.

"We don't need to," she said, according to Nathan. He continued, "And then she kicked me out of her office, saying she was Molly's attorney, not mine."

And, even though Hamilton agreed with the Forts that there was virtually no evidence to back up Lucy Perez's false allegations, she told them without hesitation that "you're going to lose; the judge always sides with CPS," again according to Nathan.

The attorney urged Nathan to admit that he did *something* and let CPS put him into a sexual offender's program. It would help to get Madison back with Molly faster. He refused.

That's when Nathan hired a lawyer of his own, Peggy Thorning, at his own expense. But she failed to win permission for him to even enter the courtroom.

"I grew up believing you have a right to face your accuser. But in family court, you are *not* innocent until proven guilty," he told me. It was a sentiment expressed by many parents whose children were stolen away from them.

The jurisdiction trial began in May 1998, in the courtroom of Judge Thomas Breen, and proceeded until December.

During the proceedings, Michael Mewborn managed to insert Madison's biological father, Robert DeVenecia, into the fray in the hopes that he could win custody of the child. DeVenecia had never paid any child support or attempted to see his daughter, Nathan told me. Despite that, he was appointed an attorney to help him get custody.

In June 1998, Molly gave birth to a baby girl. CPS made it clear that they would take the child away from Molly, citing California law requiring that they remove all the children if they remove one. Molly had no option to keep the baby. She found a suitable family from the East Coast who was willing to adopt the girl. They agreed to have an open adoption so the child would have an on-going relationship with her birth mother. Judge Breen allowed them to take her home pending a final determination of adoption. But then Breen reversed himself and ordered that the baby girl be flown back to California and handed over to her biological father. Eventually, the father's parents adopted the child.

"It was a kangaroo court with no evidence against me," Nathan said. "The doctor who examined Madison said there were no signs of abuse and that the video had proved that nothing went on. The only thing they had was this one lady, with no bachelor's degree, who said I'd touched Madison's pee-pee. But the judge still finds that it probably happened."

Without the police videotape, the judge relied solely on the testimony of Lucy Perez, to which Molly's court-appointed lawyer, Karen Hamilton, never objected, even when specifically asked by the judge if she wanted to. When pressed on this by the Fort family, Hamilton told them, "I know Lucy, and I don't believe she would lie," Nathan said.

Nathan believed that Hamilton proved to be a poor advocate for her client. She declined to vigorously cross-examine Lucy Perez while she was on the stand. "I felt sorry for her," Hamilton told Molly. "She was so nervous up there."

Perez, of course, was the prosecution's expert witness even though, in any jurisdiction surrounding San Benito County, she would have been barred from interviewing any child because she did not have a master's degree. Perez admitted on the stand that she had failed to follow proper procedure during the initial interview. Judge Breen asked her why. "I just did what my supervisor [Donna Elmhurst] told me to do," she testified. She also said there was nothing on the videotaped interview that contradicted her initial interview, something that was demonstrably false.

On every court date, the Forts had numerous character witnesses and close friends present and ready to testify on their behalf, but none were ever called by Hamilton. Her reason for failing to call these witnesses—including parents of young girls whom Nathan had babysat, and the girls themselves, now older: "She said that bringing in witnesses would just make the judge mad," Nathan said.

Then Mewborn took the stand. He accused the entire Fort family of running a "cult" and controlling Molly through mind-altering drugs. Karen Hamilton never once objected to such outlandish and unsubstantiated claims. Hamilton also made no effort to request reports from Madison's psychological evaluations and failed to call any expert witnesses to refute CPS's assertions, according to Nathan. "There was simply no effort to mount a defense," he said.

Next, San Benito County attorney Karen Forcum testified that Esther Fort was never authorized to stay with Molly and Madison while they were being held at the low-budget motel.

Karen Forcum's "sole concern was winning this case, and she fought hard to keep any evidence out that did not benefit CPS," Nathan said. The prosecutor also failed to "disclose evidence including evaluations and reports in regard to Madison and resisted the admission of the videotaped interview."

Eventually, Molly asked Judge Breen to appoint a new lawyer to defend her, but he refused. "Young lady, just because things aren't going your way doesn't mean you are not being well represented," he told her.

The court also appointed an attorney, Debra Strunk, another county employee, to represent Madison. "She was just another attorney for CPS, never questioning the validity of the charges, never interviewing Molly, Nathan, or even her own client," the couple wrote in a statement to their lawyers when they decided to sue the county years later. "In the courtroom, she was one of the most aggressive attorneys for the prosecution even though during her first appearance she did not know that her client's name was Madison (repeatedly referring to her as Molly). She assumed that Madison's best interests would be served by being removed from her mother, but had no evidence to support that assumption other than the allegations of CPS."

In the end, Breen ruled against Molly and handed provisional custody over to Madison's biological father, Robert DeVenecia. Molly was given only supervised visitation, indefinitely and under DeVenecia's control. For more than three and a half years, Molly would never see her daughter on any holiday or special occasion. Nathan, Esther, and Robert Fort were denied any visitation rights. The judge, however, did also limit Michael Mewborn's access to Madison, granting him just one hour per month of supervised visits.

The case then went into the "dispositional" phase, when the court tries to determine where the child should live and what potential steps the parents could take to win reunification. Molly's new lawyer managed to get the videotape of Madison admitted into evidence. Judge Breen viewed it, and even though it contradicted everything that Lucy Perez had said—under oath on the stand—he stated that he did not see anything that would cause him to influence his jurisdictional finding.

Ultimately, Judge Breen reaffirmed that Robert DeVenecia should have custody of Madison.

Molly and Nathan had been through enough. In late 1999, they filed an appeal of Judge Breen's ruling. It took two years for the appeals court to decide. During that time, Molly had only supervised visitation, and then only at Robert DeVenecia's discretion. At times, he did not let Molly see her daughter for weeks at a time, sending the distraught mother into deep bouts of depression.

Then DeVenecia did something that was extremely upsetting to the Forts. He moved in with Molly's parents, the Mewborns, even though Judge Breen had ordered that Mewborn could only have one hour of visitation per month with Madison. This was done with the full knowledge of Donna Elmhurst, the CPS supervisor.

"No attempt was made to even pretend that the court's orders were being followed for more than a year as Mewborn was allowed to babysit Madison alone while his wife, Pamela, and Robert DeVenecia were at work," Nathan said. The Mewborns also took Madison on extended vacations, leaving Robert behind in California.

Finally, things seemed to be breaking in favor of Nathan and Molly. In late January 2001, the appeals court ruled that, unless CPS could produce any new evidence within sixty days, it would reverse Judge Breen's decision. The appeals court went one step further, declaring that Lucy Perez was not qualified as an expert witness. It determined that two of Madison's statements allegedly made to her were "demonstrably false."

Judge Breen had retired since his ruling, but the Forts learned he was being brought back from retirement to decide whether there was any new evidence in their case. Molly and Nathan filed a motion with the appeals court, seeking a different judge to hear the case, alleging that Breen was biased against Molly. It was denied.

Judge Breen, without allowing any testimony or inquiring as to how Madison was faring under the care of DeVenecia, decided to uphold his own ruling against Molly.

Defiantly, he stated that the finding of the appeals court was "just their opinion." He repeated his contention that Lucy Perez was a reliable witness.

But the case did not end there. After Breen returned to retirement, it was handed over to a new judge, Harry Tobias. "The change in the direction and tone of the proceedings was immediate," Nathan said. "For the first time since the case began, we felt that someone seemed to care about what was happening to Madison."

In August of 2001, Tobias called for a new hearing. Attorneys for CPS argued that Breen's order should remain intact, even though Robert DeVenecia had moved in with the Mewborns, in violation of court orders.

Then, unexpectedly, Molly's county-appointed lawyer had a change of heart. Now she argued that the only damage done in the case was the removal of Madison from her mother and handing the girl over to DeVenecia.

Judge Tobias seemed to sympathize with that sentiment. He modified Molly's visitation order from two hours per week to six hours twice a week. Molly was allowed to see her mother at the Forts' home, with Robert or Esther Fort acting as supervisors. Nathan, however, was still barred from seeing Madison, and all photographs of him still had to be hidden whenever the girl visited.

More than fifty times over the next six months, until late December 2001, Nathan had to vacate his own home when Madison came over.

The new judge also ordered psych evaluations on Molly, Madison, and Robert DeVenecia, which took several weeks. Nathan volunteered for evaluations as well, as he had done twice before, despite the objections of CPS and the county's attorney. His examiner placed him, once again, at the bottom of the scales used to assess pedophile tendencies or abuse of children, the California "Child Abuse Central Index"; he exhibited zero tendencies or psychological disposition toward child molestation.

"All of the tests concerning Molly's parenting skills and bonding with Madison came back extremely positive," Nathan and Molly wrote in their statement.

During the four years while Madison was with DeVenecia, they said in the declaration, she had developed medical and dental problems from lack of proper care. "She had morphed from a happy, well-adjusted two-year-old who was completely potty-trained to a sad and confused six-year-old who wet her pants and lived in fear that someone was going to take her away."

By the end of 2001, Madison was allowed to visit both Molly and, for the first time in four years, Nathan, though he could not be alone with the child at any time. Eventually, Molly was allowed to have unsupervised visits with

Madison with Nathan present. Then she was granted fifty-fifty custody with Robert DeVenecia.

In July 2002, Judge Harry Tobias, in spite of Judge Breen's jurisdictional ruling, returned full custody of Madison to Molly, giving DeVenecia limited visitation every other week, removing all restrictions regarding Nathan, and terminating jurisdiction of the case. The following month, the court of appeals ruled an unqualified reversal of the case.

In December of 2002, Nathan's name was removed from the Child Abuse Central Index.

The nightmare was winding down, but its damage had been done. Madison was "a mess," according to Nathan, who was left broke and exhausted. Meanwhile, his marriage with Molly fell apart, and eventually she moved out of the house.

In October of 2003, Molly and Nathan filed suit in federal court against San Benito County and all the CPS workers involved in Madison's case. Robert Fort and Madison were listed as plaintiffs.

The family retained three of the state's leading attorneys who fight CPS in California: Donnie Cox and Paul Leehey of San Diego County and Robert Powell of San Jose.

"I was trying to understand how this could happen," Nathan told me. He knew that it was happening to so many other people. "And if we fought and fought these guys, we'd be able to prove, for the first time, that there was a conspiracy. And if we could get our court case on the books, we could change the laws and help others out."

The legal complaint alleged that Nathan and Molly had fallen victim to "a deliberate indifference to the rights and safety of individuals caught in the crosshairs of the power and reckless unaccountability of the CPS and its personnel." The actions of CPS staff, it added, were "malicious, oppressive, shocking to the conscience of the reasonable person, and despicable in the extreme."

The social workers had committed perjury by fabricating facts in written reports and live testimony, and obtained false statements from Madison through coercive and manipulative tactics, the suit said. Meanwhile, CPS employees failed to perform any independent, unbiased investigations into the allegations against Nathan and did not seek any exculpatory evidence that would have contradicted their position.

The suit lodged thirty-five formal complaints against the defendants. The social workers had violated the family's constitutional rights to "familial association" granted under the Fourth and Fourteenth Amendments by removing Madison from her family and detaining her for nearly four years. The removal of Madison also violated the family's Fourth Amendment protection against unreasonable search or seizure.

Molly's First Amendment right to free speech, meanwhile, was trampled when social workers told her they would have the restraining order against her father lifted if she did not stop saying negative things about them.

Forcing Molly and Madison to stay in a motel violated their Fourth Amendment protections against unreasonable search or seizure and also constituted false imprisonment. The defendants, moreover, engaged in "outrageous, unprivileged conduct, intended to cause emotional distress."

The list went on. The examinations and medical procedures that Madison underwent, without any court order, parental consent, or exigent circumstances, violated her First Amendment right to privacy. The placement of Nathan's name on the Child Abuse Central Index without even interrogating him violated his Fifth Amendment right to due process, while forcing him to leave his home at least fifty times while Madison was brought for supervised visits with Molly amounted to false imprisonment. And the initial interrogation of Madison without supervision or videotaping violated California law.

The lawsuit further alleged that CPS employees were "encouraged, trained, and/or directed to seize children immediately from their parents' custody and control, without a warrant and in the absence of exigent circumstances of imminent physical harm or emotional harm."

They were likewise directed or encouraged to "ignore, obfuscate, conceal, deliberately destroy, disregard, and minimize, information which contradicts or otherwise diminishes grounds for supporting a dependency petition, and to fabricate evidence, not disclose evidence, and commit perjury, if in doing so they can improve the chances of the juvenile court maintaining jurisdiction over minor children."

And while legal damages could compensate Molly and Nathan for their past injuries, they would not protect them, or other families in similar situations, against "actual or threatened future injury and violations of their constitutional rights."

The lawsuit requested that the court require CPS to adopt a new policy requiring "reasonable, evenhanded, good faith investigations" subject to independent review into any child's situation before seizing that child, except for cases where there was a clear and immediate danger.

Notices seeking depositions were served on all the defendants, including Paul Peterlin, the CPS social worker who had visited the Forts' home while he was in charge of the case. Peterlin had since left his job and was now an active-duty captain and military policeman in the California Army National Guard. He was stationed in Iraq.

When Peterlin received his deposition notice, he mistakenly called one of the family's attorneys, Robert Powell, thinking that he worked for the prosecution.

"He was confused and surprised that we were suing him," Powell told me.[3] "He said he had tried to help the Fort family." Peterlin said he knew there was nothing on the videotaped sheriff's interview with Madison that implicated Nathan in any way, and he believed the case should have been summarily dismissed.

"He said he took his concerns and the information he'd heard from the little girl to the county counsel and CPS supervisor Donna Elmhurst," Powell said. "In response to his telling them about this, they literally took the hard paper file from him and told him he was no longer going to be working on the case."

The revelation was precisely what Powell had been hoping for: a smoking-gun witness who could implicate CPS and the county in an unlawful conspiracy against Nathan and Molly.

On November 4, 2004, Donnie Cox and Robert Powell deposed Peterlin, who had recently returned from Iraq. He appeared in his military uniform. Molly, Nathan, and Robert Fort were also at the deposition, which lasted more than four hours. Six years had passed since Madison was first taken away from them.

The deposition was tense, but Peterlin's revelations, made under oath, were startling. He said that when Lucy Perez came out of the videotaped interview with Madison, she was "frustrated" because the girl "had not disclosed anything to her . . . there was really nothing out of the ordinary."[4]

The day after that, Donna Elmhurst had called Peterlin into her office and told him he would be taking over the case, even though he had only been on the job for a month or so. Elmhurst explained that she attended Mewborn's church and was a friend of his and his wife, Pamela, which was "potentially" a conflict of interest.

Elmhurst had told Peterlin to file the court petition to have Madison removed from her parents, a highly unusual move, since he had never interviewed the girl himself.

But Elmhurst did far more than receive updates. She instructed Peterlin what to include in the petition and personally revised several drafts that he wrote, including the claim that "the child, Madison, was repeatedly touched in the vaginal area by Nathan Fort . . . with his index finger."

"Did you do any investigation, prior to filing the petition, that led you to believe that this allegation was true, other than reviewing Lucy's notes or whatever?" Powell asked.

"No," Peterlin said.

Powell asked if Peterlin had been aware that he was required by state law to do an independent investigation before filing a petition. He had not. Then Powell asked the key question of the encounter.

"At some point did you become of the opinion that the case should be dismissed?"

"Based on what I thought were the facts, yes," Peterlin said.

"And did you communicate those facts to Donna Elmhurst?"

"Yes."

It didn't matter. Elmhurst, despite her undeniable conflict of interest, said the case would not be dismissed.

"It was pretty heated at that point," Peterlin said, under oath. "She was mad at me. She told me that I would proceed with the case against Nathan, and that was the way it was going to be. There was no opportunity for me to sway her differently . . . even though, you know, I was the one investigating the case."

At one point during the investigation, Peterlin had interviewed Madison himself. He asked the girl if the other family member had ever touched her. Madison said he had climbed into the bath "and did things with her," Peterlin said.

Peterlin had included Madison's disclosure in his handwritten notes, as well as his belief that the case should be dropped. But after he was removed from the case, none of that information would be included in CPS reports filed in court.

Peterlin, however, did discuss the matter with his boss, Donna Elmhurst, who ordered him to destroy his handwritten notes in the case.

"I argued with her that we had other suspects that needed to be followed up on before we focused on somebody that, in my view and my investigation, didn't have anything to do with what he was being accused of," Peterlin said.

"What did she say?" Powell asked.

"She told me that we were definitely going forward with Nathan as the suspected perpetrator and that that's what I needed to focus on," Peterlin said. Elmhurst made no mention of Madison's allegations against the other family member. Soon after that, Elmhurst removed Peterlin from the Fort case.

When the deposition ended, Powell knew the Forts would prevail. He could tell by the looks on the faces of the county attorneys.

"A jury would have a field day in this case," Powell told me. "That poor little girl was taken from them and made to go live with that loser, DeVenecia, and with her grandfather, the same guy who fabricated allegations against Nathan Fort to have her taken away."

Donna Elmhurst, Powell said, was determined to have Madison kept away from her parents no matter what. It was like she was under some kind of "spell" cast by Mewborn, her pastor.

"People do outlandish shit," he said. "And maybe 5 percent get fired or fined, but most just go on about their business and continue on up the ladder." Indeed, Elmhurst eventually became head of the county's Adult Protective Services.

Months after the Peterlin deposition, the county offered to settle the case, in the end handing over $1.25 million to the Forts, half of which was kept by the family's attorneys. It also agreed to write a letter of apology for what had been inflicted on an innocent couple and their young daughter. As part of the settlement, the county instructed those involved not to discuss the case. Several emails I sent to county officials for comment went unanswered.

Significantly, San Benito County also agreed to review the deceitful practices deployed by its CPS workers and put an end to such unconstitutional abuses of power.

"Money was not our goal," Molly told the *San Benito Pinnacle* at the time. "Our goal was to stop the people who did this to us from doing it to anyone else."[5]

"But no one got fired," Nathan added. "This town is a cesspool of corruption."

Donnie Cox, one of the other Fort attorneys, told the *Pinnacle* that their case was hardly unique. "What happened to the Forts happens at least once if not several times a day to parents throughout the state and nation," he said.

"I have no sympathy for child abusers. They should rot in jail for the rest of their lives," Cox said. "But when someone is accused of this, in the business, it's called 'admit to get.' That means they have to admit they abused the kid to get the kid back. That's the systemic problem in these cases. It should scare anyone who has a child. It's a bloody outrage."

LEGALIZED KIDNAPPING

It bears repeating: These sorts of outrages take place every day in this country. Many professionals—doctors, nurses, teachers, day care workers, counselors, and others—are required by law to report any suspicion of child neglect or abuse. One can easily understand how that protects society's deeply held interest in not letting any child tumble into danger, injury, or death. But it also needlessly paints thousands of innocent parents as potential, if not actual, criminals. If a child shows any signs of injury or abuse, the parents are typically the first to be implicated.

Meanwhile, many parents fall victim to false, often outrageous accusations filed anonymously by ex-spouses, vengeful relatives, jealous coworkers, unethical teachers, and malevolent—or sometimes well-meaning—neighbors who report a family argument as "violent abuse."

In these cases, parents have no right to know who filed the complaint, or why. And they will never have the ability to challenge that person in court. That seems to be a direct violation of the Sixth Amendment, which guarantees that a citizen "be informed of the nature and cause of the accusation" and "be confronted with the witnesses against him." In other words, any person accused of a crime has the right to learn who is accusing him and the right to ask questions.

Massachusetts lawyer Gregory Hession, one of the most outspoken, and thus controversial, attorneys working with families who have been victimized by the system, told me that the deck was perpetually stacked against parents.

"If you cannot justify to the doctor's satisfaction how your kid got an injury, like a broken bone, then forget it. CPS will be called, and they will label it abuse," he said. And even though kids break their bones all the time, "It's still assumed that it's abuse," he said. "In other words, it's guilty till proven innocent. It is very common."[6]

According to Hession, about 40,000 child-abuse reports are called in to the Massachusetts hotline every year, in a state with 2.4 million households. In other words, 1.6 percent of all households are investigated each year, or roughly one in six households over a decade (although some homes are surely reported more than once).

"I tried to think if I ever heard, in the twenty years I've done this, one family say they were benefited by the agency," he said with a sigh. "I could not think of one."

Then he described a typical case.

"Little Johnny goes to school and says, 'My daddy slapped my sister.' So then the teacher gets CPS on the speed dial and, *boom,* they wait for him and his sister at the bus stop and take them both. That's one of their favorite ploys—to take them off the bus. There's no muss, no fuss."

In other cases, CPS agents arrive at school and snatch the kids out of class. Nobody tells the parents. "When the kids don't go home that day, of course the mother's frantic, wondering where they are," he said. "I wish I could tell you all of what I've seen. It's a lot. Not *one* case but tons of cases."

If the authorities don't nab your kids at school, they'll come right to your door. "It's like a SWAT team," Hession said. "Sometimes they literally bust down the door, running, screaming, going in." He said that CPS agencies have "roaming teams of child kidnapper units that work on a nightly basis to take these kids."

Joshua Covert, an attorney from Michigan, said his work on CPS cases has caused him to fear for his own family.

"I've seen so many cases where they start attempting to take away a child and put the people through the system for something that occurs in my house probably on a daily basis," he told me. "And I feel like I'm a great parent—I take care of my children perfectly. But if someone comes into my home, at any one time, like a snapshot in time, that does not necessarily reflect how my home is. You may come to my house at one minute and there may be a diaper lying on the floor. A dirty diaper that fell when I was changing and I got busy chasing after my kid, right?"[7]

That would be enough for CPS to get involved in Covert's life, he said, and to take jurisdiction over his child because "they say I keep an unclean home because I've got a diaper on the floor."

A dirty diaper on the floor may seem a bit extreme, but it has been used as evidence to at least partially justify removing children from their homes. The general messiness of a household is often cited in court jurisdiction reports. Again, children found living in filth and squalor should be delivered from their wretched conditions without delay. But who is to determine what constitutes a "dirty" house that is dangerous for kids? How many of us would pass an unannounced inspection? And what right does anyone in the government— let alone unelected, virtually unaccountable public "servants"—have to make a judgment that is, more often than not, subjective and arbitrary?

Many parents of special needs children feel particularly vulnerable to unjustified interference by CPS. I spoke with parents of children with autism, for example, who worry that neighbors might mistake the screams of a full-blown meltdown for cries of physical pain and abuse and call CPS, something that does happen. Other parents have been reported to CPS out of spite and in retaliation for arguing with school officials over their children's special education plan.

"Schools don't like that," attorney Robert Powell said. "They don't like having to deal with the kid who pisses his pants or whatever his deal is. Sooner or later, you get the CPS referral. You've pushed too hard. You pissed off the wrong person. And then it just goes from there."

CASE STUDIES

I encountered a story in Escondido, California, north of San Diego, where the rantings of an insane relative were enough to remove two small children from their home.[8] Police officers, falsely claiming to have a court order, seized the children, aged two and five, and sent them to a county-run institution. Days later, without any authorization by a judge or notification of the parents, they brought the kids to a hospital for intrusive anal and vaginal physical examinations.

CPS workers already knew about the family. Four years earlier, the mother's sister, who suffered from a long history of psychiatric problems, including severe dissociative and multiple personality disorders, made a false report to San Diego County social workers accusing the father of sexually abusing his son. CPS investigated and found no credible evidence to support the allegations and the case was closed. The couple cut off all relations with the woman, who, before long, began making even more bizarre, and dire, statements to her therapists.

The sister had recounted a recently "recovered memory" of being in the woods with the children's father, who was bedecked in a cult robe and chanting hypnotically, "On the third full moon after two blue moons, a child will be killed," one of her multiple personalities told the therapist, insisting that the incantation referred to the boy, who would be sacrificed to Satan on the fall equinox, one of the satanic "High Holidays."

The children were not returned to their parents for two and a half months.

In another case, in Elizabethtown, Kentucky, a downstairs neighbor (and, interestingly, a CPS employee, who obviously knew how the game is played) filed repeated and false accusations against two loving young parents. The complaints, made in 2015, always came late at night while the family, Corey Chaney and April Rodgers and their infant daughter, Summer, slept. They alleged that the parents upstairs were being "too loud."[9]

So many calls were made that the parents begged CPS to consider whether someone was fabricating the allegations. The agency said it had no choice but to respond to each call.

The severity of the allegations increased as the calls continued. One call claimed the mother was holding the baby upside down over a balcony; another alleged the father was violent and high on methamphetamine. Each time the police showed up, they found no evidence of the allegations.

Still, every call triggered a new investigation from a new state social worker with a new round of questions about their personal lives, such as whether they used drugs (they did not), whether they fought violently (no), or whether they had abused or neglected their child. All investigations were closed as unsubstantiated or unfounded.

Anticipating a new hotline call, the parents took their daughter and left their home to stay with relatives.

The couple alerted Elizabethtown police about their plans. The first night they were away, a call came into the abuse hotline reporting that the father had turned violent and hurled the baby against the wall. Another call followed on May 23, 2015, alleging a disturbance at the couple's apartment. Police went to the apartment but found no one home.

Finally, the couple discovered that the anonymous accuser was their downstairs neighbor with a grudge, thirty-seven-year-old social worker Beth Bond from the Kentucky Cabinet for Health and Family Services, and her fiancé, forty-two-year-old Joseph Applegate Jr.

The neighbors were arrested, but the couple decided to move to avoid any encounters with Bond and Applegate.

"We moved that weekend," the mother told the *Courier Journal*.[10] "It took every single dime we had." No one from the agency contacted them to explain or apologize, the couple said. They decided to go public with their story to expose what happened. "We don't want this stuff swept under the rug," she said.

"This could happen to anyone," their attorney told the *Courier Journal*. "The bottom line is that there was a social worker allowed to run amok because there's a system in place to protect anonymous callers."

Bond and Applegate later pled guilty to misdemeanor charges of filing false statements, for which each received a twelve-month suspended sentence. Two years later, however, in May 2017, Bond was reportedly convicted on four counts of official misconduct and four counts of falsely reporting incidents against a former friend and a church pastor.

In yet another case, on May 16, 2011, a young California mother received a call from her children's day care provider telling her that one of them, her son, had developed "some redness" on his face. The provider had no idea what had caused the discoloration. Maybe it was an allergy, she ventured, or perhaps he'd hurt himself on the trampoline. Whatever it was, it appeared after the child had arrived at day care.

But when the mother, Joanna Swartwood, picked her two kids up that afternoon, she noticed that it did not look like a fall or an allergic reaction. Apart from the redness, there was also bruising under her son's eyes. The next day, her pediatrician determined that the redness was caused by "non-accidental/inflicted trauma," and advised that both children should undergo further medical testing at an emergency room. The doctor, as required by law, reported the injury to the local CPS agency.

The ER physicians examined both children and did not believe that the boy's injuries were inflicted by either of his parents.

Despite the exoneration by trained medical professionals, CPS social workers showed up at the couple's home and whisked away the kids, without a court order, parental consent, or any evidence that either child was in imminent danger of bodily injury, according to court documents, filed later.[11]

While in state custody, the kids underwent invasive physical exams without medical need or court order. There was no parental consent; the parents weren't even allowed to be present.

Two days later, the children were returned without explanation or apology. The parents were lucky to get them back so quickly, but the episode understandably left them traumatized. In 2012, they filed suit in federal court and were awarded $1.1 million for violation of their rights.[12] "In addition, the county stipulated to a judgment and agreed to change their policies, although it appears their *practice* is still an issue," attorney Donnie Cox said in an email.[13]

Finally, there are parents whose children were taken away because they rejected the advice of one doctor over the advice of another. "You get into a battle of the doctors over diagnosing and treating a kid, where one doctor says this; another doctor says that. It's not uncommon," Massachusetts lawyer Gregory Hession said. "Pediatricians have become an extension of the system by feeding it more and more cases."

Other parents seeking a second, third, or even fourth medical opinion are reported for "shopping around" for a diagnosis that confirms their beliefs or yields the greatest benefits. Others are falsely accused of fabricating, exaggerating, or even causing their children's symptoms, something known as Munchausen syndrome by proxy, triggering a CPS intervention.

They call it "medical kidnapping."

The most highly publicized case was that of Justina Pelletier, a young girl from Connecticut who was held against her parents' will for sixteen months by doctors at Boston Children's Hospital and officials at the Massachusetts Department of Children and Families.

Justina had been diagnosed with a disorder of her mitochondria—the tiny batteries of the body's cells that convert sugar and oxygen into energy—at Tufts Medical Center, where she was undergoing an outpatient treatment plan overseen by Dr. Mark Korson, chief of metabolic services and a leading expert in mitochondrial disease.

In early 2013, Justina developed flu-like symptoms and stopped eating for about a week. Korson directed her parents to bring her into the emergency room at Boston Children's Hospital to see a gastroenterologist, who had been treating Justina before transferring to the hospital one month before.

While in the ER, Justina was examined by a resident who, just seven months out of medical school, unilaterally decided to change her diagnosis to "somatoform disorder," meaning her symptoms were caused by mental, not physical illness.

The resident barred any of Justina's specialists at Tufts from examining her and likewise refused access to the GI specialist she had come to see.

The new diagnosis, that Justina's physical ailments were all in her head, were confirmed by a Boston Children's Hospital psychologist after spending just twenty-five minutes with the girl and without consulting any other physicians, according to a civil complaint filed by the family. As it turned out, the psychologist had received a National Institutes of Health grant to study somatoform disorder. Justina, once she became a ward of the state, could legally be used in somatoform research, without her consent or that of her parents, and regardless of whether it benefited her or not.

Justina's parents, Lou and Linda, were understandably angry. Hospital officials were insisting that they sign forms authorizing a new treatment regimen, including placement in the psychiatric ward and halting all her current medications. The parents would be barred from seeking a second opinion, from speaking to their daughter about her condition, and even from speaking with her new physicians without hospital approval. They refused.

The Pelletiers demanded that Boston Children's Hospital discharge Justina at once and return her to the care of Dr. Korson at Tufts. Instead, hospital officials called the Massachusetts Department of Children and Families, who charged Lou and Linda with "medical abuse"—even though their only transgression was to follow the treatment plan established by a worldwide medical expert at one of the nation's leading teaching hospitals. Although the Tufts geneticist supported the mitochondrial diagnosis, a juvenile court judge deferred to Boston Children's Hospital. An emergency hearing assured that the parents' custody was removed and that Justina became, essentially, a full-time detainee of the state.

The juvenile court not only sanctioned the abduction of the Pelletiers' daughter, it eviscerated their First Amendment rights by imposing a gag order against discussing the case with the media. When Lou Pelletier spoke to reporters, DCF sought to hold him in contempt.

Justina's case became a cause célèbre among conservative Christians and pro-family organizations. The drama was fueled by coverage on Breitbart and Fox News. Republicans and libertarians alike blasted the hospital and state agency for trampling on the Pelletiers' rights to make medical decisions for their own daughter.

The public furor changed nothing. The despair that engulfed the Pelletiers' lives without warning or recourse would endure for sixteen months. Justina would spend most of that time in the psych ward, with just one hour per week for parental visits and one twenty-minute phone call per week. The calls were monitored by DCF workers.

The family, aided by the conservative legal foundation Liberty Counsel, fought back in court.

In March 2014, Suffolk County juvenile judge Joseph Johnston approved an agreement between the Massachusetts Department of Children and Families and the Pelletiers to jettison the contempt charges against Lou Pelletier, drop the gag order, and transfer medical care for Justina back to Tufts Medical Center.[14]

"DCF should be held accountable for the tragic abuse inflicted by this incompetent agency on the family," Mat Staver, founder and chairman of Liberty Counsel, told reporters.

Just three weeks later, Judge Johnston, citing evidence provided by the Massachusetts and Connecticut DCF agencies that the Pelletiers had been verbally abusive with authorities and haphazard in their decision-making, granted permanent custody of Justina to the Massachusetts DCF.[15] The fifteen-year-old was likely destined to remain in state custody until she turned eighteen—unless her parents could convince the court otherwise.

Finally, in June 2014, the same Massachusetts juvenile court judge who removed her from her parents' care ordered that Justina be returned to her parents.

In February 2016, the family filed a lawsuit in state superior court against Boston Children's Hospital, four of its physicians, and Massachusetts DCF for gross negligence, medical malpractice, and civil rights violations.

"I'm very angry, and I just don't understand how this happened, and I just really don't want this to happen again to another family," Justina, who was now seventeen, said at a news conference announcing the lawsuit.[16]

That June, the judge in Justina's case rejected the immunity claim by Dr. Alice Newton, a hospital pediatrician who allegedly headed the effort to detain Justina, who argued that she was a mandated reporter of suspected child abuse.

The lead attorney on the case, John T. Martin of Boston's KJC Law Firm, said in an October 2018 email that the proceedings were still in pretrial discovery, adding that the parties "are subject to a gag order regarding all discovery materials." Trial was set for January 2020. "What we have discovered is, quite frankly, heinous and shocking," Martin said. "Much more disturbing than what was widely reported. I wish I could provide you with more detail."

In a landmark piece of reporting, *The Boston Globe* discovered at least five other cases of children being commandeered by Boston Children's Hospital under similar circumstances: unfounded allegations about medical treatment leading to DCF taking custody and permitting the hospital to do what it claimed was medically required.

A SYSTEM IN CRISIS

"We have an unconstitutional and barbaric agency that gets away with financially incentivized mass removals of kids, 85 percent of them not being for physical or sexual abuse," attorney Robert Powell told me.

He said that investigators are often "terribly trained," their evidence-gathering practices can be "horrendous," and that some parents are left destitute just trying to disprove claims against them. "These are whole justice systems that are financed through unjust practices," Powell said. "That's the truth about child protective services."

Once again, poorer families, the most vulnerable citizens with the fewest resources to fight back, bear the brunt of injustice.

At first glance, the incessant drive to remove children from their homes seems inexplicable. After all, the stated goal of *all* CPS agencies is the ultimate reunion of children with their parents, if possible, as soon as possible, even if the parents must first receive psychological evaluation and counseling, anger management classes, substance-abuse therapy, or other mental-health services.

But it often does not work that way. "Pervasive and serious agency-wide dysfunctions continue to result in corruption, mismanagement, coercion, bullying, and intimidation," say Julian Dominguez and Melinda Murphy, two seasoned former social workers at the L.A. County Department of Children and Family Services (DCFS), who coauthored a 2014 exposé of the agency, *A Culture of Fear.*[17] "Most importantly, tragically and unconscionably, these problems have caused us to harm families."

I consulted dozens of people involved with CPS agencies, including parents, attorneys, reformist lawmakers, and child-protection workers. Their testimonies left me to conclude that this is an abusive system, rotting from the inside, and in desperate need of a top-to-bottom, nationwide overhaul. And while some agencies needlessly remove children and often conspire to keep them separated from their parents, a minority of incompetent, underfunded entities fail to intervene in cases where children truly are at imminent risk and their removal is clearly warranted. In neither case are the "best needs" of the children being met.

We will never know exactly how many parents have had their children needlessly taken away by harried social workers laboring to appease a revenue-hungry machine constantly demanding more cases to process. But, as you will see, we can get some idea.

"The majority of the parents who come to the attention of DCFS are not horrible people," Dominguez and Murphy wrote. About 20 percent of their cases involved parents who were "completely innocent or the situation doesn't merit having their kids taken away. The damage done to these families is unconscionable."

Many children will never go home: Family reunification was the "case plan goal" for just 55 percent of those kids in L.A. County.

Dominguez and Murphy estimate that another 20 percent tended to "have a myriad of issues," but were denied financial assistance, affordable health care, and other services that would have kept them out of a system in which they did not belong. "Their only crime is that they are poor, with limited resources," they wrote.

In fact, only 20 percent of their cases involved parents whose behavior toward their children was so "egregious and heinous" that courts had no choice but to permanently remove the kids from home.

That leaves 40 percent. "These are the only cases that DCS should focus on," Dominguez and Murphy wrote.

Meanwhile, even the most idealistic young social workers entering the system can be indoctrinated into its culture of nanny-state authoritarianism.

Those that do try to build a case on the parents' behalf and conclude that a child's removal is unwarranted often slam into an impenetrable wall of resistance.

"Pity the poor social worker who tries to correct the wrong and alert the court or supervisor. Neither DCFS nor the DCFS attorneys admit to making mistakes, so even if parents are innocent, DCFS's tendency is to make them appear guilty in some way," they wrote. "And that could include making things up if need be or blowing things out of proportion. DCFS does not have a mechanism for backing down."

Social workers, Murphy and Dominguez said in their book, "go unrewarded for trying to tell the truth, for putting forth facts that actually represent the best interests of the family, based on verifiable events confirmed by credible sources."[18]

Murphy and other former CPS agents say that, in their experience, many social workers who try to help families stay together quickly learn they have a stark choice: lie or leave. "These good people are subtly and overtly rewarded, encouraged, praised, coerced, threatened, and even ordered to lie," she said. "That ensures that attorneys will use the harshest language possible in the petitions and/or court reports. Then the court accepts it all as truth."

One supervisor even had a term for the practice: FUCMA—fuck you and cover my ass.

Murphy and Dominguez went on:

Reports and petitions are routinely rewritten by "phantom authors," supervisors, administrators and other higher-ups. They remain in the shadows behind the curtain, routinely censoring, slanting, and omitting facts and sometimes even tampering with court reports, day in and day out. These are the very same court reports that can and do determine if a family is made whole again. They compel social workers to write anything they decide should be written or omit anything they feel should be omitted. Then they don't have to sign the report, so they're not the actual authors in the courts' eyes and don't have to hold themselves responsible or accountable.

WHY DOES THIS HAPPEN?

What possible motives could CPS employees have for taking so many children away from safe and loving environments—and the zeal with which they fight, scheme, and yes, sometimes lie to keep kids under state control?

From what I can glean, the answer is sometimes a combination of fear, arrogance—and money.

It is not hard to understand the fear factor. All too often, shocking headlines appear in the media about a CPS worker who ignored the dire straits of a child and failed to take action, only to have the youngster killed or seriously hurt. Imagine the pressure, imagine the apprehension swirling among social workers and their superiors. *Err on the side of caution,* it's easy to imagine them thinking. *It's better to be safe than sorry and remove the kid now. It can all be sorted out later.*

"There exists a pervasive fear in CPS offices where CPS does not want to be held responsible for anything unfavorable that might happen should a child go home," former L.A. County caseworker Murphy said.

Once children have been removed from their home, no matter how spurious the allegations against the parents, the system is often rigged to keep them away. Why? Based on my conversations with many in the system, I came to believe that some CPS officials are loath to admit making a mistake: If a child was separated from his family, there *must* be a rational reason, they tell themselves.

"Once CPS has made the determination, it will fight like hell to be proven right—and it usually wins," family court attorney Robert Powell told me. "There is a God complex that runs through that crowd that you cannot believe. The root of all evil isn't money, it's power. It's just that money's one of the objects of power. And you give people this unbridled power over other human beings."

"Up until the last, say, ten or fifteen years," he said, "when my colleagues and I began suing the crap out of them, they walked free."

Courts, which routinely take CPS reports at face value, are of little help. One civil case in Florida revealed that during a fifteen-month period in 1999–2000, 2,857 children were removed from their homes. Only 86 of them, or 3 percent, were returned home within twenty-four hours. That means that

97 percent of the time, the court agreed that CPS had correctly estimated probable cause to legally remove the child.[19]

"It may be that Florida's caseworkers are remarkably good at what they do," law professor Mark R. Brown wrote in the *Ohio State Law Journal*.[20] "More likely, Florida's judges simply proved unwilling to return rescued children to their parents. DCF was uniformly given every benefit of the doubt, even when probable cause was plainly lacking, [with] its judges simply acting as 'rubber stamps.'"

Robert Powell, who represented the Fort family in their CPS battle, agreed that the entire child-protection "racket" is rigged from the bottom up. "You go to CPS court and lose, pretty much every time," he said. "I consider myself one of the best attorneys in California doing this, in terms of juvenile dependency work. And my win rate, in terms of an outright dismissal, is like 15–20 percent."

AS ALWAYS, FOLLOW THE MONEY

Foster care and adoption are big businesses in the United States. The federal government offers cash incentives to states for each child they adopt out of foster care in excess of the previous year's target goals. It's a complicated formula, depending on the age of the child and whether the child has "special needs." But bonuses can range from $4,000 to $10,000 per child.[21] That translates into serious money. Between 1998 and 2013, Texas collected $63.6 million and Florida $43.2 million.[22] Little wonder, then, that the number of children adopted each year from foster care nearly doubled, from about thirty-one thousand in 1997 to annual numbers between fifty thousand and fifty-seven thousand in each fiscal year between 2002 and 2010.[23]

CPS systems also receive federal and state money based on how many foster-care placements they have made. Funds are available for recruitment of suitable foster parents and monthly maintenance payments, which are certainly worthy expenditures. But funds are also allotted for administrative costs to manage the program and for the design, implementation, and operation of statewide data collection systems.

The amounts are often significant. In fiscal year 2010–2011, for example, the Los Angeles County child protection agency was allotted slightly more than $1 billion—with $444 million allotted for foster care assistance and $490 million for child welfare assistance, but another $32.6 million for administration.

"If children go home to their parents, states do not receive this bonus money," former CPS worker Murphy said. "CPS will recommend adoption in those cases where it clearly is not in the best interest of the child to sever parental ties."

But funds come from other sources as well. "They get Medicaid reimbursements, because every kid goes into therapy," Massachusetts family attorney Gregory Hession told me. "They get educational reimbursements because every kid goes into special ed. It's a spiderweb. They're pulling money from completely different, disparate departments of the federal government to get reimbursements from all over the place."

The bottom line is this: The more children that CPS can get into the system—and keep there for as long as possible or put up for adoption—the more public funds will spill into their coffers. From my reporting on this issue, I have come to believe that many social workers know this, their supervisors know this, and program administrators know this. They might not say it, but everyone is aware of how the game is played. And those who refuse to play along are too often dealt with harshly.

PARENTAL RIGHTS AND REFORMS

The Constitution makes no mention of children or their rights, or of any rights explicitly reserved for parents, although over the years courts have upheld certain parental freedoms inherent in the Bill of Rights. Even so, violations of constitutional rights underpin most lawsuits filed by families against CPS agencies. For example, removing children from their homes and keeping them away for extended periods, without any proof of harm or neglect inflicted by their parents, violates the right to "familial association" protected under the Due Process Clause of the Fifth and Fourteenth Amendments.

The act of removing children without a warrant or probable cause of imminent danger, in turn, violates the Fourth Amendment's protection against unreasonable search or seizure. Medical exams and other procedures performed on children without their parents' consent violates the right to privacy under the First, Fourth, and Fourteenth Amendments.

When parents are placed on child-abuse registries without so much as a hearing, their rights to due process under the Fifth and Fourteenth Amendments are shredded. And when they are told not to discuss the case with their children, as often happens, their First Amendment rights go out the courtroom window.

"Parenting as one sees fit is one of the so-called unenumerated rights. There are a lot of rights that we have that the courts have declared are constitutional rights that aren't actually mentioned in the Constitution," Michigan attorney Josh Covert, who works on CPS cases, told me. "It was so obvious that you have a right to parent your own child that they didn't even need to put it in the Constitution."

That leaves interpretation of our unenumerated rights to the courts. Federal courts are divided over whether children can be taken away without prior authorization from a judge. The Second, Ninth, and Tenth Circuits have maintained that, generally speaking, children cannot unilaterally be removed from their homes by state officials and that judicial preauthorization is required. But the First and Eleventh Circuits have concluded the opposite, upholding that traditional Fourth and Fourteenth Amendment limitations do not apply to child abuse investigations, and police and social workers may remove kids without any judicial oversight whatsoever.

This problem has been out of control for years. While some victimized parents have fought back against their constitutional abusers in court and won, there is little evidence to suggest that any type of fundamental reform is even on the horizon. It's just not a hot-button issue in our national discourse. Too many innocent parents are being tossed down the legal, financial, and emotional rabbit hole of CPS entanglement, and hardly anyone in a position of power is doing anything to stop it.

Given all the evidence of a corrupt and broken system—the outcry from parents, the testimonies of former CPS workers, the growing number of lawsuits filed for wrongful removal of a child—the number of lawmakers speaking out for reform is scant.

Only a few brave politicians have been willing to take on the CPS system, and calls for reform usually die a quick death. "They can't do anything about it; they don't want to get in trouble," Hession told me. "It's a big money machine. And their political opponents could really use it against them. Can you imagine? *Oh, yeah, look at that, they're for child abuse!*"

Still, there are a number of reforms that lawmakers could enact, if they could summon the political courage, to guarantee that the rights of parents (and children) are respected without compromising the state's imperative role of rescuing kids who are truly at risk.

First, critics say, the state must stop rewarding agencies for each additional child they decide to place in foster care or up for adoption over the previous year. "The agency itself is the feeder for the money, for the foster care part," Hession said. "Foster care is the money machine. But the same agency also has the taking function. So what if you decoupled it? What if the decision to take children had absolutely nothing to do with the department that cared for the children?"

As cash incentives disappeared, so would the pressure put on social workers to exaggerate or fabricate damning evidence and omit information that might exonerate parents. Without financial incentives, far fewer children would be torn needlessly from their homes, while those who are actually being abused and neglected would receive targeted intervention and improved care as available resources were directed to their cases. Taxpayers, meanwhile, would save billions of dollars a year by no longer financing an unconstitutional system that relies on deceit and intimidation to keep revenue flowing.

The next step: Provide far more transparency throughout the process. In most jurisdictions, parents and their attorneys are barred from the initial detention hearing, even though social workers and lawyers for CPS, the county government, and even the children themselves are present. With no one there to speak on behalf of the parents, judges routinely side with the state.

Members of the media, meanwhile, are barred from covering most child-custody cases in order to protect the kids' anonymity. "We desperately need the disinfectant of the press and the public in these courtrooms," Hession said. "It all would end right there."

Many critics contend that rescuing children from abuse needs to become the function solely of law enforcement, and not social workers, because of the built-in due process protections involved in police work.

Other reform ideas include providing parents with their rights in writing; mandating jury trials where evidence for both sides can be presented and evaluated before permanently removing children; upholding laws against perjury and obstruction of justice by government officials; if a parent declares fraud, providing for a hearing with the right to discovery of all evidence; rescinding all immunity for CPS agents who behave illegally; providing automatic punitive damages to parents who are falsely accused of child abuse or neglect; requiring CPS caseworkers to wear dash and body cameras; requiring anyone reporting abuse and/or neglect to swear under penalty of perjury that their accusations are true; forcing all medical facilities to provide records to parents within seven days; and requiring a warrant to examine or search children.

To their credit, *some* politicians and pundits, mostly conservatives, have railed against the trampling of parental rights, but it's going to take more than Fox News, InfoWars, and Breitbart to change things. The issue was rarely if ever raised during the bruising eighteen months of the 2016 campaign, and so far, it does not seem to be a priority of the Trump administration.

For now, the small cadre of attorneys filing lawsuits against CPS agencies in federal court will be left with the task of chipping away at the flagrant denial of basic civil rights that has injured so many innocent Americans. Some of their winning cases have set precedents and changed procedures in a handful of jurisdictions. In 1999, for example, the U.S. Ninth Circuit Court of Appeals held that government officials cannot conduct invasive bodily searches of children in suspected abuse cases without parental permission, unless a judge has ruled it warranted, and that parents have a right to be present or nearby during permitted searches.

Children have a right to "the love, comfort and reassurance of their parents while they are undergoing medical procedures," the judges wrote in a 2–1 decision, "particularly those . . . that are invasive or upsetting," such as vaginal and anal exams.[24]

The ruling, forcefully authored by Judge Stephen Roy Reinhardt, balanced the needs of the state against the rights of the accused, and came down in favor of parents:

> *This case involves a conflict between the legitimate role of the state in protecting children from abusive parents, and the rights of children and parents to be free from arbitrary and undue governmental interference. Such conflicts occur with increasing frequency these days. The problem of child abuse is a critical one, with deep personal and social costs. For too long, intra-familial sexual abuse was considered to be a "private" matter.*

*Today, the law is changing. As we develop a greater awareness of the
extent and severity of this difficult and painful problem, society has finally
begun to treat intra-familial child abuse as a serious criminal offense.*

Then, Reinhardt offered a cautionary tale about not keeping state power in
check.

*Because the swing of every pendulum brings with it potential adverse
consequences, it is important to emphasize that in the area of child
abuse, as with the investigation and prosecution of all crimes, the
state is constrained by the substantive and procedural guarantees of
the Constitution. The fact that the suspected crime may be heinous—
whether it involves children or adults—does not provide cause for
the state to ignore the rights of the accused or any other parties.
Otherwise, serious injustices may result. In cases of alleged child abuse,
governmental failure to abide by constitutional constraints may have
deleterious long-term consequences for the child and, indeed, for the
entire family. Ill-considered and improper governmental action may
create significant injury where no problem of any kind previously
existed.*

Who can argue with that?

3

YOUR MONEY OR YOUR FREEDOM

"You don't go to jail for walking your dog without a leash, making an illegal left turn or burning leaves without a permit," Pulitzer Prize–winning author Tina Rosenberg wrote in a March 2015 opinion piece for *The New York Times*. "But in many states you will go to jail if you can't pay the resulting fees and fines. We have a two-tier system: The rich pay fines. The poor go to jail."[1]

Most Americans are unaware that they could go to jail if they are unable to satisfy a debt, whether criminally related or even civil in nature. The problem has grown worse over the past decade or so, experts say. Today in the United States, thousands of people—perhaps even tens of thousands—are languishing in jail, not because they *won't* pay a debt but because they simply cannot afford to. The practice—although considered illegal and unconstitutional by many experts—locks people away in what amounts to modern-day debtors' prisons.

Debtors' prison: The very name conjures archaic images of Dickensian dungeons where indifferent societies incarcerated people, most of them poor, and fed them gruel because they could not pay what they owed. Debtors' prisons flourished in Europe, the United States, and elsewhere until the mid-1800s, when bankruptcy laws and social reforms finally made the practice obsolete. The notorious prisons were designed to instill terror into anyone who might owe money to creditors, including the government, and to exact restitution from those who couldn't pay by forcing them to work off their debts while incarcerated.

There is, of course, a gaping distinction between someone who can't pay a debt and someone who simply won't. If you owe money and have the resources to pay it, refusal to do so can and should result in prosecution. But no one should ever be incarcerated because she is too poor to pay what she owes.

That, however, is not how things work in twenty-first-century America.

TEEN JAILED AFTER TRAFFIC TICKET

Kevin Thompson, a teenager from the Atlanta suburbs, never dreamed that a paperwork technicality could ultimately land him in jail. Now, like thousands of other Americans, many of them people of color, he knows that even the most minor violation can lead to incarceration—if you don't have the means to cover fines, court fees, and other legal costs.

When Thompson was first arrested, he was an average eighteen-year-old, living at home in a comfortable one-story, three-bedroom house with his mother, sister, and newborn niece. He never had any run-ins with the law. "I kept out of trouble," he told me. "I had great parents; they raised me right." He was a diligent student with average grades. He had a girlfriend and played on the high school football team. But his real passion was cars. He loved going to car shows and working on his own car.[2]

Thompson's hometown of Decatur is solidly upper middle class, with a median household income of $82,000. Still, 15 percent of the population—and a quarter of people under age eighteen, including Thompson, who is African American—live below the poverty line.[3] In the summer of 2014, Thompson was getting by on about $200 per week, picking up sporadic jobs in auto-repair shops and driving a tow truck. Some of that money went to pay rent to his mother.

On July 18, 2014, Thompson left home on his way to a job interview at National Tire and Battery. As he was halfway out of his driveway, a DeKalb County police officer blocked his way. The cop leaped from the patrol car and demanded to see Thompson's license. Thompson obliged. He was surprised to learn that it had been suspended.

"I think he ran the plate number," Thompson recalled. "He started hollering and screaming, asking me if I wanted to go to jail." The officer handcuffed the teenager and shoved him into the patrol car just as Thompson's mother was pulling up into the driveway.

He was charged with driving with a suspended license and booked into the

DeKalb County jail, where he spent the rest of the day before being released that evening. "It's not a place you ever want to be," he told me. "I thought it was crazy for me to be in there, but I also wondered why my license was suspended."

Thompson would soon learn the reason: Earlier in the year, he had been ticketed for a minor traffic violation (he'd missed a "no left turn" sign) and was ordered to appear in Atlanta Municipal Court. But Thompson arrived late for the 8:00 a.m. hearing and was barred access to the courtroom, he said. "It was the first time I had ever been called to court," he explained. "I thought I could arrive any time during the morning." His tardiness cost him dearly. He was charged with one count of failure to appear in court.

When Thompson cleared up the matter, the court said his license could be reinstated. But Thompson didn't know that he was supposed to mail in a form notifying the Georgia Department of Driver Services that the suspension was withdrawn. He was never told that, barring that, the suspension remained in effect.

At the time, traffic violations were handled by the DeKalb County Recorders Court, part of the county's executive branch, which has an interest in generating revenue, rather than an independent member of the judiciary, which is the third pillar of American democracy.

On October 9, Thompson appeared before a court judge and pleaded guilty to driving on a suspended license. He was sentenced to a fine, fees, and court costs totaling $838, an enormous amount of cash for the financially struggling youth.

"Can you pay the fine today?" the judge inquired.

Thompson said he was unable to comply.

The judge ordered him to pay the fine, court costs, probation fees, and a fee for the Georgia Crime Victim Emergency Fund within thirty days, and to serve one year of probation. Meanwhile, his driver's license was suspended for an additional six months.

As part of his sentence, Thompson was assigned to a private probation company, Judicial Correctional Services Inc. (JCS), which contracted with the county to manage probation cases and collect fines and other assorted fees from the convicted. Like most private probation firms, JCS provides its service— called "pay only" probation—free of charge to the court. It generates revenue by charging probationers monthly fees to manage their own cases.

In late October, Thompson went to meet with the JCS probation officer assigned to him, Shanekia Thomas. Once again, he explained that he did not have the money to cover his fine and had no way to gather that much cash within thirty days. Thomas told Thompson to report once a week to the JCS office and to pay whatever he could at each visit.

But without a driver's license, Thompson found it extremely difficult to get or even look for work. His weekly income had plummeted to just eighty dollars, mostly from doing odd jobs at an auto body shop within walking distance. It was barely enough to cover food, transportation, and rent. Thompson turned to his family for whatever help, however meager, they could muster. One week, his sister lent him a small sum, followed by his mother and grandmother.

During that time, Thompson also submitted an application to the Recorders Court to issue him a limited driving permit, which he believed would allow him to drive for work purposes if it was signed by a court judge. The court clerk said she would give the form to her supervisor. He never heard back about the request.

By early December, Thompson was out of options. On his weekly visit to JCS, he told Thomas he simply had no money to hand over. Thomas was unmoved. Without providing the teen with the opportunity to show evidence that he was, indeed, indigent, she served him with a petition for the Recorders Court to revoke his probation.

The petition accused Thompson of violating the terms of his probation by failing to pay his fines and fees, including a twenty-eight-dollar charge for JCS's management of his case. It made no mention of the fact that Thompson could not afford to pay, that he was chronically underemployed, and that he had difficulty looking for work without a valid driver's license in car-dependent Atlanta.

The petition also had an "acknowledgment" from Thompson that he was aware he could retain an attorney for his probation hearing—which, of course, he couldn't afford—"or be represented otherwise as the Court may direct."[4] Thompson didn't realize that meant he had a right to request a court-appointed lawyer to represent him and that those services were provided for free to indigent probationers in revocation proceedings. Thomas did ask Thompson if he wanted a public defender, but Thompson did not understand the term.

The private probation officer said Thompson could pay $150 for someone to speak for him in court, or he could speak for himself if he waived his rights. The actual public defender fee was $50. No one informed Thompson it could be waived if he was unable to pay. Thompson, of course, did not have $150. He told Thomas he could not afford it and signed the bottom of the petition. She then checked the box saying, "Right to Public Defender Waived."

On December 8, Thompson, clad in slacks and a dress shirt lent by his father, rode with his mom to the Recorders Court for the hearing. Thompson hoped the judge might give him an extension of time or maybe community service. "Of course I wanted to pay the full amount and was trying my best," he said. "But it just was not possible.

"I was nervous on the way to court," he said. "But my mom said everything would be okay. She said we'd get something to eat after the hearing and then come back home. I was under the impression we were going to leave court and continue with our day."

Things did not turn out that way.

The Recorders Court was packed with defendants, most of them there on failure-to-pay charges. Thompson sat and watched as, one by one, they were sentenced to jail, some for up to several days, and taken away in handcuffs.

Eventually, Judge Angela Brown called Thompson's case. She held up a copy of his petition and asked him to verify his signature on the "acknowledgment" section, when he'd waived his right to court-appointed counsel. Brown did not ask why he declined to have a public defender, nor did she inform him that he could still request one at that point. Brown then called on the attending JCS probation officer (not Thomas), who recommended that the judge order Thompson to pay his fines and fees in full that day, or serve ten days in jail. The officer made no mention of Thompson's previous payments to JCS.

When it was Thompson's turn to speak, he explained that he had paid what he could, but without a valid license he could not get to work or drive a truck, making it impossible to cover the balance due. He said he had applied for a driver's permit from the court. "I'm doing the best I can," Thompson said quietly, asking the judge for more time to pay his debts.

"I also asked her if there was a driver's permit that allows you to go to work, so I could work to pay the fine," he told me. "She just brushed me off and said, 'I am not the DMV.'" Judge Brown asked Thompson if he had served any jail time when he was arrested. He said yes, for a day. She then sentenced him to ten days, with one day off for time served.

Thompson trembled. The idea of spending nine more days in jail over an unpaid traffic debt made his head spin. He fought back tears as he turned to face his mom.

"May I hug my mother?" Thompson asked before being handcuffed. Judge Brown said no. Thompson broke down and cried after he was led away and locked in a cell adjacent to the courtroom.

Judge Brown, according to the civil rights lawsuit Thompson would eventually file, never asked him if he was able to pay his debt or not. She did not inquire about his ability to borrow money, or if staying out of jail would help him find a job and retire his debt. She also failed to determine whether Thompson had willfully failed to pay or make an effort to acquire the funds, and she refused to consider any alternatives to jail, such as a waiver or reduction of his fines, an extension of time to pay, or community service.

In short, Thompson asserted that Brown made no effort to determine if he was indigent, which clearly he was. It was just another business-as-usual day in her courtroom.

In 2014, Human Rights Watch issued a damning report on the judicial abuse going on in DeKalb County and other localities called *Profiting from Probation: America's "Offender-Funded" Probation Industry.*[5] Although it looked at cases in Alabama, Georgia, and Mississippi, the report detailed the "patterns of abuse and financial hardship inflicted by the 'offender-funded' model of privatized probation that prevails in well over 1,000 courts across the U.S."

Human Rights Watch placed DeKalb County on the "lucrative end of the spectrum" when it came to private probation companies in 2014, the year of Thompson's arrest. It estimated that JCS was raking in more than $1 million in annual revenues in that one court alone. Judge Brown's courtroom, according to the report, was a putative cash machine for the county—and the company:

> On March 21, 2013, roughly 600 people were subpoenaed to appear
> in the DeKalb County Georgia Recorders Court. The summons they
> received by mail did not explain why they were being requested to appear
> in court. Of the 300 people who obeyed the summons only one had legal
> representation, through the office of the county's public defender.

*Unknown to them, all 300 people had been summoned to court because
they had not kept up with payments on fines and on supervision fees owed
to the Court and JCS. The cases had been appended to a docket of animal
control cases and listed on the Court's calendar as "Animal Control."*

The first few cases proceeded. But as lawyers and at least one probationer
in the courtroom told Human Rights Watch, Judge Brown "called probationers forward and then turned to a JCS employee seated next to her to ask whether
there was a warrant out for the person's arrest."

And, the report continued:

*In each case, the JCS employee responded in the affirmative—though she
did not actually produce evidence of that warrant for the court. Judge
Brown then told the probationer the total amount they allegedly owed in
fines and JCS fees and asked whether they could pay that amount
immediately and in full. Whenever a probationer said that they could
not, Judge Brown ordered their arrest.*

No offender had a chance to explain why they had not paid, nor did the
judge attempt to determine if their failure was willful. "Most cases were dis-
posed of in under a minute," the report said. "All told, some 60 probationers
on the 'Animal Control' docket reportedly went to jail that day for want of
money."

And that's what happened to Kevin Thompson, who was dispatched directly to the DeKalb County Jail.

"It was horrible, it was cold, it smelled awful, and the guards were allowed
to talk to you in any kind of way they wanted," he told me. "And it was lonely
in there with a building full of crooks and thieves. I didn't belong there. I was
a kid trying to figure everything out." Thompson missed his family, his girlfriend, and "real" food. "I have no idea what that food was," he said. "It was
just a terrible place to be."

The next day, Thompson received an unexpected visitor.

It was Laura Huizar, a legal fellow and attorney with the ACLU Racial Justice Program. Laura and other ACLU staffers had been poring through jail
rosters to identify people incarcerated in DeKalb County for probation violations based on their inability to pay fines. ACLU lawyers had been looking for

a case to bring against the court, and JCS, for engaging in practices they felt were blatantly unconstitutional.

Thompson was wary. He knew that a lawsuit of this type would get publicity. "I thought about it. I thought about lawyers I wouldn't be able to afford, and newspeople running up to me and being in my face and Channel 2 chasing after me," he said. "I thought about all that stuff and wasn't too excited about any of it. But I knew they [ACLU lawyers] were there for a reason, so I just went along with it and listened."

Thompson learned belatedly that his rights had been violated. Still, for the cold, frightened young man, a lawsuit was not foremost in his mind. "All I was thinking about was doing those nine days in jail and then getting back out and living the regular life I knew," he said. Thompson agreed to have the ACLU file a civil rights complaint on his behalf, pro bono.

On Thompson's fifth day in jail, his name was called over the PA system. A guard approached his cell. "Pack it up," he was told. "It's time for you to go home." No one explained why he was being released four days early. But Thompson didn't care. He was out of that place.

Thompson wrote about his ordeal at the ACLU website. "I felt ashamed, scared, and sad during those five days," he said. "And even after I was released, I felt scared that the police might arrest me and jail me again for no good reason. After all, DeKalb County and JCS essentially jailed me for being poor."[6]

For weeks after his release, and wary of being jailed again, Thompson always made sure to carry a document confirming his legal release. To this day, he remains fearful of all law enforcement officers.

After his release, Thompson met extensively with Laura Huizar and Nusrat Choudhury, another staff attorney at the ACLU's Racial Justice Program, to prepare for the lawsuit. "They kept following up with me; they must have spoken with me a hundred times," he said. "They sat me down to explain what was about to happen. They called me every day and night, in conversations that lasted up to three hours."

On January 29, 2015, the ACLU filed suit in United States District Court for the Northern District of Georgia, challenging a debt-collection system that jails people because they have no money. The lawsuit charged that DeKalb County and Judicial Correction Services conspired to "engage in a coercive debt collection scheme that focused on revenue generation at the expense of protecting poor people's rights."[7]

The lawsuit also claimed that Thompson's right to an attorney and to an indigency hearing under the Due Process and Equal Protection Clauses of the Fourteenth Amendment were violated by the county, JCS, and the chief judge of the court. The DeKalb court had also failed to offer legal counsel to Thompson, the lawsuit said, noting that the Fourteenth Amendment "affords all probationers a due process right to request court-appointed counsel in probation revocation proceedings." Low-income probationers have the right to court-appointed counsel at no cost.

Thompson sought damages for "the humiliation, anxiety, stress, emotional distress, and other irreparable injury he suffered" after being handcuffed and taken to jail in front of his mother, forcibly separated from his family, and held for five days in a cold, dirty cell without enough food to eat following probation revocation proceedings "in which he lacked representation by counsel."

Within two months, DeKalb County and Judicial Correction Services agreed to settle the case. Without admitting any wrongdoing, the defendants would pay Thompson $70,000.[8] The county also agreed to adopt a number of reforms, including issuing a "bench card" for judges. That missive instructed judges to offer defendants an indigency hearing, outlined alternatives to jail time, and reminded judges that defendants have a right to court-appointed legal counsel in probation revocation proceedings.

The county also agreed to provide training and guidance to court personnel working on misdemeanor cases of probationers' right to an indigency hearing and legal counsel. It likewise agreed to revise courtroom forms that let people charged with probation violation know about their right to counsel and to request a waiver of public defender fees if they could not afford to pay.

Shortly after the settlement, the Georgia General Assembly abolished the DeKalb County Recorders Court. All pending and new cases were given to two traffic courts, and major reforms were adopted.

"It was a landmark case," Nusrat Choudhury told me.[9] She said that, due in part to Thompson's victory, the Georgia General Assembly also took up and passed sweeping reform legislation to require judges to determine if failure to pay fines or fees was willful or the result of indigency.

"The Thompson case really did help propel that legislation into passage," Choudhury said. "The case made a constitutional argument regardless of any statutes. And the press helped keep the issue in the forefront of the legislature and the public mind that there are real human consequences to these practices."

The statute, she said, makes it clear that people can't be jailed for failure to pay without a hearing and follows the three-pronged procedure established by the Supreme Court: assessment of ability to pay, assessment of ability to secure resources, and assessment of alternatives to incarceration.

It's hard to assess exactly what impact the new law has had statewide (there is no central repository of information on this issue), but in DeKalb County, it has been significant. In January 2016, *The Atlanta Journal-Constitution* reported that traffic fines there fell from an average of $159 in 2013 to about $100 or less in 2015. County residents now have up to six weeks to pay their fines and have the option of working off those fines through $8-an-hour community service jobs instead of going to jail. Meanwhile, private probation companies are no longer used in such cases.[10]

According to Choudhury, traffic courts in the county are imposing probation dramatically less often, and there have been few, if any, reports of anyone being jailed because he could not pay fines or fees.

Despite his legal victory and the changes it helped bring about, Kevin Thompson remained skeptical about the entire episode.

"I just hope what happened to me doesn't happen to someone else because, like me, they didn't know what their rights were," he said. "But judges feel like they can determine whatever they want to do. At the end of day, they will find a way to get their way, so it won't necessarily stop the problem."

Choudhury was a bit more sanguine. "What we need are more municipalities that have these line items in their budgets for court fines and fees to realize that they can't prioritize meeting those targets over protecting the rights of the poor . . . and they should voluntarily change their system before they're sued."

DEBTORS' PRISONS V. U.S. CONSTITUTION

Punishing people for their inability to pay a debt has been rejected by the U.S. Supreme Court on three separate occasions. In 1970, the court ruled that it is unconstitutional to extend a maximum prison sentence because an offender is too poor to pay fines or court costs.[11] The following year, the justices said it was unconstitutional to impose a fine and then automatically convert it into a jail term "solely because the defendant is indigent and cannot forthwith pay the fine in full."[12]

But the most significant decision came in 1983, in a landmark case known as *Bearden v. Georgia*. The court ruled that judges cannot sentence probationers to jail time for failure to pay fines and fees without first holding an "indigency hearing" to determine the person's ability to pay and whether appropriate alternatives to incarceration are available.[13]

Charging people fees as part of a criminal penalty is allowed by the Constitution (and many legal experts agree with that practice), as is jailing people who have the ability to pay but still refuse. But incarcerating people without giving them a chance to demonstrate their inability to pay is unconstitutional.

Despite that, it happens every day in this country.

It is unsettling to learn how many judges around the country, either through laziness, ignorance, or willful defiance, disregard *Bearden v. Georgia* in their own courtrooms. Investigations conducted in recent years by the ACLU, Human Rights Watch, NPR, and the Brennan Center for Justice at New York University Law School have documented several hundreds of cases where judges sent debtors to jail in violation of the Constitution and, seemingly, the will of the Supreme Court.

Meanwhile, many defendants, including Kevin Thompson, are being arrested inside the courtroom itself, without a warrant—a violation of the Fourth Amendment's prohibition against unreasonable search and seizure. And the fact that judges routinely fail to inform defendants of their right to a court-appointed lawyer violates the Sixth Amendment's requirement that the accused *have the Assistance of Counsel for his defence.*

If judges are ignorant of such basic rights, it's fair to say that most defendants are unaware of them as well.

Still, a surprising number of judges believe that jail time is warranted in failure-to-pay cases, just to hold people accountable when they break a law. "If they won't pay the money, the only thing we can take from them at that point is their time," Benton County (Washington) District Court judge Robert Ingvalson told NPR.[14]

In other words, judges can deprive people of their Fifth and Fourteenth Amendment rights against deprivation of liberty, without meeting any burden of proof.

Many judges have noted how difficult it is to determine who can and who cannot afford to pay their fines and fees. Some also contend that, while the Supreme Court said they must determine an individual's ability to pay fees, the ruling left them with wide discretion in how to go about carrying that out. They also say there simply are not enough resources—or time—to hold a hearing on the personal finances of each offender. Instead, judges often create their own criteria. If a defendant is wearing an expensive jacket, for example, a judge may use that as evidence of that person's ability to pay.

Some judges tell defendants that they could somehow land a high-paying job or even win the lottery in the near future, so they should pay. Others tell the accused that if they quit smoking cigarettes or give up their cell phones, they could afford to pay their obligations. Many tell defendants to borrow money from friends and family (something that is not always possible, of course) or tap into public assistance money such as welfare, social security, or even veterans' benefits.

"Instead of looking at the likelihood of [the offender's] ability to pay, judges are simply saying it's *possible* at some point in the future that money can come in, and so these motions to lower or waive fees are not granted," Nick Allen, an attorney at the Seattle-based Columbia Legal Services, told me. "Common sense goes out the window. In some counties, this is very rigid and they're not taking any excuses, they're not taking any explanations. If that money is not here by this date, this is the punishment you're going to get."[15]

LFOS: MAKING CRIME PAY, OVER AND OVER

No one knows exactly how often people are jailed for not paying a legal debt. "It's hard to know nationwide how many people are being victimized by debtors' prison, because there could be a community that isn't jailing people for poverty and then right next door, that town is," said the ACLU's Nusrat Choudhury, who worked on Thompson's case.

So how did we get to this "pay or stay" state of affairs?

In the 1980s and 1990s, the nation's inmate population exploded, partly due to mandatory minimum sentences and "three strikes and you're out" rules that became more popular in a crime-and-drug-weary country. As more people were carted off to jail or prison, and as anti-tax sentiment flourished, state and local lawmakers began viewing offenders as a reliable source of revenue, shifting the financial burden of prosecuting and jailing them away from the taxpayers and onto the accused.

Much of that money finds its way back into the coffers of the courts and prosecutors—not to mention private probation companies—in a clear conflict of interest that encourages them to demand more and higher fees, even for minor offenses. Meanwhile, the ever-present threat of jail time is a powerful incentive—some would call it ransom—for offenders to pay up.

Choudhury said things really deteriorated with the Great Recession that began in 2007. "Now, it's happening all over the country: Urban and rural. Small towns. Big cities. North and South," she said. "And the problem is getting worse."

In twenty-first-century America some people even go to jail for their inability to pay civil debts—including store credit, rent, child support, or alimony. But most, like Thompson, spend time locked up because they could not afford to cover unpaid criminal fines, plus the costs levied by private probation companies to manage their case.

But there are also an uncounted number of people who were convicted of crimes and completed their sentences—whether jail time, fines, probation, and/or community service—but were *still* locked up because they owed money to the judicial system. Why? Because of so-called legal financial obligations, or LFOs—a laundry list of costs associated with a criminal case.

Many defendants are, essentially, handed a bill for much of their own prosecution, including court costs, bench warrants, jail time, filing fees, crime victim programs, probation fees—and even public-defense lawyers, whose services most people assume are always free. As it turns out, in forty-three states, defendants can be billed for public defenders, according to a 2014 survey by NPR.[16]

A few decades ago, very few courts levied defendants' fees, but now it is common practice in all fifty states. In 1991, one-quarter of prison inmates owed court-imposed costs, restitution, fines, and fees, NPR reported. By 2004, the last year for which government data are available, the figure had climbed to around 66 percent. Today it is estimated to be somewhere around 80–85 percent, sociologist Alexes Harris of the University of Washington told the radio network.

The NPR investigation revealed a "long list of government services that were once free—including ones that are constitutionally required." In the United States today, inmates can be charged for room and board in at least forty-one states. Offenders can be charged for their own probation and parole supervision in at least forty-four states, and in all but one state, offenders are charged a fee for the electronic bracelet that monitors them when they're out of jail.

Making matters worse, once again, we see state power and private corporate interests in collusion with each other, all in the name of revenue generation. In at least thirteen states, private probation companies—such as JCS, which handled Thompson's case—may charge fees to supervise offenders. These companies depend on a steady stream of debtors to keep their coffers full. And, as Human Rights Watch pointed out in 2014, "it's not in the interest of private probation companies to let probationers know about their rights," including their rights to an indigence hearing and court-appointed counsel.[17]

Georgia is one of the worst offenders, according to Human Rights Watch. Officials began using private probation in 1991 and quickly became "the state most dependent on it," the report said. As of 2014, fully 80 percent of all residents in Georgia on probation for misdemeanor convictions—some 175,000 people at any given time—were managed by these for-profit firms, yielding them about $40 million a year.

And then there is the cost to taxpayers for all of this. On paper, LFOs make sense. Why shouldn't convicted offenders be ordered to offset the costs of their own prosecution and jail time to help fund the legal system and valuable programs such as victim restitution?

As Nick Allen pointed out, "It only begins to make sense if you assume that the people coming through the system are generally reflective of society. But in practice, 80–90 percent of people coming through our system are indigent. Yet our policies say, how are we going to fund our court system? And it comes on the backs of the poor."

When you look at the imbalance between those with the ability to pay and those without, "you can't possibly think this is a good idea for funding," he said. "If you keep incarcerating people at this rate, specifically people who are low income, you're never going to be able to dig yourself out of this hole. You're never going to be able to fund your criminal justice system. There needs to be a more efficient way."

In many cases of people who were jailed for failure to pay fines or fees, the costs to the state or county were considerably higher than the amount of money collected. "It's expensive," Allen said, "when you account for court time, law enforcement time to serve the warrants, jail time at about seventy dollars a day. And then there's the human cost—people who are arrested and now can't go out and find a job, people who have been separated from their families because they're being incarcerated for failing to pay."

AN UNYIELDING CYCLE OF DEBT

The overall cost of an offense increases once supervision fees are added to the tab, Nick Allen said. One Washington State commission determined in 2008 that the average amount of costs, fees, and fines levied in felony cases was $2,500.[18] In Washington, before reforms were enacted in 2018, offenders were also slapped with a 12 percent interest charge on the money they owed (the 12 percent interest still applies for restitution payments). The typical amount that these debtors pay is $5–$25 per month, according to Allen. If someone paid this amount every month, without missing a single payment, his debt would continue to rise. In fact, at that rate, after four years of consistently making monthly payments on a $2,500 debt, his total debt would have *grown* to $3,000.

"These costs follow an individual around for the rest of their lives, in many instances, because they'll never be able to pay them and interest is accruing," Allen said.

The costs are considerable. Anyone convicted of a felony or gross misdemeanor in Washington State Superior Court, for instance, is required to pay a $500 "victim penalty assessment," even if there were no victims associated with the crime. Many offenders, of course, have more than one conviction.

Before the 2018 reforms, "We saw people with, say, seven or eight nonviolent drug convictions—each one of those cases with the $500 victim penalty assessment. And each one of those cases accruing interest at 12 percent a year," Allen said. "So, in a case where you could have seven or eight crimes where you never had a victim involved, yet be $4,000, $5,000 in the hole just in principal, and once the interest accrues, you could easily have found yourself in a situation where you owe $7,000 to $10,000 in LFOs."

Allen cited cases of individuals whose licenses were initially suspended, who were later arrested and convicted of driving with a suspended license, and ordered to pay fees and fines as a result, couldn't pay those fees and fines, and then tumbled into a relentless cycle of constantly being arrested for failing to pay them.

In Washington State, in addition to racking up 12 percent interest on their debts, offenders also face fees up to $100 per year, levied by county clerks, to help collect the LFOs they owe. That might not sound like much, but to a truly indigent person, it can perpetuate the cycle of debt. As Allen explained it, if someone owes restitution on a case, then whenever they've sent in their minimum monthly payment, it should first go toward the outstanding restitution that's owed. But in Washington State, clerks don't believe this fee is a legal financial obligation, and they collect the $100 fee before crediting *anything* to restitution. Most people who can't afford to pay their LFOs at once are making installment payments in very small amounts, say, $5, $10, or $25 a month.

If someone is making $10-a-month payments toward her LFOs, those first ten payments will go directly to the clerk's office, while only two payments will be applied against her restitution. When the next year begins, so does the same vicious cycle. "It doesn't allow that person to address their underlying legal financial obligations," Allen said. "Plus that 12 percent interest that's been accruing. So there's no way to catch up. It's going to accrue during your entire sentence. And so when you get out, oftentimes people are seeing that the amount has doubled or tripled, based on how long they served that time."

In some cases, people charged with failure to pay may get credits against their debt for every day they spend in jail. Under the district court system in Washington State, for example, they receive a set amount per day—such as $50 per day. But that can still mean a long time in jail.

"We've seen in some counties that folks have sat up to a year or more in jail for district and municipal court failure to pay fines and fees they can't afford, where the underlying offenses are low-level crimes such as driving while license is suspended, minor possession, or DUIs," Allen told me.

Those convicted in the state's superior court system are even less fortunate: There is no monetary credit for time served. "It's just going to be dead time,"

Allen said. "You're definitely going to come out with more owed in LFOs than when you went in."

LEGAL FINANCIAL OBLIGATIONS: CASE STUDIES

It is not uncommon for people to take years to pay off their LFOs, with the threat of jail time always hanging over their head as a grim incentive to comply. David Ramirez, a single father of four in Washington State, was still paying off his debt more than a decade after his conviction.

Ramirez was profiled in the 2014 report *Modern-Day Debtors' Prisons* by the ACLU of Washington State and Columbia Legal Services, which documented that the average LFO in Washington's superior court system was $2,540. In one county, Benton, one in five inmates were serving time for failure to pay their LFOs.[19]

In 2003, Ramirez had pleaded guilty to residential burglary after entering his ex-wife's home without permission. His sentence? Pay $2,144 in restitution and roughly $1,150 in penalties and other fees related to his case. At the time, he was making about $10 per hour and paying $500 a month in child support. With four kids at home to support, Ramirez was just getting by on very little money.

Ramirez didn't have the nearly $3,300 being demanded of him. For years following his conviction, he was under constant threat of arrest for failure to pay. In 2008, the court issued a warrant against him. The judge said Ramirez would need to pay $800 to have the warrant lifted.

"I didn't have that kind of money, and they wouldn't take a partial payment," he said. "So I basically lived in fear of arrest for a year until a lawyer in my church agreed to help me negotiate a lower payment to quash the warrant."

Although he was now unemployed and living on public assistance to keep his family afloat, Ramirez was able to borrow enough money to remove the warrant and be put on a payment plan of $30 a month. But medical problems kept him from returning to a job in his field. In 2014, Ramirez was still paying off the debt, with no relief in sight. He had paid off the initial amount but still owed $1,831 in interest. His continued financial hardships have won him little sympathy from the criminal justice system.

"I've had judges tell me that they don't care what my other obligations are—LFOs come first," he said in the report. "Sometimes, I have to choose between paying the electricity bill and paying LFOs, or between buying my kid a winter coat and paying LFOs. The message the courts have sent to me over and over again is that if I don't pay in full every month, I'll go to jail and I'll lose everything."

Then there is the case of Stephan Papa, an Iraq War veteran who returned home to Michigan with neither a home nor a job. According to reporting by the ACLU, one night he got drunk and went on a rampage, earning him a conviction on charges of property destruction and resisting arrest. He was ordered to pay $2,600 in fines and court fees.

Upon conviction, the judge told Papa he could pay $50 at the time in order to avoid going to jail, but Papa only had $25 with him. He explained to the judge that he had just landed a new job and would begin making regular payments as soon as he got his first paycheck, the following week.

"I tried really hard to get this job, and I'd really like to keep it," he said in court.[20]

The judge was unmoved. Because he was $25 short on his first installment, Papa was sentenced to twenty-two days in jail. Incredibly, the judge ordered Papa to "maintain stable employment" after leaving jail and going on probation. But of course, you can't stay away from work for twenty-two days and expect to walk into your former place of employment and find your job still there waiting for you. Papa's wasn't. Eventually, he managed to get another job, and he struggled to keep up with his subsequent payments.

"Let's take stock of what this government action 'achieved,'" wrote Carl Takei, an ACLU senior staff attorney. "One veteran mired in debt after being needlessly jailed for the better part of a month. Taxpayers out thousands of dollars for locking someone up for twenty-two days because he couldn't pay $50 on the spot."[21] It doesn't make much sense.

MINORITIES HIT HARDEST: FERGUSON, MISSOURI

Kevin Thompson told me he went to jail "for being poor," but it's possible that he was also incarcerated for being black. As with so many civil liberties crises, the debtors' prison problem disproportionately affects people of color. In

DeKalb County, for example, African Americans are 54 percent of the population, "yet nearly all probationers jailed by the DeKalb County Recorders Court for failure to pay are black," the ACLU notes on its website. "[It's] a pattern replicated by other Georgia courts."[22]

The use of fees in criminal cases to generate municipal revenue was part of a landmark March 2014 Justice Department report that followed the police killing of unarmed African American teenager Michael Brown in Ferguson, Missouri, sparking days of unrest and dozens of arrests.

Ferguson's law enforcement practices "are shaped by the City's focus on revenue rather than by public safety needs," the DOJ report said.[23] By emphasizing revenue for the city budget, the "institutional character" of Ferguson's police department had been compromised, leading to a pattern of unconstitutional policing. The questionable practices also impacted the local municipal court, "leading to procedures that raise due process concerns and inflict unnecessary harm on members of the Ferguson community."

The City of Ferguson, where municipal fines and fees were found to be the second-largest source of revenue, "each year exhorts police and court staff to deliver those revenue increases, and closely monitors whether those increases are achieved," the DOJ said. "City officials routinely urged Police Chief Jackson to bring in ever more revenue through enforcement." Indeed, Ferguson officers of every rank told federal investigators that revenue generation "is stressed heavily" in the department.

The report confirmed that many judges around the country are indeed ignoring the Supreme Court by denying defendants their constitutional rights to due process and equal protection.

Put in that context, it's easier to comprehend the rage and rioting in and around Ferguson following Brown's death.

Again, race played a big role here. Both the Ferguson police and its municipal court "reflect and exacerbate existing racial bias, including racial stereotypes," the DOJ said. "Ferguson's own data establish clear racial disparities that adversely impact African Americans." Many cops in the city view some residents, especially African Americans, "less as constituents to be protected than as potential offenders and sources of revenue."

This dependence on revenue from offenders is driving police to make arrests that are often unconstitutional. "The result is a pattern of stops without reasonable suspicion and arrests without probable cause in violation of the

Fourth Amendment; infringement on free expression, as well as retaliation for protected expression," the DOJ said.

And of course, the heavy-handed practice is sending a lot of people to jail. The Ferguson court "abused its authority" to compel payment of fines and fees, the DOJ found. In 2013 alone, the court issued more than nine thousand arrest warrants, mostly for minor violations such as parking and traffic tickets, and even building-code violations. "Jail time would be considered far too harsh a penalty for the great majority of these code violations," the DOJ said, "yet Ferguson's municipal court routinely issues warrants for people to be arrested and incarcerated for failing to timely pay related fines and fees."

Even the most minor offenses can result in crippling debts, the DOJ report said. It mentioned the 2007 case of an unnamed black woman in Ferguson who had illegally parked her car and was given two citations and a $15 fine, plus fees. The woman had struggled financially for years, including being homeless on more than one occasion. Between 2007 and 2010, she was hit with seven charges of missing court dates or not paying her increasing fines.

For each failure to appear, the court issued an arrest warrant and imposed new fines and fees on the woman, who was arrested twice and spent six days in jail—all because of a parking ticket. Court records show she tried to make two partial payments for $25 and $50 each, but the judge refused to accept anything but payment in full. As of 2014, she was on a payment plan and making regular payments. But more than seven years after her parking ticket, and despite owing an initial fine of $15 and having already paid $550, she still owed $541, the DOJ report found.

Reform Efforts

Because so many innocent victims of the modern-day debtors' prison system stood up and fought back, efforts to remedy the problem have advanced when it comes to jailing offenders for inability to pay fines and fees related to a charge. In some places, reform is being delivered through legislation, while in others, it's through litigation.

In Ohio, badly needed change came about through public pressure on the courts to simply educate judges about the rights of defendants.

In April 2013, the ACLU of Ohio published a report called *The Outskirts of Hope: How Ohio's Debtors' Prisons Are Ruining Lives and Costing Communities,* a scathing critique of courtroom practices in seven Ohio counties that were sending hundreds of people to jail each year for inability to pay fines and fees. In one county, Huron, in the second half of 2012, more than 20 percent of all jail bookings were related to failure-to-pay fines. In all seven counties, there was no evidence that anyone jailed for nonpayment was offered a hearing to determine if he was able to pay his debt or not, even though Ohio state law (not to mention the Supreme Court) requires such an opportunity.

The ACLU sent the report to the Ohio Supreme Court along with a letter to Chief Justice Maureen O'Connor, asking her to devise a way to eliminate debtors' prisons in the state.

The following February, the court issued a bench card to every judge in Ohio, with instructions on how to comply with the law by offering alternatives to incarceration, including payment plans, community service, driver's license forfeiture, or even dismissal of the debt owed.[24] It outlined the required procedures for determining a defendant's ability to pay and reminded judges of the right to legal counsel. The bench card was the first of its kind in the country. Since then, the supreme courts of Washington and Missouri have issued similar guidelines to judges.

"I don't think judges were intentionally not following the law," Chief Justice O'Connor told *The New York Times.* "It wasn't: 'I don't care what the law is and I'm going to do it my way.' This was clearly an area they needed to brush up on."[25]

"Ohio actually had very good statutes on the books affirming the right to counsel, affirming that people can't be jailed for failing to pay fines as well as fees," the ACLU's Nusrat Choudhury told me. "The problem in Ohio was that judges weren't following the law, and the training and guidance resulting from the report produced there have brought about really important changes. So sometimes the solution is not a legislative one; it has to do with education, it has to do with creating a culture where we don't look to our poorest residents as sources of municipal revenue."

After the bench card was issued, "the results were nothing short of remarkable," two ACLU of Ohio lawyers wrote in the *Michigan Journal of Race & Law.* "Courts across the state reformed their practices," according to the article.

"While we cannot state with any certainty that debtors' prison is completely eradicated in Ohio, we do note that the number of complaints to the ACLU of Ohio offices have decreased precipitously."[26]

Meanwhile, in Washington, in addition to passage of the reform bill (HB 1783), the ACLU also filed a lawsuit in Benton County, which resulted in settlement. Meanwhile, Washington was one of five states awarded a U.S. Justice Department Price of Justice Grant, with which state officials and other stakeholders "have been working to acquire more data, track policies and practices, and assess the costs of collection, with the goal of improving the LFO scheme in Washington," Nick Allen told me in October 2018.

Another Washington case, *State v. Wakefield,* held that "ordering people to pay money toward LFOs violates the anti-attachment provision of the Social Security Act, if the person's sole source of income is Social Security Disability," Allen said.

Reform is also happening at the municipal and county levels. In 2014, a U.S. district court in Montgomery, Alabama, ordered that city to stop jailing people who can't afford to pay fines and fees arising from minor traffic violations. The move came after the Southern Poverty Law Center and a group called Equal Justice Under Law sued the city on behalf of fifty year old grandmother Harriet Cleveland, who lost her job and was unable to pay her fine. Cleveland was arrested by police as she was babysitting her infant grandson and sentenced to thirty-one days in jail for failure to pay the old tickets and fees collected by Judicial Correction Services, the same group that handled Kevin Thompson's DeKalb County case.

As part of the settlement, Montgomery Municipal Court judges were ordered to offer an attorney to all defendants and provide them with an Affidavit of Substantial Hardship form to determine if they are indigent. Those living within 125 percent of the federal poverty level (or less than $25,000 a year for a family of three) are automatically recognized as indigent. Anyone who qualifies now has the choice of paying $25 per month or doing community service—at $10 per hour—until the debt is paid off.[27]

But there is still far to go to achieve nationwide reform. "Even now [in 2016], after a half dozen high-profile lawsuits challenging these practices, we know the problem is still going on, and we're trying to change the culture so that judges know what the law is," the ACLU's Choudhury said. The threat of civil rights litigation, she predicted, will compel judges to enforce the law.

Most people would agree that a system of justice that treats the haves and have-nots differently is contrary to who we are as Americans. Our jails are filled with people who are there because they are poor, not because they have done something that deserves jail time. It does little to help society, it is wasting taxpayers' money, and it's degrading human dignity. And of course, in many cases, it violates the Constitution.

Is that really the kind of country we want to live in?

WHEN POLICING PAYS FOR ITSELF

Most Americans are probably aware that the government can seize money or property if connected to criminal activity. Most people would agree with that rationale. But how many realize that the government can gain title to those assets without prosecutors even charging the property owner with a crime, let alone gaining a conviction? And how many know that some, most, or even all of those forfeited assets will be kept, and spent, by law enforcement—with police, prosecutors, and sometimes federal agencies getting a cut of the loot? It goes right back in the budgets of the very people who seized the assets and litigated the forfeiture cases in the first place.

"People are shocked when I tell them about it," Lee McGrath, managing attorney and senior legislative counsel at the Institute for Justice, a public interest law firm that defends clients in asset forfeiture and other civil rights cases, told me. "They just can't believe that it's happening in a country that's supposed to respect private property rights and rights to due process.[1]

"But it absolutely happens; it happens every single day. And to all different types of property as well—homes, businesses, cars, cash, trucks, boats—just about any type of real or personal property is subject to forfeiture," he said. "It's something the vast majority of Americans oppose, and as I said, quite frankly, they are stunned when they find out about it."

Under civil forfeiture laws, property is seized by local police or federal agents, and the owners must engage in litigation with the government to get it back. If they fail to file their claims on time, or if they lose in court, the state then "forfeits" the assets and keeps them.

The idea of civil (as opposed to criminal) forfeiture has been around for centuries, although it fell out of use in the modern era—that is, until the late 1960s and the U.S. war on drugs, when cartels and traffickers eschewed the financial system in favor of cash. The shakedown system gained new footing in 1984, when Congress permitted local law enforcement to outsource forfeiture litigation to federal prosecutors, for a fee, in a practice euphemistically referred to as *equitable sharing.*

In 2014, *The Washington Post* published a groundbreaking analysis of some four hundred civil-asset seizures in seventeen states. While it got some notice in media, legal, and political circles, it never raised the alarm bells it deserved. The most common practice, *Post* reporters found, was to use minor traffic violations as pretexts for stops, allowing police to look for signs of unlawful behavior, such as nervousness or evasion. This in turn led to warrantless searches of vehicles, with "a focus on cash." In most of the cases, police never made an arrest. This wasn't crime fighting; this was corruption.[2]

Interstate highways known to be drug-running corridors are considered cash cows by some local police departments. A long stretch of I-40 connects California to North Carolina and runs through a sizable swath of the crystal-meth and opioid belt. It is a favorite thoroughfare for police looking to make a fast and easy buck. A 2016 investigation by a Tennessee television news team found that 90 percent of all asset seizures along I-40 in that state happened on one side of the road: the westbound side, otherwise known as the "money side."[3]

If the police were really intent on putting a dent in interstate drug running, critics point out, they would focus on the eastbound side—the "drug" side of the interstate. Of *course* some people on the "money" side are ferrying drug-related cash, but most of them are not. That's why the vast majority of victims are never arrested for a crime. Why should police and prosecutors bother with the cost and time it takes to arrest, indict, try, and punish someone, when they can just pilfer the cash and be on their way to relieve the next hapless fool of his valuables?

Many cops seem to have little interest in turning cases over to prosecutors for criminal prosecution. "In all the cases that we're involved with, there's been no prosecutions whatsoever of the people," said Scott Bullock, president and general counsel of the Institute for Justice. "Because they know that a judge is going to say, 'What? Who is this, this small business owner, and why are you accusing him of a crime?' It's all about getting the cash."[4]

There is a lot of cash for the getting. The Justice Department's Asset Forfeiture Program took in more than $28 billion in the decade from 2007 to 2017, the agency's Office of the Inspector General reported. The Drug Enforcement Administration collected 80 percent of all federal cash seizures in civil cases.

In a sample reviewed by the Inspector General's office, a minority of the seizures led to charges or even arrests, and in two-thirds of the sample's cases, the seizures did nothing to advance ongoing investigations or instigate new investigations. Again, it appears that money, not prosecution, was the motivating factor.[5]

As in similar issues explored in this book, cash forfeitures disproportionately victimize people of color, the poor, and anyone who cannot afford a knowledgeable attorney to muster a fight, versus other types of property. These people are less likely to own homes, boats, or luxury cars. What they stand to lose most is their money.

A 2017 analysis from *Reason* magazine and Lucy Parsons Labs—a police oversight nonprofit—plotted the location of thousands of forfeitures in Chicago and found that most of them took place in poor, largely African American neighborhoods on the South Side and West Side. Of the roughly twenty-three thousand seizures between 2012 and 2017, just under half, about eleven thousand, involved amounts less than $1,000, most of it in cash.[6] These were hardly drug kingpins.

"If they find cash, they can seize it and claim, 'Well, we suspect that you're a drug dealer or you're money laundering,' which is another common catch-all provision that they use," said Scott Bullock. "And because it's a civil proceeding, the burden is on you to try to get the property back. And so they give you a receipt and then they say, 'Well, we'll see you in court.' And what oftentimes happens in those proceedings is that, again, if it's $6,000, or whatever it might be, and you start raising a stink about it, they might say, 'I'll tell you what—we could fight this out in court,' and sometimes they do go to the bitter end on it. 'But why don't we just settle this case? And we'll keep three and we'll give you back three.'"

Many victims accept the settlement. After all, losing $3,000 is better than losing $6,000. And if they don't take the deal, their case might languish for a year or more before it is brought to adjudication: In most states, they have no right to a prompt hearing. Even worse, they have no right to a court-appointed attorney. Some of them could easily spend $6,000 on legal fees, making it a wash.

"It just doesn't make financial sense to go through the whole civil forfeiture process," Bullock said. "And that simply shows the incredible burdens that are placed on property owners and the very substantial benefits that the government has in these proceedings."

It's astonishing that the mere possession of what the police deem to be a suspiciously large amount of cash is now, practically speaking, supposed evidence of a crime. This is particularly troubling since there are many legitimate reasons why people travel with cash. Professional gamblers or anyone who deals in cash sales for goods and services might be on their way to make a bank deposit, for all that the cops know. Others carry cash for cultural reasons. And many working-class Americans and undocumented immigrants don't have bank accounts and therefore conduct transactions, even larger ones, in cash. That makes them prime targets for greedy cops. They know that most can't afford a lawyer and will simply walk away or accept only part of what was taken away.[7] Some of them lose their life savings.

Despite all this impropriety, the U.S. Justice Department, especially under the Trump administration, makes no bones about defending the system. The feds insist that asset forfeiture wields both punishment and deterrence against anyone engaged in or contemplating criminal activity, especially drug trafficking. It also boosts cooperation among local, state, and federal agencies and raises new revenues to help fight crime.

But many legal experts—and some politicians on the left and right—contend that the whole thing amounts to nothing less than sanctioned highway robbery of law-abiding citizens. The tactic pads the budgets of police departments struggling with cuts in public spending, even as the clamor for more "law and order" has grown louder.

Like most Americans, I had never heard of civil asset forfeiture before starting this book, and I was startled by what I learned. It is difficult to fathom why the specter of police taking your things without the requirement that prosecutors charge and convict you of a crime is not a subject of greater scrutiny and alarm by the public, the media, and lawmakers around the country. Few people realize that it can happen to them—until it does happen to them. Thanks to that apathy and willful ignorance, the problem is only getting worse.

BUDGET MOTEL: A RIPE TARGET

When it comes to selecting targets, police and federal agents have a penchant for low-hanging fruit—individuals and small companies without the means to challenge the forfeiture in court. This is especially true when agents home in on big-ticket items like cars, homes, and especially mom-and-pop businesses. Why pick on corporate-owned enterprises with their bottomless resources and batteries of lawyers? The cops seem to think it's faster, easier, and cheaper to go after the little guy—and gal.

The Motel Caswell was a glaring case in point. The family-owned business was an unassuming one-story budget lodge in the town of Tewksbury, located in the northeastern corner of Massachusetts. It was built in 1955 by the father of Russ Caswell, who took over the place with his wife, Patricia, in 1984. It was not a huge moneymaker, but the mortgage was paid and the income was enough to support the family and allowed them to save up for retirement.

For years, the motel attracted vacationing families and truckers plying two nearby interstate highways. The Caswells toiled continuously to maintain the property. But like many towns in the area, crime, drugs, and gang activity began to infect the once-tranquil community. As truckers began sleeping in their rigs and vacationers bypassed the town, they struggled to hang on. They turned to lodging local families who were evicted or foreclosed upon and needed temporary housing, and other residents struggling to get by on welfare, including clients of Catholic Charities. Rooms went for under $50 a night.

Eventually, the motel began attracting transients and petty criminals. What the family, who lived next to the lodge, didn't anticipate was that some guests would consume illicit drugs behind locked doors in the privacy of their rooms.

Caswell did what he could to prevent criminal activity on the premises. He installed lighting and security cameras in common areas and photocopied the IDs of all guests, permitting local law enforcement to routinely review the records. He and staff members called the police on several occasions to report suspicious activity—and gave them access to rooms whenever asked. Caswell even provided cops with free rooms during stakeouts. Despite that, at no time did any police or town official offer to work with Caswell to reduce crime and drugs at the premises. No one warned him of the potential consequences if he failed to take action.

But then, in 2009, an envelope arrived in the mail that would hurl their quiet lives into chaos.

The packet, from the U.S. Drug Enforcement Administration, accused Caswell of running the motel as a hotbed of illegal drug activity. Neither

Caswell, his family, nor any employees were accused of any crime. Still, the DEA was poised to conduct a government-sponsored land grab.

"There were these forfeiture notices in there, and it had a lot of legal terms and so on, but basically what the letter said is, 'We're taking your property,'" Caswell told me. "And I was shocked. I'd never heard of such a thing.[8]

"But that's the way they do these things—they move against the property, not the owner," he said. "The complaint wasn't against me; it was *The United States Government v. 434 Main Street, Tewksbury.*"

Despite the free access he had allowed cops, Caswell had never been informed of any drug convictions against any motel guests. "But they used those cases anyway, just the fact that they'd arrested these people on the property, that's all it took," he said.

Other national chain motels in the area had notorious reputations as havens for drugs and crime, as well as the nearby big-box-store parking lots, Caswell said. But these corporate outfits were not targeted. And though there were other small, privately owned motels in the area, with similar clientele problems, the cops chose to target the Caswell.

Why Motel Caswell? Because its mortgage was completely paid off. Caswell was sitting on equity worth about $2 million.

A lien was put on the property, meaning the Caswells could still conduct business there until the forfeiture matter was settled, but they were barred from doing anything else with the property, including selling it. They hired a lawyer and prepared to fight. A few years and $100,000 later, they were still in jeopardy of losing the property and the family's livelihood.

At one point, after many months, the government made a settlement offer: If Caswell paid a fine of $167,000, he could hold on to the motel.

"I thought about it, but I said I'm not going to do this—this is just totally wrong," he said. "It's like something you'd expect in Cuba or Russia—certainly not the United States. I don't know how I'm supposed to know when somebody's doing drugs inside a locked motel room. I mean, legally I *can't* know about it."

The nightmare did not end. "That's what they were trying to do, just anything to drag it out, to break people so you have to keep spending money and spending money until you can't afford it, so that you just fold, and then they can take your property," he added. "You're guilty, and you have to go prove your innocence."

Eventually, Caswell got in touch with the Institute for Justice, the Arlington, Virginia–based libertarian nonprofit law firm, which took the case pro bono. Attorneys moved to have the forfeiture overturned under the "innocent owner" clause of a federal law approved by Congress in 2000. That statute covers cases in which the owner, by "a preponderance of the evidence," can show that he or she was unaware of illegal activity or, once discovered, "did all that reasonably could be expected under the circumstances to terminate such use of the property."

During depositions, Caswell's attorney asked the DEA agent in charge why Motel Caswell was seized, while the others were left alone.

"And the agent says, 'Well, we'll come in to try and find, you know, any place that's had a kind of drug arrest. And then I go to the Registry of Deeds to see how much equity is in the property,'" Caswell recalled. "And my lawyer asks, 'What does the equity have to do with anything?' And he says the DEA won't go after a property unless the owner has at least $50,000 worth."

DEA agents then approached the Tewksbury Police Department with what is known as an *equitable sharing deal:* The police would seize the property, the DEA would forfeit it and then hand over 80 percent of the haul back to the local police department.

The nonjury trial was held in November 2012, before a U.S. magistrate in Boston. During the proceedings, Carmen Ortiz, the U.S. attorney for Massachusetts, announced there had been one heroin overdose and fourteen incidents that led to drug arrests on the property from 1994 through 2008. She implied that the Caswells were aware of the illicit commerce, if not directly benefiting from it.

Forfeiture of the Caswell property would "send an important deterrent message" to others who "may turn a blind eye to crime occurring at their place of business," she said. The drug arrests proved that the motel was a "dangerous property," ripe for seizure.

But Institute for Justice attorneys argued that forfeiture would be illegal and unconstitutional. During the period in question, they said, the motel had about two hundred thousand room rentals. Fifteen isolated drug arrests hardly constituted a public danger. Clearly the government overstepped its bounds.

Two months later, magistrate judge Judith Dein was ready to make her ruling. It was a jurisprudential broadside against the government.

In all fifteen arrest cases, she noted, evidence found by police could have easily been hidden from view when motel staff entered the room to clean if the business were trying to cover up illicit activity.

The judge also found that the government had identified an extremely limited number of unrelated incidents spanning more than a decade, "none of which involve the Motel owner or employees." Likewise, there were no reports of any efforts that were undertaken to work with Caswell to reduce crimes at the motel, "nor was any warning given as to the possibility of forfeiture prior to the suit being filed."[9]

"This Court concludes that the Government has failed to meet its burden of establishing that the Motel is subject to forfeiture [and] that the Claimant has met his burden of proving that he is the innocent owner of the Property," Dein wrote.

After Caswell and his family had endured more than four years of litigious hell, the forfeiture action was summarily dismissed.

In the end, the government had to pay the Institute of Justice some $500,000 in legal fees, and $100,000 to Caswell for the money he had borrowed to protect his motel.

"I can't prove this, it's just something I heard through the grapevine, but I would say a pretty good grapevine—that this whole thing cost the government about $4.5 million when all was said and done," said Caswell, who remains shaken by the saga.

"We hire these people, these police and prosecutors and all these people," he added. "We pay our taxes, and they're supposed to be protecting us. But they're stealing from us—and not only stealing from us, they are rewarding themselves for their own failure. I mean, drugs come in—I guess a lot are probably from Mexico or wherever. And they come into Massachusetts, and nobody catches it: all the federal people, the local police, everybody. Everybody misses it, until it gets on my property, and now they want to steal my property for their own failure, and reward themselves.

"They're no better than somebody coming into your business with a gun," Caswell said. "Only they do it with a computer."

The Caswell case "epitomizes so much of what is wrong with modern civil forfeiture laws," Scott Bullock told me. "There was no allegation, they didn't even attempt to show he knew about it, he was in on it, he turned a blind eye toward it. But there was only so much that Caswell could do. And every time he heard about something, he tried to work with the cops."

Caswell and his wife, wearied by the ordeal, sold the property and retired.

AN EXPLODING NATIONAL CRISIS, WOEFULLY IGNORED

Because civil asset forfeiture is a lucrative and sustainable cash machine, the practice is growing. In 1986, the federal Assets Forfeiture Fund took in $93.7 million. By 2014, that number had mushroomed to $4.5 billion—an increase of nearly 5,000 percent, according to the report *Policing for Profit*, by the Institute for Justice.[10]

"We've seen forfeiture really grow, and it's only increasingly become very aggressive," the institute's Scott Bullock told me.

Data on state-level forfeitures are extremely limited, thanks to lax reporting and spotty monitoring laws in most jurisdictions. But among the fourteen states for which sufficient data were available for an extended period, forfeiture revenue more than doubled from 2002 to 2013, according to the institute.

The situation will only deteriorate in the current era of budget cuts that threaten law enforcement agencies, combined with the exceedingly pro-forfeiture posture of the Trump administration. "Many departments are facing cutbacks, and you see more and more of an effort on doing things that will obtain property for the local police departments," Bullock said.

What's truly shocking is how easy it is for police to seize assets and for prosecutors to gain title to those assets through forfeiture litigation without charging and convicting the property owner of any crime.

In most states, all that is required for prosecutors to win a forfeiture case in court is a "preponderance" of evidence (at least 51 percent), although in ten states that evidence must be "clear and convincing" (substantially more likely than not that it is true). In only three states—California, North Carolina, and Wisconsin—must the evidence prove "beyond a reasonable doubt" that a crime has been committed. Worst of all are Massachusetts and North Dakota, where the standard of proof prosecutors must meet is "probable cause," well below 50 percent certainty.

Still, twenty-nine states and the District of Columbia have enacted some form of restraint on the system. In fifteen states, a criminal conviction is now required before civil assets are forfeited, while two states, New Mexico and Nebraska, have abolished civil forfeiture entirely, replacing it with criminal forfeiture.

If there is one silver lining to this unfortunate situation, it's that, as officers and prosecutors become more aggressive in seizing and forfeiting property, more negative publicity will flood the airwaves, fueling calls for a complete overhaul of the system. So far, that clamor has yet to lead to nationwide reform.

DRIVING WHILE CHARITABLE

On February 27, 2016, Eh Wah, a forty-year-old refugee from Myanmar, was pulled over in his black four-door Suzuki by sheriff's deputies in Muskogee County, Oklahoma, for driving with a broken taillight. It was 6:30 at night, and Eh Wah had been on the road for more than twelve hours, on his way home to see his family in Dallas. He was managing the finances of a Christian rock band from Burma, which was touring the United States to raise money for a Burmese Christian school and an orphanage in Thailand that helps displaced members of his native Karen tribe. Eh Wah, a U.S. citizen for more than ten years, is a soft-spoken man who is not proficient in English, according to a suit later filed. The police suspected narcotics trafficking and brought in a drug-sniffing dog. It reacted with a positive alert. They searched the car, and, though they found no drugs or paraphernalia, they did discover that Eh Wah was carrying just over $53,000 in cash.[11]

The cops demanded to know where it came from. Eh Wah struggled to understand the questions and explain his situation: About $35,000 was from proceeds at nineteen concerts, he told them, $9,000 came from merchandise sales, $8,000 was a gift to a band member for his family, and the rest was reimbursement for expenses. The cops scoffed at his halting explanations and transferred the frightened Eh Wah to the station. There, he was threatened with jail and interrogated for several hours. He used his one phone call to put the police in contact with the bandleader to corroborate his accounts. The cops, unimpressed with the man's pleadings, kept the money and sent the shaken

Eh Wah on his way at about 1:30 in the morning—without any criminal charges but still with a faulty taillight.

Tellingly, the police let Eh Wah keep a $300 personal check written out to him even though it was allegedly tied to drugs as well. They couldn't cash it.

It was a long four-hour drive home.

Oklahoma has a low burden of proof for civil forfeiture. Prosecutors are required to prove merely a "preponderance of evidence" that there is a link between the property and the suspected criminal activity. Between 2000 and 2014, nearly $100 million was forfeited in the state, 72 percent of it in cash.[12]

In fact, Oklahoma has some of the most lenient U.S. forfeiture laws, according to a 2015 report by the Institute for Justice, which gave a grade of D-minus to the state on the issue. No conviction is required, "innocent owners" are not adequately protected, and law enforcement gets to keep up to 100 percent of what it takes away—a clear profit motive that confirms conflict of interest.[13]

As with so many roadside seizures, which typically start with a minor infraction, Eh Wah happened to be driving on the southbound "cash" side of U.S. Route 69 toward Texas—a favored route for drug traffickers. Muskogee County sheriff Charles Pearson denied that his deputies target the southbound lanes, insisting to *The Washington Post* that "we work both sides of the highway." But he did accuse *other* departments of focusing on southbound travel.[14] Put bluntly, they are more eager to seize the cash than the drugs that generate it—drugs that kill tens of thousands of Americans each year.

Five weeks later, the Muskogee County DA issued an arrest warrant against Eh Wah for "knowingly and intentionally acquiring, transporting and concealing proceeds . . . known to be derived from the trafficking of controlled dangerous substances."[15]

The deputy's affidavit supporting the charges said the cash was seized "due to inconsistent stories and Wah unable to confirm the money was his" and noted the canine's "positive alert" as probable cause.

But drug-sniffing dogs are surprisingly bad at their jobs. One meta-study of three years' worth of data conducted by *The Chicago Tribune* found a 44 percent accuracy rate for positive alerts, while research at UC–Davis revealed an 85 percent false positive rate.[16]

Eh Wah was not a drug trafficker. He worked at a refugee resettlement charity, helping persecuted Karen people to escape Myanmar and immigrate to the safety of America, just as he had. His family and friends rose to his defense, calling him a simple, quiet, humble man who "didn't even know" how to smoke or drink beer.

As if further evidence were needed, the Omaha church that sponsored visas for the band's fund-raising tour, the Thai orphanage, and the band members themselves not only corroborated his story, they also demanded the confiscated money be returned to its intended beneficiaries in Southeast Asia.

The Institute for Justice agreed to take the case and, on April 22, filed a motion in state district court to challenge the seizure and demand that law enforcement return the money at once and drop the criminal charges. On the morning of April 25, *The Washington Post* published its article on the case, and hours later, the DA ruled that law enforcement must return the money and drop all criminal charges.[17]

But the irony was not lost on Eh Wah and other members of the Myanmar refugee community in the United States, who fled their native country precisely to escape its corruption and repression.

FOLLOWING THE MONEY

In forty-three states, police and prosecutors can keep anywhere from 45 percent to all the proceeds they grab from civil forfeiture cases, according to the Institute for Justice. Critics say there is a direct connection between the percentage they can keep and the likelihood of abuse and corruption. The shiny lure of new patrol cars (including refashioned forfeited vehicles), state-of-the-art weapons, remodeled offices, and slush-funded trips to law enforcement conferences are impossible to resist, at least among some, though certainly not all, departments.

States such as Maine, Missouri, and North Carolina now compel law enforcement to hand over most or all seized assets, depositing them into the treasury's general fund or a neutral fund like education. Instances of abuse in those states are much less prevalent, according to a 2015 Institute for Justice report, *Policing for Profit*.

"If you give people perverse incentives, it's not surprising that they're going to act on them," Bullock told me. "This is not just the story of a couple of bad cops; it's the laws themselves that create this type of behavior. And it perverts law enforcement away from thinking, 'Well, what am I going to do to truly stop crime and to capture the bad guys,' to thinking, 'What am I going to do to improve my life, the life of my colleagues, the life of the department?'"

Can the seized funds be used for bonuses to officers who bring in the most valuable assets? "I think it is, in certain instances it's permissible, but it's mainly for overtime pay," Bullock said while noting that money in budgets is fungible. "Either way, the officers themselves get very direct benefits."

Ezekiel Edwards, director of the ACLU's Criminal Law Reform Project, told me that many officers view seized civil assets as a feather in their cap waiting for them back at the station house. "It's kind of like any organization," he said, "whether you're talking about a firm lawyer bringing in clients, or an ACLU lawyer winning cases, if you can get money that can then be distributed throughout the organization, you look good."[18]

Edwards said he is sure that there are officers "who are heralded because they made a big drug bust, so I'm sure there are departments that say, 'Joe brought in—whatever—$30,000 last year that went straight to our training program; congratulations, Joe.' That to me is just common sense. I think most departments are going to be thrilled about that." In some cities, he noted, police departments openly boast about all the new equipment they attained through forfeiture.

Edwards said the problem "has certainly gotten worse over the years, both in terms of how it's used and the money that's seized." And with that growth in seizures, "you see also an increase in abuse."

It doesn't help that local district attorneys also often get a cut of the take, placing them in financial cahoots with the police. "One of the ways that liberty is protected in this country is that prosecutors have discretion to charge or not to charge," the IJ's Lee McGrath told me. "And that's exacerbated by the fact where the cop comes over and says to the prosecutor, 'Please take this case to court. We want to win so we get the money.' All sorts of biases exist, putting pressures on prosecutors, both in terms of their own budget and those of police officers."

ACCUSED CRIMINALS ARE TREATED BETTER THAN THIS

Civil forfeiture is quite distinct from the criminal variety. If a kid is selling pot from his parents' house and gets busted, the police can arrest the kid and have prosecutors take the case to criminal court, but the cash that police seize at the time of the case goes to a different court system. Prosecutors litigate the transfer of the cash's title to the state in a separate procedure in civil court.

Criminal forfeiture is different. Unlike with civil forfeiture, criminal forfeiture cases happen in the same courtroom and before the same jury and judges in a single process. Prosecutors must show beyond a reasonable doubt that the assets came from drug sales and must comply with all constitutional requirements.

From a citizen's perspective, criminal forfeiture is better than civil forfeiture for additional reasons.

In criminal forfeiture, if someone can't afford a lawyer, the court must appoint one for them. Public defenders not only defend the person's liberty but also his property because it all is happening in criminal court.

In civil proceedings,[19] the government routinely wins. If people can't hire a lawyer, if they don't file a claim by a certain date, if they don't show up in court, the government simply concludes that nobody is claiming the property. That's it. It wins by default, the property is found "guilty," and the case is resolved without any sort of judicial review or resolution.

This two-track system of asset forfeiture, where accused criminals—even gang members and murderers—receive more legal and constitutional protections and benefit from a higher burden of proof than property owners, discourages many from seeking restitution. Nearly nine out of ten civil forfeitures are completed "administratively," meaning through default, because the property owner failed to challenge the seizure in court for any reason.

That is precisely why civil asset forfeiture has become big business with an impressive profit margin. According to the Institute for Justice, 87 percent of all federal forfeitures were civil, not criminal, from 1997 to 2013. The government did not have to spend a dime on arresting, charging, or convicting a single person in order to take title to seized property through forfeiture litigation.

In a just world, there would only be the criminal system, where the accused receive all their due constitutional protections, including the right to an attorney. Property, not people, are the accused in these cases, and public defenders are prohibited by federal law from representing your 2012 Honda or that $1,200 in cash you were bringing to a relative.

Consider this: All the police time spent shaking down innocent citizens for their civil assets is time spent not fighting crime.

"When you have police departments where they're sworn to protect entire communities but are driven by profit motive and looking not to stop crime or react to crime or arrest people who they have probable cause to believe they've committed crimes but are instead out to supplement their budgets by conducting legalized robbery, that does put everybody at risk," said the ACLU's Edwards.

"And then there's just the generic argument," he added, "even though I know it's not that persuasive. But if police are violating constitutional rights, whether they're yours, mine, your neighbor's, the next community over, I think people should care about them."

"EQUITABLE SHARING" OF PLUNDER

The federal Equitable Sharing Program permits local police departments to outsource to U.S. attorneys in the Department of Justice civil forfeiture litigation with federal agents under a joint task force to assist with civil forfeiture cases. Under the arrangement, the feds "adopt" the litigation of property that was seized by state law enforcement agents for alleged violations of state law. Under the second, state law enforcement agents team with officials from the Drug Enforcement Administration or other federal departments to form task forces.

Under each arrangement, the laws enacted by state legislators are ignored. Federal agencies not only have greater resources, their prosecutors face a lower burden of proof than prosecutors litigating forfeiture cases in many state courts.

Even more enticing to cops, federal law requires federal prosecutors to return cash and the proceeds from the sale of forfeited property to the state law enforcement agency that did the initial seizure—as opposed to many state laws, which require that it go into a neutral fund. Typically, under such federal arrangements, the local cops get up to 80 percent of the haul and the feds keep the rest.

Between 2000 and 2017, the DOJ returned more than $6 billion to state and local law enforcement through equitable sharing, although, it should be noted, an additional $4 billion was paid out to crime victims—many of them people who lost everything in the Bernie Madoff scam.[20] During the decade between 2007 and 2017, "forfeitures through the Department's Asset Forfeiture Program have grown to over $28 billion," a report from the DOJ's Office of the Inspector General found.[21]

"It's like money laundering, really," says the Institute for Justice's Scott Bullock. "You see the local officials, saying, 'Well, we're not going to go through the state system because we're not going to get any money; we'll pass it along to the feds.' You see this complete end run and really defying the will of the people of that state in order to financially benefit the local police."

The police in Tewksbury, Massachusetts, must have known that equitable sharing with the feds in the Caswell Motel would increase the chance of success in court—and also increase the overall haul. Under Massachusetts law, police receive only half of the assets they seize, as opposed to the 80 percent they get through equitable sharing. Meanwhile, Massachusetts law says that in order for it to be forfeited, property must be used not only to facilitate a drug crime but "for the business of unlawfully manufacturing, dispensing, or distributing controlled substances." The local cops knew that was a case they would never win in state court.

It should come as little surprise, then, that findings from a 2011 study in the *Journal of Criminal Justice* "indicate that agencies in jurisdictions with more restrictive state forfeiture laws receive more proceeds through federal equitable sharing." The results, the authors concluded, "suggest that state and local law enforcement agencies use federal equitable sharing to circumvent their own state forfeiture laws when state laws are more burdensome or less financially rewarding to these agencies, providing additional evidence that police operations are influenced by financial incentives."[22]

For a brief while, it seemed as though some of the abuses of equitable sharing would be halted. In January 2015, U.S. attorney general Eric Holder surprised civil libertarians with sweeping changes to equitable sharing cases, instructing federal agencies to accept only those that involved firearms, ammunition, explosives, child pornography, or other materials that endangered public safety.[23]

But the new rules were so riddled with loopholes, especially in drug cases, that local police could still find ways around them, critics said. Civil libertarians quickly reined in their enthusiasm. Victoria Middleton, executive director of the ACLU of South Carolina, called the move a "step in the right direction," but lamented that it did little to resolve financial incentives at the local and federal level.

In December 2015, the DOJ suspended equitable sharing payments to local agencies "for the time being," citing budget cuts from the previous year.[24] But that did not last long; three months later, the department said it would resume payments.[25]

Things only grew worse under the new Trump administration. In July 2017, Attorney General Jeff Sessions, struggling to please his forfeiture-loving boss and, perhaps, help keep his job, issued a new directive to expedite equitable sharing, regardless of state and local laws that prohibit or severely limit the practice. After a modest period of decline, this move would increase seizures of cash and property, the DOJ predicted.[26]

"With care and professionalism, we plan to develop policies to increase forfeitures," Sessions warned. Forfeitures to the feds are appropriate, he said, as is sharing proceeds with "our partners." Sessions contended that criminal activity was involved in the "vast majority" of cases; he cited evidence that four out of five federal civil forfeitures were never challenged in court.[27] Of course, the low ratio of challenges may also be a consequence of the time, money, and daunting burden of litigating in civil court in cases involving middle-to-lower-income people. Failure to challenge the loss of property is hardly an admission or even evidence of a crime.

Equitable sharing is cash catnip for local police and prosecutors looking to circumvent state laws that require a higher burden of proof or limit the amount of money, if any, that law enforcement gets to keep. After Attorney General Holder placed new restrictions on the profit-sharing system in December 2015, the number of DEA cash seizures fell by more than half, and the total value of seizures fell by more than a third, the U.S. Department of Justice's inspector general reported in March 2017.[28]

YOUR HOME'S WORTH: A SMALL BAG OF DOPE?

Some of the most egregious forfeiture cases involve the seizure of private houses because of drug possession. Consider the case of Christos Sourvelis, who built his dream home in the Somerton district of northeast Philadelphia for his wife, son, and two daughters. He worked sometimes seven days a week to support his family and couldn't always supervise his children. He could never have known, he insists to this day, that his son, Yanni, twenty-two, was using or selling heroin.[29]

He was about to find out.

According to a legal complaint later filed by the family, on March 27, 2014, police raided the quiet household, armed with an arrest warrant for Yanni. "By the time I got to the door, they had already opened the door, with his hand in, and put a gun to my dog's head," Yanni's mother, Markela, told CNN.[30] According to the police report, Yanni was in the bathroom with the door locked, allegedly flushing something down the toilet. They broke down the door and found the young man with a small bag of heroin. Yanni, they said, had been previously observed by an officer selling $40 worth of drugs to an informant outside the home on a previous day.

Yanni was an honors student at a local community college, preparing to transfer to Temple University. While working at a restaurant bar, he had fallen in with the wrong crowd, his parents say, though he had never been in trouble with the law.

After searching the rest of the house, the cops arrested Yanni on seven drug charges. As they dragged the young man out of the house, Markela said an officer barked at her, "This house is gonna be ours! We're gonna break your walls and throw you out. You will be living in the street."

A month later, prosecutors dropped most of the charges against Yanni in exchange for him pleading no contest to possession with intent to distribute, and conspiracy. He was directed to check into a residential addiction treatment program. Christos and Markela took a deep breath and took stock of their situation. They reasonably assumed that, with their son now getting help and his criminal case resolved, the worst was behind them.

But they would not go back to life as normal.

On the morning of May 8, 2014, as Christos drove his son to the rehab center to begin treatment, the authorities returned to the home, wielding sledgehammers and power tools. They had come to empty, seal, and take possession of the property.

"As he was explaining to me what was going on, there were people closing the doors with screws, locking them. They had the electric company here to turn off my electric and gas," Markela told CNN's Jake Tapper.[31]

Markela protested. An officer scoffed. "We do this four, five times a week," he told her. "You will see a judge in a week. You can plead your case to him."

The family (and dog Max) were forced to leave their property immediately, without most of their personal belongings, even though they never were formally charged with a crime. The house they had built, now worth some $350,000, was snatched away. Now homeless, they moved in with their eldest son, where they slept on sofas.

"I didn't do nothing wrong; I didn't bother anybody, but still they came in and moved us out of our house," Christos told reporters at a press conference.[32]

A hearing was set for May 14 at city hall. The day before, the Sourvelises were permitted to fax a letter to Assistant District Attorney Daren Waite, explaining why the family should be allowed to return home.

That would turn out to be a big mistake.

Like all Philadelphia homeowners whose property has been seized, the Sourvelises were ordered to appear in the city's infamous Courtroom 478 to appeal their case. In this fourth-floor courtroom, a dingy little chamber in the Beaux-Arts city hall, they discovered that the same people who pilfered their house and land now controlled the entire process of whether or not to return it. There was no judge, no jury, not even a court reporter. There were only the prosecutors presiding over the case, whose department was set to profit handsomely from a forfeited $350,000 home.

Complaints abounded about the treatment of citizens in Courtroom 478. Those who requested counsel, including the Sourvelises, were routinely told that it was unnecessary, that their cases were not complex and would not "go to court"—just before being handed a hefty ream of complicated, jargon-filled paperwork to complete, all of it under oath. If owners failed to appear on time, they would automatically be in default and lose their property. As if those weren't enough hurdles, the prosecutors constantly "relisted" hearings—on average five times each, according to the Institute for Justice—and commanded property owners to return each time, on time, or face default.

At the Sourvelis hearing, ADA Waite presented the letter they had faxed to him. In order to have their home unsealed, he explained, the letter had to be transcribed onto a legal document for them to sign, before it went to the judge. Once the judge signed it, they could get back into their house.

The distraught couple, eager to have their home returned, signed the transcribed document without reading it, assuming they were merely signing the same letter they had faxed over.

The Sourvelises left for home, but their case was hardly over. Although the property was no longer considered "seized," the forfeiture case against it would grind on. Their case was "relisted," and they were ordered back to Courtroom 478 in one month.

On the ride home, Markela read the paper and her heart nearly stopped. It barred Yanni from stepping foot on their property ever again. There were other stipulations, too, but without a lawyer to explain everything, the couple didn't fully comprehend what they had just signed. They had unknowingly agreed to waive the "innocent owner" defense in any future forfeiture action and, even worse, any challenge to the forfeiture of their home based on the Excessive Fines Clause of the Eighth Amendment, which is best known for its prohibition on "cruel and unusual punishment."

The family settled back into their Somerton house and tried to regain some sense of normalcy, though nothing was normal about this situation. Yanni was still in rehab and not coming back soon, so they decided to wait a month for the June 13 hearing to get clarification and then resolve the whole thing.

That didn't happen.

Instead, Waite ordered the Sourvelises to respond in handwriting to each allegation contained in the forfeiture petition, declaring each as true or false. They complied. The case was relisted, once again, for July 10.

At that hearing, Waite personally handed Christos a copy of the questionnaire and relisted the case for August 12.

Over the summer, Yanni was discharged from rehab and sent to an outpatient program, sleeping at his brother's house because he could not return home. His attorney, a public defender, urged Waite to let Yanni return safely to his parents. Waite agreed to draft the necessary paperwork.

Christos and Markela were overjoyed. Now, they hoped, their nightmare would finally end at the August 12 hearing. But it didn't. Instead, Waite offered a settlement: Prosecutors would void the forfeiture petition, but only if Christos agreed to waive his right to a trial, admit that his home was being used to commit or facilitate a drug-related crime, agree that any future drug offenses in or near the home could result in forfeiture, allow the state to screen and veto any future tenant or even new owner of the home, and waive his Excessive Fines Clause rights in any future forfeiture case.

He refused to sign. Instead, in August 2014, the Sourvelises filed suit against the city in the United States District Court for the Eastern District of Pennsylvania.[33] Four months later, prosecutors dropped the forfeiture case against them.[34]

Even with the forfeiture case dropped and their house returned, the Sourvelises still demanded justice. Finally, the family's attorneys convinced the court to let Yanni come home. But they also wanted justice for every Philadelphian who had lost property, or would lose property, because of the abusive and unfair practices in Courtroom 478. They teamed up with three other forfeiture victims—two of whom had their houses threatened in similar drug cases. In November 2014, they filed their class-action suit against the city and its mayor, district attorney, and police chief. The Institute for Justice agreed to partner with a local law firm and take the case.

The civil complaint accused the city of "unconstitutionally" using civil forfeiture to grab property from private owners, even when they "have no involvement in or even knowledge of the crimes alleged." It called Philadelphia's program "robo-forfeiture" because it used confusing legal documents and endless proceedings "to generate millions of dollars in revenue outside of its appropriated budget."

Philadelphia has one of the largest municipal forfeiture programs in the country, the suit claimed, raking in an average of $5.8 million each year. Compare that with Los Angeles County, with a population more than 6.5 times greater: In 2010, it took in just $1.2 million.

"The Philadelphia D.A.'s Office has turned this tool into a veritable machine, devouring real and personal property from thousands of residents, many of whom are innocent," the lawsuit said. In an eleven-year period (the years were not provided), it seized more than 1,000 homes, 3,200 vehicles, and $44 million in cash, or $64 million in total assets—nearly 20 percent of the DA's budget, generated outside the oversight of the city council.

Much of that money went to salaries, including for the prosecutors who administer the civil-forfeiture program. In Philadelphia, forfeited assets earmarked for salaries worked out to nearly $17 for every resident of the city, as opposed to the $1.11 per capita spent by all other Pennsylvania counties combined.

Under increasing public pressure and media scrutiny, District Attorney Seth Williams defended the "seize and seal" program in a *Philadelphia Inquirer* guest column. "Drug dealers and the social rot that comes with their trade ruin neighborhoods—they bring addiction, illegal firearms, death, despair, and destruction," Williams wrote. The forfeiture process, he insisted, "makes it harder for dealers to operate by removing their profits and profit motive. Don't believe the claims that we are just snatching up property, mostly homes and autos, owned by random individuals who have nothing to do with drug dealing."[35]

But the class-action suit handed down a clear and concise indictment of Philadelphia's unfair, illegal, and unconstitutional practices. Specifically, it alleged that the city was violating Fifth and Fourteenth Amendment guarantees of due process, among other constitutional protections, because it:

permitted the seizure of property without providing any evidence to justify proceeding or an opportunity for owners to be heard;

forced owners to waive their legal and constitutional rights in order to return home or have the forfeiture petition withdrawn;

failed to provide a prompt preliminary hearing before a neutral arbiter, where owners could argue for permission to remain at home, pending an ultimate hearing on the merits;

repeatedly "relisted" hearings, forcing owners to appear in person over and over again or permanently lose their property;

retained all proceeds from forfeiture for use by the Philadelphia District Attorney's Office and Police Department; and

allowed prosecutors and their staff to control hearings in Courtroom 478.

In June 2015, the city agreed to settle part of the case. It would no longer bar people from staying in their homes until forfeiture proceedings were decided by a judge. It would permit relatives accused of crimes to stay on the property, end state veto power over all new tenants and owners, and no longer limit the rights of property owners to challenge future forfeiture attempts.[36]

The city then moved to dismiss the Sourvelis complaint. But in March 2017, the court rejected that motion. After that, the parties agreed to settle.

City officials agreed to "a set of reforms that will end the perverse financial incentives under which law enforcement keeps and uses forfeiture revenue," the Institute for Justice announced on September 18, 2018. The settlement would also "fundamentally reform procedures for seizing and forfeiting property, and establish a $3 million fund to compensate innocent people whose property was wrongly confiscated."

That same day, the preliminary paperwork for a settlement was filed in federal court. A hearing on the matter was scheduled for mid-October, with a ruling on whether the case meets the criteria of a class-action suit expected in November. The court would also have to approve any final settlement as well.

In the meantime, thanks to the lawsuit and the enormous amount of media attention it garnered, Courtroom 478 is no longer used as a forfeiture kangaroo court. "After we filed in August 2014, that fall, the DA's office started a little bit of change, such as actually recording the proceedings," said Darpana Sheth, senior attorney at the Institute for Justice. "But it took them until January 2016 before they stopped holding forfeiture proceedings there and effectively shut down Courtroom 478." Today, all forfeiture hearings are held across the street in the state criminal courthouse (even though these are civil cases), where they are presided upon by a judge or trial commissioner. "Our settlement will make it legally binding and enforceable," Sheth said. If approved by the court, city prosecutors will never be able to go back to their old, unconstitutional ways.

Even as the Sourvelis suit slowly wound its way through the halls of justice, a similar case produced a landmark court decision that, perhaps, will end or at least reduce abuses in a state that is rife with them.

On November 19, 2009, seventy-one-year-old grandmother Elizabeth Young was startled by a loud knock on the door of the West Philadelphia home where she had lived for four decades. It was the police narcotics division, wielding a search warrant. The cops claimed that her fifty-year-old son, Donald Graham, who lived in the home with his two children, had sold $40 bags of marijuana to an informant on several occasions from the house. They found a scale and six baggies containing small amounts of pot.[37]

Graham was not at home at the time and was not arrested or charged with a crime. Over the next few weeks, he continued to sell drugs to informants from the house, or sometimes from his mother's 1997 Chevrolet Venture minivan parked out front. After a deal on January 7, 2010, he was arrested. The police confiscated a small bag of marijuana, a cell phone, $176 in unmarked currency, and $60 in "prerecorded currency" (marked for use by the informant). They also took the keys to Elizabeth Young's minivan.[38]

After getting a warrant, they searched the house again, this time finding a tiny amount of pot in the living room and about a quarter ounce more in the van. Graham pleaded guilty to possession of marijuana and possession with intent to deliver. He was sentenced to eleven to twenty-three months of house arrest with no fine imposed.

Elizabeth Young thought the trouble was behind her.

But more than eight months after her son's arrest, in October 2010, the Commonwealth of Pennsylvania filed a petition for the forfeiture of Young's house and vehicle, in the case titled *Commonwealth v. Real Property and Improvements Commonly Known as 5444 Spruce St., Philadelphia.*

Young chose to fight, filing a challenge with the Philadelphia Court of Common Pleas, in Courtroom 478.

The court was not sympathetic. It ruled that the commonwealth had established a link between the house and the illegal sale of drugs. Specifically, it said, Young facilitated the sale of drugs or stored them in her house and vehicle. The court also rejected her "innocent owner" defense because even though police told her of her son's drug dealing and served a search warrant on the property, she "refused to take any proactive measures or steps to demonstrate her lack of consent to this illegal activity."[39]

It went on. Young neither vacated her home nor barred her son from entering it, the court said, and she turned "a blind eye" to the crimes being committed at her property (the exact same language that federal prosecutors used in the Caswell Motel case).

Perhaps most ominously, the court rejected Young's claim that the forfeiture of an entire house for a minor drug offense violated the Excessive Fines Clause. The seizure was not "grossly disproportionate" to the supposed gravity of her son's offenses. (It's worth noting that the U.S. Supreme Court has determined that criminal forfeitures cannot be grossly disproportionate to the offense, but it has never ruled on civil forfeitures.) Graham, the court noted, faced maximum penalties of $80,000—more than the combined value of his mother's house and minivan.

The fact that Young was never charged with a crime was "irrelevant." This was civil forfeiture.

Young appealed to the state's Commonwealth Court, which reversed the trial court's decision, concluding that it had not properly evaluated whether the forfeiture violated the Eighth Amendment and failed to consider all relevant circumstances in Young's innocent owner defense.

The Commonwealth of Pennsylvania, apparently eager to maintain such an easy revenue stream, appealed to the state supreme court and, in May 2017, lost in what became a landmark case.[40]

The high court ruled that property could not be seized unless it was "uniquely important to the commission of the offense." It further held that the Excessive Fines Clause does in fact forbid forfeitures where the loss of value is grossly disproportionate to the severity of the crime. And even though the house was assessed at just $54,000, its value was worth much more to the person who owned and lived in it, Elizabeth Young.

The ruling "ends years of uncertainty in the law regarding the constitutional limits on civil forfeiture where the property owner is not charged with any crime," an attorney on the case, Joanna Kunz, wrote in a blog. And though the powerful ruling only applies to future cases in Pennsylvania, it has emerged as a legal model that other state courts could adopt, Kunz said.[41]

Why, after all, should someone lose her property, especially her own home, just because it was somehow implicated in a minor drug crime committed by somebody else?

WHAT DOES THE CONSTITUTION SAY?

Civil asset forfeiture, on its face, appears to violate several fundamental principles of the U.S. Constitution. To begin with, it defies the separation of powers doctrine, the basis of our famous system of "checks and balances." Article I reserves the raising of revenue and appropriation of funds as the sole purview of the legislative branch, most scholars agree. But with civil forfeiture, law enforcement, as part of the executive branch, gets to raise and appropriate its own funds.

"Law enforcement agencies need more money? Well, they go out and assign more cops and prosecutors to pursue crimes that have a forfeiture component to them, so that they can supplement their budgets," said Lee McGrath of the Institute for Justice. "The legislature has abdicated its responsibility. Legislators have turned over the means of funding budgets and setting priorities to the executive branch and law enforcement agencies."

McGrath quoted George Mason, principal author of the Virginia Declaration of Rights of 1776, the basis for the federal Bill of Rights, who with blunt eloquence once wrote, "When the same man, or set of men, holds the sword and the purse, there is an end of liberty."

The right to due process, meanwhile, as guaranteed by the Fifth and Fourteenth Amendments, also seems to be thrown under the constitutional bus in civil forfeiture cases. The amendments' Due Process Clause requires a neutral administration of justice, where defendants are informed of their rights, given a fair hearing, and presumed innocent until proven guilty. If government actors are biased by the lure of remuneration from purloining other people's property, citizens are not getting a fair hearing or a fair process.

It's akin to a judge who pockets part of a fine he imposes on somebody, only much subtler. In civil asset cases, the police decide what crimes to pursue and prosecutors decide what the penalty should be. They are both sharing in the spoils. "Due process is sometimes a difficult concept to understand," Lee McGrath told me. "But if you think of it as getting a chance to a fair and thorough hearing, the amount of process you are due must be proportional to the liberty or property being taken from you."

Civil forfeiture, in most cases, also seems to violate the Sixth Amendment's guarantee of the right to a "speedy trial." Getting a hearing on a case could take up to a year. The right to a speedy trial exists for someone in criminal court but not for his car or cash in civil court. Most states still do not require a prompt hearing on getting stuff back, although a 2000 federal law does require it in cases involving seized homes and businesses.[42]

Oddly, the Supreme Court has never ruled on whether one has a right to a prompt hearing in civil asset cases. A precedent-setting decision on this matter would help to address the many constitutional issues surrounding civil forfeiture.

Then there is the question of Eighth Amendment protections against excessive fines. If seizing an entire house as punishment for harboring minor drug offenses does not qualify as an "excessive fine," then what does?

BE CAREFUL WHAT YOU DEPOSIT

Federal law says that any bank deposit or cash transaction greater than $10,000 must be reported to the IRS, as well as the Departments of Homeland Security and Justice. It's not illegal to deposit less than $10,000 when you have legitimate business-related reasons for it. But if you own a small business that deals in cash—a restaurant or a shop, say—and you consistently make large deposits that approach but do not reach that mark, the IRS will notice. It can and does swoop in to seize your account. They call the crime "structuring" and claim that businesspeople are trying to circumvent the $10,000 reporting rule for nefarious reasons.

You read that right: Innocent people get their bank accounts frozen and then may lose their money based solely on governmental suspicion as to how they put their money in a bank.

From 2005 to 2012, the IRS confiscated $242 million in more than 2,500 alleged structuring cases, a study from the Institute for Justice found. One-third of those cases involved people making a series of sub-$10,000 cash transactions. The median amount seized was $34,000, while legal costs to attempt to retrieve the money can easily surpass $20,000.[43]

In 2012 alone, the IRS made 639 seizures based on structuring allegations, way up from 114 in 2005. Only one in five was prosecuted as a criminal case.

And in 2017, the Treasury Department's inspector general found that out of 278 sample cases investigated, 91 produced zero evidence that the funds came from an illegal source or involved any illegal activity at all.[44]

Justice, however, can be served when the disinfectant of public scrutiny, coupled with high-powered legal counsel, comes to bear on something that is so patently unfair. One high-profile case roped in the owner of an extremely popular restaurant in the northern Iowa vacation town of Spirit Lake, Iowa, where Carole Hinders lives and owned Mrs. Lady's Mexican Food for more than forty years. During peak summer season, the place routinely drew crowds of a hundred or more patrons every meal, who packed the two modest dining rooms. Everyone knew the rules: This was a cash-only business. Hinders did not want to pay the fees charged by credit card companies.

One morning in August 2013, Hinders was enjoying breakfast at home with her grandchildren when there was a loud rapping at the door. Two federal agents informed her they had just emptied Mrs. Lady's bank account of nearly $33,000. The sixty-three-year-old woman and her community institution of a business had been "structuring" deposits, they said. They accused her of money laundering due to her frequent cash deposits.

The agents had reviewed the restaurant's bank statements from mid-April 2012 through mid-February 2013, they said. They found more than

$315,000 in deposits, none of them for more than $10,000—most were between $5,000 and $9,500. They also found deposits on consecutive business days that amounted to more than $10,000 on multiple occasions.[45]

The seizure was done with a secret warrant, without warning or notice. The agents said they would quickly file papers with the U.S. Department of Justice to keep all that money under federal civil forfeiture laws.

Hinders insisted she was a law-abiding citizen who had never been in trouble. *This must be a mistake,* she thought. In fact, her mother, who used to keep the books at Mrs. Lady's, always made deposits under $10,000 because, that way, tellers would not have to do "extra paperwork." Besides, after a robbery, she made sure never to keep excessive amounts of cash in the restaurant. Hinders had followed that practice for thirty years after taking over the bookkeeping, without so much as a whisper of warning from the government or the bank.

"I'm going to get my money back," Hinders told the agents as they left.

"You can try," she recalls one of them responding.

Without cash on hand, Hinders quickly fell into debt—for the first time in her life. Using borrowed money, credit cards, a second mortgage, and extended credit begged from vendors, she struggled on, scared, bewildered, and demoralized.

Where could she turn? Hinders called one of the agents who had been part of the seizure. He didn't respond. Attorneys told her the legal fees would likely exceed the $33,000 snatched from her. One lawyer volunteered to take the case pro bono, expecting the government would listen to reason and return the money. He got nowhere against a wall of federal officials who offered no clemency.

When Hinders called Republican senator Charles Grassley, staff members were in disbelief and told her to call the police. She clearly had been the victim of a scam by con men posing as revenue agents, they said. The IRS does not do things like that.

More than a year and a half passed without any offer of a hearing before a judge.

In October 2014, Hinders secured the pro bono help of the Institute for Justice. Beaten down, her business in disarray, she had decided to sell the restaurant. Her son was suffering from a worsening case of multiple sclerosis, and she wanted to take care of him. Besides, the business's cash flow never fully recovered after the government seizure.

"They still haven't charged me with anything," she told *The Des Moines Register* at the time. "If I'm guilty of something, lock me up. They're just taking my money."[46]

Hinders filed suit in federal district court, arguing that seizing the entire bank account because of lawful deposits violates the Eighth Amendment's Excessive Fines Clause.

The Hinders lawsuit attracted attention from the media, including *The New York Times,* which asked the IRS to provide an explanation for what happened in the Hinders case and others like it.

Unexpectedly, the agency backed down and issued a new policy statement.

"After a thorough review of our structuring cases over the last year and in order to provide consistency throughout the country . . . regarding our policies, I.R.S.-C.I. [Criminal Investigation] will no longer pursue the seizure and forfeiture of funds associated solely with 'legal source' structuring cases [i.e., money that was legally acquired] unless there are exceptional circumstances justifying the seizure and forfeiture," the agency said.[47]

Accordingly, in December 2014, U.S. Justice Department lawyers moved to dismiss the Mrs. Lady's case, known as *United States of America v. $32,820.56 in United States Currency,* and return the money. But the government offered no admission of wrongdoing and asked the judge for summary judgment "without prejudice," meaning it could still file charges against Hinders and seize her assets at some later date.

This was unacceptable to Hinders. She filed a motion in federal district court, urging the judge to dismiss her case with prejudice, meaning it could never be reopened, or else let it proceed to trial. She also asked for all legal fees, court costs, and interest on the seized assets and loans she took out to be reimbursed.

"I actually wanted a trial, which would have cleared my name and helped to protect others, but it is good to get the money back. My fight is far from over, though," Hinders said in a statement provided by her lawyers. "I am willing to tell my story to Congress to help change forfeiture laws so that no one else has to go through what I suffered."

The court refused Hinders's requests. She appealed to the Eighth Circuit Court of Appeals, which sided with the government.[48] She had lost the battle, but she had somehow still won the war. In addition to the return of her $33,000,

Hinders's case had helped to rewrite IRS policy in favor of innocent business owners across the country.

WHAT CAN WE DO?

Most efforts at civil-forfeiture reform have arisen at the state level. On the federal side of things, Eric Holder's short-lived experiment of placing even modest restrictions on equitable sharing will not be repeated any time soon.

Donald Trump has proven to be a big fan of seizing people's property, a distinctly anti-populist approach. Early in his term, Trump sympathized with a group of law enforcement officials who were complaining about local efforts to curb civil forfeitures. Harold Eavenson, sheriff of Rockwell County, Texas, bemoaned in front of the cameras that certain politicians in Texas's state legislature were threatening the war on drugs by trying to enact modest reforms of the state's asset forfeiture laws.

"There's a state senator in Texas that was talking about legislation to require conviction before we could receive that forfeiture money," Eavenson griped.

"Do you believe that?" Trump responded, frowning dramatically for the cameras.

"And I told him that the cartel would build a monument to him in Mexico if he could get that legislation passed," Eavenson said.

Trump looked animated. "Who is that state senator? I want to hear his name," he demanded, only half in jest. "We'll destroy his career!"[49]

The attempt at bombast sparked awkward chuckling. But even the sheriff, who refused to name the rogue lawmaker, looked stunned.

When it comes to fighting government overreach, civil asset forfeiture should be near the top of the conservative agenda. But Trump seemed far more concerned with burnishing his "new sheriff in town" bona fides than taking a more libertarian tack.

"This is a portrait of Trump in full law-and-order mode, where all of the emphasis is on order and none on law," *CounterPunch* magazine scoffed. "Any real conservative would object to asset seizure as a 'taking' of property without compensation or judicial review, a constitutional crime by the state."[50]

If libertarian-minded politicians from the Right *and* Left want to take on asset-forfeiture reform, they will have to do so against the will of Donald Trump, who suggested he would fight any efforts in Congress that would roll back Obama-era rules that protect and even promote civil asset forfeiture. Politicians seeking to limit the authority of police, he said, "could get beat up really badly by the voters."[51] Meanwhile, Attorney General Jeff Sessions had a long history of supporting the system, making federal reform even more of an uphill climb.

Libertarian National Committee chair Nicholas Sarwark told Fox News how "disappointing" it was to learn of Trump's fondness for legal highway robbery. "He campaigned on the idea of helping people who are on the low end of the economic spectrum and this [law] disproportionately affects minorities and those who do not have the means to hire an attorney," Sarwark said.[52]

Undaunted by the president's zeal for forfeiture, reformists vow to press on. There are several avenues of attack, but success is dependent on steadfast lawmakers, an unblinking media, and a general population that is fed up enough to demand change. Here is an agenda to work toward policy reform:

Keep Track

Before effectively tackling civil forfeiture, we need a nationwide audit of the system: a thorough accounting of all the assets seized, their net value, how much was returned to lawful owners, and how the rest of it was appropriated and spent. In many states, there is a lack of reporting for this. Officials are mum as to how much revenue they are collecting. "In some states, the cops or prosecutors are supposed to keep track of it; but they don't report it," Bullock said. "It really cuts down on accountability when people say, 'Well, how much did you bring in last year?' and there's really no good answer."

End Incentives

Anyone with a hand in seizing or forfeiting assets should have zero say in how those funds are spent. All moneys should go into a state's general treasury or to designated agencies such as the Department of Education. Some could be earmarked for return to law enforcement, but if local police and district attorneys want some of the forfeiture booty, they should seek it through regular budgetary mechanisms decided by the state legislature just like every sector of government, instead of simply pocketing it.

The corrupt judge analogy applies here, too. If judges have a financial interest in the outcome of a case, they must, by law, recuse themselves. So what about cops and prosecutors? They are not judicial officials, but they are public officials nonetheless, and the Constitution is supposed to apply equally to them. How much—if any—interest in the outcome of a case should they have? If we can end the financial incentives, we will see most problems curtailed. This isn't really about fair and effective law enforcement; it's about a giant cash-grab game encouraged by the state.

Move to a One-Track System

Civil libertarians have been heartened in recent years by talk among some lawmakers of wholly eliminating civil asset forfeiture and replacing it with criminal forfeiture. Right now, offenders face a two-track system: Their *person* might go into the criminal justice system, but their property goes through the civil system, which does not offer the same constitutional protections and burdens of proof as criminal prosecution.

A much better system, Bullock said, would be to have only a criminal forfeiture process, in which the suspect is first convicted of the crime by a jury of his or her peers, after enjoying the presumption of innocence and having any evidence illegally seized suppressed "and then, after being convicted, the jury could find that the vehicle and the cash were an instrument in, or proceeds of, a crime. You would have a single process, as New Mexico and Nebraska have enacted in 2015 and 2016, which would also ensure that only those who are convicted lose their property."

Litigate

More victims of unconstitutional forfeitures are now fighting back in court, not only to retrieve their homes, cars, or cash but to compel cities, counties, and states to police their police—to restore all of those "guaranteed" rights that are trampled upon in the escalating rat race for revenue. These civilian complainants, often guided by the considerable help of nonprofits such as the Institute for Justice and the ACLU, have a surprisingly good record against the state. More judges, aware of the growing situation, have sided with victims of governmental greed, graft, and overreach.

One particularly effective tactic at trial: Identify the percentage of the local law enforcement budget that depends directly on forfeited assets. If it can be shown how desperately police and prosecutors need civil forfeitures to underwrite costs, especially their own salaries, and if conflicting self-interest can be proven, then a good case for overreach can be made. These are the cases that tend to prevail in federal court.

End Equitable Sharing

It wouldn't be a cure-all, but it certainly would help. In states with tougher laws on how property is seized, forfeited, and allocated, police would no longer be able to get around the limits by partnering with the federal government, which requires that all assets be used to benefit law enforcement. In states where the rules are laxer and police and prosecutors can keep most or all of what they grab, an end to equitable sharing would help, but not as much as in the stricter states. Many cops will stop outsourcing and simply do the work themselves to make up for lost revenue.

Reform "Structuring" Laws

Should innocent people really be parted from all of their savings in the bank, without warning, without charges, without a criminal trial, just because they made deposits under the $10,000 reporting threshold? Of course not. This insidious practice is unfair and unconstitutional, since the IRS does not have to prove intent or even knowledge of a crime. It seizes enormous sums at will, based on computerized algorithms and a hunch, without adequate independent oversight or due process guaranteed under the Fifth and Fourteenth Amendments. At the minimum, all depositors should be given advance written notice from the IRS and/or their bank when suspicious or illegal activity first appears. In other words, fair warning. If an account is seized, provide a fair and impartial hearing as quickly as possible. And even if actual structuring has occurred, make the punishment fit the crime. Don't just swoop in, wipe out their bank account, and ask questions later.

Legislation

Calls for reform have been muted, at best. At the national level, several bills on the matter currently languish in the House or Senate, largely because asset forfeiture just hasn't received the coverage it deserves.

That's a major reason why the Fifth Amendment Integrity Restoration (FAIR) Act, the sole sponsor of which was über-libertarian Senator Rand Paul, could not even get out of committee during the 2015–2016 Congress. His bill—which should appeal to Americans across the political divide—would have eliminated the Equitable Sharing Program and completely ended monetary incentives among federal law enforcement by directing all seized assets in federal cases to the Treasury's General Fund. None of it could be sent to state and local law enforcement, eliminating a sizable chunk of their conflicting incentives.

In addition, the FAIR Act would lift the burden of proof in federal (though not state) civil assets cases, from a "preponderance of evidence" to the much more rigorous "clear and convincing evidence" that a crime had been committed. "Innocent owners," meanwhile, would no longer have to prove that their property was not involved in a crime, restoring the presumption of innocence. Poorer property owners would receive appointed counsel. The act would also hobble forfeitures based on "structuring" by forcing the IRS to prove that the defendant made the deposit with criminal intent. The agency would have to demonstrate knowledge that a crime was being committed and provide a probable cause hearing within fourteen days of seizing any funds.

During the 2017–2018 Congress, a few bills tried to chip away at civil forfeiture abuses. One proposal, introduced in each house by Senator Tim Scott (R-SC) and Representative Peter Roskam (R-IL), proposed similar reforms to "structuring" that were included in Rand Paul's far more robust legislation. As of this writing, the nonpartisan website govtrack.us gave the bill a 1 percent chance of becoming law.

Despite a few other efforts at reform in Congress, there is just not enough appetite for reform in Washington. Progress in state capitals, meanwhile, has been more mixed.

A bill to require criminal conviction before civil asset forfeiture, introduced in Georgia in 2015, was making its way through the legislature when the Georgia Sheriffs' Association and other law enforcement agencies prevented its passage out of committee, according to Bullock. "They just came out and said, 'Absolutely not, we will not stand for this, and if you vote for it, that shows you're not fit for the cops,'" he said.

Lawmakers in other states are moving forward to confront the problem, with varying degrees of success. Some have taken remarkably bold steps; others have drafted more milquetoast reforms, watered down by the intrusion of police and prosecutors. Connecticut, for example, in July 2017 approved requiring a criminal conviction before any assets could be seized. Even so, the law did not restrict equitable sharing with the feds, handing law enforcement a big legal loophole to sail through. That same year in April, Arizona passed a law that barred equitable sharing in cases with property worth less than $75,000—the vast majority of all cases—and raised the burden of proof to "clear and convincing" evidence. It did not, however, include a provision requiring conviction before seizure. Other reform measures have been adopted in Colorado, Illinois, and Pennsylvania, where legislation was inspired by the case of Elizabeth Young, explained earlier in this chapter, whose Philadelphia home was confiscated after her son was arrested for selling marijuana on the property.

In other states, reform efforts have fallen flat. In Idaho, Republican governor Butch Otter vetoed a widely supported bipartisan bill in April 2017 that would have required criminal conviction in seizures involving suspected drug crimes. The bill was a "solution in search of a problem," Otter scoffed. "There have been no allegations that Idaho law enforcement officers or agencies are illegally or inappropriately seizing property from alleged drug traffickers."[53]

Without an adequate and sustained outcry from the public and media alike, it will be difficult to slap constitutional shackles upon this legalized robbery. But reforming, or ending, civil asset forfeiture is an especially urgent task, protecting the American people from those who are paid to protect *them*.

"Legislative change is not impossible by any means," Bullock said. "But it is tough."

FREE SPEECH AND THE INDIVIDUAL AMERICAN

The First Amendment prohibits "abridging freedom of speech, or of the press; or the right of the people peaceably to assemble." In a subsequent chapter, I explore ways the media and peaceful organized protestors have been cowed, surveilled, harassed, beaten, teargassed, pepper-sprayed, arrested, and/or prosecuted for crimes—a situation that was bad under Obama and is growing direr under the current administration. But what about everybody else, ordinary individuals going about their daily lives, carrying with them a mixed basket of beliefs, emotions, attitudes, outrages, and political viewpoints? In many ways, the current climate is even more treacherous for them, because the threat is both under the radar and far more widespread than most people realize.

In today's America, law-abiding citizens face harassment, detention, and even prosecution for their posts on Twitter and Facebook, for asking heated political questions in a library, for swearing in public, for disrespecting police officers, and for desecrating the flag, among other purported crimes.

Happily, when they choose to fight back, they tend to win (though not always, as we will see). The government does not take kindly to efforts to restrain its ability to stifle speech—even protected speech—and it has all the resources it needs to prosecute. Most of the people I profiled here endured intense emotional duress and sometimes financial hardship in their long, arduous battles to have their charges dismissed and, in some cases, seek damages for the infringement of their free-speech rights and an injunction to prevent officials from punishing that particular form of speech in the future.

But most people don't fight back or even worry about free speech. Then they wake up one day to discover that *their* speech is not so free anymore. Such apathy is dangerous for the future of human expression in America. Two recent trends, in particular, should be alarming to all civil libertarians: an intrusive, abusive, authoritarian federal government under President Trump and Attorney General Jeff Sessions, followed by Acting Attorney General Matthew G. Whitaker and then Attorney General William Barr; and a simmering, pro-censorship undercurrent of beliefs—especially among progressive millennials—that has gained steam on college campuses and elsewhere.

Nearly all forms of speech are protected under the First Amendment, with a few exceptions, including obscenity, child pornography, direct incitement to violence or criminal acts, a personal threat of violence, defamation, perjury, and false advertising.

The government also reserves the legal authority to prohibit certain forms of speech on its own property. Government employees can lose their jobs for making racially offensive remarks, uttering profanities, or saying something that interferes with the efficiency of the workplace. Students in public schools can be disciplined or expelled for language that disrupts class, includes vulgarity, or offends other people. Protestors cannot disrupt government functions. And the government retains considerable control over speech in the judicial, immigration, military, and prison systems.

But the state need not outlaw speech in order to repress it: Government gag orders and injunctions, casting a "chilling effect" through scare tactics meant to dissuade political suppression, and enforcement of outdated or obscure laws are just three of the tools at its disposal. When those fail, a battery of prosecutors and Justice Department lawyers are at the ready to protect the government's interests by any legal means available.

Americans of every political persuasion should be unsettled by any attempt to chip away at what they are free to say. Otherwise, we might all find ourselves in a country where we watch our mouths assiduously, even in the supposed privacy of our own homes.

As the nonprofit civil liberties legal foundation the Rutherford Institute puts it, "Remember, the only way to safeguard our freedoms is to know when they're being threatened."

NO FREE SPEECH ON SOCIAL MEDIA?

America has lost itself. We have lost who we truly are.[1] The words, posted on Facebook in 2011, seemed innocuous enough. But the author, Brandon Raub, was "trying to start a revolution," he told me.[2] They were the opening lines of what would become a somewhat rambling anti-government online manifesto. He did so despite knowing that, like many politically expressive veterans returning from Iraq and Afghanistan, his social media was being monitored by the feds. He had a sense that something was going to happen to him.

Raub, of Chesterfield, Virginia, about ten miles south of the site where Patrick Henry and George Mason argued in Richmond over the powers of government versus the rights of individuals, was an opinionated twenty-six-year-old, a decorated former U.S. Marine who served from 2005 to 2011 as a combat engineer sergeant before being honorably discharged. He was enraged by what he considered to be people leading the takeover of Washington by a "shadow government," and the central bank (the fed). His distrust of the modern world economy led him to open a home business dealing in silver coins.

On November 11, 2011, Sergeant Raub offered an online honor roll of historic American figures, from early Republic patriots to more contemporary icons. "This is the land of Thomas Jefferson," he wrote. "This is the land of Benjamin Franklin." It is also the land of Frederick Douglass, John F. Kennedy, Martin Luther King, and Smedley Butler, a decorated Marine general, a Quaker, opponent of U.S. military adventurism, and author of the book *War Is a Racket.*

The government "is in bed with the Fed," he charged. "They want to enslave you to the government so they can control every aspect of your lives. It is an empire based on lies." The reasons given for America's twenty-first-century wars were also lies, and "September Eleventh was an inside job. Your leaders betrayed you."

But there was a "better way," he continued. "It's called freedom . . . you have the right to do whatever you want as long as you don't infringe on the freedoms of other people."

By the following year, 2012, Raub's musings turned darker. He launched a new Facebook page, "Dear Illuminati," aimed at what he describes as a "Satanist mafia and leaders of the shadow government." In August of 2012, he really started pouring forth, with anti-government alarm bells blaring.

"There has been an overwhelming amount of evil enacted and planned against you, your children, and your countrymen," Raub wrote.[3] "Your government is evil. And the Cavalry is coming." Two days later he wrote, "I'm starting the Revolution. I'm done waiting." And the next day: "Sharpen up my axe; I'm here to sever heads."

A series of cryptic, quasi-violent posts ensued:

This is revenge. Know that before you die.
This is the start of you dying. Planned spittin with heart of Lion.
I'm gunning whoever run the town.

Raub said the lines were taken from rap-song lyrics that he had composed, several of which contained "terrible lyrics that I don't agree with. I am not proud of a lot of the things I included," he told me. "I don't actually believe in revenge. I believe in justice for the innocent and the oppressed." The words were not meant in "the literal sense," he added, but "more as metaphors and frames of mind."

Raub launched the page as a private one, with just his brother and sister as members. But then he decided to make it public. Raub had no idea, but two Marines from his former Iraq platoon came across the page online and reported their brother in arms to the FBI. They were concerned by Raub's "increasingly threatening" Facebook posts. One of them, Howard Bollen, told agents that the posts used "typical extremist language," but added that Raub "genuinely believes in this and is not simply looking for attention." He said Raub's "threatening and action-oriented" rhetoric had only grown worse in recent months.[4]

Someone in the government was now paying close attention and didn't like what they were reading. "I think there was someone within the government who had been watching me for a long time," Raub told me. "Someone in power saw an opportunity."

On August 16, there was a polite knock at the front door of Raub's home. He opened it to find an FBI agent and a Chesterfield County Police Department liaison to the FBI. They had no warrant but asked to speak with him about "what was going on," according to Raub. After a minute or two, he said, the police liaison began stumbling and passed out. That's when more than a dozen uniformed and plainclothes agents and officers from the FBI, Secret Service, and Chesterfield County Police Department rushed onto the property.

Clad only in shorts, Raub spoke to the officers through the screen door. He admitted he wrote the posts. And though he had never threatened violence, the police said Raub refused to answer directly when asked if he intended to commit violence. "We will all see very soon what all of this means," he allegedly told two of the cops, according to the police report.[5] Raub denied ever saying that.

One detective, Michael Paris, later said that the ex-Marine's demeanor "shifted wildly over the course of the conversation, alternating between calm and extremely intense and emotional." Raub asked the police why they weren't arresting government officials for launching a missile into the Pentagon on 9/11, running a child sex-slave ring, or exposing citizens to radioactive metals.

They asked him to come out into the street to talk, and he agreed.

Raub's half-naked interrogation went on for a half hour as agents called state and federal prosecutors for legal guidance. They all said the same thing: Raub's statements, by themselves, did not provide sufficient grounds for criminal charges.

With arrest not an option, Detective Paris decided to confer with a mental health professional working for the county. He got on the phone with Michael Campbell, a certified "pre-screener" with the local EMS.[6] Paris described the Facebook posts and told Campbell that Raub appeared "preoccupied and distracted" and exhibited "rapid mood swings and roving, intermittent eye contact." He was also worried about Raub's military weapons training and his potential access to weapons, even though—perhaps somewhat surprisingly—Raub owned no firearms.

That was all it took—a third-party phone consultation with a low-level government pre-screener—to diagnose Raub, someone he had never met or even seen, as a probable psychotic. Campbell recommended that Paris seize and detain Raub "for an evaluation."

While waiting, Raub grew increasingly impatient and began raising his voice, shouting, "What are you guys here for?" That's when the officers tackled Raub and piled on his body. "I resisted for a second and then stopped," he told me. "But I wanted them to know I could defend myself." As Raub's brother and his brother's girlfriend arrived and began shooting video, the cops pulled Raub to his feet. "You're coming with us!" one of them shouted, without saying where Raub was going or why he was going there.

He was going to jail.

Still shoeless and clad only in shorts, Raub was handcuffed to a metal bench in the jail's intake room. That's when Campbell arrived. He questioned Raub about the posts and Raub's beliefs in government conspiracies and the impending revolution.

Raub was not in a chatty mood, declining to answer some but not all of Campbell's questions, according to court documents. "I was angry about my rights being violated," he explained to me.

Campbell determined that Raub seemed "preoccupied and distracted," which is not surprising given what he had been through. That, paired with his belief in a coming revolution that he would lead, led the EMS staffer to conclude that Raub likely suffered from paranoia and delusion and was "responding to some internal stimulus."[7]

Raub, who had no criminal record, was not mentally ill. He had returned from a tour in Afghanistan about a year before the incident and, as his mother insisted in an interview conducted by Michael Campbell, did not have PTSD or any other mental-health issues.

Why, then, was it so urgent for law enforcement to take him into custody? No one had a ready answer. Campbell determined that Raub, given his "recent change in behavior," met the statutory criteria for involuntary temporary detention as provided for under Virginia Commonwealth law. Campbell then petitioned for, and received from a magistrate judge, an official detention order.

That night, Raub was transported to John Randolph Medical Center in nearby Hopewell, where he was held against his will and forced to undergo a more thorough psychological examination. The psychologist concurred with the bureaucrat Campbell: Raub exhibited "symptoms of psychosis." Hospital staff immediately petitioned a state court for an order of involuntary admission for treatment.

Days went by, and neither the FBI nor the Chesterfield County Police Department charged Raub with committing any crime. Still, he was not released.

Raub pleaded for his freedom. His postings were little different from those questioning the government's version of the 9/11 attacks, he noted, or the Federal Reserve. He believed the government is "corrupt and ready to fall," which may have explained his home business in silver coins.

Four days later, Raub finally got to see a judge—in this case, a special magistrate who came to the hospital to hold a detention hearing. Raub's lawyer argued that, although his postings mentioned the beginning of the revolution and his role in leading it, and despite some mild threats, "those words came mostly in conversations between friends on a private page, in the context of a game," he told the judge.

Raub's younger brother, Brent, and his mother, Cathleen Thomas, testified as character witnesses. "The only threat he is, is to the corruption that is
in this government," Brent said.[8]

But government officials argued that Raub's detention was based on "the
controversial nature" of lines from lyrics, messages, and virtual card games he
posted to his Facebook pages. Those statements, they said, were "terrorist in
nature."

And they dismissed Raub's claim that he had been taken out of context.
They scoffed at his attorney's allegations that First Amendment rights were being violated.

They won.

Instead of being released, arraigned, or offered bail, instead of being
charged with *anything,* the former sergeant was sentenced to thirty days' further confinement in a psychiatric ward—this time at a VA hospital in Salem
more than three hours across the state, away from his family, friends, and
legal team.

Raub's mother was dumbfounded. "He never was violent or psychotic or
anything like that," she told a Richmond news station. Her son, she said, explained himself well before the judge, arguing his case rationally. "The judge
also allowed me to give some facts and basically a character representation of
my son," she added.

That's when Raub secured the high-caliber counsel he needed to match his
deteriorating legal-medical hostage predicament. On August 20, 2012, the
Rutherford Institute leaped to the young man's defense.

Founded in 1982 by outspoken constitutional attorney and author John W.
Whitehead, the Charlottesville-based civil liberties nonprofit offers pro bono
legal services "to people whose constitutional and human rights have been
threatened or violated." A hero in conservative and libertarian circles, Whitehead gained renown as cocounsel in Paula Jones's sexual harassment suit against
President Bill Clinton.

Rutherford attorneys filed an emergency motion with a Hopewell District
Court special justice, trying to stop Raub from being forcibly transferred to
the veterans' psychiatric facility. The motion was denied, and Raub was dispatched to the psych ward at the VA hospital in Salem.

The ward, as Raub described it to me, sounded like something out of a
1950s horror film.

"They escorted me into this room filled with doctors, and there was this doctor who was going crazy. He was so angry at me," Raub told me. "He was pulling his hair with both hands and raising his voice, saying, 'We're going to force medicate you, we're going to brainwash you!'"

For government officials to not only detain Raub for exercising his First Amendment rights "but to actually force him to undergo psychological evaluations and detain him against his will goes against every constitutional principle this country was founded upon," Whitehead said in a statement.[9]

"This should be a wake-up call to Americans that the police state is here," he added. Raub was no different from most people who use private Facebook pages to "post a variety of content, ranging from song lyrics and political hyperbole to trash talking their neighbors, friends, and government leaders.

"This is not how justice in America is supposed to work," he continued, "with Americans being arrested for doing nothing more than exercising their First Amendment rights, forced to undergo psychological evaluations, detained against their will, and isolated from their family, friends, and attorneys."

Asked why Raub was placed in a psychiatric ward, an FBI spokeswoman told a Richmond news station that the bureau "typically doesn't make determinations such as that."[10]

Then who did?

"Because of complaints that our office had received about people coming across his posts and perceiving them as threatening . . . we went there . . . along with Chesterfield County Police Department," the FBI spokeswoman said. "When we left, we had not arrested him, we had not placed our hands on him, we did not detain him, and we did not charge him."

Secret Service spokesman Brian Leary admitted that his agency "assisted" the FBI with Raub's interview but insisted he was not arrested by the Secret Service. "The Secret Service will continue to monitor the situation," he said. "We have no further comment."

The Chesterfield Police Department said the situation "was an FBI matter and we were just there to assist them."[11] After speaking with Raub, however, the police officers believed he required "further evaluation." They contacted Chesterfield Mental Health Crisis Intervention, where Michael Campbell recommended Raub be taken into "emergency custody" to undergo psych testing, in accordance with Virginia code.

Today, in the home state of Jefferson, Henry, and Mason, an emergency detention order, or "green warrant," can be used to forcibly evaluate anyone considered a threat to himself or others. Whitehead estimated that some twenty thousand Virginia residents were being held against their will under the same law. He added that veterans around the country were contacting him because they had been subjected to the same type of psychiatric detention due to their political views they had posted on Facebook.

The officers who went to Raub's home had determined that that was the case with him—according to Raub, with no rational basis. They said he was handcuffed only after resisting attempts to take him into custody.

Reaction was predictable, swift, and damning from the Right. "This story, this is an outrage," Glenn Beck seethed on television.[12] "There were some things that stick out to me—as flares of caution. But the one thing we should be reckless with is our defense of people who have opinions that we don't agree with." Beck continued, "If we can't meet on the battlefield of ideas, as George Washington said, if we can't speak to each other openly, if we are paranoid and watching over our shoulder, we lose the essence of who we are and we will never be a great nation again."

John Whitehead went on Beck's show to claim that, while Raub was in detention, a psychiatrist threatened to "brainwash" him and force him to take medication. Beck asked if people of left-wing ideology, specifically members of Occupy Wall Street, which was raging at the time, were also being detained.

"I can't say for sure," Whitehead said, "because people all over the country are just disappearing."

Many on the Left, while generally dismissive of Raub's "Truther" views about 9/11 and theories on the Federal Reserve, agreed that what he endured was morally and constitutionally wrong. After all, if vaguely violent right-wing rhetoric posted on a private Facebook page can land someone in psychiatric detention, in a state that was run by right-wing Republicans no less, then what is to become of left-wing rhetoric?

"Despite the violent nature of some of his Facebook posts, Raub is well-spoken and articulate when writing for *Don't Tread on Me,* a blog with obvious conservative/libertarian leanings that appears to be more geared toward the preparation for socio/economic collapse and as advocates for change by the implementation of more conservative policies," wrote a blogger on the left-wing site *Daily Kos.*[13]

"To me, he seems a bit deluded, but didn't appear to be so deluded that he could present a danger to himself or others," the blogger wrote." With my Marxist tendencies, I have often said 'eat the rich,' and made allusions to revolution myself on Facebook. This is chilling, that anyone of us could be labeled a terrorist because we said something ill-conceived."

Raub remained locked up in the VA psych ward, without charges, against his will, but with his fighting spirit intact. "I really love America," he told a Richmond reporter, "and I think that idea that you can be detained and sent somewhere without due process and a lawyer is crazy."[14]

A full week after he was dragged from his home in handcuffs without a warrant, Raub's lawyers filed a motion in state district court to have him released from the hospital or, at the very least, have him returned to the municipal hospital in Chesterfield, where he was first held, "so that he may fully participate in his own defense." His detention, they added, was "procedurally improper, and legally unjustified," and done "based entirely upon statements that constitute protected free speech under the First Amendment."[15]

Without any lawfully obtained reports, they added, the court "lacked *any* basis (much less clear and convincing evidence) to conclude that Raub has a mental illness, and that there was a substantial likelihood that, as a result, Raub will, in the near future, cause serious harm to others."

The district court ruled for the government. Raub would remain confined to the psych ward.

The following day, Rutherford attorneys filed an appeal at the state circuit court. Judge Allan Sharrett surprised just about everyone and dismissed the government's petition for involuntary commitment, calling it "so devoid of any factual allegations that it could not be reasonably expected to give rise to a case or controversy."[16] Raub's immediate release was ordered.

"The doctor who said he was going to brainwash me told me he wasn't going to let me go. That he didn't care what the court said, he was going to ignore it," Raub said. Soon enough, however, he was free. A friend of John Whitehead's picked Raub up. Raub says a suspicious car followed them part of the way home. "We took an exotic route with twists and turns, trying to lose them," he said. When he got to his house, he learned that someone in an unmarked car had driven up to his brother and pointed a gun at him "multiple" times. It would not be the last attempt at intimidation.

So why did this happen to a young former sergeant in the Marine Corps? Raub thinks it has to do with his unorthodox beliefs and stated viewpoints on a number of issues, and in particular, his call for revolution, attacks on the Federal Reserve, and the 9/11 theory that the attacks were an inside job perpetrated by the Bush administration "to get us into a war with an oil-rich nation and usher in a fascist police state in the United States and launch multiple invasions in the Middle East."

Had his philosophy changed at all in recent years? He said no. And though his words are unorthodox, they are hardly uncommon in countless posts, blogs, and online comments.

As Raub sees it, the Russian Revolution and resulting Soviet Union was funded by an international banking cartel controlled by the Rothschild financial empire, which gave Lenin and Trotsky a bunch of gold, freed people in jail, turned them into a proxy army, and took over the Soviet government.

"The people were under complete tyranny, and now they are trying to bring it to the U.S.," Raub told me. "They want to silence people by throwing them in psych wards."

Raub believes the goal of the entire operation was more sinister than just getting him off Facebook. "It's unconstitutional, and it's messed up on multiple levels," he said. "Maybe they wanted to make me disappear. And it looked like that was what really was going on. It felt like they were being very evasive about what they were going to do with me and where they were going to move me. No one would look me in the eyes. They knew what was going on. Maybe," Raub added, quite casually, "they were attempting to kidnap me, or something nefarious, like using MK-Ultra."

I had never heard of MK-Ultra.

"It's a CIA torture technique designed to fracture someone's psyche and split their personalities, causing them to be different people who do certain things," he explained. "It's a form of brainwashing where you traumatize them and break them down."

MK-Ultra was real, though the CIA claims that it ended the grisly practice in 1965, after twelve years of experimentation on extreme psychological metamorphosis. Brutal mind-control tactics on the unsuspecting left them "emotionally crippled for life," as Ed Bradley, on CBS's *60 Minutes,* reported in 1983, when details of the program were declassified. More than 160 MK-Ultra operations were conducted at prisons, universities, and hospitals across the United States. The CIA, Bradley said, was "learning how to make people do things they would normally not do by controlling their minds."[17]

Raub, a history buff, said it all reminded him of the tyranny of Soviet Russia. "They used to take political dissidents and do to them similarly what they did to me," he explained. "You throw people in psych wards to discredit them or make them look crazy if they are exposing corruption or something like that."

As for the EMS pre-screener Michael Campbell, Raub chalked up his zeal for bringing him in for evaluation to "hypervigilance" and, although the court ultimately would not share his view, using psychology as a weapon against dissenters.

"Psychology used to be an illegitimate course of study until the army started dabbling in it and then mainstream America picked up on it," he told me. "Personally, I believe if you can control what a society can say by labeling certain ways of thinking or certain belief systems as a disorder, then you can control that entire society."

Raub was emotionally battered but ready to fight back. It was time for some justice. But he had no idea of the litigatory nightmare that was about to consume the next two years of his young life.

During those trying times, "I was followed extensively by cars, quite a few SUVs, and big white vans," he recalled. "Someone would drive by and glare menacingly. It was more of the same. My family was not cowed; we just kept doing everything that we were doing."

On May 22, 2013, Rutherford attorneys filed a civil rights lawsuit against Michael Campbell on Raub's behalf at the U.S. District Court for the Eastern District of Virginia.[18] The complaint alleged that Raub's illegal seizure and detention resulted from a federal government program code-named Operation Vigilant Eagle, which entails "the systematic surveillance of military veterans who express views critical of the government," the institute said in a statement.

It may sound like something out of a Clancy novel, but Operation Vigilant Eagle is a real, if rather secretive, undertaking. It was launched by the FBI in 2009 to target white supremacists and "militia/sovereign-citizen extremist groups," including a reported focus on veterans from Iraq and Afghanistan, according to memos sent from the FBI to field offices and obtained by *The Wall Street Journal*.[19]

The attempt to label Raub as "mentally ill" and his involuntary detention were mere pretexts "designed to silence Raub's speech critical of the government," the lawyers argued.

Campbell had violated Raub's Fourth Amendment right to freedom from unreasonable seizure, they alleged, by recommending he be apprehended and forced to undergo a psychological evaluation against his will. Likewise, his First Amendment right to free speech was trampled when Campbell concluded that Raub was "delusional," based solely on his Facebook posts and responses to Campbell's questions. And even if those claims fell, they argued, Raub was still entitled to "injunctive relief" to keep Campbell away from him.

Raub was seeking an undisclosed amount in damages "for the harm caused by the deprivation of his constitutional rights" and a permanent injunction against Campbell to ever seize, detain, or harass Raub again.

Government attorneys quickly moved to quash the suit. Their defense? Essentially, they didn't understand that their actions were unconstitutional.

"For any government official to suggest that they shouldn't be held accountable for violating a citizen's rights on the grounds that they were unaware of the Constitution's prohibitions makes a mockery of our so-called system of representative government," Whitehead said at the time.[20]

Raub's attorneys pleaded with the court to reject the government attempt to dismiss.

On August 2, 2013, Judge Henry Hudson handed a stunning victory to the former sergeant. He rejected the government's rather implausible argument and ruled that Raub's civil rights lawsuit could indeed move forward. Rutherford attorneys, he said, had offered sufficient facts to indicate that Raub's involuntary commitment violated the First and Fourth Amendments.[21]

The legal triumph was sweet but short-lived. Exactly seven months later, in February 2014, the same federal district judge found Raub's contention that the government was suppressing dissident speech to be "far-fetched" and summarily dismissed his case against the feds. The judge also agreed with defendant Campbell's claim of legal protection under "qualified immunity," which shields public officials from civil liability, provided they did not violate an individual's "clearly established" legal or constitutional rights.[22]

Three weeks after the dismissal, Raub's attorneys went to the Fourth Circuit U.S. Court of Appeals to seek relief. Oral argument in *Raub v. Campbell* was scheduled for January 28, 2015, in which Rutherford lawyers would ask the court to "reinstate the lawsuit of a decorated Marine who was seized by a swarm of Secret Service, FBI, and local police," the institute said.

The attorneys argued that Campbell had violated Raub's constitutional rights because "a reasonable mental health professional" would not have relied solely on a detective's report to recommend seizing Raub, but rather would have spoken to him first. And no "reasonable mental health professional" would have conducted an interview in a jail intake room while Raub was shirtless, shoeless, and handcuffed to a bench, nor would he conclude that a detainee be kept for mental evaluation based on Facebook posts and a jailhouse interview.

On April 29, 2015, the Fourth Circuit handed down its decision. It did not go well for Raub.

"In sum, we think it doubtful that Campbell violated Raub's Fourth Amendment rights," the three-judge panel ruled unanimously.[23] Besides, the question was moot because Campbell was, as the lower court had found, protected by qualified immunity. As for the First Amendment claim, "the district court concluded that Raub failed to advance facts sufficient to support [it] and we agree."

The claim for injunctive relief was likewise rejected. Raub had failed to prove any "real or immediate threat that [he] will be wronged again," by Campbell, the judges wrote. "Past wrongs do not in themselves amount to that real and immediate threat of injury." Raub's contention that he would be subject to future "unreasonable seizures and retaliation because of his political beliefs," they added for good measure, was merely "speculative."

It was a slam dunk for the government. There was only one more place to turn: the U.S. Supreme Court.

On November 17, 2015, the justices refused to hear the case. Game over.

"Rutherford Institute attorneys were seeking to overturn lower court rulings dismissing the case, which characterized concerns over government suppression of dissident speech as 'far-fetched,'" the group said in a statement. "In rejecting the appeal, the Supreme Court also refused to establish standards to guide and constrain mental health professionals when they seek to commit individuals and to prevent commitment on the basis of a person's exercise of his right to free speech."[24]

Raub was not surprised by the decision. "It could have been some hyperactive, un-American social worker, combined with other elements," he conjectured. "I think it went up very high in the intelligence community because I was talking about 9/11 and . . . they are not going to let that hit the Supreme Court and have the whole country look at what actually happened."

Was Raub really implying that the justices were unduly influenced by intelligence officials to refuse the case?

"Do you think it's not possible?" he answered.

What about his mental health status? Had Raub ever been evaluated by an independent professional? Had he been diagnosed with a psychological disorder?

"We hired a psychologist to evaluate me for the lawsuit," he told me. "She said I was completely normal."

What about continued state surveillance of his words and whereabouts? He said he wasn't worried. "I don't know, and I don't really care. I'm going about my life, I'm going to do what I'm going to do." As far as posting online was concerned, "there are a lot of programs you can use to not be spied on by commercial entities tracking and selling your info," Raub said.

And what about Raub's views on the United States in general? Have they changed since his ordeal?

"It doesn't make me see America any differently," he said. "I still love America. There's a lot of really good people in America."

The Raub story raises troubling questions about civil liberties and public safety in the wake of so many bloody mass shootings from Sandy Hook to Parkland and beyond. If people display signs of impending violence, what are the authorities to do? Ignore it and hope nothing happens?

The question in justice's other hand, however, is at what point do we allow bureaucratic mental health "experts" to determine if someone is in imminent danger of harming others or himself and then deprive him of his liberty without probable cause or due process? Remember, Raub never committed a single crime, and he made no direct or even indirect threats to anyone.

How many other Brandon Raubs are there?

More than most people realize.

It is not difficult to track down other cases of people being hauled in for questioning, harassed, or worse by local or federal agents after posting quasi-seditious comments on Facebook, Twitter, and other platforms.

In the relatively liberal Northeast, for example, adjunct professor Kevin Allred taught gender studies at the New Brunswick, New Jersey, campus of Rutgers University, including a wildly popular course called Feminist Perspectives: Politicizing Beyoncé. Just after Donald Trump won the election, Allred led a discussion among his students in a question about white people and the Second Amendment. Why were conservatives so enthralled with it, he asked, when more white people were being killed by guns? He also led discussions on the constitutionality of flag burning, which he feels is protected speech.

Then there were his postelection tweets—dozens of them:

> *Rutgers, did you send out an email addressing the fears of MANY RU students for their safety in Trump's amerika yet? did i miss it?*[25]

Others expressed support for flag burning and, in a postironic way, gun control.

> *Would conservatives care as much abt the 2nd amendment if guns killed more white people? a question meant to expose double standard.*

And there was this, more sinister post:

> *Will the Second Amendment be as cool when I buy a gun and start shooting at random white people or no . . . ?*

But, he quickly added:

> *that tweet was not a threat. it was a hyperbolic question posed to show a double standard—look at context/tone of most every tweet i make.*

One week after the election, NYPD officers arrived at his home in Greenpoint, Brooklyn, saying that police and other officials at Rutgers had requested they speak with him.

NYPD officers, without placing Allred under arrest or accusing him of any crime, insisted that he undergo a psychiatric exam. In theory, it was voluntary. But if he refused, they would "take you by force," the cops allegedly told the professor. With no way to resist, Allred was loaded into an ambulance and driven across the East River to Manhattan's Bellevue Hospital for "evaluation." Allred tweeted:

> *And this is for exercising my fucking first amendment rights. i'm being labeled a threat and put in a psych hospital.*

He spent two hours in custody before doctors agreed: He was neither crazy nor a danger to himself or anyone else.

"The doctors were like, 'This is ridiculous, why did they bring you here?'" Allred told *The New York Daily News*. "And I said, 'That's what I thought, but they told me they had to do it.'"[26]

NYPD said its officers had detained Allred because "we were informed by Rutgers PD that he made threats to kill white people" and he was taken to Bellevue for a "wellness check." Rutgers officials had no comment other than to confirm that it happened.

Allred returned to work, but now his Twitter account was no longer functioning. The tech giant had suspended him until he removed the post about guns that kill white people. He tweeted:

THAT IS WHAT THEY DEEMED A THREAT ENOUGH TO SEND POLICE FROM 2 DIFF STATES AFTER ME & FORCE ME INTO A PSYCH HOSPITAL, wow.

Soon after the incident, officials at Rutgers, a publicly funded school, told Allred that his contract would not be renewed. In the meantime, he was placed on leave and barred from teaching at the school.

Was Allred's termination justified? Rutgers seemed to think so. Was it constitutional? Not according to Robert L. Shibley, executive director of the Foundation for Individual Rights in Education (FIRE), a leading free-speech watchdog for college campuses.

"Given that the NYPD and the mental health authorities appear to have determined that this was hyperbolic speech and not a true threat, it's hard to see what justification Rutgers has for removing him from teaching," he told *Inside Higher Ed*. "While Rutgers is free to express its disagreement with Allred's speech, it cannot, as a public university bound by the First Amendment, punish him for controversial speech."[27]

John K. Wilson, an independent scholar and authority on academic freedom, told the magazine that the Allred case raised urgent concerns about civil liberties. The question, as in the cases discussed above, was not over the violent content of the rhetoric but its intent. Did Allred, who is white, really intend to go shoot white people? Of course not.

"The key issue for a threat is whether it is serious and directed—that is, whether it is an actual threat," Wilson said. "Hypothetical discussions about whether support for the Second Amendment has a racial component do not constitute an actual threat." After all, Allred's tweet was not the equivalent of tweeting "I'm going to start shooting at random white people," he added.

Stories like these, civil libertarians note, make people think twice before posting personal and especially political viewpoints anywhere on social media. Big Brother really is watching, and there is nothing quite like human fear to stifle speech. It's chilling, it's cumulative, and it works.

A HISTORY OF REPRESSION

Freedom of speech is more at risk today than many of our citizens realize. Barack Obama prosecuted more whistle-blowers than all his predecessors combined, while Donald Trump and other administration officials are threatening the free press through their rhetoric and their machinations of the law. And though it may be uncomfortable to discuss, our entire history is stained with acts of censorship. It's important to understand the root causes of these dark periods if we are going to defend our most basic, cherished freedom: deciding what to say, think, write, or otherwise to express ourselves.

Most Americans assume that the First Amendment occupies its preeminent position because of its importance, but the original Bill of Rights submitted to Congress by James Madison contained twelve amendments. The first two, pertaining to limiting the population size of congressional districts and the ability of lawmakers to increase their own pay, were not ratified, so the Third Amendment was adopted as the First:

Congress shall make no law respecting an establishment of religion, or prohibiting the free exercise thereof; or abridging the freedom of speech, or of the press; or the right of the people peaceably to assemble, and to petition the Government for a redress of grievances.

But power has a way of corrupting even the most honorable men. Leaders of the new government soon launched a federal assault against free speech and dissent. The censorious streak inherited from their British forerunners had not been extinguished. Throughout much of the nineteenth and twentieth centuries, successions of laws on sedition, anarchy, and criminal conspiracy were deployed to stifle the speech of abolitionists, religious minorities, feminists, labor organizers, pacifists, and left-wingers. Before the Civil War, all Southern states passed laws limiting criticism of slavery.

Then there was the infamous 1873 Comstock Act, which banned sending any "obscene, lewd, and/or lascivious" materials through the mail, including contraceptives or even information *about* them. It was named after anti-obscenity crusader Anthony Comstock of the New York Society for the Suppression of Vice, known for conducting postal inspections, far overstepping his powers in a form of quasi-legal vigilantism.

Fortunately, in recent decades, the Supreme Court has rejected the notion that speech can be punished just because it offends some people's sensibilities. At times, the court's defense of free speech has bordered on radical libertarianism. In the 1949 case *Terminiello v. Chicago,* for example, the justices overturned the conviction of an anti-Semitic priest charged with disorderly conduct after provoking a violent confrontation while denouncing Jews at a rally.

The court's majority, voiced by William O. Douglas, ruled that "the function of free speech under our system of government is to invite dispute. It may indeed best serve its high purpose when it invites a condition of unrest, creates dissatisfaction with conditions as they are, or even stirs people to anger."

Advocating violence in general is considered protected speech under the First Amendment, though that protection ceases when speech becomes "directed to inciting or producing imminent lawless action." By that measure, Sergeant Brandon Raub's Facebook postings, though perhaps unsettling and arguably violent at times, should clearly fall within the realm of protected speech.

Meanwhile, artistic expression is also under attack, "as some groups of citizens seek to impose their morality on the rest of society," warns the ACLU on its website. Book censorship in schools (*Huckleberry Finn* and *Catcher in the Rye* are still banned in some libraries), record labeling, and obscenity prosecutions of rap singers, record distributors, and museum directors "are just some of the recent manifestations of suppression efforts. Artists, performers and authors now occupy the same vulnerable position that political radicals did in the 1950s."[28]

All Americans need to remain vigilant of everyone's free-speech rights, regardless of the repugnance of what they have to say. "Whenever government gains the power to decide who can speak and what they can say, the First Amendment rights of all of us are in danger," the ACLU cautions. "But when people are allowed to express their views and ideas, democracy and liberty are enhanced."

ARRESTED FOR SWEARING

The First Amendment is not, and was never meant to be, pretty.

As Colorado civil rights attorney David Lane told *The Denver Post* in 2011, the amendment "lives in a rough neighborhood and if you can't stand the neighborhood move to China . . . or somewhere the First Amendment does not exist."[29]

In that freewheeling neighborhood, even the most foul, obnoxious, and offensive words and gestures imaginable are protected speech. With a few key exceptions, swearing in public is perfectly legal and protected by the Constitution (although employers can fire you for it and judges can throw you in jail for swearing in court). But that doesn't stop police from arresting people for dropping the F-bomb.

When is swearing not protected speech, apart from inside a courtroom? First, when "obscene" words are uttered on broadcast television or radio airwaves, which belong to the public and are heavily regulated. (Cable channels have no such restrictions and follow their own standards and practices, from PG-13 language on MTV to Larry David profanities on HBO.) Here, the government can prevent obscenity on the air and censor or even punish it when it occurs, even accidentally (think Janet Jackson at the Super Bowl).

Meanwhile, obscene words are not protected if uttered as part of a direct threat of harm or immediate breach of the peace (legally called "fighting words") or incitement to other criminal activity.

Other than that, the police have zero right to punish you for potty-mouthing under any circumstances. Saying, "Fuck you, you fucking asshole," to just about anyone you please, except for judges, is as legal as drinking beer on your back porch.

Or so you would think.

The First Amendment did not stop cops from arresting Danielle Wolf, twenty-two, who was shopping at a Kroger supermarket in North Augusta,

South Carolina, with her husband and kids in August 2014 after saying the word *fuck* in the bread aisle. A woman shopping in the store followed Wolf and her family as they selected groceries. When Wolf's husband tossed some frozen pizzas into the shopping cart, squashing some loaves of bread, she cursed at him.

The woman confronted Wolf and accused her of swearing at her kids. Wolf said she was speaking to her husband. Still, the other shopper whipped out her cell phone and called the police.

Wolf was arrested for disorderly conduct, which, under North Augusta law, includes to "utter, while in a state of anger, in the presence of another, any bawdy, lewd or obscene words or epithets."

She was transferred to a local jail, cited, and later released but ordered back to court in a few days.

Wolf and her family had just moved to conservative South Carolina three weeks previously from Ohio. She was shocked by her treatment in the Deep South. "I didn't harm nobody," she told a reporter. "The lady said she was having a bad day. So, because you're having a bad day, you're going to ruin somebody's life?"[30]

After the incident, the shopper who had called the cops called Wolf. She felt horrible, she said. She never meant for the young mother to be arrested. The shopper, who identified herself as "Michelle," explained that the cursing in front of children triggered memories of her own childhood abuse.

Wolf's case was hardly an outlier. In May 2014, nineteen-year-old Colin Andersen of Brighton, Michigan, was fined $200 for using "unsanctioned speech on public property"—in this case, a city park. After cops cited one teen for illegal skateboarding, they ordered Andersen and a group of friends to leave the park for no apparent reason. The teenager lost his cool.

"This is fucking bullshit," Andersen muttered, under his breath, to no one in particular.

A cop overheard him and arrested the teenager. He was charged with disorderly conduct and slapped with a $200 fine. Brighton police chief Tom Wightman told the local *Livingston County Daily Press & Argus* newspaper that Andersen's speech was classified as "misbehavior."[31]

Although no local statutes explicitly banned lewd speech in the town, Wightman insisted that offensive words would never be tolerated in "the immediate vicinity of a municipal playground occupied by very young children," the newspaper reported.

The teenager argued that no children were in the area at the time and, at any rate, he mumbled the foul language quietly and to no one in particular.

Civil libertarians objected that it didn't matter who heard the profanity or how loudly it was spoken. Free speech is free speech, they said. And public property is public property.

"Clearly this is a violation of our right to free speech," wrote James Weeks II, a Libertarian candidate for U.S. Congress at the time. He accused the Brighton Police Department of acting in violation of another case in which the Michigan Court of Appeals struck down an identical statewide anti-profanity law as unconstitutional.[32]

Any law that criminalizes speech on the grounds that someone else may find it offensive "has no basis in the First Amendment to the U.S. Constitution," said Weeks, who organized a free-speech demonstration on May 31, dubbed the "This Is Fucking Bullshit Rally."

Rana Elmir, deputy director of the American Civil Liberties Union of Michigan, also weighed in. "If we allowed police to ticket individuals for swearing, our jails and courts will be filled with people with filthy mouths."[33]

What about swearing directly *at* a police officer? They sometimes swear at us, so why can't we swear back at them? The truth is, we can—even though many officers, and some prosecutors and judges, think that foul language directed at cops is still, somehow, against the law.

The same question applies to gestures. Protected speech doesn't have to be spoken. Flipping the middle finger, for example, whether aimed at law enforcement or that jerk trying to cut you off on the highway, is perfectly legal. No officer—at least on paper—can arrest you for it.

Many of us have felt the urge to swear at or flip off a rogue or rude cop, but not that many have acted on it. We harbor a common gut instinct: primordial fear. Doing so will only enrage them. It might even land you in jail.

It's not supposed to be this way. The police are here to serve and protect us, and if their feelings get hurt or their egos inflamed by one middle finger, well, that's just too bad. Sometimes "serving" means taking public abuse. It's why the U.S. Supreme Court has ruled repeatedly that swearing at or flipping off a cop is protected speech.

In the 1987 U.S. Supreme Court decision in *City of Houston v. Hill*, for example, the justices wrote that the First Amendment protects most "verbal criticism and challenge directed at police officers." It added that "we have repeatedly invalidated laws that provide the police with unfettered discretion to arrest individuals for words or conduct that annoy or offend them."

An extended middle finger counts among "the most common insulting gestures in the United States," wrote American University legal scholar Ira Robbins in a seminal paper on the constitutionality of flipping off cops, *Digitus Impudicus: The Middle Finger and the Law*. The term *digitus impudicus* comes from the Latin (the Romans were prolific digital displayers) for "impudent finger."

"A number of recent cases demonstrate that those who use the middle finger in public run the risk of being stopped, arrested, prosecuted, fined, and even incarcerated," Robbins wrote. Even though most cases are eventually dismissed or overturned on appeal, the fact that people are still being arrested for flipping off the police "infringes on First Amendment rights, violates fundamental principles of criminal justice, wastes valuable judicial resources, and defies good sense."

As Robbins noted, cops typically cite disorderly conduct or "immediate breach-of-peace" laws to charge those who flip them off, and trial court judges often, though not always, convict the offenders. Such was the case with John Swartz, a New York resident who spent several exhausting, expensive years fighting police and prosecutors over a common, if offensive gesture.

It happened in Saint Johnsville in upstate New York, a quiet hamlet of about two thousand residents in the Mohawk Valley. One balmy May evening in 2006, Swartz, a sixty-two-year-old Vietnam vet and retired airline pilot, and his fiancée and now wife, Judy Mayton-Swartz, were on their way to see a family member. Judy was driving. When they reached a main intersection, John saw a village policeman, Officer Richard Insogna, sitting in his patrol car, wielding a handheld radar device. The radar detector on the Swartz's dashboard went off. It infuriated John that local cops were wasting their time on a speed trap instead of patrolling neighborhoods and solving crimes.

John reached his arm out the window and let the cop know how he felt by extending the middle finger of his right hand over the car roof.

The couple continued on their way. When they arrived at their destination, a car with lights flashing raced toward them. It was Insogna. John got out of the car, but the officer shouted at him to get back inside. John refused. Insogna then demanded Judy's license and registration, but John told her not to show the officer anything, insisting they had committed no wrongdoing.

"Shut your mouth!" the cop shouted. "Your ass is in enough trouble!"[34] Judy handed over the documents.

Within minutes, three more officers arrived. After fifteen minutes, Insogna gave Judy her documents back and told the couple they could go. John got out of the car and said to Insogna, "I'd like to speak to you, man to man." He approached the officer, who was more than twenty feet away. The next thing he knew, the backup cops blocked his path. John stopped, then turned and walked away.

"I feel like an ass," he mumbled to himself.

"*What* did you say?" one of the cops barked. John repeated his remark, this time loud enough to be heard. That's when Officer Kevin Collins rushed John and slapped him into handcuffs. He was hustled into a squad car and taken to the station, where he was given an appearance ticket and released. He was charged with disorderly conduct.

John hired a lawyer, who filed suit against the two officers for false arrest in federal district court in 2011. But the police moved for summary judgment, and they won. The court dismissed John's case, buying Insogna's explanation that the arrest was legal because "the odd and aggressive behavior" that Swartz displayed created a reasonable suspicion that he was "either engaged in or about to be engaged in criminal activity, such as violence against the driver of the vehicle." The two officers were granted qualified immunity. As public servants, they couldn't be sued.

It is baffling to think how flipping off a cop could conceivably equate to "threatening imminent violence" against one's spouse. But those were the judge's words.

The couple brought the case to the Second Circuit Court of Appeals, which, in early January 2013, nearly six years after their constitutional ordeal began, overturned the dismissal and said they could indeed sue the police. The fourteen-page opinion described "giving the finger" as "a gesture of insult known for centuries." And it rejected Insogna's testimony that Swartz had been "trying to get my attention for some reason" and that he "was concerned for the female driver."[35]

"This ancient gesture of insult is not the basis for a reasonable suspicion of a traffic violation or impending criminal activity," the judges wrote. "Surely no passenger planning some wrongful conduct toward another occupant of an automobile would call attention to himself by giving the finger to a police officer." On the night in question, John Swartz's conduct was a paradigm of orderliness, the court noted. The police had not witnessed any "disruptive conduct, any threatening conduct, any shouting, or anything that risked a public disturbance," the judges found.

It was a significant legal victory. But the Swartzes' case would not end there. John and Judy Swartz had spent hundreds of hours and thousands of dollars defending their right to express displeasure at an officer. But they felt the need to press on. Their case would now head back to the same federal district court for a jury to sort out the claims and counterclaims at trial. The jurors ruled entirely in favor of the two officers, Swartzes' attorney, Elmer Robert Keach III, told me.[36]

Looking back, John said he regretted his action that night. "I never did it before and I haven't done it since," he told *The New York Times*. "It's not something I'm proud of."[37]

Other people who fought back after being arrested for the same action were directly compensated for the abuse of their rights. On Easter Sunday in the spring of 2012, Amy Barnes, a civil rights activist in a largely African American community in Marietta, Georgia, was riding her bike down the street when she saw two Cobb County Police Department officers harassing a man outside a convenience store.

"It was yet another African American stopped for doing nothing other than being outside while black," Barnes told reporters.[38] It prompted her to lob profanities at the cops.

"Cobb police suck!" she cried. "Fuck the police!" For those six words, the police locked her up in solitary confinement—overnight.

What reason did they give for their behavior? "The officers argued that it was a bad neighborhood and you shouldn't disrespect the police because it could create issues," Cynthia Counts, Barnes's attorney, told *The Atlanta Journal-Constitution*. The police had kept Barnes in solitary "for her own protection," because she is hearing impaired.[39]

The next year, Barnes was acquitted at a criminal trial.

"The Defendant was not engaged in a face-to-face confrontation with the officers which tended to incite an immediate breach of the peace when the words were spoken," wrote Judge Melodie Clayton, who added some interesting observations: "In addition, the word 'su*k,' used as an epithet, is now common enough in modern society that it cannot reasonably provoke a threat of violence. The defendant's other statement, '(expletive) the police,' was a fleeting epithet that was insulting and inappropriate, but it did not create an immediate threat and danger of violence."[40]

Barnes, although acquitted, was understandably livid. She wanted, sought, and ultimately received justice. She filed a lawsuit against the police, who settled the case in 2014 for $100,000.

Barnes called her lawsuit "a shot across the bow." She told public radio station WABE that "it basically sent a message across this whole nation that free speech shall remain free or somebody's going to keep paying."[41]

Some have suggested that we should all consider swearing at or lifting our middle finger to a cop every now and again, just to remind them that we *do* have that right. But should you find yourself throwing verbal or "impudent digit" profanities at police, try to use your phone to record it, preferably on video, legal experts say. It will make it harder for them to charge you with uttering fighting words, disturbing the peace, or obstructing police work.

And consider this: The time, hassle, and expense of being arrested, posting bail, hiring a lawyer, and fighting your case in court may not be worth the extremely fleeting satisfaction of insulting an officer.

But in the final analysis, no citizen should be afraid of legally expressing her opinion to anyone, even if that person has a gun, a badge, and handcuffs.

"PRIOR RESTRAINT" AND THE GAGGING OF LIBRARIANS

When it comes to repressing speech, the government has two powerful tools at its disposal: censorship and something known as "prior restraint."

Censorship typically occurs *after* something has been produced, published, or broadcast that is deemed to be obscene, libelous, a fraudulent misrepresentation, or some other form of unprotected speech. With prior restraint, the government prevents certain types of speech *before* it can take place. Except for a few extraordinary situations—shouting "Fire!" in a movie theater, say, or issuing a direct threat to human safety or property, known legally as "fighting words"—prior restraint is considered extremely oppressive and, generally speaking, is unconstitutional.

With few exceptions, the government has no right to tell you, in advance, what you can—and cannot—say.

Consider the gag order. In some cases, it makes sense: Jurors, for example, are placed under prior restraint not to discuss the trial until it is over; national security officials are barred from revealing secrets (which is why it is, in fact, illegal to leak national security secrets). But what about librarians?

Yes, librarians.

In May 2005, George Christian was working at his generally placid job as executive director of the Library Connection, Inc.—a Windsor, Connecticut–based nonprofit that uses a common computer database to provide book tracking and other services among thirty libraries in the state—when his network operator ran down the hall and burst into his office.

"The FBI called," he told Christian, catching his breath. "They're going to serve us with a national security letter and want to know who should it be addressed to."[42]

Neither of them had any idea what a national security letter (NSL) was. Christian called the nonprofit's pro bono attorney to find out.

"She didn't know either," he told me. After doing some research, the lawyer called back. An NSL, she explained, is an "administrative subpoena" issued mostly by the FBI to tech companies, phone providers, credit reporting agencies, financial institutions, travel agencies, and others demanding they turn over certain usage data (though not usually actual content) concerning their customers' activities online or over the phone. The FBI's power to demand and seize the information without probable cause or judicial oversight was extended under the controversial anti-terror USA Patriot Act of 2001, following the attacks of 9/11.

The act gives the FBI authority to obtain "any tangible thing," including telephone, banking, educational, and medical records, databases, and, of course, computer histories and library records.

The attorney said not to worry about it too much. A federal district court in New York had already ruled that NSLs were unconstitutional because they violate the First (free speech), Fourth (unreasonable search and seizure), and Fifth (guarantee of due process) Amendments. The case was still under appeal, she cautioned, but Christian felt relieved. The thought of handing over personal data on thousands of library users across the state was both dreadful and draconian. There was no way he would ever consent to that, at least not without a court order. The very idea smacked of fascism.

A few weeks later, two FBI agents showed up at work and handed Christian an envelope.

"You are hereby directed to provide to the FBI any and all subscriber information, billing information, and access logs of any person or entity related to the following," the letter said. It then listed a Library Connection IP address and demanded information on everyone accessing the site on any library computers on February 15, 2005, between 4:00 p.m. and 4:45 p.m. eastern time.

It cited "international terrorism or clandestine intelligence activities" as the reason for the request and assured Library Connection that the action "is not conducted solely on the basis of activities protected by the First Amendment."[43]

But Christian was hardly assured. How could the government compel his organization to hand over highly personal and confidential information about the browsing habits of library patrons? This alone, he knew, was an assault on the First Amendment because of the chilling effect it would have on patrons using library computers for research or communication, if they were to find out about the government's snooping.

But according to federal law, the public would not, and could not, ever find out anything about the request.

"You are further advised," the letter said, "that [the Patriot Act] prohibits any officer, employee or agent of yours from disclosing to any person that the FBI has sought or obtained access to information or records released under these provisions."

Under Section 505 of the Patriot Act, it is a felony to discuss the matter with any other person, often for the rest of one's life, with penalties up to five years in prison if convicted.

The gag order was authorized by FBI director Robert Mueller III, who would later go on to investigate the Trump administration and Russian interference in the 2016 election, among other potential crimes.

"It's a federal criminal offense to discuss this matter with anyone," the agent warned Christian with a stern law-and-order grimace. "Do you understand?"

So, not only was Christian being ordered to violate the First, Fourth, and Fifth Amendment rights of library patrons, those same rights were being eviscerated for him and his top staff: Barbara Bailey, president of the Library Connection; Peter Chase, its vice president; and Jan Nocek, its secretary.

The four librarians were barred from communicating with each other by phone or email about the case, which they could not even discuss with their families. Christian was deeply shaken but defiant.

It was the first time the government had used the Patriot Act to seize personal user information from libraries. "We would be turning over tens of thousands of individuals with no idea that they even warranted suspicion by the FBI," Christian told me. "So when the estimate is that there are hundreds of thousands of national security letters, I have no problem assuming that that means there are millions of individuals being surveilled."

It turned out that someone had sent the FBI an anonymous tip on potential terrorist activity, via a library computer, according to Christian, and agents wanted to know who it was. How they would identify that person from the records was unclear, and, as Christian pointed out, "if it's the FBI policy to turn heaven and earth upside down in order to find out who's giving them anonymous tips, then how many anonymous tips do they expect to receive in the future?"

Christian was ready to fight, all the way to the Supreme Court, if needed. "If they lost, then they would lose all their powers to issue these national security letters," he said. "You can't really expect any law enforcement agency to have subpoena-like powers unless there's been a review by a judicial agency, who says yes, there's probable cause here."

But the FBI, he added, "can really do whatever it wants to issue its own subpoenas, and that's totally against the separation of powers in the Constitution."

Christian consulted with the three other librarians. They concurred: File a lawsuit, challenge the gag order, and refuse to hand over any data. "They came at it as librarians, and librarians have a long tradition of protecting patron privacy," he told me. "In fact, forty-eight of the fifty states have laws that compel librarians to go to extreme measures to protect patron privacy. So they all said no, not without something from the court saying yes, there's probable cause here. We want to resist."

Christian called the lawyer, who typically only handled the foundation's workaday legal matters pro bono and had no experience dealing with federal gag orders and domestic espionage.

"You have to sue Attorney General Gonzales," she told him. "And that's a bit beyond my mandate." The following day, she called back to say that the ACLU was looking for just such a case and wanted to take it on at its own expense. Christian agreed.

The days grew tense and frightening. The ACLU was worried that the librarians could be prosecuted for breaking the law simply by consulting with them. ACLU attorneys told the four to *never* send them emails and keep phone calls to a minimum. Communications were likely being intercepted (Christian reported strange beeping sounds on his cell phone at the time). If they needed to speak, they would have to travel to New York to do so in the private security of the ACLU office.

Despite the risks, the ACLU and the "Connecticut Four," as they would come to be known, filed suit in August 2005 for a preliminary injunction in federal district court against U.S. attorney general Alberto Gonzales and FBI director Mueller to lift the gag order.[44]

Doing so would permit the librarians to take part in the raging national debate over the Patriot Act, which was up for imminent reauthorization in Congress. Two sections of the act pertaining to NSLs and gag orders were set to expire on December 31, 2005, unless Congress voted to retain them. The librarians' free-speech clock was ticking.

"Plaintiffs did *not* seek to disclose any information about the subject of the NSL or any other specific details about the NSL's issuance," court records show. They argued for relief because the gag was preventing them from "disclosing firsthand information that is vital to the ongoing public and congressional debate about the Patriot Act."

Because of the nondisclosure provision, the suit was filed under seal, and the names of the plaintiffs and their organization were redacted. The four could not even attend any legal proceedings in their own case, due to "national security" concerns, the government insisted.

Meanwhile, the librarians were eager to testify at a scheduled congressional hearing about the dangers of reauthorizing the Patriot Act, but they were legally barred from doing so.

On September 9, 2005, the district court found in favor of the plaintiffs (known collectively as "John Doe"), and issued an injunction against the gag order. Without the right of free speech granted to the librarians, the court ruled, a critical component of the national Patriot Act debate would be muzzled, under penalty of imprisonment.[45]

"It is apparent to this court that the loss of Doe's ability to speak out now on the subject as an NSL recipient is a real and present loss of its First Amendment right to free speech that cannot be remedied," the judge ruled.

"Doe's speech would be made more powerful by its ability to put a 'face' on the service of the NSL, and Doe's political expression is restricted without that ability," she said. As a recipient of an NSL, their testimony would carry considerable weight.

The court further held that the Connecticut Four had demonstrated "a clear likelihood of success on the merits because the gag was an unconstitutional prior restraint."

But the court, anticipating an appeal by the government, issued a stay on the injunction until the appeal could be heard. The ACLU tried to block the stay but failed. Oral arguments on the appeal were tentatively scheduled for the week of October 31, too late for any Library Connection official to testify in Congress before its hearings on legislation to limit or expand the Patriot Act.

And then the story took an odd turn. The judge in the case ruled that all documents, including briefs filed by the four, would be posted on the court system's PACER site, which tracks the dockets of all federal cases. All identifying information was to be redacted, and there was little time to do so. In their haste, the government failed to draw a thick black line through Christian's written statement that he was the executive director of a "library consortia in Connecticut" and the statement from Peter Chase, the group's vice president, that he was chairman of the Intellectual Freedom Committee of the Connecticut Library Association.

That piqued the interest of a *New York Times* reporter, who pieced together the puzzle, spoke to some key people, and concluded that those in question were Christian and Chase. The story ran.[46]

"Our phones just rang off the hook, both at work and at home," Christian said. The ACLU said not to answer. "But that made it a real strain on my staff because we're there to really help the libraries out. And now I had to tell them no, you must always let it roll over into voice mail first." Meanwhile, at home, Christian said he had to tell his family, "'Look, a lot of people are going to be calling, wanting to talk to me, and none of us can talk to them. Don't answer.' It was hard on my staff, it was hard on my family."

After the article appeared, the PACER site scrubbed the offending identifications. But the government was still desperate to keep the operation under wraps. Despite being written about in *The New York Times,* the librarians remained under prior restraint: They could not discuss the case, they could not testify in Congress, and worst of all, they could not warn their own library users that their government had attempted to spy on them.

The ACLU, arguing that the proverbial cat was now out of the bag, moved once again to lift the gag order in time for the librarians to testify in Congress. But the Second Circuit Court of Appeals bought the government's rather flimsy argument that it had since removed the PACER references, and no one could have "confirmed" *The Times'* article's veracity via the website. Therefore, national security was not compromised. The librarians would remain gagged, pending appeal.[47]

The ACLU and the American Library Association (ALA) filed for an emergency vacate of the gag order at the U.S. Supreme Court. It was delivered to Justice Ruth Bader Ginsburg, who handles cases from the Second Circuit.[48]

Time was running out.

Now that Library Connection had been identified as John Doe, the petition said, "the prior restraint on speech is utterly useless as a national security measure." It was, however, "highly effective as an impermissible means to exclude a critical voice from the national debate about the Patriot Act."

As the only known recipients of a national security letter demanding library records, the Connecticut Four were "perhaps the most powerful messengers for educating the public and Congress about the dangers of the NSL power and its permanent gags operated by the government," it said.

On October 8, Ginsburg denied the librarians' petition. While sympathetic toward them, she felt the proper venue for deciding the case was back in the lower court. The gag order was upheld. There would be no Connecticut Four testimony in Congress.[49]

Five months later, Congress reauthorized the Patriot Act. We will never know what impact the librarians' testimony would have had on the vote, because their First Amendment rights were squashed.

The new legislation did carry some modest reforms, even though national security letters and their accompanying "nondisclosure provisions" would remain in the federal statute. But under the new law, a federal judge could repeal or modify an NSL if the request for information was deemed to be "unreasonable, oppressive, or otherwise unlawful." As for gag orders, federal courts could now repeal nondisclosure provisions that they found were made in bad faith, and recipients of an NSL could finally confer with their attorneys without fear of prosecution. Modest reforms indeed.[50]

A few weeks later, the federal government began taking measures to drop the Library Connection case, and a federal judge ordered the gag lifted. Many analysts believed the move was intended to head off a possible court challenge, and defeat, of the Section 505 nondisclosure provisions in the Patriot Act.

Despite this victory, NSLs still get handed to companies and other institutions every day in America. In fact, between 2001, when the Patriot Act was passed, and 2011, more than 300,000 NSLs were issued, including a record 56,507 in 2004 alone, according to the Electronic Frontier Foundation (EFF).[51] Hundreds were sent to libraries. The year before the act was passed, in 2000, just 8,500 NSLs were issued. Things got bad under George W. Bush and continued in the Obama years. In 2013, Obama's Intelligence Review Group said the government was issuing nearly 60 NSLs each day.[52] I could not find data on NSLs issued under the Trump administration at the time of this writing, but I did learn that NSLs were reportedly used to launch the DOJ investigation into Russian interference in the 2016 election and possible connections to the Trump campaign, including communications with former aides Carter Page and George Papadopoulos.[53]

If you don't think that NSLs could ever touch your daily life, you're probably wrong. Between 2016 and mid-2017, Microsoft, Facebook, Apple, Yahoo!, Adobe, Twitter, and Cloudflare all announced receipt of at least one security letter but had been forbidden to disclose them to anyone, including the customers who were being spied upon.

Happily, some of these corporations have pledged to respond to NSLs with a reciprocal notice challenge, seeking permission to disclose each federal request for personal-usage data. According to the 2017 edition of the EFF report *Who Has Your Back?,* those high-profile companies were Adobe, Airbnb, Apple, CREDO, Dropbox, Lyft, Pinterest, Slack, Sonic, Uber, Wickr, and WordPress.

But don't celebrate the protection of your privacy just yet. Fourteen other companies, all of them legendary tech giants with hundreds of millions of users, refused to take the pledge: Amazon, AT&T, Comcast, Facebook, Google, LinkedIn, Microsoft, Snap, T-Mobile, Tumblr, Twitter, Verizon, WhatsApp, and Yahoo!, according to the 2017 report.

Of course, the federal government has the right—and indeed, the duty—to surveil those people for whom they have probable cause, determined by a court, of planning harm to Americans. But concerned citizens everywhere should push Congress relentlessly to adopt further reforms to the Patriot Act that pile even more judicial review onto the NSL process and make it easier

for companies—and libraries—to warn their customers that the feds are looking at their usage data.

ARRESTED FOR ASKING QUESTIONS . . . AT A *LIBRARY*

When it comes to free speech and libraries, patrons sometimes find themselves
just as restrained as the librarians. On May 9, 2016, Jeremy Rothe-Kushel of
Lawrence, Kansas, who is a video documentarian and "self-identified Jewish
American patriot of conscience with a public background as a 9/11 researcher
and peaceful critic of U.S. and Israel covert policy," arrived at the Plaza Branch
of the Kansas City Public Library to attend a public lecture. The speaker was
Dennis Ross, former United States ambassador to Israel. Ross, who had been
active in Middle East diplomacy since the 1970s, was slated to discuss the attitudes toward Israel of every president from Truman to Obama. The library,
the Truman Library Institute, and the Jewish Community Foundation (JCF)
of Greater Kansas City cosponsored the event, which was titled "Truman and
Israel."

Rothe-Kushel had arrived and met up with a friend, Greg McCarron, whom
he knew from various events and exchanging political thoughts on Twitter.
Rothe-Kushel planned to record the event, for which they both had RSVP'd,
for his documentary archive. Arriving early, they sat near the entrance and chat-
ted for a while.

"That's when we saw a man in a suit, who we later found out was the JCF's
head of security [for the event], come outside and take a real careful look at
us," Rothe-Kushel told me.[54] The man would later testify that he took photographs of them.

When they finally entered the auditorium, an off-duty police officer hired
for the lecture said he needed to search them first.

"I asked whether I had to submit to the search in order to get into the
event," Rothe-Kushel recalled. "He said, 'There are private cosponsors here, and
they might be able to say that you can't come in.'" The guard was polite and
respectful.

No one else entering the room was being searched, noted Rothe-Kushel,
who offered a reason to the cop as to why he had been stopped. "I ask political
questions that some public figures find uncomfortable, and I document the

response for the public record." The officer said that was within the activist's rights. They submitted to the search, which revealed Rothe-Kushels notepads, a video camera, and other "items of First Amendment activity," as he described them to me.

They entered the auditorium to watch—and record—Ambassador Ross's talk. When Ross finished the lecture, library staff set up microphones for questions. Rothe-Kushel was first in line.

He lobbed a broad-brush yet challenging query at the former ambassador about "the issue of tribalism and terror." He brought up letter bombs allegedly sent to President Truman by the militant pro-Israel Stern Gang in 1947, and the 1946 King David Hotel bombing, carried out by the far-right Zionist underground militia, the Irgun, against Palestine's British administrative headquarters, which were housed in the hotel. The violence took ninety-one lives and injured forty-six. The bombers had dressed in Arab clothing, hoping to frame Palestinians for the attack, an event known as "false flag" terrorism.

"Jews were amongst the dead involved in that *necessary statecraft*," he said. "So you see, this long history of not only the United States but Israel utilizing terrorism that includes potentially the death of its own tribe to advance its own geopolitical cause all the way up into the twenty-first century, including September 11.

"So, at what point does the Jewish diaspora . . . have to have the ethical courage—I'm a Jewish American—to point out that . . . both the countries that operate in our name have used terrorism way too long, including against its own citizens, to protect power at home.

"When are we going to stand up and be ethical Jews and Americans?" he asked.[55]

On Rothe-Kushel's video of the event, Ross is seen shuffling as he demurred, with a look of disdain etched on his face. "Well, look, I don't think that as a matter of policy, that the United States or Israel engage in acts of terror. Terror is you target deliberately civilians for an expressed political purpose. The idea that Israel had something to do with 9/11 is just outrageous—they had nothing to do with it," he replied, to loud applause.

But Rothe-Kushel wasn't finished. He tried to press his point further, but his mic was suddenly cut off—just as the security chief hired by the JCF grabbed him with force from behind and pushed him toward an off-duty cop, also part of security that night, standing nearby. The off-duty detective, it turns out, was the police department's intelligence liaison with the Kansas City Regional Terrorism Early Warning Interagency Analysis Center, one of the dozens of Homeland Security Fusion Centers nationwide.[56]

Ross did not seem to object to the censorship. "This former US ambassador, minutes after he spoke about one country in the Middle East that respected freedom of speech, press, and assembly, was standing there smirking at his Jewish American interlocutor getting jacked up at a public event in an American library," Rothe-Kushel told me.

Rothe-Kushel pulled away and said, "Do not touch me! Get your hands off me right now! You can ask me to leave. I will leave if asked." The confrontation drew the assistance of Steve Woolfolk, the library's director of public programming, who helped organize the event. Woolfolk stepped in and de-escalated the situation. Once everyone took their hands off Rothe-Kushel, they all began walking out. McCarron, who was still recording, was told to leave. Woolfolk showed them out the back to the lobby while the entire security detail followed. Just outside the lobby, Rothe-Kushel was stopped by another off-duty officer and then handcuffed with no warning and no explanation why he was under arrest. Woolfolk turned to go find his supervisor, deputy director of public affairs Carrie Coogan, when he was grabbed from behind and shoved into a pillar by the cop affiliated with the anti terror fusion center, he told me.

Another cop showed up and kneed Woolfolk in the leg. He sustained damage to a ligament on the inside of his knee. As the officer handcuffed him, several people came by to ask what was happening.

"We don't know," one cop reportedly replied. "We can't say," mumbled another. "The word *arrest* was never used until I was in the paddy wagon," Woolfolk later told reporters. The library's Coogan followed both men to the jailhouse, where she, along with library director R. Crosby Kemper III, managed to secure their release.

Woolfolk was charged with interfering with an arrest and Rothe-Kushel with trespassing and resisting arrest. Nearly a full year after his arrest, prosecutors had heaped two more charges on Woolfolk: obstruction and assault, because Woolfolk allegedly pushed a detective.

After the incident, Woolfolk told the journal *American Libraries* that "we agreed to the additional [outside] security on two conditions." First, guards were told not to remove anyone just for asking an unpopular question. Second, unless library staff concluded there was an imminent threat of danger, security would not take any action without consulting with the staff. The library protested that the arrests were a violation of the First Amendment.[57]

On August 10, 2016, Rothe-Kushel's lawyer said the city prosecutor had offered Woolfolk and him a plea deal: thirty hours of community service and no jail time if they agreed not to file any civil lawsuits over their arrests.

Both Rothe-Kushel and Woolfolk rejected the deal and demanded to go to trial. Kansas City prosecutor Lowell Gard said his office was prepared for the legal challenge. "If the police say, 'We're going to handcuff you,' you need to not fight," Gard told *The Star*. "We don't want to encourage anyone to resist arrest."

A few weeks before Woolfolk's trial was due to start, prosecutors dropped all charges against Rothe-Kushel. One year later, on September 8, 2017, Kansas City municipal judge Joseph H. Locascio acquitted Woolfolk on all three counts against him.

In April 2017, the American Public Library Association awarded the Kansas City Public Library the Paul Howard Award for Courage, given for "unusual courage for the benefit of library programs or services." Woolfolk, meanwhile, was bestowed with the wonderfully titled Lemony Snicket Prize for Noble Librarians Faced with Adversity.

R. Crosby Kemper III, the city library system's executive director, told *The Kansas City Star* at the time that the arrests didn't "pass any kind of smell test. . . . It's absurd and it's Dickensian and it's outrageous. They're playing games with the law. It's disgraceful. We're going to be living in a different kind of country" if people can be arrested for asking questions in a library, he warned. "If this kind of behavior is unacceptable to the police, then I guess we're going to have to shut the library down."[58]

Rothe-Kushel, meanwhile, was eager to fight back against having been ejected from a public library simply for asking a question during a Q&A session. In April 2018, he filed a lawsuit at the U.S. District Court for the Western District of Missouri against the Kansas City police chief, Rick Smith, five members of the Kansas City Board of Police Commissioners, two city police detectives and a sergeant, as well as the Jewish Community Foundation of Greater Kansas City, two of its employees, its (by then) former security director, and one staffer at the Truman Library Institute. The various defendants faced a total of eight counts, including violation of First Amendment rights, wrongful arrest, battery, conspiracy to violate civil rights, and inadequate training and supervision of police officers.[59]

The Kansas City Public Library, despite "deep concerns" of some library staff, "had supplied the RSVP names to their cosponsors, who we now know had documented intent, in the case of the Jewish Community Foundation, to share the names beforehand with security," Rothe-Kushel told me.

The cosponsors knew that Rothe-Kushel was coming to the event. The sergeant that searched him testified that the head of security had "intelligence" to that effect. But how did they recognize him when he arrived? Aside from Rothe-Kushel and McCarron, only one other attendee was searched when entering the auditorium, he said.

"Either they Googled hundreds of attendees and had my photo on hand," he said, "or more likely, they flagged names and photos via a database."

"A key piece of our discovery inquiry," Rothe-Kushel continued, "is to follow up and clarify whether facial recognition mobile technology was used in conjunction with RSVP information and security databases of unknown origins to set up an 'invisible checkpoint' based on political viewpoint and activity in an American library," he said. "There are factual indicators both on and off the record that head in this direction."

If biometrics and facial recognition are being used in public spaces to identify those with a certain political viewpoint, "that is a blatant constitutional violation, in that it likely creates unequal, politically determined access to public space and resources," Rothe-Kushel told me. "If they were using it to target viewpoint, which it looks like they probably would have been . . . then it brings up the question of invisible checkpoints for core political speech or press."

The defendants moved to dismiss Rothe-Kushel's suit, but as of this writing, the judge had not yet ruled.

STIFLING RELIGIOUS EXPRESSION

Congress shall make no law respecting an establishment of religion, or prohibiting the free exercise thereof. Those first sixteen words of the Bill of Rights, the Establishment Clause, were meant to construct an impervious barrier between church and state.

But that wall is springing leaks, and it seems to be getting worse.

More and more government officials are increasingly trying to impose a "Christian-Judeo" order on society (the "establishment" of a religion), while simultaneously constraining certain forms of religious expression (the "free exercise thereof"), particularly if that religion happens to be Islam.

The debate over religious freedom in this country is as heated as it is complex. What type of expression of faith should be tolerated, and what should be banned? Many conservatives, and libertarians, too, believe the government has no right to tell small business owners that they must provide goods and services to all members of the public—including same-sex couples—and that they can pick and choose their customers based on their own religious beliefs.

Where do we draw the line in this expression of religious freedom? Should Muslim merchants be allowed to refuse to sell to Jews? Can a Pentecostal doctor deny services to a known adulterer? Should Hindus be able to legally discriminate against carnivores? Of course not, because their rights of religious expression end at the doorstep of trampling the rights of anyone else.

But that hasn't stopped conservative Republicans—and Donald Trump—from touting what is known as the First Amendment Defense Act (FADA), which would put this blatant discrimination into federal statute. It would even cover corporations and nonprofits. Imagine disasters like Hurricanes Harvey, Irma, and Maria, where companies and religious relief organizations, even those who receive taxpayer funds, could legally turn away same-sex couples and their families because their marriages offended someone's religious beliefs. FADA and the idea behind it will cause real harm to real Americans. And that is simply unconstitutional.

But what about acts of religious faith that harm absolutely no one at all?

Take, for example, the right of a Muslim woman to wear a headscarf known as a hijab, a right that is routinely violated in modern America.

In July 2014, twenty-seven-year-old Malak Kazan was stopped by police in Dearborn Heights, Michigan, for a minor traffic violation. Her license was expired, and she was arrested and taken in for booking. While at the station, Kazan was ordered to remove her hijab for her arrest photo.[60]

"I can't do that," she replied. "It's a violation of my faith."

The officer told her it was standard police procedure and there were no exceptions. All head coverings were banned to prevent detainees from concealing weapons or other harmful items.

Kazan appealed to a supervisor, with no success. Her request for a female officer to photograph her was denied. The police threatened to extend her detention time if she did not remove the scarf and keep it off during her entire stay in jail. Humiliated, she complied.

The following January, Kazan filed suit in federal court against the city, the police department, and its chief, alleging violations of her First, Fourth, and Fourteenth Amendment (equal protection) rights.[61] She sought compensatory and punitive damages, as well as a permanent change in police policy to allow headscarves worn for religious purposes, and sensitivity training of officers.

"The prohibition on Ms. Kazan's use of a religious headcovering . . . violated her right to the free exercise of her religion, violated her rights under federal law, and caused her extreme mental and emotional distress," the complaint alleged.

"Your religious freedoms are not stripped at the jailhouse door," Kazan's attorney, Amir Makled, told the local Fox News affiliate. "It's part of the canons of the Muslim faith for a woman to wear a headscarf. For her to have it removed in front of a nonrelative male would be a very unpleasant situation for her."[62]

"I honestly don't want other women to be put in my position, where they are forced to take off their scarf in front of men they don't know," Kazan said in an interview with *The Arab American News.* "I've worn my scarf for twelve years, and my religion says that I can't take it off. It's not just a religious issue; this is a part of me."[63]

Most Americans have no idea how important it is for devout Muslim women to cover their head, neck, and shoulders when in public or even at home with men who are not immediate relatives. Being without it, to them, is like walking around naked. Kazan's lawsuit spelled the violation out.

"Ms. Kazan has studied religious texts, thought deeply, and prayed about her practice of covering her head and hair," her lawsuit noted. "Wearing a headscarf is a reminder of her faith, the importance of modesty in her religion, and her religious obligations, as well as a symbol of her own control over who may see the more intimate parts of her body." Removing the garment was a "serious breach of faith and religious practice, and a deeply humiliating, violating, and defiling experience."

Dearborn Heights city attorneys vowed to fight the claims at trial, calling Kazan a "scofflaw and an individual who habitually drives on a suspended license," in their legal response. The city didn't always have a female officer on hand (there were only three women on the force), the city said, adding that women "may be hiding contraband in the hijab, such as a razor blade, or an illegal substance."[64]

By July 2015, under increasing pressure in a city where 22 percent of the people are of Arab descent—most of them Muslims—Dearborn Heights was ready to settle. The city agreed to change its booking procedures to allow Muslim women to keep their headscarves during photos and to be searched only by female officers without men present.[65] The legal victory came as Muslim women across the state of Michigan stepped up the fight to wear hijabs while in custody, and just days after another Muslim woman, Maha Aldhalimi, sued the City of Dearborn for being ordered to remove her headscarf during booking. The lawsuit was later dropped.[66]

The idea of barring someone from expressing ones religious beliefs—as long as one doesn't break the law—is as much anathema to American sensibilities as it is to the First Amendment. Still, the debate over whether that protection extends to private businesses that serve the public is still playing out.

In 2014, the Supreme Court ruled that Hobby Lobby is not required to offer birth control as part of employee health care plans because it violates the owners' religious beliefs.[67] In October 2017, President Trump signed an executive order exempting companies from offering birth control in their health plans, if the practice violated their religious or *moral* beliefs (emphasis mine, because "moral beliefs" are mentioned nowhere in the Constitution).[68] And in June 2018, the court ruled on the case of a Colorado bakery owner who refused to make a wedding cake for a same-sex couple and was charged with violating the state's antibias laws.[69]

In a 7–2 decision in favor of the owner, Jack Phillips, the justices found that the Colorado Commission had exhibited "hostility" against his religious beliefs by comparing them to those that were used to justify slavery or the Holocaust. The commission ruling was overturned. But the decision has little to no impact going forward as to whether public accommodations can discriminate against members of the public simply because of their faith. That monumental decision will be left for another day.

Regardless of the outcome or its impact, discrimination—even when motivated by religion—is still discrimination, many civil libertarians believe. It should not be protected speech.

In its wisdom and eloquence, the Establishment Clause of the First Amendment protects us from state-sponsored religious tyranny in two ways: "Congress shall make no law respecting an establishment of religion," meaning the government cannot impose any faith on its citizens, "or prohibiting the free exercise thereof," meaning it cannot restrain that faith and the right to practice it (such as by wearing a hijab in jail).

Coercing someone to worship an entity in which he does not believe is no less detestable, and no less unconstitutional, than barring someone from worshipping any god he pleases.

But it happens.

Barry Hazle Jr., a computer network administrator from Shasta County, in Northern California, spent a year at the state rehabilitation center in Norco from 2006 to 2007. He had pleaded guilty in 2004 to possession of methamphetamine and was sentenced to probation, which was revoked when he continued to use the drug and was sent to prison. In exchange for release from Norco, Hazle's parole officer ordered him to complete a ninety-day residential drug treatment program in Shasta County at the Empire Recovery Center in Redding, California, where he would attend daily classes and meetings. Most important, he had to obey all rules established by Empire staff.[70]

After settling in, Hazle learned that the rehab center used a twelve-step recovery program based on that created by Alcoholics Anonymous, a treatment protocol deeply rooted in faith, with distinctly religious components. Among them: One must acknowledge the existence of a God and take part in prayer.

But Hazle is a lifelong atheist.

Hazle had specifically requested of Empire officials and his parole officer not to be sent to a recovery center that included religion in its program.

Empire staff assured him they weren't "picky" about which higher power he chose to acknowledge. "They told me, 'Anything can be your higher power. Fake it till you make it,'" he later told *The San Francisco Chronicle*.[71] It did nothing to change his mind.

The request for transfer was denied. "All of the programs in Northern California are twelve-step programs," Hazle's parole officer informed him.

Hazle filed a formal petition of appeal against his coerced participation in a religious program, citing legal authorities who confirmed that his parole conditions were in blatant violation of the First Amendment. Three days later, while studying in class, Hazle's parole officer showed up and cuffed and arrested him.

What was his crime? Violating the terms of his parole by refusing to participate in residential treatment. Hazle was transferred to the Shasta County Jail, then to the High Desert State Prison, and ultimately back to the same prison in Norco, which, according to Hazel's lawsuit, California's governor had labeled overcrowded and "very dangerous for . . . the inmates."

He spent a total of 125 days in custody for not believing in God.

In September 2008, Hazle filed a civil rights lawsuit in U.S. district court against his parole officer, the California Department of Corrections and Rehabilitation (CDCR), and WestCare California, a Fresno-based organization that coordinates parolee rehab placements. He sought punitive damages for the violation of his rights under the Establishment Clause, and for suffering "an extended period of deprivation of liberty, the indignity of incarceration, and financial loss, stress, humiliation and emotional distress." His lawsuit also asked for a court injunction "prohibiting the illegal expenditure of state money to fund unconstitutional parole practices."

Just six weeks later, the CDCR issued a directive stating that parole agents could no longer force parolees into rehab programs with religious components and must offer a secular alternative for those who object. The department cited a federal court case in Hawaii that found in favor of a parolee who had been ordered to attend Alcoholics Anonymous against his will.

Hazle's lawsuit, however, dragged on.

In 2010, U.S. district court judge Garland E. Burrell Jr. found in favor of Hazle. Forcing him to undergo treatment at Empire ran "afoul of the prohibition against the state's favoring religion in general over nonreligion," Burrell ruled. Hazle's subsequent "loss of freedom" violated his First Amendment right against government imposing religious beliefs upon him.[72]

With that civil liability decided, it was now time to determine the amount of damages to be awarded. How much are 125 days of false imprisonment in a dangerous and overcrowded penitentiary, and the trampling of one's rights, worth in dollars?

The case went to trial. The jury awarded Hazle nothing.[73]

But that was not the end of it. In August 2013, the Ninth U.S. Circuit Court of Appeals threw out the jury's unreasonable verdict. The three-judge panel ruled that Hazle must be compensated for the violation of his First Amendment protection against enforced religion. They sent the case back to Burrell for another trial, this time telling the judge to instruct the jury that Hazle was, in fact, entitled to damages.

The court further found "a genuine issue of material fact" that WestCare abetted the violation of Hazle's rights by contracting with facilities that rely solely on religious-based programs and sending Hazle to one, despite knowing he was an atheist who strongly objected to the treatment.

Even though he had still not been compensated, Hazle's victory was significant. It was now precedent-setting case law in the Ninth Circuit, made up of nine western states and two Pacific island territories.

Hazle's attorney, John Heller, said the victory would send a clear signal to the authorities that all parolees have the right not to have any form of religion foisted upon them. "It informs [them] what they can expect if that right is violated," he told *The Sacramento Bee*. That might keep things like this from happening in the future."[74]

The following year, six years after his ordeal had begun, the defendants agreed to settle. The Department of Corrections agreed to pay Hazle $1 million, and WestCare disbursed $925,000.

At the time, Hazle told reporters that he was drug-free and intended to become active in drug rehabilitation efforts around Redding. Meanwhile, he would work his family's ten-acre farm and, one day, build a home up in the mountains, where nobody can make you pray if you don't want to. He certainly has the funds to do so.

NO FREE SPEECH IN COURT?

Among the few venues where normally protected speech by ordinary civilians can legally, constitutionally be restrained by the state—apart from schools, prisons, and the military—is the courtroom. Judges have enormous discretion in prohibiting foul or abusive language, or vulgar disrespect for their positions of high honor. Many people have been fined, or even sent to jail, on criminal contempt of court charges—which judges can impose on the spot, without a jury or any other proceedings—for what they alone deem to be inappropriate speech or behavior.

There is nothing wrong with demanding decorum in a court of law. The rules are set by the judge, and breaking them can land you in jail for criminal contempt. But even though judges have the legal power to enforce prior restraint on certain types of speech, they sometimes overstep their constitutional authority and convict innocent people of contempt—perhaps out of pique, or worse, an ignorance of the law itself. Either way, it's an abuse of power.

It happened to Karen Hudson, a corn and soybean farmer and grandmother of five in the western Illinois hamlet of Elmwood, outside Peoria, where she is a leading national activist against the hazards of animal factory farms, officially known as concentrated animal feeding operations, or CAFOs. Hudson was one of three figures that I profiled in my 2010 book, *Animal Factory,* about industrial-scale animal production and its indisputably detrimental impact on human health and the environment.

As a founding member of Illinois Citizens for Clean Air & Water (ICCAW) and regional representative for the national nonprofit Socially Responsible Agricultural Project (SRAP), Karen helps property owners try to stop CAFOs from coming to their area, and to protect themselves from the putrid, toxic stench of rotting animal feces and urine and the contamination of local surface and groundwater from existing facilities.

In 2004, Karen learned about ten people in Scott County, about two hours from Elmwood, who had filed a nuisance suit against a local hog CAFO, with its fifteen thousand cramped animals drawing flies and emitting clouds of methane, ammonia, sulfur dioxide, and other harmful gases. Oral arguments were scheduled for the morning of April 1 at the Scott County Courthouse in Winchester, Illinois.

Karen and Susan Turner, also a member of ICCAW, showed up to witness the trial. They arrived early, along with Karen's husband, Rocky, and another friend, Judy Koehler, a former state legislator and judge who owned property in an area where she was planning to retire and where a CAFO had been built.

Karen routinely travels with books and pamphlets about factory farms, "just in case I run into someone who is interested in reading about it,"[75] she told me. On that particular day in her car trunk, there was a box of ten or so paperback copies of *The CAFO Reader,* a collection of thirty essays that catalog the worst aspects of factory farming. Karen thought, why not bring them inside? Rocky carried the box up to the third-floor courtroom.

Well before court was called into session, Karen spoke briefly with one of the plaintiffs' attorneys, Charles Speer. She asked him if it was appropriate to wear her anti-CAFO button in the courtroom. He said it was better to take it off. Karen removed the pin and asked a few other spectators wearing similar buttons and stickers to do the same. They agreed.

Karen visited with one of her grassroots contacts in the hallway before court began and handed him a promised copy of the book as Rocky entered the gallery and stowed the rest beneath the bench in front of him. Karen spotted an acquaintance and asked her if she would like a copy. The woman said yes, and Karen handed her one.

Court was called to order by Illinois circuit judge David Cherry. Prominent anti-CAFO attorney Richard Middleton went first, on behalf of the plaintiffs. Judging by his body language and dismissive questioning of Middleton, Karen believed that Cherry, a local, elected circuit court judge, was sympathetic to the animal agriculture industry. "He had a chip on his shoulder against anti-CAFO activists," she told me. "It was obvious."

When Middleton finished, the court recessed for lunch. As Karen filed out, she asked a spectator she did not know if she would like a copy of *The CAFO Reader,* and the woman said yes. Karen handed her one.

After the lunch break, Judge Cherry returned to the bench with an announcement. A lawyer for the CAFO operator had reported that a "lady known to plaintiffs' counsel" had arrived with a box of books. During lunch, "someone" had told the lawyer they had observed her handing out copies in the courtroom. The books were "prejudicial to the defendant," the lawyer had alleged in the judge's chambers, adding that he was concerned they would make it into the hands of jurors.

Judge Cherry said he recalled seeing a woman with a box but did not observe her distributing any material. He said he would investigate the matter right there in the courtroom and question the jury—which was sequestered in the deliberation room—to see if they had been influenced.

Cherry ordered everyone in the courtroom not to leave, due to a "security

breach." He asked those in the gallery if they had any information about someone with a box of books who was passing them out to members of the audience. Eleven people raised their hands.

The judge demanded to know who had received the books. Two women
said that they had. Eventually, Karen and Susan were identified as the culprits.
Cherry ordered them to approach the bench.

"Did you bring those books into the courtroom?" he asked Karen. She said
she had, and distributed one before court was in session and one during re-
cess.[76]

The judge neither hesitated nor held back in his retaliation. "You are here
to influence a jury," he scolded Karen. "That is jury tampering. That is a felony!"

He found Karen guilty of direct criminal contempt, right there on the spot,
without any further consideration of the facts.

The judge then asked Susan if she had handed out any books. She admitted to distributing a few small pamphlets, but no books, to some people.

"This is not the proper venue for you to get on a soapbox," he growled, also
finding Turner in direct criminal contempt. He said the two women would be
taken into custody and charged with jury tampering. They would remain in
jail until bond was set.

"This taints everything we stand for. And this deserves, this deserves prison,"
he said.

Turner apologized to the judge. "Apologies don't make it," Cherry replied.
"When you come in and ruin almost three, four years of work that these attorneys have worked for, in an attempt to forward your personal agenda, you
are using the wrong forum." He ordered that the women be handcuffed and
taken away.

Karen began sobbing and shaking. She was having a panic attack and, as
the cuffs were slapped on her wrists, thought she would surely pass out. Rocky
looked on in disbelief as his shaking and shackled wife was removed from the
courtroom.

"I was shocked that I was being arrested for something that I did not think
was wrong," Karen told me, fighting back tears as she recalled that day. "I was
trying to hold it in, but I couldn't. I just couldn't believe this was happening.
The judge wouldn't let us talk. We weren't allowed to say anything. And I still

didn't know what I had done wrong. I was in his crosshairs," she felt, as a CAFO opponent "and he took me down."

And, Karen added, her friend, the former state senator and appellate court judge Judy Koehler, was seated next to her in court the entire time. "If I was doing something wrong, she would have told me," she said. "If anyone had told me not to do it, I never would have."

Karen and Susan were led across the street to the Scott County Sheriff's Department headquarters, where they were fingerprinted and had their mug shots taken. Karen had never been in trouble with the law before. She was terrified.

What happened next in the courtroom is rather odd. Attorneys for both sides disavowed any knowledge that anyone intended to distribute any material. The judge also said he did not see anyone distributing books, although he again noted witnessing one of the women carrying a sealed box.

Likewise, the bailiff did not observe anyone passing out books or anything else.

The judge called the jury back into the courtroom to question them. One juror said he had seen a woman passing out a book in the gallery but did not see its title or have any contact with it.

Cherry then addressed the entire jury. "You are a target now, you know," he said. "For you to be improperly influenced by some outside source is hard enough to put up with all these lawyers, but to be influenced or [for] somebody outside of this to try to influence you is criminal and, in fact, it is a crime in Illinois to try to tamper with the jury."

He then declared a mistrial. The CAFO would be spared litigation, at least for now.

An hour later, the women were told that Judge Cherry wanted to talk to them. They were handcuffed once again, paraded across the street, and led back up to the third-floor courtroom.

Judy Koehler, who is also a lawyer, stood next to them in front of Judge Cherry in the courtroom. But because she was not formal counsel in the case, Cherry never called on Koehler to present evidence, argue, or make a recommendation.

The judge informed the women that they were in direct criminal contempt for performing an act "in front of the court" and "in derogation of admonishments given to the jurors, potential jurors, the jury pool, and the gallery not to talk about this case." He fined each of them $500 and said they would remain in custody until it was paid. There was no opportunity for them to present evidence or provide statements. Other than verifying their identities, the only question he asked was whether Karen was a "Ms." or "Mrs."

Karen and Susan were taken back across the street to the sheriff's office. There was no jail in town, they learned. If the fine was not paid immediately, they would spend the night in the Jacksonville Correctional Center, a state prison.

Rocky did not have $1,000 to pay both women's fines. He dipped into his pocket and pulled out what cash he had. Then he passed the hat. Sympathetic spectators chipped in, including the plaintiffs' lawyers—an action that was later protested as unethical, unsuccessfully, by the CAFO attorneys.

Finally, Karen and Susan were free to go.

"I cried the entire way home," Karen told me. "I sat in the kitchen, and Rocky sat nearby with his head in hands, sobbing. That's how much it affected our family. It was all so horrible."

The next day, Cherry entered a written order of contempt. There was no need to entertain any allegations, as the violation took place in front of him, he said. Besides, Karen and Susan had "admitted passing out the objectionable material during the trial, apologized to the court for their actions, and indicated they did not know they could not do so," he wrote. "There is no burden of proof required."

Then, in June 2014, Karen and Susan filed a motion to vacate the court's judgment. The judge did not rule on the motion for over a year and then denied it. After that, Karen and Susan appealed to the Illinois Fourth District Appellate Court. That court ultimately held that their alleged misconduct did not take place "in the physical presence of the trial court or any of the parties." As a result, the judge improperly conducted an investigation. Meanwhile, the books in question were never found, nothing in the record showed that the two had caused any disruption or distraction, there was zero evidence that the jury had any knowledge of the contents of any materials, the judge "improperly interrogated" the defendants through leading questions and denying them the chance to fully respond, and he "improperly refused to entertain" their apologies.

In short, the court "failed to provide them with the constitutional safeguards necessary for a finding of indirect criminal contempt."

Judge Cherry scheduled a hearing for September, where Karen and Susan argued that they were unaware they had broken any court rules that would subject them to criminal-contempt proceedings, nor did the judge directly witness their conduct, which was necessary to find them in contempt. And, they added, they were given no chance to make a statement before sentencing, a procedure known as *allocution*.

In a second filing, the pair asserted there was no evidence that their conduct was "calculated to impede, embarrass, or obstruct the court," which had "denied their fundamental constitutional rights with respect to contempt petitions."

But the judge, it seemed, was disinclined to overturn his own ruling. Karen and Susan had been offered a hearing and an opportunity to make a statement prior to sentencing, he said curtly. He would make a ruling following depositions in the case.

Meanwhile, as part of discovery, Karen was ordered to turn over all emails she had sent or received to the lawyers representing plaintiffs in the original nuisance lawsuit. She complied.

The following months were hell for the Hudsons. Karen was pulled into court for her deposition and ordered to sit in the witness chair, a highly unusual and intimidating tactic. Judge Cherry looked on as the CAFO attorney, Stephen Kaufman, grilled her about her activities and asked whether she wanted people to stop eating meat.

"No," Karen answered. "I am an educator."

Then it was brought to Karen's attention that the CAFO attorneys were in possession of an email she had sent to the plaintiffs' lawyers but not disclosed during discovery. She had inadvertently missed it. "If you want anything, go through my computers," she said.

A few days later, Karen's attorney called. A court-ordered forensic specialist was on his way to the farmhouse to confiscate her desktop and laptop. The judge had authorized the specialist to search the hard drives for keywords like *CAFO* or *factory farm*. He arrived soon after and seized the computers.

Why? Because the CAFO lawyers had alleged that Karen was working in cahoots with the opposing legal counsel. They accused her of deliberately planning the whole thing with them in advance in order to disrupt the trial and influence the jury. Karen said the allegations were "ludicrous."

In the end, some ten thousand personal emails were copied off Karen's hard drives and archived. "They were emails to my son, my daughter, and I don't know how many clients. I can't know everything that was copied—there were ten thousand of them," she said. "The industry still has all of those."

Karen's computers remained in custody for about eight weeks, she said. During that time, she could not work, she could not post things on social media, and she could not be in any internet contact with her clients. Karen did not buy a replacement computer, she said, because her lawyers had told her to go underground. "Anything that I said at that point could have been held against me," she said. "So I dropped out of sight."

Sadly, Karen added, "the CAFO industry got exactly what they wanted."

For fourteen months, Karen, Susan, and their families waited. It wasn't until March 2016 that Cherry finally entered a brief one-sentence order: "Motion denied, this case is now appealable."

It took a few months to prepare the appeal. Meanwhile, Karen and Susan retained two new lawyers, paid for by SRAP, John Cunningham, and criminal-defense attorney Kevin Sullivan. They filed a motion at the Illinois Fourth District Appellate Court, in the capital, Springfield. Oral arguments were scheduled for December 7, 2016.

Karen and Rocky drove down from Elmwood for the hearing, but Susan was not able to attend. The proceedings lasted ten minutes.

The circuit court judge "never really found out what had happened," Sullivan told the three-judge panel. And besides that, "nobody had improperly influenced anyone, including jury members," he argued. "I think Judge Cherry made the wrong call."

Neither Karen nor Susan had been advised what the "appropriate courtroom decorum was," Sullivan said. While most people know not to swear at a judge, how many were aware that discreetly handing someone a book, before court was even in session, was cause for a criminal contempt charge?

"A person should be given notice before being held accountable for direct criminal contempt," he pleaded, noting that Karen had asked other spectators to remove their anti-CAFO paraphernalia before entering the courtroom. "There was no interference, no willfulness in this situation," he said. "Please, reverse this and vacate these findings."

A few seconds passed. "Is Ms. Turner here?" one of the judges inquired. Sullivan said she was not.

"Well, you can give Ms. Turner a call," the judge said, nodding to his colleagues. "We're reversing."

It was a highly unusual and rapid judgment. Typically, appellate courts take their time for deliberations and preparing written opinions, and finding out a ruling can take weeks, if not months. But this was instantaneous; after more than two and half grueling years, Karen Hudson and Susan Turner were officially cleared of any wrongdoing, and there was nothing Judge Cherry could say or do.

The written decision was handed down a few weeks later.

Karen and Susan had been denied "procedural safeguards"—the judges ruled in a unanimous opinion—including the chance to answer the accusations, confront and question witnesses, and be proved guilty beyond a reasonable doubt.[77]

"A finding of direct criminal contempt is strictly restricted to acts and facts seen and known by the court, and no matter resting upon opinions, conclusions, presumptions or inferences should be considered," they wrote.

On the day of the incident, when the judge first slapped the women with contempt charges, he failed to explain any of their rights to them, including the right to remain silent, the right to counsel, and the protection against self-incrimination. The judge did not give them notice that he was even considering criminal contempt before he began asking his "leading questions." And though Judge Cherry assured Karen and Susan that he would give them a chance to speak before sentencing, "this opportunity never arose."

As for their second appearance before Cherry, the judges unleashed a measured heaping of scorn. Those proceedings "constituted less of a 'hearing' and more of a lecture by the court."

The official vindication was sweet, but as Karen said, "We really didn't win in the end. I feel like there's so much more to do, and they are still getting away with stuff like this." The attorney for the CAFO in the original lawsuit, she told me, had recently warned her that lawyers were constantly monitoring the social media activity of Karen and her organizations, waiting for any reason to go after her again.

"My rights were stolen that day," Karen said, looking back on all that had happened. "I felt like I had been raped. It's a long, sickening, but ultimately empowering story."

I asked if she was going to file a federal lawsuit for violation of her First, Fifth, and Fourteenth Amendment rights. She replied that she thought judges had immunity against such claims.

"I guess now I'm willing to put myself under more moral duress to do it," Karen said, adding that she still needed to petition the state to have her criminal record expunged. She did, however, say she had received a check for $500 in the mail to reimburse her for the fine she paid. No apology was included.

These days, Karen told me, "my goal of educating the public about intensive animal agriculture now includes empowering citizens to stand up to anyone and anything that practices bullying and defies justice. My battle for justice is worth every tear I shed."

DESECRATING OLD GLORY

In early October 2017, controversy roared over the red-hot feud between President Trump and NFL players who kneel during the national anthem in protest of America's racial inequalities and police brutality. Proper respect for the flag and the anthem is perhaps the most critical aspect of public life among many Americans, especially conservatives. That's fine. It's also unquestionable that protected speech does not always extend to the workplace. While you can't be prosecuted for political protests at work, you can be fired.

Likewise, the president has every First Amendment right to call players "sons of bitches." He can legally demand that they be deprived of their livelihoods, as long as it is not done for politically partisan reasons, which is actually a felony.

However, just because you *can* say something doesn't mean you should. For someone as powerful as the president to call for the firing of players in an attempt to quell their protected speech produces a chilling effect on others contemplating similar behavior. And not just rich football players. Where does it stop? What if, say, a postal employee, schoolteacher, sanitation worker, or other government employee wanted to kneel during the anthem at a game but was afraid that he or she might be fired or retaliated against?

The chilling effect is cumulative. It is a direct threat to the First Amendment and the free speech it enshrines. No president has any business dabbling in it.

Coercing patriotism is not only a bad idea, it is unconstitutional. In 1943, U.S. Supreme Court justice Robert Jackson penned a decision in *West Virginia State Board of Education v. Barnette,* overturning a law in that state that made it a crime for students to refuse to say the Pledge of Allegiance—punishable by expulsion and the fining and jailing of their parents. Cases were brought against the rule by Jehovah's Witnesses, who pledge a verse from the Bible.[78]

In his decision, Jackson decried the dangers of what he called "compulsory unification of opinion," the stuff of Soviet gulags, and "the fast failing efforts of our present totalitarian enemies."

Justice Jackson believed that our republic is better than this and certainly stronger than this.

"To believe that patriotism will not flourish if patriotic ceremonies are voluntary and spontaneous, instead of a compulsory routine, is to make an unflattering estimate of the appeal of our institutions to free minds," he wrote.

In short, the court ruled, no official, including the president, "can prescribe what shall be orthodox in politics, nationalism, religion, or other matters of opinion."

Not standing for the flag or anthem is one thing. But what about actually burning, shredding, or stomping upon our nation's symbol of freedom and democracy? Doing so is fully protected under the First Amendment. It shocks and upsets people to see someone desecrating the Stars and Stripes. But if someone wants to burn the flag—a piece of private property—*on* private property, it is nobody else's business, especially the government's.

The flag exists—and generations of Americans fought for it—*precisely* so that you, I, or anyone else can set the thing on fire without fear of retribution by the state. If you burn the U.S. flag, you are not attacking the freedom for which it stands, you are exercising that freedom.

We have many national symbols—copies of the Constitution, Declaration of Independence, and Emancipation Proclamation, statues of bald eagles, and portraits of the presidents. Should people go to jail for burning those? There were many burnings—and hangings—of President Obama in effigy during his time in office. Should those people have gone to prison? What about burning a photo of Trump?

Speaking of the president, Donald Trump supports an amendment to the Constitution to make flag burning a serious felony. Such a radical measure is needed, die-hard conservatives say, because the Supreme Court, on not one but two occasions, has ruled that burning the U.S. flag is a perfectly protected form of free speech as guaranteed by the First Amendment.

In a 5–4 decision in 1989, the Supreme Court upheld the right of protestors to burn the flag, with the late justice Antonin Scalia, somewhat surprisingly, siding with the protestors.[79] He later said he based his ruling on a "textual" reading of the Constitution.

"If it were up to me, I would put in jail every sandal-wearing, scruffy-bearded weirdo who burns the American flag," Scalia said during a speech in 2015 in Philadelphia. "But I am not king."[80]

Neither is Donald Trump. Still, the following year, in November 2016, the new president-elect let the world know his policy position on this apparently urgent issue that somehow threatens democracy itself. It came, of course, in the form of a tweet: *Nobody should be allowed to burn the American flag - if they do, there must be consequences - perhaps loss of citizenship or year in jail!*[81]

Not only is Trump unaware of past Supreme Court decisions on flag burning and free speech, he's also unfamiliar with *Trop v. Dulles,* a 1958 Supreme Court case in which the justices ruled that a federal law allowing the expatriation of criminals, in this case a convicted military deserter, violates the Eighth Amendment's protection against "cruel and unusual punishment."[82]

For now at least, no American will be deported for flag burning. And, at least for now, nobody will be prosecuted, much less spend a year in jail. Still, at least forty states continue to log flag-desecration laws on their books, with penalties that include fines or even incarceration. Some Southern states also passed statutes against desecrating the Confederate flag.

And regardless of the Supreme Court's decisive rulings on this question, people are still being arrested for a "crime" that should not even exist.

In October 2009, Frank Snider of Cape Girardeau, Missouri, grew incensed that the U.S. Social Security Administration had turned him down for disability benefits, and he believed the government was preventing him from getting a job. As a form of protest, he took his American flag and, brandishing a lighter, walked out into his front yard.[83]

Snider tried to incinerate the flag, but it wouldn't catch fire. Instead, he took a knife to it, shredding it and tossing scraps to the ground. A neighbor saw him and called the local cops.

Officer Matthew Peters of the Cape Girardeau Police Department was dispatched to the scene shortly after that. He climbed from his patrol car, collected the remnants of cloth, and confronted Snider, who calmly explained that he was merely protesting U.S. policies.

Before Snider knew it, he was taken to jail, where he would spend the next eight hours. He was charged with violating a state law against flag desecration, a Class-A felony punishable by up to a year in jail, a $1,000 fine, or both.

Now Snider was really upset with the government. On July 6, 2010, with the assistance of the ACLU of Eastern Missouri, he filed a lawsuit in federal district court against Officer Peters for violating his First Amendment rights, and the City of Cape Girardeau for "deliberate indifference" to constitutional freedoms and failure to train police in recognizing legally protected speech. He sought a declaration that the law was unconstitutional, monetary damages and legal fees, and an injunction against the city to never enforce the statute— and to better train its officers.

It took nearly two years for a ruling. The district court on March 20, 2012, declared the Missouri statute was indeed unconstitutional and permanently barred the state from enforcing it.[84]

That's because burning a flag is no more illegal than saying "fuck you" to a cop.

"Here the State does not, and likely could not, articulate an interest that would justify restricting expression," the judge wrote.

After a follow-up trial, on August 24, 2012, Snider was granted $7,000 in compensatory damages, and the ACLU was awarded attorneys' fees and costs.[85]

But it wasn't over quite yet. Officer Peters appealed the ruling because it denied the qualified immunity he had asserted and included legal fees for the plaintiff. The State of Missouri intervened on Peters's behalf and the court ruled in his favor, dismissing the judgment. Snider and the ACLU then took his case to the U.S. court of appeals, which ultimately restored justice. It found that Snider's "expressive actions" were completely protected, that Peters was not entitled to immunity, and that the Missouri law was, on its face, unconstitutional.[86]

Another case took place in 2017 over Independence Day weekend, ironically enough, when twenty-two-year-old Bryton Mellott of Urbana, Illinois,

posted some photos of himself on Facebook "celebrating" the Fourth by setting fire not to sparklers or bottle rockets but to the Stars and Stripes itself, in
a protest of government treatment of women, minorities, and gay people, such
as himself.

"I am not proud to be an American," Mellott said in his post. "In this moment, being proud of my country is to ignore the atrocities committed against
people of color, people living in poverty, people who identify as women, and
against my own queer community on a daily basis.

"Too many people are allowed to be slaughtered for the sake of gun manu-
facturer profits. Too many Americans hold hate in their hearts in the name of
their religion, and for fear of others. And that's only to speak of domestic issues."[87]

Mellott made no threats. His words harmed no one. His photos and commentary were both legal and constitutionally protected.

Many Facebook users threatened the young man's life—something that
truly is illegal, unprotected speech—but nothing ever happened to them. It
was Mellott, the *victim* of those threats, who was now suspect: Some Facebook
users alerted the local police about his post. The cops immediately arrested Mellott under an unconstitutional Illinois law that is almost identical to that of
neighboring Missouri.

Urbana police took him to the Champaign County Jail for, they say, violating the statute, a Class-IV felony in Illinois, and for disturbing the peace—
not only of the public but, in yet another irony, his own.

That's right, the police, who also received illegal threats against the flag
burner, arrested Mellott in part to protect his own safety. George Orwell would
have appreciated the roundabout Newspeak that ensued.

"It's an unfortunate situation when freedom of speech issues come into conflict with safety issues," Sergeant Andrew Charles told *Forbes* magazine with
chilling understatement. "Concerns have to be balanced."[88]

Charles said that Mellott had mentioned the name of his employer, possibly putting his coworkers at risk as well. "When you say things that are incite-
ful and make it clear that you are associated with someone that doesn't share
your ideas, it got raised to a level where a reasonable person there would fear
for their safety," he said. "It's similar to yelling 'fire' in a movie theater."

Only there is a big difference. Yelling "fire" is not protected speech.

The saga kept getting stranger.

When Mellott was arrested, the cops asked him to wipe the photos from his Facebook page, and he declined. Soon after, while Mellott was still in custody, with no access to his cell phone, the Facebook images disappeared, according to *Forbes* magazine.

Ultimately, the cops called the state attorney's office. They said to release Mellott, even though he could still face arraignment on the charges. But State's Attorney Julia Rietz announced that no charges would be filed, citing the 1989 Supreme Court decision upholding this inflammatory form of protest.

Rietz's office said it would urge state lawmakers to review the law and "the constitutional issues it presents." What she didn't ask is, why did the legislature even bother to pass such a statute in 2013, knowing that it had been shot down by the Supreme Court more than two decades earlier?

Remember, in the 1989 Supreme Court decision, the ruling was 5–4, with Scalia breaking the tie. He is no longer on the bench, and it's easy to see his replacement, Justice Brent Kavanaugh, overturning the right to burn. Imagine if the High Court were to uphold such draconian state laws as those on the books in Missouri or Illinois, which make it illegal not only to deface, defile, or trample upon the flag but to "cast contempt upon, satirize, deride or burlesque, either by words or act, such flag, standard, color, ensign, shield, or other insignia of the United States."[89]

U.S. troops did not die for a flag; they died for freedom and justice. In short, perhaps mangled syntax, the flag is the symbol of your right to burn it.

THE FIRST AMENDMENT AT SCHOOL

Free speech on campus. Four explosive words. The fight over who can say what, where, and when on college property will not be resolved any time soon. And while the First Amendment does not protect all speech in publicly funded elementary, middle, and high schools, it does extend to universities, at least on paper.

It was disappointing to see students at the University of California–Berkeley, the birthplace of the free-speech movement and my alma mater, among other schools, trying to shut down appearances by far-right speakers such as Ann Coulter and Milo Yiannopoulos, the British provocateur associated with the alt-right.

When I was at Berkeley and controversial figures from the Reagan administration and its advocates came to speak, we went, we listened, and then we protested. I don't remember anyone trying to shut down the lectures.

Ridiculing attempts to silence Coulter, Yiannopoulos, and others became a cause célèbre among the Right, calling the students "snowflakes" who needed their "safe spaces." But it has also been condemned by some on the Left, including Senator Bernie Sanders.

"I think people have a right to speak. And you have a right if you're on a college campus not to attend. You have a right to ask hard questions about the speaker if you disagree with him or her," Sanders said in June 2017 on CBS's *Face the Nation*.[90]

Unpopular but protected speech is under assault on many, though not all, American college campuses. Robert Corn-Revere, an attorney who represents students fighting to protect First Amendment rights at their schools, says the problem arose from what he calls "politically correct speech codes" that began in the late 1980s. Many of those codes were eventually thrown out by the courts.

Indeed, as far back as 1960, well before the free-speech movement, the U.S. Supreme Court ruled in *Shelton v. Tucker* that "state colleges and universities are not enclaves immune from the sweep of the First Amendment" and "the vigilant protection of constitutional freedoms is nowhere more vital than in the community of American schools."[91]

"Most people believed that the problem was over because the courts had ruled on it and upheld First Amendment rights," Corn-Revere told the right-wing news site *The Daily Signal*. But that did not stop schools from enforcing speech codes, he said, "and created what is laughably referred to as 'free speech zones,'" small, enclosed areas dedicated to protests—as if protesting anywhere else on campus could or should be off limits.[92]

Happily, in recent years, speech codes on campus have been on the decline. The Foundation for Individual Rights in Education (FIRE) conducts an annual survey of colleges and universities to track the prevalence of such restrictions. In 2007, it found that 259 out of 346 surveyed institutions of higher learning, or 75 percent, maintained policies that "both clearly and substantially restrict freedom of speech." A decade later, in FIRE's 2017 report, that figure had dropped to 39.6 percent.[93]

Speech codes aside, many schools still impose onerous and unfair burdens on student groups that want to get their message out on campus, including the insistence on free speech zones. As of March 2017, only four states, all with conservative legislatures, had passed laws prohibiting the establishment of free speech zones on campuses: Virginia, Missouri, Arizona, and Kentucky.

Still, the abridgment of free speech on campus persists—as do efforts to fight the censorship.

Look at what happened at Dixie State University, in St. George, Utah.

In October 2014, students belonging to Young Americans for Liberty (YAL)—an approved student club and self-proclaimed "Pro-Liberty" organization with more than 204,000 activists and 500 chapters—decided to promote weekly meetings by posting flyers around school.

The students followed the rules: They first sought permission from the dean of students before posting anything and submitted them for official review two weeks before their meeting, as required by school rules (making spur-of-the-moment organizing virtually impossible, by the way).

"Learn to hold your leaders accountable," said the first flyer, with a photograph of President George W. Bush and the all-caps caption "MISS ME YET?" Next to that was an image of a cat with the caption "WHY AREN'T YOU IN PRISON?"[94]

The second flyer had a photo of President Barack Obama speaking into a microphone and the words "Get in my BELLYYYY!" over the caption "Don't be consumed by the state!" The third displayed a drawing of South American revolutionary Che Guevara, enclosed in a red circle with a slash through it.

"REAL REBELS DON'T SUPPORT CENTRALIZED STATE AUTHORITY," it said, above the statement "No More Che Day / You've seen him on Shirts. You've seen him on Mugs. Now see him as he really is with Young Americans for Liberty."

All three flyers were rejected by the school because they "mocked individuals," a violation of school policy, which required that all materials be "professional," "not derogatory," and in "good taste," without offering any criteria for judging such things.

School policy also prohibited the posting of anything in student dorms that the Office of Resident Life deemed to be "racist, sexist, indecent, scandalous, illegal, inciting, advertising alcohol or illegal substances, or in any way oppressive in nature," again without defining what *oppressive* means.

The officials said they would approve the flyers if the images of Bush, Obama, and Guevara were deleted. YAL president William Jergins complied with the request, out of fear of punishment, but it did not sit well with the group. To them, the unchecked power of officials—at a publicly funded school—to make such arbitrary, subjective decisions about what constitutes "good taste" amounted to the improper use of prior restraint.

That same fall, YAL members planned to erect a "Free Speech Wall" covered in giant blank sheets of paper on which students could compose any message about constitutional free-speech protections they wanted. Again, YAL followed every approval step required, this time by the school's "Activity Approval Guide," and obtained all necessary permits at least three weeks prior to the event, as required by Dixie State policies.

But there was one problem: The students had requested to put the wall up in a central area of campus with heavy foot traffic, known as the "Diagonal." Instead, a school official marked "Free Speech Zone" on top of the group's application.

The free speech zone at Dixie was a small concrete patio—YAL members estimated its size as less than one-tenth of 1 percent of Dixie State's one hundred acres—outside the Gardner Center, home to faculty offices and the student cafeteria. It has no classrooms, and there are none in the immediate area. The cafeteria entrance is on the other side of the building, meaning students have little reason to walk past this part of the school.

Nonetheless, the Free Speech Wall went up on October 27, 2014, from 9:00 a.m. to 2:00 p.m. Not many students showed up—although a campus security officer did. The school had offered to have a police presence at the wall, but the group declined, fearing a chilling effect on student participation. But there he was, hanging out, watching, for at least thirty minutes. He told the group he had been sent there to "look out for hate speech." During that time, even fewer students came to look at or write on the wall.

It was time to push back. The following March, Jergins, along with YAL vice president Joey Gillespie and member Forrest Gee, filed suit in U.S. District Court, Utah Central Division. They were represented by attorney Robert Corn-Revere.

"Dixie State, a public institution, has adopted and enforced excessive restrictions on the rights of student organizations, and limited student speech in open areas of the campus," the legal complaint said. "Further, Dixie State unconstitutionally restricts access to open areas on campus for expressive activities by requiring that students request permission to speak several weeks in advance. And once approved, Plaintiffs were relegated to a previously unknown 'free speech zone.'"[95]

The students sought monetary damages and legal fees, a permanent injunction against Dixie State policies, and a court declaration that the school's posting policies, free speech zone policy, and club event policies were unconstitutional. They claimed emotional injury "as a consequence of being denied their First Amendment rights" and alleged that assigning a security official to monitor the wall for "hate speech" violated their free-speech rights and their Fourteenth Amendment rights of equal protection under the law.

The school's small and off-the-beaten-track free speech zone, meanwhile, "impermissibly restricts student expression, does not serve a significant government interest, and is unconstitutionally overbroad," the lawsuit charged. School policies that required student groups to obtain permission from at least four separate entities at the university—and then to wait two to three weeks before holding an event—were "cumbersome and time-consuming," forcing the students to limit the number of events they could sponsor. It was "an unconstitutional prior restraint on free expression."

In September 2015, the school settled out of court. Officials agreed to revise campus policies targeted in the lawsuit, train campus officials about the new free-speech policies, and award the plaintiffs $50,000 in damages and attorney's fees.[96]

Attorney Corn-Revere has handled several similar cases, including a student who was threatened with expulsion from the Citrus Community College District in Glendora, California, in Los Angeles County. His offense? Asking another student to sign a petition outside the campus free-speech area. The student won a $110,000 settlement that included an agreement by the college to revise its policies, allow free expression in all outside areas of campus, and adopt a definition of "harassment" against speech in compliance with the First Amendment.[97]

In another bizarre case, a student at Modesto Community College in California sued the district after it barred him from distributing copies of the U.S. Constitution—on Constitution Day. That case resulted in a settlement: The district agreed to permit free speech in all outdoor areas open to students and the public and paid the student $50,000 in damages.[98]

When attempts to restrain free speech on college campuses are challenged in court, the plaintiffs usually stand on solid constitutional grounds, and quite often they win. But when it comes to K–12 students in public schools, the legal deck is so heavily stacked against them, they rarely prevail.

Consider the "BONG HiTS 4 JESUS" case.

On a dismal January day in 2002, the streets of Juneau, Alaska, were packed with people anxiously waiting for the Olympic Torch to pass by on its journey to the Utah Winter Olympics. Joseph Frederick, an eighteen-year-old senior at Juneau-Douglas High School, was meeting classmates gathered outside to watch the torch relay.

The young man had a silly senior-class prank in store and asked for assistance: He carried a handmade, twelve-foot banner and needed help unfurling it. Several friends volunteered. They waited for the TV cameras passing by.

Written on the cloth were the words: BONG HiTS 4 JESUS.

Principal Deborah Morse saw the banner and seized it. Frederick was in trouble. Called in to explain himself, he said he had first seen the phrase on a snowboarding sticker and found it amusing. He thought it would attract the attention of the TV crews, just as a joke.

Morse was anything but amused. His banner was a violation of the school district's antidrug policy, she told Frederick. She suspended the prankster for five days.

The student began uttering libertarian quotes from Thomas Jefferson, but Morse only doubled his suspension, to ten days. Morse later could not recall if Frederick had quoted Jefferson but said that was not the reason for the ten-day suspension.

According to Frederick, an assistant principal told him that "the Bill of Rights does not exist in school" and does not apply until "after graduation."

Frederick filed an administrative appeal with the district superintendent. It was denied, though his suspension *was* capped at eight days, the time he'd been out of school. Undaunted, he took his case to the Juneau School Board, which likewise denied his appeal, on March 19, 2002.[99]

The young student was livid. His free-speech rights were being trampled, he felt, and the school district didn't care. A month later, he filed a civil suit against Morse and the school board in the U.S. District Court for Alaska, seeking an official declaration that his First Amendment rights had been violated, in addition to the removal of the suspension from his academic record, compensatory and punitive damages, and legal fees.

The case was dismissed without trial. The court ruled that no rights had been violated because the principal "reasonably interpreted" the banner as promoting marijuana, which was contrary to school policies.

That was not going to stop Frederick. He took his case to the Ninth Circuit Court of Appeals. Even though Frederick was not on school grounds during the incident, the appeals court held that school-speech doctrine (limiting students' freedom of expression) still applied in this case.

But that didn't necessarily mean the school had a right to suspend the student.

The question came down to whether a school may "punish and censor nondisruptive, off-campus speech," when it caused no disruption of school activities, just because it "promotes a social message contrary to the one favored by the school," wrote Judge Kleinfeld in the unanimous opinion. "The answer under controlling, long-existing precedent is plainly 'No.'"

Prior cases had upheld limits on student speech, but they pertained to things like pervasive sexual innuendo, which can be punished, "as contrasted with the 'political viewpoint' of protected speech," Kleinfeld wrote. Frederick's speech was not sexual. And it is not so simple, he added, to distinguish speech about marijuana "from political speech in the context of a state where referenda regarding marijuana legalization repeatedly occur."

It was a joyous and hard-fought victory, but the celebrations would not last long.

Shortly thereafter, district superintendent Peggy Cowan complained that the ruling "could compromise our ability to send a consistent message against the use of illegal drugs." The school board petitioned the U.S. Supreme Court to review the decision. In December 2006, the court agreed to hear the case.

Oral arguments were made on the morning of March 19, 2007. Representing the school district was none other than Kenneth Starr, of Whitewater and Monica Lewinsky fame. He noted there was no constitutional right among students to "disruptive" speech, which, he claimed, included any behavior that goes against the educational mission of the school. Given that this school's announced policy was to support the control of marijuana laws, student speech to the contrary was not protected by the First Amendment.[100]

Justice David Souter challenged Starr's assertion. The banner's wording "sounds like just a kid's provocative statement to me," he said. But Starr insisted it was crucial to allow the school official to interpret the message "as long as that interpretation is reasonable."

When Frederick's attorney, Douglas Mertz, began his argument, he claimed, "This is a case about free speech. It is not about drugs." But Chief Justice John Roberts was unmoved. "It's a case about money," he snapped. "Your client wants *money* from the principal personally for her actions in this case."

Mertz ignored Roberts. He went on to stress that the torch relay was not school-sponsored, that his client had not stepped foot on school property, that "BONG HiTS 4 JESUS" was intended to be purely humorous, and that, at any rate, the banner had caused no disruption.

Two months later, in a 5–4 decision along conservative-liberal lines, Frederick lost his case.[101]

Chief Justice Roberts, in his majority opinion, said the school had not violated the First Amendment by seizing the banner and suspending its creator. The school speech doctrine applied, he wrote, because Frederick displayed his message "in the midst of his fellow students, during school hours, at a school-sanctioned activity."

The speech itself was "reasonably viewed as promoting illegal drug use," Roberts wrote. The wording may have been "cryptic," but there were only two possible meanings. "The phrase could be interpreted as an imperative: 'Take bong hits . . .'—a message equivalent to "smoke marijuana," Roberts wrote. "Alternatively, the phrase could be viewed as celebrating drug use—'bong hits are a good thing,' or 'we take bong hits.'"

Regardless, the majority could "discern no meaningful distinction between celebrating illegal drug use in the midst of fellow students and outright advocacy or promotion," Roberts said. Schools, he added, have an "important—indeed, perhaps compelling interest" to discourage student drug use in any way possible.

In concurring, Justice Clarence Thomas argued that the history of public education "suggests that the First Amendment, as originally understood, does not protect student speech in public schools." American schools trace back to colonial times, Thomas asserted, when they were intended as substitutes for private tutors and could discipline students as they pleased. "Teachers commanded, and students obeyed," he wrote.

But Thomas was not concerned about the content of the banner. He was worried that *not* punishing Frederick would send the wrong message. Protecting the youth's free speech in this case would be to "surrender control of the American public-school system to public school students."

Liberal justices—and progressive commentators—were horrified. Justice John Paul Stevens, in a harshly worded dissent joined by Souter and Ginsburg, lamented that "the Court does serious violence to the First Amendment in upholding—indeed, lauding—a school's decision to punish Frederick for expressing a view with which it disagreed."

The school's interest in discouraging drug use, no matter how well reasoned, was no justification for punishing the student for trying to make "an ambiguous statement to a television audience simply because it contained an oblique reference to drugs," Stevens wrote.

There were many reasons why civil libertarians of all political stripes (groups as diverse as the American Center for Law and Justice, the Christian Legal Society, the Drug Policy Alliance, and Liberty Counsel filed Supreme Court briefs on Frederick's behalf)[102] were alarmed by the High Court's ruling, given the precedent it could set and the slippery slope it risked. After all, if references to drug use can be banned, then what's next? What about schools that have policies to fight teen obesity? Would a student wearing a T-shirt to school that extols, say, greasy fast food, be subject to suspension?

Repressing of speech in public elementary, middle, and high schools is commonplace. Here are just some of the other violations I encountered:

Suspended for Sitting During the Pledge

India Landry did not want to stand during the Pledge of Allegiance in school, in protest of police brutality and, more recently, the policies of Donald Trump. She had remained seated, she says, more than two hundred times in classes taught by six different teachers since the ninth grade, always without incident.

But then the fierce public battle over NFL players "taking a knee" broke out, and things changed at school.

On October 2, 2017, the seventeen-year-old senior at Houston's Windfern High School was sitting in the principal's office when the pledge came over the loudspeaker. She did not stand up. The head principal, Martha Strother, expelled her from school on the spot.

Yet India remained seated. She was taken to the office of the assistant principal.

"Call your mother," she ordered the student. "Tell her to come pick you up." If that didn't happen within five minutes, she warned the shaken girl, a police officer would be summoned to physically remove her from school.[103]

"This is not the NFL," the assistant principal scolded, according to court documents that were later filed. India was going to stand for the pledge "like the other African Americans in your class," she said.

"I was actually terrified; I see what's going on with the country," India's mother, Kizzy Landry, told *The New York Daily News*.[104]

Kizzy called school officials, asking that India be allowed to return to class.

"No one can sit for the pledge at my school," was the message relayed back from Principal Strother.

Three days after India's expulsion, the Landrys managed to get a meeting with Strother, who insisted that India had to stand for the pledge as a condition of her returning to school. Sitting was "disrespectful," she said. It would not be tolerated. She declared the meeting over.

That's when a local TV reporter from KHOU Channel 11 called Strother about the "pledge controversy." The resulting broadcast did not portray the school in a favorable light. "I don't think that the flag is what it says it's for, for liberty and justice and all that," India told the reporter. "It's not obviously what's going on in America today." The news account noted that India was just months away from graduating. "She may only have two options: stand or get her diploma. She knows her decision," the reporter said.

"I wouldn't stand because it goes against everything I believe in," India explained.

The next morning, at around 8:40 a.m., Principal Strother called Kizzy. She had changed her mind. India could return to school, and she would not have to stand for the pledge. By 10:30 a.m., India was back in class.

Still, the Landrys were upset.

The two engaged legal counsel from the respected civil rights attorney Randall Kallinen, and on October 7, Kizzy Landry filed suit on behalf of her daughter in federal district court in Houston against Principal Strother and the Cypress-Fairbanks Independent School District, the nation's third largest.[105]

The lawsuit, which was brief, simple, and to the point, alleged that the district had violated India's rights to free speech and due process under the First, Fifth, and Fourteenth Amendments. Due process, it noted, "requires, in connection with a suspension of 10 days or less, that the student be given oral or written notice of the charges against him and, if he denies them, an explanation of the evidence the authorities have and an opportunity to present his side of the story."

Kizzy Landry sought "declaratory and injunctive relief" (a determination that the practice was unconstitutional and a court order to forbid it in school), plus monetary damages.

"The right for a student not to be forced to stand for the pledge is an old one," the complaint said, citing the landmark 1943 Supreme Court ruling that upheld Jehovah's Witnesses' right to remain silent during the pledge in public schools. "Furthermore, it said, "instant expulsion from a public school is not allowed if a student is not a danger."

Principal Strother, the lawsuit alleged, "had recently been whipped into a frenzy by the publicity of African American National Football League players kneeling during the National Anthem at NFL football games."

A district spokeswoman told *The Daily News* that she had not seen the lawsuit, but insisted, quite erroneously, that "a student will not be removed from campus for refusing to stand for the pledge," adding that "we will address this situation internally."[106]

In September 2018, the State of Texas supported the school in its decision to remove India from campus. State Attorney General Ken Paxton filed a motion to intervene against the former student's case, saying in a news release that "school children cannot unilaterally refuse to participate in the pledge," though he added that they could get written consent from their parent or guardian to do so.[107]

Yearbook Redacted

In June 2017, students at Wall High School in Wall Township, New Jersey, were excited about summer vacation and the ritual year-end distribution of the school's yearbook. But some students immediately noticed that something was amiss—or more accurately, missing.

For his school portrait, Grant Berardo, seventeen, wore a black "Make America Great Again" T-shirt, in support of Donald Trump. Another student, Wyatt Dobrovish-Fago, put on a sweater vest festooned with Trump's name, and his sister, Montana, the freshman class president, selected a Trump quote, entirely innocuous and apolitical, to appear beneath her photo: "I like thinking big. If you're going to be thinking anything, you might as well think big."

Now, they were all gone; someone had Photoshopped the two photos, obliterating any references to the president, and removed the quote. Other students had selected quotes from their favorite presidents, but those were not redacted.

School rules do not prohibit political messages. The students and their parents protested vigorously.

"I think it was probably politically motivated," Grant's father, Joseph Berardo, told reporters. "It was inherently offensive to somebody, and they made a decision to Photoshop it—and without discussion, which is the worst part." He said he would have been equally opposed if messages about Hillary Clinton were removed. It was the first election to attract his son's attention, and censoring the youth was a terrible introduction to politics.[108]

The school did suspend the teacher who was the yearbook advisor that year.

The school board apparently got the message, as well. Board president Allison Connolly called the redactions "disturbing" and said the board "takes the charge that students have had their free speech rights infringed upon very seriously."[109]

The censorship caught the attention of one Donald J. Trump.

Thank you Wyatt and Montana—two young Americans who aren't afraid to stand up for what they believe in, the president posted on his Facebook page. *Our movement to #MAGA is working because of great people like you!*[110]

Hairstyles

African American schoolchildren are not only harassed for their political be-liefs but for their hairstyles, Shaun King, a columnist for *The New York Daily News,* wrote in July 2016. "I received an email from a genuinely angry parent from my home state of Kentucky," King wrote.[111]

When the woman went to enroll her teenage daughter at Butler Traditional High School in Louisville, she was handed a notice about a new version of the school's hair and dress codes. The rules on "Personal Grooming" declared that "hair styles that are extreme, distracting, or attention getting will not be per-mitted. No dreadlocks, cornrows, twists, mohawks, and no jewelry will be worn in hair." It also banned "afros more than two inches in length" and any "cut-in designs."

The school rule was "disgusting," King wrote. "It basically bans every popu-lar form of natural hair African Americans wear today. My sons and daughters, every single one of them, would be in violation of the policy."

"My son, who always gets designs cut into his hair, would be in violation," King noted, adding that New York City mayor Bill de Blasio's son, Dante, "with his huge afro," would have been kept out of school as well.

Bible Verses and the County Sheriff

Most mornings, Christina Zavala would slip a note containing a Bible verse into the lunch bag of her seven-year-old son, a first grader at Desert Rose El-ementary School in Palmdale, California. At lunchtime, her son would some-times read them to his friends. Before long, some of the kids asked for copies of the verses, and Zavala happily supplied them.

The biblical writings apparently went unnoticed until, on April 18, 2016, Zavala received a phone call from a teacher. A student had shown her one of Zavala's handwritten notes, telling her "this is the most beautiful story I've ever seen."[112]

Zavala's son, the teacher said, was "not allowed to share such things while at school," citing separation of church and state. He could only share such things after school, outside the school gate. Zavala explained that the Estab-lishment Clause of the First Amendment protected her son's rights to share Bible passages. The teacher was unimpressed.

Zavala and her husband directed their son to follow the rules. But three weeks later, on May 9, a new edict was handed down: The sharing of Bible verses would have to be done at a distance, on a public sidewalk. Again, the parents complied.

But even that wasn't the end of it. That afternoon, a knock came at the family's front door. It was a deputy from the Los Angeles County Sheriff's Department, summoned by school officials to have a talk with the devout Christians. He said the school was concerned that "someone might be offended" by the Bible verses.

The Zavalas, understandably unsettled, contacted Liberty Counsel, a conservative, nonprofit organization that takes up issues of religious freedom.

The prior restraint on religious expression "should shock the conscience of every freedom-loving American," Liberty Counsel attorney Horatio Mihet told Fox News. "Apparently all the real criminals have been dealt with in Palmdale—and now they're going after kids who share Bible verses during lunch time."[113]

Mihet said the situation was like something out of Communist Romania, where he attended elementary school, "but cops don't bully seven-year-olds who want to talk about Jesus in the Land of the Free."

Raul Maldonado, the superintendent of the Palmdale School District, told Fox News that officials were reviewing the incident. He confirmed that a deputy was sent to the Zavalas' home, but he declined to answer additional questions.

Liberty Counsel attorneys wrote to Maldonado, reminding him that the speech of public school students is protected by the First Amendment, including distribution of printed material, as long as the words are not obscene or libelous, and do not constitute an imminent danger of criminal acts. The letter accused the school of "unconstitutional suppression and censorship of student religious speech" and warned that Liberty Counsel attorneys would "take further action" if officials persisted in abridging the child's First Amendment rights.[114]

The district wrote back with a compromise: The Zavalas' son could "freely discuss his religious beliefs" on campus as long as it took place "during non-instructional time." The Zavalas and their son could distribute Bible passages to anyone, including those on the sidewalk just a few feet away from the school gate. The boy could also "invite any of his peers to join him on the sidewalk" after school for Bible discussions.[115]

An equitable ending to a sorry story. But it does beg at least one question—namely, if a child were to share passages from, say, the Holy Koran and pass notes from his mother touting the virtues of Muhammad, would the school be equally tolerant in that case?

PROTESTORS, THE PRESS, AND
AN EMBATTLED FIRST AMENDMENT

It may be true that Donald Trump has read the Constitution.
But it's unclear if he understands it.

—*POLITICO*, AUGUST 2016[1]

I'm not convinced that Donald Trump has read the Constitution. His disregard for the founding principles of our republic is evidenced by his shocking ignorance of it. In July 2016, during a meeting with GOP leaders—many of them jittery at his authoritarian rhetoric and wary of his impending nomination—some lawmakers sought reassurances that Trump would respect Article I, which establishes the powers of the legislative branch and separates them from those of the executive and judicial branches.

"I love Article I," was his reply. "I love Article II. I love Article XII."[2]

There are only seven articles.

In trying to boast about his knowledge of the Constitution, the future president betrayed how little he knows or even cares about it. Trump may love Article XII, but he seems to harbor a personal distaste for Amendment I, especially when it comes to harassing, threatening, surveilling, suing, jailing, and otherwise exacting retribution from his perceived enemies—not only among the organized civil resistance that has risen up around him but in the media as well.

It's as if he had never read the amendment and its prohibitions against *abridging the press,* or the *right of the people peaceably to assemble* or to *petition the Government for a redress of grievances.*

As a keen observer of the Obama years, I was deeply troubled by that administration's treatment of the press. Freedom of Information requests became more and more difficult to fulfill, and those dreaded black lines of redaction grew more common. Even more alarming, Obama's Justice Department was caught red-handed spying on U.S. journalists. Incidents included the secret collection of personal phone records at the Associated Press, the seizing of phone records of Fox News's James Rosen, tapping of his parents' phone, and tracking his movements around the State Department, where he worked, and accusations of hacking into the home of CBS News investigative reporter (and thorn in the Obama administration's side) Sharyl Attkisson. Other journalists were intimidated, roughed up, pummeled, and sometimes jailed during this period. Some were arrested for their pointed, aggressive questioning of high-level officials.

The abusive treatment of nonviolent protestors was even more widespread. In 2011, when thousands of demonstrators took over Lower Manhattan's Zuccotti Park and launched Occupy Wall Street, and tens of thousands more took part in protests across the country, they were secretly monitored by the FBI and DHS through their Joint Terrorism Task Force, even though Occupy had been declared a peaceful movement and had nothing to do with domestic terrorism.[3]

Five years later, private and public security agencies used attack dogs, pepper spray, water cannons, and other tactics against protestors who occupied land in North Dakota to decry the Dakota Access Pipeline and the ruinous effect it could have on the drinking water supply of the Standing Rock Indian Reservation. Nearly two hundred people were arrested. Many of them complained of being confined to what amounted to "dog kennels," where they were marked with numbers and subjected to high-pitched "sound cannons." Many women alleged that they were strip-searched in front of male officers.[4]

It's also worth noting here that at least twenty-six people who identified themselves as journalists were arrested while reporting on Occupy Wall Street, as were ten reporters at Standing Rock.

But when it comes to the freedom of gathering news or protesting policies, if the Obama years were bad—and there is plenty of evidence in the pages that follow that they were—then the Trump era is sending us on a collision course with catastrophe.

As I write this, in early August 2018, the president has once again called members of the media "enemies of the people," a phrase that White House press secretary Sarah Sanders refused to refute. The same month, Trump tweeted:

> *The Fake News hates me saying that they are the Enemy of the People only because they know it's TRUE. I am providing a great service by explaining this to the American People. They purposely cause great division & distrust. They can also cause War! They are very dangerous & sick!*[5]

Trump has elevated his rhetoric to such dangerous levels that I now fully expect that journalists will be physically harmed—as nearly happened in October 2018 when pipe bombs were sent to CNN, among other critics of the president. His attacks have escalated over the past year, during which he threatened to revoke the broadcasting license of NBC, citing unfavorable coverage, even though he does not have that authority; called First Amendment liberties "frankly disgusting" because "the press is able to write whatever they want to write"; called for reform of libel laws to make it easier for public officials to file suit against reporters; and directed press secretary Sarah Huckabee Sanders to call on ESPN to fire journalist Jemele Hill for criticizing him.

And ominously, on January 15, 2019, William Barr, President Trump's selection to replace former attorney general Sessions, told the Senate Judiciary Committee that he believed journalists can be prosecuted as a "last resort." He added that such prosecution would be proper for news organizations that were knowingly "putting out stuff that would hurt the country."

These constitute a small fraction of Trump's repeated attempts to cow and delegitimize the American media.

As for protestors and other vocal opponents, Trump has called for them to be beaten, even offering to pay the legal bills of anyone who assaulted a protestor at one of his rallies. He has called for the firing of NFL players who protest policy brutality by silently kneeling during the national anthem and said flag burners should spend a year in prison before having their citizenship stripped away.

Under Attorney General Jeff Sessions, Trump's Justice Department tried to seize huge swaths of personal information on millions of Americans who visited a key anti-Trump protest website and the Facebook pages of protest organizers—even those visitors who merely "liked" the pages. The DOJ also prosecuted protestors—and even journalists—just for being in an area where violence occurred. Some of them faced up to eighty years in prison.

PROTESTS, PEPPER SPRAY, PROSECUTION

The Trump crackdown on reporters and protestors began during the very first hours of his administration.

On January 20, 2017, Inauguration Day, thousands of protestors who had been banned from assembling at or even near the National Mall and other federal properties (an affront to the First Amendment in itself) amassed along a four-block stretch of downtown D.C. to express their alarm. Most were entirely peaceful. Some were not: They had come to incite bedlam.

Among the crowd was a relatively small group of black-bloc anarchists and Antifa members, clad in their trademark black clothes, their heads covered in bandannas, hoods, and goggles. Armed with crowbars, hammers, and other weapons, they hurled objects at police and bystanders, set fire to a limousine, and shattered the windows of local businesses, including Starbucks, Bank of America, Wells Fargo, and McDonald's. The police fought back relentlessly with pepper spray, tear gas, rubber bullets, water cannons, and stun grenades as they tried to corral the demonstrators into a confined space in an action known as *kettling*.

It was a roiling kettle, from which some of the corralled protestors allegedly hurled "rocks, bottles, flares and unknown liquids" at the cops, according to the Metropolitan Police Department (MPD) report. Six officers received minor injuries, including three who were struck in the head by projectiles.

The wanton dragnet was indiscriminate as cops assaulted and rounded up just about anyone in their path, regardless of whether they were rioters or not, including peaceful demonstrators, working journalists, and volunteer legal observers.

It was an ugly scene. A video posted on Facebook showed D.C. police pepper-spraying an elderly woman and a man trying to flee on crutches. In no way could they be mistaken for violent anarchists. One woman was seen carrying her ten-year-old son through the melee, shouting, "My child! My child!"

as she ran with the fleeing crowd, desperately but unsuccessfully trying to protect the boy's eyes from the stinging mist.

The woman, Gwen Frisbie-Fulton, is a single mother from North Carolina who works for a nonprofit and is active in community organizing and protesting abuses of social justice. She is trying to raise her son, whom she called A. S., to value political participation. A. S. had been keenly interested in the 2016 election and was stunned when Trump won. The two decided to head for Washington for the Inauguration Day protest and the next day's Women's March.

"I wanted to make sure that my son had the space to express himself, and I wanted to show him how people respond in a democracy to election results they disagree with—by letting our leaders know why we're unhappy and how they ought to change," she later told the ACLU-D.C.[6]

Frisbie-Fulton and A. S. had seen police begin to pepper-spray people down the block and were scrambling to flee the area when another group of officers, unprovoked and without warning, rushed toward them from the opposite direction. Two of the cops slammed into A. S. and knocked him to the pavement. Frisbie-Fulton dove atop her child to protect him. "We were soon engulfed in a tangle of bodies," she said. "My son was crying underneath me on the sidewalk. I was terrified that he would be crushed or that I would be injured myself and unable to get him out safely."

Finally freed from the scrum, the terrified mother picked up her son and began running. Still more police blocked their way. One screamed at her for bringing a child to a demonstration. Another tried to lead them away from the confusion and the spray but lost them in the crowd. They fled down a street, choking with pepper spray.

The military-style tactics also shocked Shay Horse, a freelance photojournalist whose clients have included Getty Images, the Associated Press, *Rolling Stone,* Al Jazeera America, and *The Intercept.* Although a self-described anarchist on his Twitter feed, he had not traveled from his home in New York to riot. He'd come to cover the protests and the police. Dressed that morning in dark jeans, a hooded sweatshirt with the hood down, and a leather jacket, with a professional camera around his neck, and a camera bag, Horse also did not look like an Antifa agitator.[7]

Around 10:30 a.m., as hundreds of protestors marched south on Thirteenth

Street NW, from Logan Circle toward the National Mall, Horse accompanied the demonstration down the street, shooting photos of the marchers.

Suddenly, a group of protestors, dressed all in black with hoods over their heads and masks over their faces, began vandalizing local businesses.

As Horse and others approached Franklin Square, they were diverted by the MDP and forced to head east, away from the Mall. They complied, heading down side streets. There, other officers were waiting for them. Armed with gallons of pepper spray, they doused the marchers, over and over again.

Horse readied his camera. He photographed one officer soaking peaceful protesters in pepper. The cop spotted him, saw his large, expensive camera, and sprayed him, too, without warning.

Horse gagged on the searing gas and gasped for breath. His eyes were on fire. As he and others began to flee, the police confronted them yet again, this time with concussion grenades, stingers, smoke flares, earsplitting "sound cannons," euphemistically known as Long Range Acoustic Devices (LRADs)—and more pepper spray. None of those around him threatened the officers in any way. Indeed, they were fleeing away from the cops, not charging toward them.

Shay Horse was corralled into the kettle, along with some 230 detainees, including seven other journalists.

Jack Keller, for example, was working as a producer for the web documentary series *Story of America,* gathering video of the fracas when police grabbed him. Detained for a day and a half, he repeatedly told the officers he was a journalist and had nothing to do with the rioting. It did him no good.

Also arrested were Matt Hopard, an independent journalist who was livestreaming the protests; Evan Engel of Vocativ; Alex Rubinstein of RT America, the Russian-owned news network; photographer Cheney Orr; Alexander Stokes Contompasis, an independent journalist who films and hosts an Albany Public Access TV news show; Alexei Wood, who live-streamed the protests and their aftermath; and Aaron Cantú, a freelance journalist who has contributed to Al Jazeera America, *The Nation, The Baffler,* and *The Intercept.*

"I had a press badge and tried to tell them I was press," a journalist, who asked not to be identified, told the lefty website *AlterNet.* "Two flash-bang grenades fell within three or four feet of me. I had tinnitus in my ears for a couple of minutes. I yelled out for a medic, and by the time I could see, we were completely kettled. I was incapacitated."[8]

MDP officers reportedly let some journalists out of the kettle after they showed their credentials, but others who produced ID were not freed. None of their arrest reports made any specific allegations of wrongdoing. It was guilt simply by association.

Like the journalists, several of the protestors caught up in the teeming, terrifying kettle had nothing to do with anarchy or destruction.

Elizabeth Lagesse, a twenty-nine-year-old grad student from Baltimore, had arrived a bit late at Logan Circle along with her fiancé, Michael Webermann. Lagesse, a computational chemist (a writer of computer programs to simulate molecules), had just decided to leave school to pursue a Silicon Valley programming career in her native California.

Lagesse told me she had come to have her voice heard and show solidarity with so many Americans who were angry at the incoming president and mortified by his proposed policies. "He had major problems when it came to the way he treated women and minority groups," she said. "And I was really concerned about where the country was going to go with him: down."[9]

Lagesse, who said she had never been involved in any kind of violence, political or otherwise, had been to other protests and saw demonstrators pepper-sprayed by the police. She brought along a bandanna and old pair of lab goggles she had used as an undergraduate.

Lagesse and Webermann began walking down Thirteenth Street NW about a half hour after most of the marchers had left. She was dressed in a black-and-white T-shirt and a brightly colored jacket, carrying a long gray rain jacket under her arm. She was not wearing the bandanna or the goggles at the time.

Even so, the two were swept up into the kettle, despite not having participated in any acts of violence or vandalism. They had been too far away, in fact, to even witness any.

The police continued to spray people even after they were trapped in the kettle, with nowhere to escape. A toxic fog settled in, causing some detainees to panic when they couldn't breathe. They were caged there for hours in the chilly air, without food, water, or access to a toilet. Officers took their time as, one by one, they processed the arrests.

When one woman said she needed to use a toilet, an officer allegedly laughed and told her to shit in her pants to prove she had to go. With no other place to urinate, some relieved themselves in the street or alongside buildings. Others were seen rummaging through garbage cans looking for empty bottles in which to go. Someone crouched against a building and defecated into a paper bag.

One of the protestors who badly needed a toilet, Milo Gonzalez, had come down from New York to peacefully demonstrate. Now, wary of a public urination charge, he held his bladder, throbbing in pain. An officer saw his distress. "If you wanted to go to the bathroom," he sneered, "you shouldn't have gotten arrested."[10]

At that moment, just a few blocks away on the Washington Mall, newly sworn-in President Donald J. Trump was delivering his inaugural address. Trapped in the holding pen, Elizabeth watched it on her cell phone, gaping in disbelief as Trump went on about ending the "American carnage" that he said had been engulfing the nation.

It wasn't until early afternoon that the police finally began handcuffing people and putting them into transport vehicles. Shay Horse had been detained for seven hours and had not used a bathroom.

The zip tie cuffs were excruciatingly tight. They lashed through the skin of Lagesse's wrists, while Horse lost feeling in several fingers. When he complained, a cop told him, "They're not supposed to be comfortable." The pepper spray remained lodged in his long hair, which burned his face every time it made contact.

Horse, Gonzalez, and several other men were delivered to the Metropolitan Police Academy near the Maryland state line and led into a building that, with its mock street, looked to be a training area. Officers began searching Horse and Gonzalez. One cop patted Horse down and then jabbed into his anus, pushing his fingers through Horse's loose-fitting pants and underpants and into his rectum, ordering him not to "flinch."[11]

Several minutes later, the same officer patted down Gonzalez and ordered him to spread his legs, then to spread them again, this time wider. He reached inside Gonzalez's underwear and fondled his testicles. He then jammed his finger into Gonzalez's rectum, causing the man to cry out. He was ordered not to resist.

There was no reason to suspect that either man was hiding contraband, and none was found. The rectal searches were reportedly done with the same latex glove, an exceedingly unhygienic practice that can spread hepatitis, HIV, and other infectious diseases.

Horse was detained for a total of thirty-three hours. After his release, he became withdrawn and had nightmares and difficulty sleeping. He suddenly found it hard to perform daily tasks, such as typing or using his camera. His left wrist was scarred from the zip tie. His anus was sore for several days. He felt as if he had been raped. It would be emotionally taxing to report on future demonstrations, a big part of Horse's livelihood.

"I've covered several protests over the course of my career, but I've never seen police act like this in America and in broad daylight," he told me in November 2017. The effects of his arrest and detention that day were still with him. "A couple of fingers on my left hand are still numb. I continue to suffer stress and anxiety." He said he also has trouble sleeping, waking up every three hours.[12]

The arrested reporters and protestors may have begun their morning under the Obama administration, but their alleged misdeeds would now be punished, mercilessly, by the incoming regime that took power at noon that day.

Most faced felony rioting charges, the highest level of offense under Washington's anti-rioting law, which carries a maximum penalty of ten years in prison and a $250,000 fine. Most detainees were released and ordered to return for hearings in February or March. Virtually all of them had their cell phones confiscated, which, as we shall see, became yet another threat to free speech protected under the First Amendment.

Many of them said that they, their dignity, and their rights were abused by police.

"I felt like they were using molestation and rape as punishment," Horse told reporters after the incident. "They used those tactics to inflict pain and misery on people who are supposed to be innocent until proven guilty. It felt like they were trying to break me and the others—break us so that even if the charges didn't stick, that night would be our punishment."[13]

Lagesse, who had been detained overnight in a holding cell with twenty other women with little food and limited water, said she came to D.C. "to do a good thing: to express my concern about the direction of our country. You would think that of all the cities in the world, Washington, D.C., would respect my freedom of speech and right to peaceably assemble."

The arrests outraged First Amendment defenders. Carlos Lauría, senior Americas program coordinator at the internationally renowned Committee to Protect Journalists, called the charges "clearly inappropriate" and said they "could send a chilling message to journalists covering future protests." The committee demanded that D.C. officials drop the charges immediately.[14]

Jason Flores-Williams, an attorney representing three of those arrested, told the liberal news site ThinkProgress that the federal prosecutor's office in D.C.

"is now engaged in an all-out repression of dissent and sending the message across the country that we are going to crush you. Under the Sessions DOJ, states are going to have carte blanche to pass whatever local ordinances they want to eliminate, outlaw, and make protests extremely difficult."[15]

The new policies under Trump and Sessions, Flores-Williams said, were designed to "chill" the right to free and open expression. "They're prosecuting people for their associations, which violates the First Amendment," he said.

Over the next two months, charges were dropped for five of the journalists, who first had to suffer being sprayed, kettled, arrested, jailed, and indicted, incurring considerable legal bills in the process.

But Aaron Cantú and Alexei Wood were not off the legal hook.

Then, in April 2017, federal prosecutors from Sessions's Justice Department unexpectedly filed new charges against the protestors in a "superseding indictment" that added allegations of felony inciting or urging to riot, conspiracy to riot, destruction of property, and misdemeanor assault on a police officer.[16] If convicted on all charges, offenders now faced an astonishing seventy to eighty years in prison—some of them for throwing a rock through a Starbucks window, many of them for doing nothing illegal at all, including reporting on the event.

"The superseding indictment is sheer government abuse of power," Flores-Williams told *The Washington Post*. "They are prosecuting people not based on evidence, but for who they know and who they associate with. It's unconstitutional and repressive."[17]

Gregg Leslie, legal defense director for the Reporters Committee for Freedom of the Press (RCFP), told *The Post* that prosecutors "know that a handful of people threw bricks through windows and one person threw something at an officer. And they arrested over two hundred people. They know that everyone they arrested was not participating in a crime."

The first of the trials was not scheduled until November 15, 2017.

In May, attorneys for twenty-one of the defendants moved to have their cases dismissed (others soon joined the action or made similar motions). The prosecutions, according to the motion, were "based on a set of vague, nonindividualized allegations that can be interpreted, at best, as seeking to hold [those arrested and indicted] criminally responsible for engaging in a large political demonstration that was marred by the unlawful actions of a small number of other protestors."[18]

The following month, a federal grand jury indicted Aaron Cantú on eight felony charges. Cantú had since become a staff writer at *The Santa Fe Reporter,* an alternative weekly newspaper, which published an article in his defense. "Video from the conservative media group The Rebel shows glimpses of Cantú off to the side of the protests with other journalists, washing what appears to be pepper spray from his eyes," the paper reported. "He's standing next to a conservative journalist as she narrates the scene."[19]

The Reporter's editor and publisher, Julie Ann Grimm, called Cantú "an experienced journalist who disclosed this pending case during the hiring process. We stand behind him and look forward to his continued good work in his new home in Santa Fe."

The U.S. Attorney's Office would not say why charges were dropped against all the journalists except Cantú and Wood. A spokesman refused to comment on any of the pending cases.

In the case of Cantú, who was clad in black that day, the indictment said he was dressed "similarly" to rioters and carried certain safety equipment with him.

"That does not demonstrate that he participated in the protest," wrote Emily Miller of the Reporters Group for Freedom of the Press, on its website. "Wearing specific clothing should not be considered evidence of guilt. In addition, gas masks and other face-protecting items are legitimate tools journalists may use to protect against pepper spray and tear gas."[20]

What's more, Cantú made every effort to obey police orders, and, though he needed to be near the unfolding drama, he never took part in any violence. Indeed, the indictment against him repeatedly stated that he "did no more than move with the protestors through the city streets as others engaged in various violent or illegal actions," Miller wrote. "These and other statements demonstrate that . . . there is no evidence or indication based on the government's facts that he actually participated in the protests or committed any crimes."

For doing nothing illegal, Cantú and Wood now faced prison sentences that could outlast their lives.

In late June 2017, the ACLU-D.C. filed suit against the District of Columbia, Metropolitan Police Department officers, and D.C. police chief Peter Newsham on behalf of Shay Horse, Elizabeth Lagesse, Milo Gonzalez, and Judah Ariel, a volunteer legal observer whose neon-green hat clearly identified him as such and who was monitoring conditions within the kettle when the cops pepper-sprayed him without warning or justification.[21]

The complaint sought unspecified compensation "for making unconstitutional arrests, using excessive force, denying arrested people food, water, and access to toilets, and invasive bodily searches of protesters exercising their First Amendment rights on Inauguration Day," the group said.

In addition to violations of the plaintiffs' First, Fourth, and Fifth Amendment rights, the lawsuit also alleged assault and battery and false arrest, among other abuses, and violation of D.C.'s First Amendment Assemblies Act, which says that MPD officers cannot "substantially encircle" protestors without probable cause or the ability to identify those individuals who actually committed crimes.

Scott Michelman, a senior staff attorney at the ACLU-D.C. representing the four plaintiffs, said the police "did not make any efforts to single out any people who may have broken the law that day from innocent journalists. Actions like MPD's that punish journalists for being near the action will inevitably chill freedom of the press and, with it, First Amendment rights not only of the journalists themselves, but of all of us."[22]

"So many of us suffered tremendously just for exercising our First Amendment rights to cover the demonstrations or participate in them," journalist and now civil-suit plaintiff Shay Horse said in a statement. "With this lawsuit, I want to stand up for all the protesters who were abused and bullied and assaulted and molested."[23]

As for those who actually did conspire to and carry out acts of violence and vandalism, that is a crime with zero First Amendment protections and should be punished. But, I would ask, should it be punished to the full extent of the law—should they really face eighty-year sentences? Isn't it "cruel and unusual punishment," as prohibited by the Eighth Amendment, to lock someone up that long for throwing a rock through a Starbucks window?

THE EFFECT THAT CHILLS

The events of January 20, 2017, produced a ripple effect that could make some people think twice before joining any type of organized resistance.

A message is being sent to anyone considering dissenting in the public square. It's an unspoken threat that is getting more menacing by the day:

We know who you are. We know what you think. We know where you live. We know where you work. We know what you're up to, and we don't like it.

This insidious form of intimidation aimed at repressing dissent through fear has a legal name: It's called the "chilling effect"—when government tactics in one action dissuade people from participating in subsequent actions.

The chilling effect descends on free speech when working journalists are arrested for doing their jobs, and it sets off warning bells for anyone contemplating coverage of public dissent that they risk injury, arrest, humiliation, and prosecution, even if they commit no wrongdoing whatsoever.

"Restrictions on speech resonate over time and may constrain not only present speakers, they also chill future speakers," as Shahid Buttar, director of grassroots advocacy at the Electronic Frontier Foundation, a leading First Amendment rights group, explained to me. "Every act of repressing speech is accumulative."[24]

And, he added, "it not only threatens the rights of people whose speech is inhibited, it also undermines the rights of other people to hear those views."

In other words, when you arrest journalists, you block the free flow of news, which is critical to the health and well-being of any democratic republic.

Few specific legal protections exist for journalists gathering information, especially during situations of unrest. In 1972, the Supreme Court ruled in *Branzburg v. Hayes* that "without some protection for seeking out the news, freedom of the press could be eviscerated." But the justices never said what those protections should be, leaving reporters with no specific legal rights beyond those extended to the general public.[25]

It is hardly a cliché to state that free speech in America is under assault. Arresting journalists, legal observers, and peaceful protestors is just one use of the chilling effect in what many worry has become a full-scale war against the First Amendment. And if we lose that war, we will surely descend into a dystopian society of Orwellian-level repression, where free speech, and perhaps even free thought, have no safe haven, no place to live.

It is up to us, then, to protect and preserve this most fundamental right. The founders knew that without public dissent, democracy withers and dies. As George Orwell once said, "If large numbers of people believe in freedom of speech, there will be freedom of speech, even if the law forbids it. But if public opinion is sluggish, inconvenient minorities will be persecuted, even if laws exist to protect them." Purveyors of the chilling effect, I am certain, are acutely aware of this principle.

ARRESTED FOR QUESTIONING PUBLIC OFFICIALS

What sort of message is sent when security agents are allowed to harass, apprehend, and even arrest members of the media simply for posing questions of government officials in a public place? It happens. And if it continues to happen, it will set us on a course toward a country in which no person of power can be approached, except at a state-authorized press conference.

Take, for example, Shahid Buttar, who in February 2015 was executive director of the Bill of Rights Defense Committee (now called Defending Rights & Dissent), who went to Capitol Hill one day in February on a mission: to confront President Obama's director of national intelligence, James Clapper, over a false statement he had made, under oath, during a Senate hearing two years earlier.

At that March 2013 hearing, a rare open session of the Senate Select Committee on Intelligence, Oregon Democrat Ron Wyden had asked Clapper if the NSA "collects any type of data at all" on American citizens.

"No, sir," Clapper responded. "Not wittingly."

Soon after, Wyden asked Clapper's staff to explain his answer, which the director declined to do, at least in public.

Just three months later, former NSA analyst Edward Snowden dropped an electronic bomb in the form of thousands of pages of agency documents leaked to *The Guardian* and *The Washington Post,* issuing a wake-up call to Americans that the NSA was in fact collecting and storing data on them. In other words, Clapper had lied. This was domestic espionage.

Despite the overwhelming Snowden evidence, Clapper stuck to his guns and would not correct the record, even when given the opportunity. "What I said was, the NSA does not voyeuristically pore through U.S. citizens' emails. I stand by that," he told the *National Journal* on June 6.[26] (The NSA was collecting phone records at the time—not emails.) During an NBC interview, he said it was difficult to give a simple yes-or-no answer to Wyden's question, especially in an open hearing. "I responded in what I thought was the most truthful, or least most untruthful manner," he tried to explain, unartfully, "by saying, 'No.'"

But the "least most untruthful," of course, is still an untruth.

Buttar was incensed. By 2015, Buttar, who wrote news and opinion pieces for the Bill of Rights Defense Committee, thought that Clapper had gone unchallenged long enough over something that "one might describe as a criminal lie reflecting institutional corruption," he told me. Perjury is a felony. Bigger fish than Clapper had been punished for it, Buttar thought.

On February 26, 2015, armed with a digital recorder, Buttar entered the hearing room where Clapper was set to testify before the Senate Committee on Armed Services. He sat quietly until Chairman John McCain adjourned the hearing and everyone stood up. Clapper and his staff rose to greet the senators before leaving.

"And so, I stood up, too," said Buttar, now at the Electronic Frontier Foundation. As Clapper was heading for an exit, Buttar, from far across the hearing room, began lobbing questions in a raised voice, but not shouting.

"In March 2013, you misled the Senate Intelligence Committee about the scope of NSA surveillance," he began.[27] "What do you have to say to communities of color that are so hyper-policed that we're subjected to extrajudicial assassination for selling loose cigarettes when you can get away with perjury before the Senate?" asked Buttar, a Muslim American, referring to the July 17, 2014, killing of Eric Garner of Staten Island, New York, by an NYPD officer. Garner was being arrested for illegally selling individual cigarettes, known as "loosies," out of an opened pack. He died after a cop put him in a choke hold for nearly twenty seconds.

An officer standing near Buttar tried to silence him. "This is your only warning," he said. "If you continue, you will be placed under arrest." But Buttar persisted. Within ten seconds, he was put in cuffs.

Even that did not silence him. "Why is your agency above the law, sir?" he continued as he was led away, but still within earshot of Clapper and several senators, exiting in awkward silence. "Why can you lie to the Senate about mass surveillance? . . . And, Senators, why won't you do your job? You're charged with oversight of these officials."

Buttar was placed under arrest, transferred to United States Capitol Police, and detained for several hours. He said he was charged with crowding, obstructing, and something called *incommoding,* "which essentially entails blocking someone's path, which I certainly did not do." Video of the incident confirms his account.

"I didn't intentionally set out to get arrested that day. I went to get the national director of intelligence on tape, responding to a question," he told me. "I thought it an issue of global importance." Buttar was posing his question "in a journalistic capacity," he said. "I think my arrest indicates that, whether intentional or not, the legal reality is that it implicates the right of the press as much as the right to speak.

"It's a public space. It's a public forum," he said, noting that it is not possible to disrupt a hearing after it has ended. "But it is still somehow illegal—in a country that claims to respect the freedom of the press—to ask a question as a journalist. I'm not so concerned about my own rights but the right of someone else to ask that question."

Buttar believes the Senate committee should have demanded the removal of Clapper from his position, if not the criminal prosecution of his alleged perjury.

"False claims about the scope of mass surveillance went beyond the lawyerly impulse to bend language," he wrote on his personal blog after his arrest. "We are talking about the creation of a corrupt enterprise diametrically opposed to the founding constitutional vision that inspired the world to follow our example."[28]

Before long, the charges were dropped. Buttar considered filing a civil rights lawsuit. In the end, he abandoned the idea, reckoning that the time, effort, and money required could easily outstrip his own resources.

But he is still angry—for the arrest, for his unlawful detainment, and for the abridgment of his rights as a citizen journalist. "There was a criminal in the hearing, and it wasn't me," he said. "And yet I'm the one who ended up in handcuffs."

It is important to remember that Buttar's arrest and potential prosecution took place on federal property "under a supposedly liberal administration," Buttar said. "There is an inclination to peg these abuses to the current president [Trump]. But they are more systemic than rooted in just one personality.

"My experience," Buttar added, "was a precursor for the one that happened in West Virginia. It was a different setting, under a different president, but with the same results."

He was talking about May 9, 2017, when Daniel Ralph Heyman, a veteran health reporter working for the Public News Service of West Virginia, shouted a question at then health and human services secretary Tom Price and White House senior advisor Kellyanne Conway as they walked down a public hallway.

The two senior Trump officials had just arrived in Charleston, West Virginia (aboard a private jet at taxpayers' expense and on the same day that Trump fired FBI director James Comey), and headed straight for the state capitol for a conference on opioid abuse.

Neither the police nor Secret Service agents told Heyman, who was clearly marked as a journalist with an official press pass and shirt bearing his organization's logo, not to approach the secretary or ask any questions. He pulled out his recorder and hurried down the hall after the passing health official, repeatedly asking him if domestic violence "would be considered a preexisting condition under the proposed American Health Care Act," the Obamacare "repeal and replace" measure supported by Price and Trump but eventually doomed to failure in the Congress.

Suddenly, capitol security officers rushed Heyman, seized him by the back of his neck, and shoved the fifty-four-year-old against a wall. He was arrested and charged with "disruption of government processes," a misdemeanor punishable by a $100 fine and up to six months in jail.

The criminal complaint alleged that Heyman was "aggressively breaching the Secret Service agents to the point where the agents were forced to remove him a couple of times from the area." It accused him of "yelling questions" at Price and Conway—as if that were a crime.[29]

Heyman talked about his ordeal at a press conference, telling fellow reporters that he was "trying to do my job." But the secretary had ignored him and repeatedly refused to answer any questions. "He didn't say anything," Heyman said. "So, I persisted." He added that his arrest set a "terrible example" for other reporters trying to seek truth from power.

Witnesses told the Public News Service that Heyman's behavior had not been the least bit aggressive. "Just simple, you know, trying to get somebody's attention and ask them a question," said one woman, a health care activist, who had been in the hallway. "It seems to me there was no violation of anyone's space, or physicality, other than the arrest itself."[30]

The soon-to-be disgraced and ousted Price (for his private flights) had nothing but praise for the police. Speaking alongside Conway the next day at another opioid conference in Concord, New Hampshire, he thanked the officers for "doing what they thought was appropriate," adding that it wasn't up to him to determine if a reporter should be arrested for merely asking a question.[31]

"That gentleman was not in a press conference," Price said in defense of the officers, as if press conferences were the only places where public officials could be questioned.

The ACLU of West Virginia called the charges "a blatant attempt to chill" an independent press. "We have a president who calls the media 'fake news' and resists transparency at every turn," the group said. "This is a dangerous time in the country."[32]

Heyman's lawyer, Tim DiPiero, told reporters on a conference call that he had "never had a case in which a guy got in trouble for speaking, for talking loud." He and Public News Service CEO Lark Corbeil called on prosecutors to drop the criminal charge. "It's an overreach," Corbeil said.[33]

The case received considerable coverage.

Many members of the public agreed that arresting a reporter simply for asking a fair policy question of a high-ranking Trump administration official was a direct assault on free speech. In the days following the incident, donations to the Public News Service spiked. The Reporters Committee for the Freedom of the Press received 250 donations in the first week—as opposed to its average of two per week—including $50,000 from Meryl Streep and $1 million from Jeff Bezos, owner of *The Washington Post* and CEO of Amazon. It was the largest donation in the committee's forty-six years.[34]

Two weeks after Heyman's arrest, at a Reporters Committee award event in Manhattan, honoree Kathleen Carroll, formerly of the Associated Press, attacked the Trump administration for abusing press freedoms and excoriated the president for calling reporters an "enemy of the people."[35]

"Are you kidding me? The real enemies of the people are secrecy—and downright lies," Carroll said. "We must put our competitiveness aside when our fundamental rights are being attacked. When someone gets arrested for asking a question," she said, referring to Heyman, "we'd better be prepared for much worse."

In early September 2017, Kanawha County prosecutors issued a statement. "After a careful review of the facts," they had determined that Heyman's conduct, "while it may have been aggressive journalism, was not unlawful." The charge was dismissed.[36]

Rules do exist pertaining to how closely reporters can get in the faces of the powerful, especially those with Secret Service protection, according to Robert W. Jensen, media law and ethics professor at the University of Texas School of Journalism. But it was alarming that Trump and his regime have "engaged in something like open warfare with journalists," he told *USA Today*. "Every time there is a further infringement on the rights of journalists who both collect and disseminate information in this type of atmosphere, it's troubling."[37]

The prospect of six months in jail for asking a question as a journalist "was pretty troubling," Heyman told the Associated Press. "I don't want my arrest to have a chilling effect on other reporters because we all need to keep asking the tough questions of elected officials."

LAUGH AT SESSIONS, GET YOURSELF ARRESTED

If reporters can be arrested for confronting public officials, then it stands to reason that protestors can, too. But what if their only offense is to laugh at someone?

The incident involves former U.S. attorney general Jeff Sessions, who, on January 10, 2017, appeared before the Senate Judiciary Committee for his confirmation hearing, the same hearing where he famously denied having any contact with Russian officials during the 2016 campaign.

Desiree Fairooz, sixty-one, a grandmother, retired children's librarian, seasoned activist for gender equality, and prominent member of the women-led peace group Code Pink, was seated in the back of the spectators along with several other activists, wearing a T-shirt reading "Support civil rights! Stop Sessions," and a pink foam Statue of Liberty crown emblazoned with the words *Code Pink*.

Senator Richard Shelby (R-AL) introduced his fellow Alabaman, extolling his record and exclaiming that his long history of "treating all Americans equally under the law is clear and well-documented."[38]

Sessions, who was then an Alabama senator and the first senator to endorse Donald Trump, was also one of the most far-right members of that body, with

a record to match on civil rights, women's rights, voting rights, LGBT equality, and other issues.

Fairooz found Shelby's platitudes humorous, given Sessions's votes against
a number of civil rights bills. Spontaneously, she laughed. Twice. It was neither a loud guffaw nor a theatrical attempt at ridicule, as evidenced by a video
of the incident taken by another protester. Her offhand chuckle in no way dis-
rupted or even affected Shelby's introduction. It's not clear that he even noticed it.[39]

But a Capitol Police officer heard it. She approached Fairooz and asked her
to leave the hearing. "Why?" Fairooz asked, promising to remain quiet. At that,
the officer called over two of her colleagues, who helped forcibly lift the activist from her chair.

That's when it dawned on Fairooz that she was about to be arrested. "I was
upset, being unjustly removed from a public hearing that I had every right to
attend," she wrote in a personal account of her ordeal on *Vox*. She called Sessions's record "evil" and Shelby's comment "ridiculous" as she was taken away.[40]

The three officers led her down the hallway, out the door, and onto the sidewalk, where they searched Fairooz, confiscated all her personal property, put
her in handcuffs, and drove her in the back of a commercial cargo van to jail,
where she was repeatedly interrogated during her nearly ten-hour detention.

Fairooz was charged with disorderly and disruptive conduct intended to
"impede, disrupt, and disturb" a congressional hearing and "parading, demonstrating or picketing" on Capitol grounds. She faced a fine and up to one
year in jail.

Fairooz continued to live in shock and disbelief. "I let out an involuntary
laugh, or more of a chortle of disdain," she told NPR. "We were not warned
not to laugh."[41]

Following her arrest, Fairooz was ordered to appear at five separate hearings, about an hour and fifteen minutes each way from home. The night before every proceeding, she spent money on a dog sitter and a room at a D.C.
hotel, fearful that the Washington Metro area's notorious rush-hour traffic
would cause her to miss the hearing, potentially resulting in a $1,000 fine and
six-month jail sentence.

At trial in D.C. Superior Court, it was revealed that the officer who arrested
Fairooz had been on the job for just two weeks, and this was her first-ever arrest.

Fairooz's court-appointed attorney, Sam Bogash, had assured her that the jury would be sympathetic. On May 3, the jury returned its verdict: guilty on both counts.[42]

Fairooz was stunned.

As it turned out, some jurors were at least partially sympathetic but felt they had no choice in their deliberations. In interviews with the *Huffington Post*'s Ryan Reilly, several said they voted to convict Fairooz not because she laughed but because of her outbursts as she was led away, holding aloft a protest sign, a violation of the ban on "picketing." Some jurors thought the rookie officer went too far. But all of those interviewed "felt they had to convict because of the way the laws are written," Reilly reported. "There's almost no way that you can find them not guilty," one juror said, citing the statute. "There's not a lot of wiggle room," the jury foreperson concurred.[43]

Chief Judge Robert Morin gave Fairooz's court-appointed attorney two weeks to present evidence and arguments in motions to overturn the verdicts and scheduled sentencing for a month later.

"Ms. Fairooz's brief reflexive burst of noise, be it laughter or an audible gasp, clearly cannot sustain a conviction for either of the counts in the information," Bogash wrote in the court filing. "So the only other basis for her conviction to anything are her statements after the U.S. Capitol Police arrested her for that laughing. Those statements merely expressed surprise at being arrested."[44]

But government attorney Kimberly Paschall countered that Fairooz "did not merely laugh."

"Just as a defendant cannot resist arrest when the arrest is unlawful," she wrote, "a defendant should not be able to disrupt a hearing before Congress based on her opinion that police action was unlawful."

For her part, Fairooz wrote on *Vox* that it was "absurd that the government went to the expense of prosecuting me over such a petty action.

"I have to ask myself why," she said, noting that other attendees laughed when Sessions was asked about disagreements with his wife and one spectator cried out, "You're under oath!"

No one else was arrested. Why single out Fairooz? She was not charged for laughing, she said, but because she was there in unconcealed opposition to Sessions's confirmation—a violation of her First Amendment right to political expression.

The arrest and conviction brought ridicule on late-night TV and alarm in at least certain halls of Congress. Representative John Conyers (D-MI), the ranking member on the House Judiciary Committee, wrote to Judge Morin complaining that "substantial questions" remained in the case. "I take seriously breaches of decorum in Congress," Conyers wrote. "However, in this instance, the finding of guilt under these particular circumstances raises questions that should counsel leniency with regard to sentencing."[45]

In July, Judge Morin made his ruling. He found it "disconcerting" that the government had made the case that Fairooz's laughter on its face was cause for prosecution and sentencing.

"The court is concerned about the government's theory," Morin ruled, adding that the laughter "would not be sufficient" to submit the case to a jury and "the government hadn't made clear before the trial that it intended to make that argument."

Morin overturned the conviction and ordered a new trial. Fairooz, while pleased to be exonerated, did not look forward to going back to court. She waited anxiously to see if prosecutors would finally drop the case or file charges once again. She rejected a plea deal that would have let her off for time served, arguing that doing so would be an admission of guilt. After all, she reasoned, she never should have been arrested for laughing to begin with.

On September 1, attorneys for Jeff Sessions's DOJ told the court they would try Fairooz, yet again, for the crime of laughing at their boss. The trial date was set for November 16, 2017.[46]

Fairooz said the endless persecution should come as no surprise. "Anyone paying attention since Trump became president knows that his administration doesn't seem to stomach criticism well," she wrote. "Retribution often follows."

And then just ten days before her trial's start date, the government abruptly moved to dismiss all the charges. A spokesman for the U.S. Attorney's Office for the District of Columbia refused to comment on the reason why. Perhaps they realized how ridiculous their obvious overreach seemed to late-night comics and the average American.

But Code Pink, which called the arrest "absurd," condemned the DOJ for pursuing the case as far as it did, suggesting that the chilling effect was their ultimate motive. "The prosecution of Desiree, including one jury trial, was a waste of time and tens of thousands of taxpayer dollars," the group said in a statement. "It was part of the larger effort currently being made to crack down on activists. From the January 20 inauguration protests, the Department of Justice is prosecuting two hundred people on multiple felony charges. We hope they will scale back this massive overreach and that the success we just saw in Desiree's case will encourage more people to protest in the halls of Congress and on the streets."

OBAMA: SPYING ON REPORTERS

If anyone had thought, back in the early days of the Obama administration, that the new regime was going to keep its promise to make transparency and press freedom overarching priorities, their optimism was quickly doused when Attorney General Eric Holder renewed an about-to-expire Bush-era subpoena of *New York Times* reporter James Risen. Risen had published a 2006 book exposing a secret CIA plan to sabotage the nascent nuclear program in Iran. The Bush, and now Obama, administrations wanted to identify—and prosecute—whoever leaked the information. The ensuing legal battle, in which Risen ultimately won his fight not to reveal his sources, lasted almost as long as the Obama administration itself.

Most people in civil-liberty and media circles had expected better of Obama, including Risen himself, who blasted the president over the subpoena and called out anyone in the media who still defended Obama. "A lot of people still . . . don't want to believe that Obama wants to crack down on the press and whistle-blowers," he said in an interview with *The Times'* Maureen Dowd. "But he does. He's the greatest enemy to press freedom in a generation."[47]

Risen was hardly alone. Fourteen Pulitzer Prize–winning journalists each issued individual statements—released together—in solidarity with the seasoned *Times* reporter. "Enough is enough," wrote David Barstow, whose own reporting for *The New York Times* earned him three Pulitzer Prizes. "I've felt the chill firsthand," he said. "Trusted sources in Washington are scared to talk by telephone, or by email, or even to meet for coffee. My fellow investigative reporters commiserate about how we're being forced to act like drug dealers, taking extreme precautions to avoid leaving any digital breadcrumbs about where we've been and who we've met."[48]

Another incident, largely ignored by much of the media but well covered in conservative circles, took place outside Washington, D.C., in the Maryland suburbs on August 6, 2013. At 4:30 in the morning, Maryland State Police and a federal agent with Homeland Security's Coast Guard Investigative Service raided the home of Paul Flanagan and his wife, Audrey Hudson. Armed with guns and a search warrant, they said they had probable cause that Flanagan was harboring illegal firearms, based on his past convictions for similar crimes and an interview conducted with him by the U.S. Coast Guard, his employer.

But Paul Flanagan's guns, apparently, were not the only target of the raid. Audrey Hudson was an investigative reporter for the conservative *Washington Times* up until 2010. Her work had sparked congressional inquests and won several journalism awards, including the Society of Professional Journalists Dateline Award in Investigative Reporting. Much of it in recent years had focused on deficiencies in the Transportation Security Administration (TSA), which was created in the aftermath of the 9/11 attacks. In 2005, Hudson reported in *The Times* that federal air marshals were aboard fewer than 10 percent of all domestic and international flights during December 2004, and that department officials had inflated the actual numbers.

It was the Coast Guard agent who seemed most interested in Hudson's TSA documents. The Coast Guard, the Federal Air Marshal Service, and the TSA are all part of the U.S. Department of Homeland Security (DHS). The agent spent most of his time rifling through the reporter's belongings.

Hudson was not aware that the agent had seized anything until a few weeks later, when a federal law-enforcement official told her she could pick up the files. The agent had seized reams of papers that included government documents, personal notes, transcripts from interviews highlighting problems with the air marshal service, and papers listing confidential sources and whistleblowers at DHS. Many of the government documents were marked as not for public release. The agent seized everything, even though the search warrant made no mention of Homeland Security Department documents, and despite protests by Hudson that every piece of paper had been obtained legally through the FOIA process.

The Washington Times cried foul. "There is no reason for agents to use an unrelated gun case to seize the First Amendment protected materials of a reporter," *Times* editor John Solomon said in the paper. "This violates the very premise of a free press, and it raises additional concerns when one of the seizing agencies was a frequent target of the reporter's work."[49]

After reviewing every document, the government conceded that they had all been obtained illegally. But that was not enough: Hudson and the paper filed a federal civil lawsuit against DHS.[50] In September 2014, the case was settled. Hudson received $50,000, and DHS agreed to order a review of training for its Coast Guard criminal investigators and return all documents to Hudson with a promise not to make copies and destroy any notes taken on them. It also paid *The Times* $25,000 in legal fees, a small fraction of what was spent, according to the newspaper.[51]

"To have someone steal my source information and know it could impact people's careers is disgusting, a massive overreach," Hudson told *The Times*. "This kind of conduct is intimidation clearly aimed at silencing a vigorous press."

While the Hudson affair received scant attention—despite its frightening specter of the illegal search and seizure of a reporter's personal papers—what happened at the Associated Press (AP) ignited a media firestorm. In May 2015, the AP ran a story about a CIA operation, personally approved of by Holder, that secretly subpoenaed records from at least twenty AP reporters' phone lines, via Verizon, over a two-month period, in an attempt to identify a source. The reporters were looking into a CIA operation that foiled Yemeni terrorist Fahd al-Quso's plot to detonate an explosive device on a commercial flight.[52]

The domestic spying startled American journalism, setting the industry on a collision course, at least temporarily, with the Obama administration. It was nothing short of a "massive and unprecedented intrusion into news-gathering operations," AP CEO Gary Pruitt said. "These records potentially reveal communications with confidential sources across all the news-gathering activities undertaken by the AP [and] provide a road map to AP's news-gathering operations and disclose information about AP's activities and operations that the government has no conceivable right to know."[53]

The Orwellian surveillance was contrary to all previous customs and practices at DOJ, in which the department would notify the subject of an investigation in advance to see if some type of agreement other than a subpoena could be reached. As the AP reported, Verizon neither challenged the subpoena nor alerted the journalists whose records were being requested.

About a week later, the nation learned that the Justice Department had also monitored the activities of Fox News's James Rosen in 2010 while he was reporting from the State Department. DOJ obtained a secret order to spy on

Rosen after he filed a June 11, 2009, report that U.S. intelligence believed North Korea might respond to tighter United Nations sanctions with new nuclear tests. Rosen attributed the information to "CIA sources." According to *The Washington Post,* DOJ had tracked Rosen's visits to the State Department through phone traces, timing of calls, and his personal emails. Agents even looked at his parents' phone records.[54] The warrants issued against Rosen called him a "criminal co-conspirator" and described the highly respected reporter as a "flight risk." Eric Holder had personally signed off on the covert action.[55]

Public reaction, again, was swift and harsh.

"This is the first time that the federal government has moved to this level of taking ordinary, reasonable, traditional, lawful reporter skills and claiming they constitute criminal behavior," conservative commentator Judge Andrew Napolitano said on Fox News. Liberal journalists condemned the spying as well. *Washington Post* columnist Dana Milbank said it was "as flagrant an assault on civil liberties as anything done by George W. Bush's administration," which deployed technology to silence critics "in a way Richard Nixon could only have dreamed of."[56]

The Justice Department was unbowed, saying in a statement that it had followed "all applicable laws, regulations and policies," before seeking an "appropriately tailored search warrant" under the Privacy Protection Act.[57]

To me, however, none of the spying was as pernicious and persistent as that conducted against Sharyl Attkisson, who at the time was a respected reporter at *CBS Evening News.* Her legal battle with the Obama Justice Department over what happened to her continues today under the Trump administration.

Sharyl, whom I count as both a colleague and a friend, has been a hard-hitting investigative journalist on television for nearly forty years. Currently the creator and host of the widely syndicated Sunday morning news show *Full Measure,* she was an anchor and correspondent for CNN from 1990 until 1993, when she went to CBS, where she worked for twenty-one years.

Sharyl has taken on Republican scandals, such as the 2008 TARP bank bailout and Iraq contract waste and fraud under George W. Bush, and Democratic ones, including Obama's Fast and Furious gunrunning fiasco, the ill-fated grant to the Solyndra solar power company, and Benghazi, which was or wasn't a scandal, depending on whom you ask (Sharyl thinks it was).

That's when weird things started happening around her house in Northern Virginia.

One night early on in her Fast and Furious investigation, Sharyl woke up to a familiar sound at an unfamiliar time: Her Toshiba laptop provided by CBS was turning itself on and then off again late into the night. It continued happening intermittently, always in the wee hours. At some point, her personal Apple desktop began starting up and then turning off at night, too. Sharyl and her husband, Jim Attkisson, chalked it up to a technical glitch.[58]

What followed was a multiyear deep dive into her hard drives by forensic computer experts and former intelligence agents. They all reached a consensus: Her communications were being intercepted, likely by people inside both her phone and internet provider and the federal government.

She believes that they had spied on her in more ways than one, including keystroke monitoring, extraction of data, audio surveillance of Sharyl's conversations, and activities at home, mining personal passwords, monitoring work and private email, and probable compromise of her work and personal smartphones.

Curiously, according to forensic experts who examined her computer, the spies had also placed three classified government documents deep inside Sharyl's hard drive. She surmised that they may have been left there in order to justify the improper surveillance or perhaps implicate a whistle-blower she was communicating with for having supposedly passed along secret information. In 2014, she discovered that a communications channel in her laptop was directly connected to an IP address belonging to the U.S. Postal Service, of all agencies, indicating unauthorized surveillance.

But why the U.S. Postal Service? The USPS is known to have close ties to the FBI, the Department of Homeland Security, and DOJ when conducting computer surveillance and forensic actions, one of the computer forensic experts told Sharyl.

In late December 2014, Sharyl, Jim, and their daughter, Sarah Judith Starr Attkisson, filed suit in Superior Court of the District of Columbia against Attorney General Holder, U.S. postmaster general Patrick Donahoe, and "unknown agents of the Department of Justice, United States Postal Service and the United States."

The suit alleged "misconduct in exceeding restraints on the exercise of governmental power imposed by our country's Constitution, laws, and traditions, including illegal surveillance and cyber-attacks of personal computers and phone systems through the remote installation of sophisticated spyware and the use of an IP address owned, controlled and operated by the federal government." Such activity, it added, was in direct violation of the First Amendment, the Fourth Amendment, and a host of federal and Virginia Commonwealth laws. The spying, likewise, distracted her from her duties as an investigative reporter and "chilled her First Amendment rights," while also causing "irreparable tension in Ms. Attkisson's relationship with her employer."

In November 2017, the court abruptly granted the government's motion to dismiss.[59] "We hired a constitutional lawyer and appealed to Fourth Circuit," Sharyl told me. "The government's response is due in early November 2018. I'm fairly confident, about 70–30, that part of the dismissal will be overturned and sent back for further progress." Her confidence was well founded: The judge granted oral arguments and set them for January 29, 2019.[60]

Meanwhile, the future, Sharyl fears, is far from rosy. "It makes me think that our system is so entrenched with this sort of thing that it can never be rooted out," she told me. "It's certainly not everybody in the government that's dishonest, because people in the government are the ones that helped me expose this. But it's clear to me this is so deep, and it makes the people with those kinds of technologies and knowledge so powerful."

DONALD TRUMP'S ASSAULT ON THE AMERICAN MEDIA

"I would never kill them but I do hate them," Donald Trump once joked at a rally, pointing at the raft of reporters in the back of the hall.[61]

The hatred has been palpable since the beginning. Within weeks of taking office in January 2017, the new president began his direct assault on the free press with (what else?) an off-kilter tweet:

> *The FAKE NEWS media (failing @nytimes, @CNN, @NBCNews and many more) is not my enemy, it is the enemy of the American people. SICK!*[62]

A week later, speaking at the annual Conservative Political Action Conference (CPAC), Trump repeated the charge, with relish. "The fake news media doesn't tell the truth," he said, adding that journalists should be barred from using anonymous sources, something that would make investigative report-ing virtually impossible.[63]

"We're going to do something about it," the president said. An empty threat, to be sure, but a threat nonetheless.

Calling reporters the "enemy of the people," of course, is nothing new. The tactic was popularized by Joseph Stalin and used by Chairman Mao as well. Nikita Khrushchev, who succeeded Stalin, banned the term as maligning an entire class of citizens. As retiring senator Jeff Flake (R-AZ) told MSNBC, "I don't think that we should be using a phrase that's been rejected as too loaded by a Soviet dictator."

Trump has also routinely labeled members of the "fake news" as "foolish people," "liars," "scum," "slime," and "disgusting."

The litany of attacks seems unending. Trump reportedly asked former FBI director James Comey to imprison reporters who publish classified material, even though courts have ruled that is protected speech under the First Amend-ment. Meanwhile, he is reviewing policies for subpoenaing journalists cover-ing whistle-blower cases and once advocated the prosecution of WikiLeaks. Trump also thought it was good fun to retweet doctored video of himself wres-tling a CNN reporter to the ground and a bloody image of his campaign obliterating another CNN reporter with a steaming locomotive.

The Trump team's disdain for the media was further spotlighted in Octo-ber 2017, during the ugly controversy after the combat death of Sergeant La David Johnson in Niger. Press Secretary Sanders rebuked reporters after Chief of Staff John Kelly had called Representative Frederica Wilson (D-FL) an "empty barrel" who lied about remarks she had made at an FBI event in 2015.

Video had surfaced confirming Wilson's account and refuting Kelly's, and the press had questions.

"If you want to go after General Kelly, that's up to you," the press secre-tary said, her face etched in a stern scowl, her tone deadly serious, "but I think that if you want to get into a debate with a four-star Marine general, I think that's something highly inappropriate."[64]

Journalists and all defenders of press freedom were outraged by her attempt at intimidation. Whether Kelly was a Marine general or not was immaterial (in fact, he is a retired civilian); he was arguably, at the time, the most influen-tial advisor in the entire executive branch, someone for whom questions from

the Fourth Estate are anything but "inappropriate." Not to mention that he
went to war to defend Americans' right to question anybody, including gen-
erals.

Later in the day, in an email to CNN, Sanders walked back her remarks,
but not far enough. While conceding the obvious, that "everyone can be questioned," she went on to say that "we should all be able to agree that impugning
his credibility on how best to honor fallen heroes is not appropriate."[65] But reporters were impugning Kelly's credibility on the congresswoman's statements, not on his honor paid to dead soldiers.

And, as I write this, in mid-November 2018, a federal judge has just ruled
in a lawsuit filed by CNN against the White House after it revoked the press
pass of combative journalist Jim Acosta, following a minor dispute with a White
House press intern over a microphone during a news conference with President
Trump the day after the 2018 midterm elections. Many major national news
outlets, including Fox News, had filed friend-of-the-court briefs on behalf of
CNN. Acosta and CNN had alleged that the White House violated his First
and Fifth Amendment rights and sought a temporary injunction to restore
Acosta's credentials. The judge, Timothy J. Kelly of the United States District
Court for the District of Columbia, granted the temporary injunction and suggested that the Trump administration had violated Acosta's due process rights
under the Fifth Amendment. That question, and the First Amendment claim,
would be left for another day in court.[66] Even so, *The New York Times* called
it "a win for media advocates and news organizations in a major legal test of
press rights under President Trump."[67]

When it comes to issues regarding freedom of the press, there are few greater
experts than First Amendment attorney and constitutional scholar Floyd
Abrams, who is perhaps best known for defending clients like *The New York
Times* against Nixon's attempts to bar publication of the Pentagon Papers. At
the close of Trump's first year in office, Abrams agreed to speak with me by
phone.

"There have been throughout the president's tenure, a sort of daily deni-
gration of the press, which also takes a real First Amendment toll," Abrams
said. "We have an almost never-ending series of threatening statements, some
of them from the president himself; sometimes overtly threatening, sometimes
implicitly so, but which, taken together, do give me increasing concern."[68]

Trump's outlandish tweets, at least at first, didn't terribly alarm Abrams, he said, "in part because he didn't seem to be pressing forward on them." After all, many past presidents have lashed out against the media, sometimes virulently, usually without serious consequences. "But this is the first president that I would be really worried about in terms of trying to do something about it—not just put pressure, and not just sort of mouth off when he's unhappy with it. I think what we're seeing here is a president who is more willing to advocate publicly [for restraints on] the press and what he wished he could do about it. Problem is with this president, we don't know that they're simply wishes."

Another well-known free-speech champion, Norman Siegel, former director of the ACLU of New York for fifteen years and a First Amendment expert, was far blunter in his assessment. "Based on the policies and practices that I am concerned about, I give him a failing grade," he told me. "That's an F."[69]

Siegel recalled how candidate Trump blocked several reporters and entire news outlets from attending campaign events, and the incident in late February 2017, when the White House physically barred certain news organizations from attending a press briefing.[70] "They selectively chose those that were favorable to the Trump administration to attend," Siegel said. "They actually banned *The New York Times, The LA Times,* CNN, and others. And that's a violation of the First Amendment, because when you selectively exclude the press, based on their viewpoints, in my opinion it's not only wrong but it's prohibited discrimination under the First Amendment."

Like many civil libertarians, Siegel concedes that, although Trump's record is abysmal, Barack Obama was not without his faults. His administration blocked access to Fox News for a brief period in 2009, he said, "and that's wrong, too."

Siegel added that Obama-era policies "were also not good on the press with regard to leaks, so I'm not giving him an A-plus. There were problems . . . but there was a sense that you had someone who was thoughtful, who knew the subject matter, and so the kind of chill and the kind of clear and present danger, it just wasn't there. You didn't have the kind of widespread erosion of basic principles and freedom and liberty that's now taking place."

Abrams was equally defensive of Obama. Though the Obama DOJ "certainly did go after a few journalists," Abrams told me, "I don't believe the Obama administration had a policy of limiting the First Amendment interests. One could tell that President Obama was, in the tradition of the presidency, irritated and frustrated with the press coverage of him at times, but I don't think anyone ever had reason to fear that he would really try to stop it in some way."

With Trump, however, "there is reason for concern," he said. "If we didn't have a written First Amendment enforceable as law by judges, I would be very concerned that this administration would just ride right over any of those traditions and just go and do what the president felt like doing."

Then there is the president's dangerous, disturbing—and ignorant—stance on "reforming" libel laws. Trump, of course, is fond of issuing threats of litigation, especially when his reputation is at stake. As a candidate, after several women accused him of sexual assault, he vowed to sue not only them but the media outlets that covered their claims. It hasn't happened yet. He threatened to sue the National Hispanic Media Coalition for calling him a racist and bigot,[71] and he filed an actual $5 million claim against Bill Maher, later dropped, for making an off-color joke about Trump's mother and an orangutan that is best not repeated here.[72] By Election Day 2016, candidate Trump had threatened to sue members of the media at least eleven times during the campaign, including *The New York Times,* twice, according to *The Columbia Journalism Review.*[73]

The intimidation could chill the work of journalists and advocates alike, said Lee Rowland, senior staff attorney with the ACLU's Speech, Privacy, and Technology Project.

"There is real fear in the advocacy community right now that those who are advocating for goals that are fundamentally at odds with this administration are being looked at not as people with differences of opinion but as potential targets for lawsuits," Rowland said in an interview. "Slander and libel accusations, congressional investigations, and the like, and there's no question that that environment cumulatively has a chilling effect even on an open and freewheeling debate on these important issues."[74]

Even after taking office as the highest public official in the land, Trump has openly talked of—and actually investigated—allowing officials to file suit against media outlets over unfavorable coverage. "We're going to have people sue you like you've never got sued before," he warned journalists during a February 2017 rally.[75]

Were that to happen, the chilling effect would be immediate and enormous. All but the most powerful companies, those with enough lawyers and cash on hand to fight litigation launched by the U.S. Justice Department, could dare publish something about an elected official that might land them in a courtroom.

Fortunately, libel laws are created at the state, not federal level—and there is nothing that the president or Congress can do to change them. Moreover, a 1964 Supreme Court ruling in *The New York Times v. Sullivan*[76] and other libel cases have made it extremely difficult for government officials to sue journalists.

"To change libel law, you would need to change the First Amendment, or those who interpret the First Amendment, the Supreme Court," Abrams told me. "And that's unlikely, highly unlikely.

"But," he added, "the language of it is troubling. The thought behind it, the intention or the expressed intention, is troubling."

Trump's intention to stifle the free press with threats of legal action was revealed once again in early January 2018, shortly before the release of Michael Wolff's bombshell, if perhaps not entirely accurate, exposé of the president and his minions, *Fire and Fury*.

Trump attorney Charles Harder fired off a letter to Wolff and Steve Rubin, president of the publisher Henry Holt & Co., saying his team was "investigating numerous false and/or baseless statements" in the book, publication of which would constitute "defamation by libel."

"Mr. Trump hereby demands that you immediately cease and desist from any further publication, release or dissemination of the book," Harder wrote.[77]

The threat, while troubling and bombastic, was meaningless, thanks to the First Amendment. Instead of ceasing or desisting, the publisher pushed up the release date and flooded bookshelves with an instant bestseller.

In a letter to staff and writers, John Sargent, CEO of the publishing giant Macmillan, which owns Henry Holt, pushed back hard at the blatant, unconstitutional attempt to impose prior restraint on the release of a book.

"There is no ambiguity here . . . we cannot stand silent," Sargent said. "We will not allow any president to achieve by intimidation what our Constitution precludes him or her from achieving in court." The act of defiance was meant not only to strongly support Wolff and his book, "but also for all authors and all their books, now and in the future. And as citizens we must demand that President Trump understand and abide by the First Amendment of our Constitution."[78]

SPYING ON PROTESTORS IN THE AGE OF TRUMP

There is nothing like social media to connect millions of like-minded people and organize them into political action, including the resistance against the Trump administration. But all those calls, posts, tweets, registrations, emails, downloads, comments, photos, likes, links, and more leave a trail—a vast digital repository of anti-government organizing, activity, and rhetoric that could be of great interest, and great use, to any administration with a penchant for oppressing dissent and bullying or even prosecuting perceived enemies.

The audacity of Jeff Sessions and his department's attempts to search and seize the electronic devices and records of anti-Trump protestors was breathtaking. Just like the violent roundup and merciless prosecution of peaceful demonstrators at the president's inauguration, the insatiable drive for personal data on citizen opponents started on day one. In fact, the two were intimately related. On that cold, chaotic morning, D.C. police confiscated all the cell phones and other devices of those who had been swept up into the kettle and arrested. They would be used by the DOJ to prosecute those arrested on felony riot charges.

Federal prosecutors sought and received a search warrant to open, or "crack" the phones, which were locked by personal passwords. The warrant granted permission to search for evidence against the defendants, including call records, text messages, contact and email logs, chats, search history, websites visited, photos, or videos, provided that they pertained to Inauguration Day, the protests, or other people involved.[79]

Elizabeth Lagesse, the chemistry grad student from Baltimore who was arrested along with her fiancé, said her phone had been seized and, as of November 2017, had not been returned. "They went through all of them and did their best to crack every phone, and they got into over a hundred of them," she told me. She said phones that used encrypted technology, including her iPhone, were not invaded.

But even the encrypted phones, it turned out, were not entirely immune to snooping. In 2017, prosecutors filed court papers seeking to enter into evidence data seized from eight phones, six of which were encrypted. Although investigators could not completely analyze the devices, they were able to extract "a short data report which identifies the phone number associated with the cell phone and limited other information about the phone itself," according to federal attorneys.[80]

But in all those other cases where full access was obtained, prosecutors treated themselves to a treasure trove of data not only on the phone's owner but everyone else they had contacted, followed, been followed by, and so on, *The Daily Beast* reported. The information gleaned allowed investigators to analyze the user's social networks, map their prior locations, and generate communications timelines.

There was also video of the protest taken by the protestors themselves. Prosecutors had downloaded some six hundred hours of footage and, in a court filing, said it would show evidence that each defendant did, in fact, engage in rioting.

But Mark Goldstone, a lawyer representing six of those arrested, said the images proved nothing. "Here's your client at the beginning of the march, wearing black clothes and goggles, your client could have left but did not, and here is your client at the end, in the police kettle," he said in a March 2017 conference call.[81]

Most of those arrested were not violent anarchists or black-bloc "professional" protestors. They were students, workers, journalists, and even lawyers acting as volunteer legal observers. The cracking of their phones potentially exposed reporters' confidential sources, privileged communications between attorneys and clients, and the internet habits of friends and associates of the accused to further police surveillance.

But Attorney General Sessions was hardly satisfied with merely snooping into to the cell phones of a couple of hundred rabble-rousers arrested in D.C. He wanted much more. He wanted names—more than a million names of American citizens with the temerity to oppose Donald Trump in public—and even in private.

In July 2017, the DOJ, in pursuing its case against the D.C. protestors, obtained a warrant ordering the internet hosting company DreamHost to hand over data on *every* individual who had visited a client website, disruptj20.org, which described itself as an online clearinghouse for "mass protests to shut down the inauguration of Donald Trump and planning widespread direct actions to make that happen."[82]

The government not only wanted to know who had visited the site but what pages they viewed, when they viewed them, and, according to the warrant, "all information . . . that might identify the subscribers [including deleted information], including names, addresses, telephone numbers and other identifiers, e-mail addresses, business information, the length of service, means and sources of payment for services (including any credit card or bank account number) and information about any domain name registrations."

DreamHost balked, saying that more than 1.3 million page requests had been made on the site in just six days following the inauguration. Clearly, only a tiny fraction of those users had anything to do with the D.C. protest. Most were nowhere near Washington that day.

It was a tactic, Trump critics said, aimed at cowing any potential activist, organizer, protestor, or even curious citizen from taking part in organized activity—including merely signing petitions or volunteering to make calls.

Finally, on October 10, 2017, Chief Judge Robert Morin granted the company most—though not all—of what it sought.

The government's warrant was so broad, Morin ruled, the ensuing investigation could "implicate otherwise innocuous and constitutionally protected activity." And though the feds had the right to execute their warrant, they did not "have the right to rummage through the information contained on Dream-Host's website and discover the identity of, or access communications by, individuals not participating in the alleged criminal activity, particularly those persons who were engaging in protected First Amendment activities."[83]

In simpler terms: If you were protesting Trump, unless you had been in Washington on January 20 and were observed taking part in a riot, Jeff Sessions and the FBI had no business looking at your online stuff.

The court, asserting First and Fourth Amendment "procedural safeguards," issued a declaration "to prevent the government from obtaining any identifying information of innocent persons to the website DisruptJ20." And, even after heavy redaction, the DOJ would still have to submit proposed search protocols and procedures for review and approval by the court before proceeding with any further analysis of the data. Finally, the court must find probable cause that the information sought was "evidence of criminal activity" by a particular individual and did not identify "innocent users" of disruptj20.org.

To many, what the DOJ was in fact seeking were the building blocks for a searchable political "enemies list," one that could be used by the department to monitor, harass, and even prosecute the most vocal critics of the president.

To me, the whole approach seemed right out *The Art of the Deal*, the 1987 memoir and business-advice book coauthored by Donald Trump: Come out guns blazing. Ask for everything and then settle for the most you can get.

Most of these stories on unconstitutional snooping have at least partially happy endings. But citizens should remain extremely cautious, Norman Siegel warns.

"There is no more right of privacy," he told me. "On the other hand, all these people who do Facebook and pour everything out there—police departments now review all this kind of material on the public domain, and they have a right to do that.

"I always tell people confession is good for the soul, but bad for the case—so be careful what you're putting on the internet, and your emails, text messages. And that is chilling, right there," Siegel said. "I always tell people, talk on the phone, rather than write it. And if you're really concerned, go meet the person in the street. Or the park."

OTHER FORMS OF SURVEILLANCE

Spying on suspected domestic troublemakers is nothing new. The constitutionally questionable practice predates J. Edgar Hoover and the FBI itself. It is neither peculiar to the Trump administration nor does it always happen at the federal level. Local law enforcement has been equally guilty of stretching—and overstepping—the rule of law when it comes to monitoring certain groups. As a New Yorker for more than thirty-five years, I am not proud of the fact that the NYPD historically has been among the worst offenders. The Associated Press called the department "one of the most aggressive domestic intelligence agencies in the United States."[84] NYPD surveillance and infiltration operations have targeted leftist progressives (e.g., Occupy Wall Street), African American activists (Black Lives Matter), and Muslim American groups, including mosques and student organizations, the news service said.

The activities were carried out by the department's intelligence division, which operated with virtually no oversight and refused to make public even its own organizational chart. Investigators with the division's cyber intelligence unit monitored activist groups' websites; undercover cops signed up for email lists about planned protests and gathered street flyers promoting demonstrations—all while officers and informants were infiltrating the various groups and taking part in their rallies and marches.

"Law-abiding liberals and their organizations are now cataloged in police files for discussing political topics or advocating legal protests, not violence or criminal activity," the AP reported in a bombshell 2008 article that published details from a secret NYPD report on its own spying on civilians.[85]

The use of such counterterrorism tactics to monitor protected-speech activity—some of it coordinated with the CIA and other federal officials and much of it the subject of civil rights lawsuits—yielded virtually no information on plots of violence or terrorism, foreign or domestic.

But the monitoring did generate information that would be useful to local and federal law enforcement: a cache of intelligence files on activists planning (peaceful) protests across the United States.

The infiltration and surveillance of liberal groups was ramped up significantly in 2004 in the weeks and months leading up to the Republican National Convention at Madison Square Garden, when NYPD intelligence officers monitored anti-war organizations, environmentalists, and even church groups—not only within the Metro New York area but around the country.

The spying, however, didn't end after the balloon drop on the final night of George W. Bush's nomination for reelection.

Some of it was inexplicable. In April 2008, for example, an undercover NYPD officer was dispatched to attend the People's Summit in New Orleans, where leading liberal activists were gathering to discuss ways to oppose U.S. economic policy and trade agreements such as NAFTA. The officer returned with a list of groups fighting against U.S. immigration policy, weakened labor law, and racial profiling, the AP reported. Two activists, Jordan Flaherty, a journalist, and Marisa Franco, a labor organizer for housekeepers and nannies, were mentioned by name.

"One workshop was led by Jordan Flaherty, former member of the International Solidarity Movement Chapter in New York City," the officer wrote in his report. "Mr. Flaherty is an editor and journalist of the *Left Turn* magazine and was one of the main organizers of the conference. He called for the increase of the divestment campaign of Israel and mentioned two events related to Palestine."

Flaherty, who wrote for *The Huffington Post* and insisted he was not an organizer of the summit, said the event he attended was actually a film festival in New Orleans that same week. Flaherty introduced a film about Palestinians but spoke only briefly. He failed to see why that landed him in police files. "The only threat was the threat of ideas," he told the AP. "I think this idea of secret police following you around is terrifying. It really has an effect of spreading fear and squashing dissent."

The police report "provides the latest example of how, in the name of fighting terrorism, law enforcement agencies around the country have scrutinized groups that legally oppose government policies," the AP reported, citing other instances such as:

- FBI agents who gathered intelligence on anti-war protestors.
- Maryland State Police who infiltrated anti–death penalty groups.
- Missouri counterterrorism experts who said that supporters of Representative Ron Paul (R-TX) might also support violent militias.
- Texas officials who asked police to monitor Muslim American lobbying efforts.

NYPD officials said the surveillance was justified because terror threats did not afford officers the luxury of opening an investigation and waiting until a crime was committed. They noted that department rules permit plainclothes officers to go anywhere that is open to the public and then prepare reports for "operational planning."

A decade later, the NYPD was at it again, this time spying on Black Lives Matter activists. In April 2017, *The Guardian* reported that undercover cops had infiltrated subsets of BLM and gained access to their text messages. The officers had posed as protestors in the wake of the death of Eric Garner, the Staten Island, New York, man who died in July 2014 during a choke hold after being arrested for selling loose, untaxed cigarettes on the street.[86]

The incriminating information was gleaned from a freedom of information lawsuit filed by New York law firm Stecklow & Thompson and raised serious concerns that the NYPD had broken rules governing its operations. Previously disclosed documents showed that the NYPD routinely filmed BLM activities and sent undercover cops to demonstrations.

Included in the documents were some photos and one video of activists at a protest at Grand Central Station, much like those taken by undercover transit police during BLM protests at Grand Central in 2015. But the images showed no criminal behavior whatsoever. The fact that officers took—and more importantly retained—them is a possible violation of New York City law.

Whether legally sanctioned or not, even the possibility of surveillance had a chilling effect on the group, according to Elsa Waithe, a Black Lives Matter organizer, who said there were "whispers" about certain people being possible informants. "Whether it was real or perceived, that was the most debilitating part for me, the whispers," she said. "It's really hard to organize when you can't trust each other."[87]

As it turns out, the NYPD is not the only law enforcement agency monitoring black activists. The Department of Justice is now fully engaged in it.

In the wake of Charlottesville—where thousands of racists, well-armed Klansmen, neo-Nazis, and assorted alt-right radicals descended on the college town with tiki torches, hate-filled chants, and a violent intent that culminated in the death of a peaceful counterprotestor and the injury of many others   instead of increasing surveillance of white supremacist groups, Trump's DOJ announced it would spy on African Americans instead.

In October 2017, the FBI's Counterterrorism Division declared that "black identity extremists" (BIEs) are increasingly planning acts of violence against U.S. law enforcement. Why? Partly because so many cops were shooting unarmed black men.

"The FBI assesses it is very likely Black Identity Extremist (BIE) perceptions of police brutality against African Americans spurred an increase in premeditated, retaliatory lethal violence against law enforcement and will very likely serve as justification for such violence," the division said in a report, which was marked "for official use only" but obtained by the journal *Foreign Policy* and published on October 6, 2017.[88]

"The FBI assesses it is very likely incidents of alleged police abuse against African Americans since then have continued to feed the resurgence in ideologically motivated, violent criminal activity within the BIE movement," the report claimed.

That same year, 2017, 987 people were shot and killed by police in the United States, including at least 223 African Americans, according to *The Washington Post*'s Fatal Force database.[89]

So how can government agents tell a BIE apart from other African Americans? The FBI laid it out: "Possible indicators for BIEs posing a violent threat to law enforcement include advocating for violence against law enforcement, violent *anti-white* rhetoric [emphasis added], attempts to acquire illegal weapons or explosives, and affiliations with others in both the BSE and sovereign citizen extremist movements."

The report was dated August 3, just nine days before Charlottesville. The reference "appears to be the first known reference to 'black identity extremists' as a movement," *Foreign Policy* said. "But former government officials and legal experts said no such movement exists, and some expressed concern that the term is part of a politically motivated effort to find an equivalent threat to white supremacists."

The journal said the term itself, *BIE,* was entirely new, having found just five references in a Google search, all of them police documents about domestic terrorism over the past two months.

One former senior counterterrorism and intelligence official from the Department of Homeland Security expressed "shock" after reviewing the report. "This is a new umbrella designation that has no basis," he told the journal. "There are civil rights and privacy issues all over this."

"They are grouping together Black Panthers, black nationalists, and Washitaw Nation," he said. "Imagine lumping together white nationals, white supremacists, militias, neo-Nazis, and calling it 'white identity extremists.'"

Muslim Americans have also fallen victim to intensive monitoring operations, much of it conducted by the NYPD. Since at least 2002, the department's intelligence division—which included the Zone Assessment Unit, Intelligence Analysis Unit, Cyber Intelligence Unit, and Terrorist Interdiction Unit—engaged in religious profiling and "suspicionless" surveillance of Muslims in New York City and environs, according to the ACLU. The massive sweep included religious and community leaders, mosques, student groups, civil and social organizations, businesses, individuals, and even a wedding for "pervasive surveillance that is discriminatory and not conducted against institutions or individuals belonging to any other religious faith, or the public at large."[90]

The police also spied on every mosque within one hundred miles of New York, extending its reach into Pennsylvania, Connecticut, New Jersey, and more.

Police tactics included the mapping of Muslim communities and photo and video surveillance of activities at mosques, including license plate numbers and police informants. The department also deployed police "rakers" (teams of undercover cops who are Muslim or speak Arabic that eavesdrop on conversations at restaurants and businesses, and identify Muslim "hot spots") and the tracking of individuals and use of intelligence databases to follow the daily activities of thousands of innocent New Yorkers.

Electronic spying was another integral part of the operation. One NYPD report from November 22, 2006, described the "daily routine" of logging on to websites, blogs, and forums of Muslim student associations at Yale, Columbia, the University of Pennsylvania, Syracuse, New York University, Rutgers, and the State University of New York (SUNY) campuses in Buffalo, Albany, Stony Brook, and Potsdam, among several others.

In March 2017, the ACLU, the NYCLU, and the CLEAR project at CUNY Law School settled a lawsuit they had filed in 2013 challenging the NYPD's "discriminatory and unjustified surveillance." The action was filed on behalf of "three religious and community leaders, two mosques, and one charitable organization that had all been subjected to surveillance."[91]

The spying had clearly chilled freedom of expression of religious and other beliefs protected by the First Amendment, "profoundly harming groups' and individuals' religious goals, missions, and practices, and forcing religious leaders to censor what they said to their congregants and limit their religious counseling," the civil complaint alleged. Many leaders felt compelled to record their own sermons, to protect themselves from being taken out of context by officers or informants. Charitable donations declined.

"It also diminished attendance at mosques, prompted distrust of newcomers out of concern they are NYPD informants, and prevented the mosques from fulfilling their mission of serving as religious sanctuaries," the ACLU said. Those offenses violated the plaintiffs' constitutional right to equal protection under the Fourteenth Amendment and their right to freely exercise religious beliefs under the First Amendment, the lawsuit alleged.

The final settlement, reached in March 2017, ushered in a number of significant reforms at the NYPD, including barring investigations in which race, religion, or ethnicity is a substantial or motivating factor; requiring "articulable and factual information" before police can open even a preliminary investigation into political or religious activity; requiring the NYPD to account for the potential effect of investigative techniques on constitutionally protected activities, such as religious worship and political meetings; limiting the use of informants and plainclothes police; imposing time limits on investigations with reviews every six months; and naming an NYPD civilian representative with power to enforce the reforms.[92]

"Our clients' experience is a cautionary example of what can happen when law enforcement goes awry," Hina Shamsi, director of the ACLU National Security Project, said of the settlement. "As religious bigotry rises to a fever pitch nationwide, New York City is leading by example against it."[93]

Federal officials and local police everywhere "should take heed," Shamsi warned. "When our police departments go too far, we'll be ready to fight back."

OUTLAWING DISSENT?

Just one month into the new Trump administration, massive protests erupted over the inauguration, the treatment of women, Muslim travel bans, climate change, and other issues that brought Americans out into the streets in record numbers. By then, at least eighteen state legislatures controlled by Republicans had hastily introduced at least eighteen bills designed to curb the rights of protestors and increase penalties for anyone who broke the law while exercising their free speech rights. Some bills would make it legal for motorists to strike demonstrators on public roadways.

"Democrats in many of these states are fighting the legislation. They cite existing laws that already make it a crime to block traffic, the possibility of a chilling effect on protests across the political spectrum, and concerns for protesters' safety in the face of aggressive motorists," *The Washington Post* reported.[94]

Critics, such as the ACLU's Lee Rowland, said many of the measures were not constitutional and would either meet defeat in their respective statehouses or be overturned by the courts. "The Supreme Court has gone out of its way on multiple occasions to point out that streets, sidewalks and public parks are places where [First Amendment] protections are at their most robust," she said.

Instead of advancing public safety or keeping roads clear, the bills were all designed to increase penalties for protest-related activity "to the point that it results in self-censorship among protesters who have every intention to obey the law."

Most of the bills died in committee or were killed by one statehouse or the other. In a few cases, GOP governors vetoed the measures.

Still, in 2017, a handful of proposals did in fact become law.

Nowhere did Republicans have more success than in North Dakota, where lawmakers passed laws that criminalize protests on private property where the notice against trespassing is "clear from the circumstances" and establish a trespass offense that allows officers to issue a citation and $250 fine; allow the attorney general to appoint out-of-state officers as "ad-hoc special agents" in response to large protests; increase penalties for riot offenses; and provide penalties for wearing a mask while committing a crime (including minor offenses) to avoid recognition or identification in any public forum, or in a group on private property without written permission.[95]

In neighboring South Dakota, lawmakers approved a measure to ban protests of more than twenty people on public lands in certain circumstances and expand the crime of trespass. It also permits the state Department of Transportation to prohibit protestors from stopping on the highway and criminalizes protests that stop traffic.

In Oklahoma, a law was passed to punish protestors who willfully trespass on "critical infrastructure," with heightened sentences for anyone who intends to harm the infrastructure's operations. It allows a $1 million fine for any organization "found to be a conspirator" in such trespass.

Perhaps the most egregious bills, none of which have passed so far, seek to indemnify motorists who hit demonstrators on the roadway, such as the one that passed the North Carolina House of Representatives by a veto-proof vote of 67–48 but still awaited action by the State Senate as of February 2018.

The "hit and kill" bill does not protect drivers from liability for hitting marchers who have a permit or if their actions are "willful or wanton." But it does cover anyone who exercises "due care" and hits anybody "participating in a protest or demonstration and blocking traffic in a public street or highway."

Republicans cited recent protests in which demonstrators, especially African Americans rallying against police shootings, blocked local highways.

"These people are nuts to run in front of cars like they do . . . and say, 'Me and my buddy here are going to stop this two-and-a-half-ton vehicle,'" GOP state representative Michael Speciale told *The News & Observer*. "If somebody does bump somebody, why should they be held liable?"[96]

But Democratic state representative Henry Michaux said state law already prohibits an injured party from suing if the injured party is even 1 percent at fault for an incident. Instead of giving drivers protections they already had, said Michaux, an African American attorney, the bill would be an illegal invitation to mow down protestors, especially black ones.

"Who demonstrates more than people of color?" he asked in an interview with *US News & World Report.* "It would give some folks the idea" to intentionally run over people "because you've got a group of black folks out here or a group of Latinos out here."[97]

The bill passed the House and was awaiting approval in the Republican-controlled Senate.

A similar bill was introduced in North Dakota—after the mother-in-law of state representative Keith Kempenich said she had been mobbed in her car by activists protesting the Dakota Access Pipeline. "If you stay off the roadway, this would never be an issue," Representative Kempenich said at the time. "Those motorists are going about the lawful, legal exercise of their right to drive down the road."[98]

His measure lost by a vote of 41–50. "Hit and kill" bills also failed in Tennessee and Florida, though proponents vowed to have them reintroduced.

Other bills that failed in Georgia, Iowa, Indiana, Mississippi, and Washington would have made it unlawful to block any highway, street, sidewalk, and/or other public passages. Iowa's bill called for penalties up to five years in prison, while Mississippi added a $10,000 fine to the same sentence. The failed bill in Washington was since reintroduced.

In Arizona, a bill that would expose protestors to anti-racketeering legislation similar to laws against organized crime syndicates did not pass. Claiming that most protestors are paid for their actions, it would also allow police to seize the assets of anyone involved in a protest that at some point becomes violent. It would also redefine rioting to include actions resulting in damage to others' property.

Most startling of all, the measure would have authorized law enforcement to seize the assets of anyone involved in a protest that, at some point and for reasons beyond their control, become violent, whether they were engaging in rioting or not. It passed the Senate. Fortunately, the Speaker of the House then declared the act to be "officially dead."

Other legislation was still pending, including a Washington bill to criminalize wearing a mask or hood while on any public street, sidewalk, highway, state building, or public lobby because "of a small but dangerous group of individuals who conceal their identities while committing illegal acts under the guise of political protest."[99] A measure in Oregon would require public community colleges and universities to expel any student convicted of participating in a violent riot.

Some bills aimed at curbing the rights of protestors have originated within the U.S. Congress itself. In July 2017, Senator Ben Cardin (D-DE) introduced a bill to criminalize *any* attempt by American citizens to boycott Israel. Senate minority leader Chuck Schumer and Senator Kirsten Gillibrand, a rising star in the party, were among forty-three U.S. senators to cosponsor the Israel Anti-Boycott Act, which the ACLU dismissed as being "antithetical to free speech protections enshrined in the First Amendment."[100]

The Senate bill targets the Boycott, Divestment, Sanctions (BDS) movement aimed at forcing Israel to abandon the occupation of the West Bank and Gaza Strip.

Violators of the law "would be subject to a minimum civil penalty of $250,000 and a maximum criminal penalty of $1 million and 20 years in prison" according to the ACLU. "This bill would impose civil and criminal punishment on individuals solely because of their political beliefs about Israel and its policies." In short, the bill would punish businesses and individuals based solely on their point of view. Such a penalty is in direct violation of the First Amendment.

Soon after cosponsoring the bill, Gillibrand, a future 2020 Democratic presidential candidate faced with growing pushback from constituents, announced her withdrawal of support unless language was added to specify that only corporations, and not individuals, would be subject to criminal penalties.[101]

Nearly a year after its introduction in 2017, the measure had gone nowhere in the United States Senate Committee on Banking, Housing, and Urban Affairs.

INAUGURATION DAY ARRESTS—CRIMINAL AND CIVIL TRIALS COMMENCE

After that historic day of pomp, circumstance, and pepper spray, D.C. police arrested a total of 234 people and charged them with felony rioting or other crimes. During the course of 2017, at least 20 protestors pleaded guilty to lesser crimes and charges were dropped against another 20. The rest still faced trial.

In late November 2017, I spoke with Elizabeth Lagesse, the chemistry grad student from Baltimore who had been arrested along with her fiancé, Michael Webermann, in downtown Washington on Inauguration Day.

The arrest had upturned her life and jettisoned her plans to find work in Silicon Valley. Mounting a criminal defense—as well as filing an ACLU-backed lawsuit against the D.C. police for the brutal treatment that she and three other plaintiffs endured—was daunting and exhausting. She even moved to D.C. to fight her criminal charges. But when you are facing up to eighty years in prison and $250,000 in fines, you muster the energy, she said.

"I am angry and frustrated and feel very powerless," she told me. "And honestly, I'm a little bit embarrassed that I didn't know how disruptive it can be even to come into contact with the criminal justice system—until it happened to me."

Lagesse said that, as a person who attends protests and could be a little bit of a contrarian—"even as a scientist, I question things"—she didn't realize the degree to which the system is "just so punitive and so unfair and disempowering." She felt trapped. "I can't make plans—my life has been put on hold for over a year. I've been forced to basically learn a whole other discipline of human knowledge: I was doing chemistry and programming, and now I've been spending all my time reading the law.

"In a way, it's been interesting," she added. "And in a way, I'm just utterly disgusted with the entire system."

Given all that the defendants had endured—the tear gas, pepper spray, kettling, arrests, detention without food or water, indictments, and superseding indictments with their expanded prison sentences—"the punishment is enough at this point," said Lagesse, who managed to get pro bono representation from a criminal attorney. "Even if they don't get any convictions."

And there was another worry: the chilling effect.

"This whole thing has already given many people many second thoughts about going to a Trump protest," she told me. "Even just in the group of codefendants, I know people have basically limited their own protest activity. I know people who've been connected to the case, their friends or family, or just because they've heard about it, who feel the same way. I've seen stuff on

Twitter, mentioning how they don't know if they want to go to a thing if this is what could come of it."

Lagesse herself has attended far fewer events than she might normally have attended. Now a resident of D.C., she said, "I live right in the heart of all of this. And I've only been to a couple of protests since this happened."

ACLU-D.C. attorney Scott Michelman, who represents Lagesse in her civil but not criminal trial, agreed that the net effect of the DOJ's prosecutorial abuse was scaring people away from protesting.

"What we're seeing in the law enforcement response to the Inauguration Day demonstrations is massive overreach at every level, from the law enforcement officers on the street to the charging decisions made by the U.S. Attorney's Office, to search warrants of individual Facebook accounts for their personal and political contents," he told me. "We've seen the government go aggressively after people who were voicing views critical of the administration. And that, that should concern everyone, regardless of political persuasion, because it's going to have a chilling effect on the First Amendment–protected freedom of speech."[102]

Lagesse denied all the charges and entered a not-guilty plea. Her trial was set for July 9, 2018. Wohlermann's trial was scheduled for September 10. In addition to fending off attempts to impeach her character, her lawyer would have to counter any government-presented charges, to show that no evidence existed to implicate her in any acts of violence or conspiracy.

Most important was to argue that one cannot be convicted of a crime simply for being in a place where crimes had been committed.

The indiscriminate roundup of protestors—such as the kettle deployed by D.C. police—"in all but the most extreme situations is going to violate due process," the ACLU's Rowland told me. "There's a phenomenal Supreme Court case, one of my favorites, *NAACP v. Claiborne Hardware,* that stands for the principle that you're not guilty of a crime simply because you show up to a protest and one person out of a thousand throws a brick through a window. That that violates your due process rights and your free speech rights."

How does it violate due process?

"Due process requires the state to prove that you had a criminal state of mind, that you had intent, and caused harm," Rowland said. "And when we say that those elements are met simply because you showed up at a protest with like-minded people, that's obviously guilt by association, and that's what the principle of due process is meant to avoid."

The mere act of being arrested, she added, "is a harm. Even if they let you go, you've been stopped from engaging in constitutional activity. And as the Supreme Court said in one of its better lines, 'The loss of constitutional freedoms, even for minimal periods of time, constitutes irreparable injury.'"

A few days after I interviewed Lagesse, those same legal-defense strategies were put to the test. On November 15, 2017, the first six defendants were brought to trial at the D.C. Superior Court. They ranged in age from twenty to thirty-eight and included residents of Pennsylvania, Maryland, North Carolina, and Texas. One of them was Alexei Wood, the independent videographer who was one of the nine journalists arrested that day.[103]

During the proceedings, which would last a month, federal prosecutors were forced to concede that, despite the mountain of evidence gathered in the case—including video footage captured from security cameras, police helicopters, and by the defendants and posted to social media—none of it depicted any of them engaging in acts of property destruction or violence.

The prosecution also submitted video they had obtained from Project Veritas, the controversial right-wing group known for altering videos and fabricating accusations to support conservative causes. Operatives of the group had infiltrated planning meetings to secretly shoot footage. In one, organizers discussed civil disobedience actions, such as linking arms to block inaugural attendees at checkpoints; events like the Festival of Resistance, which organizers billed as a "family friendly" venue; and ways to defuse confrontations with the cops. There was no talk of carrying out acts of violence or vandalism.

Likewise, dozens of witnesses who were interviewed could not identify any of the defendants as a perpetrator.

But, the DOJ attorneys argued, the government had mapped the movements of each protestor, and argued that none of the defendants had distanced themselves from the demonstration, despite witnessing violence. The defendants were, in essence, guilty of supporting and providing cover for their comrades, who left the pack of protestors to smash windows and set fire to a limo.

Defense lawyers countered that their clients were merely exercising their First Amendment rights and that the prosecutors had utterly failed to prove they were guilty beyond a reasonable doubt. It would be unjust to punish citizens for legally expressed dissent because of the criminal actions of a few other people they did not know.

On December 13, as the case was almost ready for jury deliberation, lawyers for the six defendants convinced Judge Lynn Leibovitz to dismiss the most serious charge against their clients: felony incitement to riot.[104]

"Personal enthusiasm for destruction of property is different to encouraging destruction to occur," Leibovitz ruled from the bench in a nearly hour-long oral decision.

Assistant U.S. Attorney Jennifer Kerkhoff protested the decision. "The defendants arrived with the organized and agreed-upon clothing," she argued. "This was not spontaneous walking into the street." The mere fact that the defendants had made the willing choice to join the protest clad in black "inherently" encouraged others to engage in violence.

The judge didn't buy it.

"I appreciate your argument, but I disagree," Leibovitz said. "I don't agree that the state of mind of wanting a riot to occur is equal to the state of mind of aiding and abetting the incitement of a riot to occur."

The defendants were elated. They waited anxiously to see if the judge would rule on the remaining charges.

Any lingering elation quickly vanished. Leibovitz not only refused to dismiss the charges—five felony counts of property destruction and two misdemeanor counts of engaging in a riot and conspiracy to riot—she suggested that the defendants were most likely guilty, as any "reasonable juror" could conclude.

The J20 six still faced massive fines and more than a half century behind bars each.

Leibovitz then let loose with surprisingly unabashed disdain for the defendants. "This might be a generational problem but the marchers [on video] seem entirely nonplussed by some pretty serious violence . . . what am I supposed to take from their apparent indifference to violence?"

The protestors, she added, had coalesced in the street "pretty thick, pretty swarm-like, and at that point there was certainly enough violence happening that any person there, in broad daylight, could be aware things might escalate." The six, she added, could have chosen "other alternative gatherings" to protest the inauguration.

Their decision about where to spend that morning, the judge said, could lead jurors to conclude that "the persons who gathered there were clearly in a conspiracy."

Even the two volunteer medics who were arrested—such as defendant Brittne Lawson, a registered nurse and trained street medic from Pittsburgh who wore a white helmet marked with a red cross—could be found guilty of rioting, the judge continued.

"Once a riot is occurring and she is a medic tending to people engaged in a riot, isn't she aiding and abetting?" the judge asked of Lawson's attorney. "Are you saying that unless she actually put a Band-Aid on somebody, she wasn't aiding and abetting?" she said.

The judge's remarks were not made in front of the jury, of course. Their decision would come a week later, on December 21.

As it turned out, the jurors did not at all share Judge Leibovitz's dismissive view of the accused, whom they found not guilty on all charges.[105] The six defendants gasped in relief, hugged each other, and began sobbing after hearing the verdict.

Although understandably relieved, some of them still expressed anger and defiance.

"This personally has changed the way I view the way I can express my opinions and how my associations can be criminalized," Oliver Harris, a twenty-eight-year-old graduate student from Philadelphia, told *USA Today*. "Things that I used to think I had a right to or the freedom to do before, I now second-guess. And to me, that's not freedom."[106]

Jennifer Armento agreed. "The government's charges are ridiculous. They really are an attempt to criminalize dissent in this country," she said. "We're not going to buy it. The jury didn't buy it. The American people didn't buy it and they need to drop those charges."[107]

Scott Michelman, the ACLU-D.C. lawyer who had filed the civil suit on behalf of Lagesse and the others, and who had filed an amicus brief in support of the six criminal defendants, hailed their acquittal as a significant legal victory.

"Today's verdict reaffirms two central constitutional principles of our democracy: First, that dissent is not a crime, and second, that our justice system does not permit guilt by association," he said in a statement. "No one should have to fear arrest or prosecution for coming to the nation's capital to express opinions peacefully, no matter what those opinions may be."[108]

Michelman urged the U.S. Attorney's Office to drop charges against the other demonstrators facing trial—including his clients Milo Gonzalez and Elizabeth Lagesse, whose criminal trials were still many months away.

They had reason for trepidation. The U.S. Attorney's Office vowed to press on against all the remaining defendants. "This destruction impacted many who live and work in the District of Columbia, and created a danger for all who were nearby," it said in a statement. "The criminal justice process ensures that every defendant is judged based on his or her personal conduct and intent."[109]

And then, on January 18, 2018, the unexpected happened. The government announced it was dropping all charges against 129 of the defendants. Their cases were dismissed without prejudice, meaning the government reserved the right to try them again. That left 59 people who would still be charged, still on all eight counts.[110]

Those fifty-nine defendants had participated "in an anti-capitalist march without a parade permit," prosecutors alleged in their Notice of Intent to Proceed, filed with the court. "This unpermitted anti-capitalist march was advertised and planned, with instructions for participants to wear black clothing. In addition, the term 'black bloc' was used by organizers in planning meetings," the document alleged.[111]

The planned use of a black bloc was "significant," it said. "The term 'black bloc' refers to a tactic, not a particular group or organization, and is frequently used when participants within the larger black-bloc group intend to commit violence or destruction of property."

The government said it was narrowing its efforts to focus on those defendants who engaged in "identifiable acts of destruction, violence, or other assaultive conduct"; took part in the planning of that violence; and/or engaged in conduct that "demonstrates a knowing and intentional use of the black-bloc tactic on January 20, 2017, to perpetrate, aid or abet violence and destruction."

Elizabeth Lagesse and Michael Webermann were stunned to find their names on the list of those who still faced trial. "The biggest feeling that I had was, *really?* We were only there for a very short period of time, and there is not anything connecting either of us to the alleged conspiracy," she told me. "It's an incredible feeling of frustration and disgust for the whole process. It seems so unfair and ridiculous . . . it's malicious prosecution."

Also on the list: journalist Aaron Cantú and Milo Gonzalez, the New York

City activist who had joined Lagesse and two others in the pending civil suit filed against D.C. police in June by the ACLU-D.C.

On January 3, 2018, the ACLU-D.C. amended its civil complaint, providing the names of twenty-seven officer defendants previously sued as John or Jane Does, including eight supervisors alleged to have ordered, and in some cases taken part in, unlawful conduct. One of them, on-scene commander Keith DeVille, speaking of the decision to detain demonstrators, testified at the first criminal trial that "I wasn't differentiating who was demonstrating and who was rioting," according to the amended lawsuit.[112]

It also added two new plaintiffs: Gwen Frisbie-Fulton, the single mother and activist from North Carolina, and her ten-year-old son, A. S., who were tackled, roughed up, and pepper-sprayed by the police on Inauguration Day.

Michelman told me at the time that it would be left up to the jury to determine any damages, because "many of them involve hard-to-quantify amounts. I mean, how much should Elizabeth get for the denial of liberty?"

Soon after that, in March, DOJ filed a motion to dismiss the civil case. Oral arguments were scheduled for July 2018.[113]

As for the criminal trials, in March 2017, the defense began receiving evidence that the government had collected and posted on a special DOJ dropbox accessible only to prosecutors, defendants, and their attorneys, Lagesse explained to me. By now, she had immersed herself full-time, eventually poring over more than three terabytes (or 3 million megabytes) of evidentiary data—digitalized documents, social media, and mostly, videos of the D.C. protest and several planning meetings. As she reviewed the materials, including several hundred hours of video footage, Lagesse began meticulously cataloging everything into a massive, searchable database, which she shared with the defense attorneys.

"There were more than two hundred lawyers, some of whom had not handled this kind of complex, multi-defendant conspiracy case before," Lagesse told me. Overwhelmed and each working individually, the attorneys simply lacked the time to cull through such mountainous evidence.

Included in an early batch of materials were four video segments taken at a January 8, 2017, Disrupt J20 planning meeting attended by at least three defendants who were now about to face trial. But there was something odd about them. "We didn't know where the videos came from or who shot them,"

Lagesse said. "It was a suspect item, filmed surreptitiously by a third party, and it soon was on the defense counsel's radar."

Then, during the first criminal trial of six defendants, in November 2017, it was revealed that the video had been shot by operatives of Project Veritas, which had previously been caught editing footage in a way that would make the unwitting subject look bad, while advancing their own right-wing agenda.

Lagesse soon realized that other videos placed in evidence had also been shot by Project Veritas. She shared that information with various defense attorneys, who suspected that the videos had been manipulated through edits. In March 2017, a group of lawyers filed a motion to compel the government to release the unedited versions. During the hearing, in April, the government admitted that it had made redactions but had only edited two brief segments—one depicting the face of the cameraman and the other showing an undercover police detective who was at the meeting. The judge ruled that all unedited video be made available so that the defense could make their own determination about what was and was not redacted.

The government put the unedited footage into the drop-box, but prosecutors downplayed their significance. They said the unedited videos contained about fifty minutes of footage taken before the meeting got under way, "disingenuously portraying it as 'pre-planning conversations,'" Lagesse said. "Because this email disingenuously downplayed the newly disclosed materials, lawyers did not closely examine this video. I did."

The redacted portion at the beginning did not reveal much, but the edited final few minutes were significant. In it, the cameraman can be heard speaking on the phone with a Project Veritas collaborator. "I was talking with one of the organizers," he said. "And I don't think they know anything about any of the upper echelon stuff."

Lagesse was astounded. She had learned enough about the law over the past several months to know that this evidence—which was deliberately withheld from the defense by the government—was potentially exculpatory.

"Some of those on the tape were claimed [by DOJ] as leaders, organizers of the movement, and those people were going to trial next," she told me. "But they don't know anything about what is going on. To take part in a conspiracy, you must enter into it knowingly and with intent to cause crime. It's called 'knowledge and intent.' It may not be proof, but it's undoubtedly important evidence to put things in context."

Not only did prosecutors redact the video, they downplayed its content and failed to point out the exculpatory evidence found in the final minutes of the unedited version. "They have an affirmative obligation to go out of their way to point to things that would benefit the defense," Lagesse told me. "They not only did *not* point it out, they lied about the contents."

Lagesse knew that withholding such evidence from the defense is a violation of something known as the Brady Rule, after a 1963 Supreme Court decision, *Brady v. Maryland,* in which the justices established a new pretrial discovery rule requiring the prosecution to turn over any exculpatory evidence to the defense.[114] She shared her shocking discovery with defense attorneys.

On May 22, 2018, the night before the next hearing for the six defendants about to face trial, their lawyers filed a motion asking the court to find a Brady violation against the prosecution, to suppress presentation of the video at trial, and to dismiss the indictments. The following day, Judge Robert E. Morin of the D.C. Superior Court ruled that prosecutors withheld potentially exonerating evidence.

He said his decision on dismissing the charges would be made the following week.[115]

On May 31, the judge dismissed all felony charges against the defendants, without prejudice, against the government's will.[116] His ruling also severely limited prosecutors' ability to argue their legal theory of the conspiracy charges for all remaining defendants, including Elizabeth Lagesse, she told me. Those charges were then dismissed, also without prejudice.[117]

Having the conspiracy charges behind them was a huge victory for the defendants, even though they all still faced trial on several other counts, including rioting. For Lagesse, "it did bring some relief, mainly that the court was finally paying attention and believing us that there was something bad going on here." DOJ then dropped all charges without prejudice against ten defendants whose trial was set for June 4, including several of those who were depicted in the Project Veritas video.

Everyone else still faced prosecution, including Lagesse, whose first pretrial hearing was scheduled for June 15. She was actually looking forward to it—it would give her a chance to expose, on the record, the corruption of prosecutors who had withheld evidence. "And we had even more motions pending alleging additional misconduct."

But it wasn't to be. On June 13, the government moved to dismiss all charges against Lagesse and seven other defendants—this time with prejudice.[118] Unlike with other defendants, their allegations of misconduct against DOJ could never be heard in court.

"I knew I had my feet kicked out from underneath me to keep doing this stuff," Lagesse said. "They would have had to answer to a lot of misconduct allegations that they did not want to answer." But now, "I have no legal standing," she said. "I can't do anything."

Just thirty-nine defendants remained in federal prosecutorial crosshairs, including Lagesse's fiancé. "That really made me angry," she said. "And it also really made me angry that they could hold this over my head for eight months but never give me an opportunity to rebut these charges—and then unilaterally drop them when it looked difficult for them."

On July 6, 2018, all charges against the remaining thirty-nine defendants were dismissed, including Lagesse's fiancé, Michael Webermann.[119] The DOJ had not won a single conviction at trial.

In my mind, Lagesse is a shining hero in this saga. If not for her dogged diligence, evidence of prosecutorial misconduct never would have surfaced, and dozens of people, including herself, would have been put on trial. She doesn't exactly see it that way, however.

"I like to think the lawyers would have found this stuff eventually," she said, "but in any case, I definitely accelerated the timeline. And I might never have found it. There were many intentional attempts to make it difficult to defend this case."

I asked Lagesse if she had any idea how much the government had spent on all the J20 prosecutions, which yielded just twenty-one plea deals, mostly for single misdemeanor charges with small fines and no jail time. It's hard to calculate, she said, but based on the salaries of the police and prosecutors working on the cases, and the average cost to prosecute a felony, she estimated the cost at a minimum of $4 million even before the first trial began in late 2017. The total amount is likely much higher.

"We had a gun homicide epidemic this summer in D.C.," she noted. "And if the U.S. Attorney wanted to do something, they could be working on that. But instead, they diverted at least $4 million to coming after us."

Meanwhile, as of this writing, the court had not yet ruled on the government's motion to dismiss the civil case filed by Lagesse and the others.

There was one other interesting coda to this story. After all charges were dropped in the remaining criminal cases, DOJ lawyers petitioned the judge to reconsider his Brady Rule sanctions by clarifying that the government had not behaved inappropriately. "They don't like getting in trouble on the record and wanted the judge to take it back." Oftentimes, she said, such violations are referred to the American Bar Association and the DOJ Office of Professional Responsibility for review, "after which point prosecutors can face ramifications, including ending their ability to practice law."

A hearing on the matter was held on October 12, 2018. Among those arguing against the government: Elizabeth Lagesse, who was also in the process of applying to law schools.

A month later, Chief Judge Robert E. Morin ruled that "the government did not fulfill its responsibilities" in turning over exculpatory evidence to the defense, but, Morin concluded, the government's failure was inadvertent, "and not an attempt to make purposeful misrepresentations to the Court."[120] Lagesse called it a slap on the wrist. "It's like he said, 'You are one hundred percent wrong, but I'm going to give you what you want anyway,'" she told me.

LOOKING AHEAD

Constitutional attorney Norman Siegel is worried.

"What keeps me up at night, and makes me really somewhat anxious about where we're going in America, is the fact that the erosion of something like free press, the opposition to that, is not as formidable as it should be," he told me. "And people begin, over and over again on TV shows and newspapers, to rationalize it, minimize it, trivialize what's going on by saying, well, that's Trump. As if this is the new normal and more acceptable.

"If the Trump people continue on this course" until 2020 or even four years after that, "America will be different," he said. "There's no doubt about it in my mind. And it's an America that we're not supposed to be."

Siegel said he had been speaking on college campuses and telling students "what the founding documents are about, and finally give them some hope—telling them, don't give up. Speak up. Act. These are principles that are important. We fought for it. Don't let people take it away."

He also called on "people of principle" within the media, "the owners, the publishers, people whose rights are being violated, to challenge the gathering storm."

It's not hard, he added, to see the "clear and present danger" in what's happening out of the White House right now. "And little by little, there will be people who will begin to write about it, speak about it, and try to oppose and challenge it—an umbrella of resistance to what's going on."

All is not dark. "We've always been aspirational," Siegel said. "Not a description of what is, but what we must strive to become. And we've had dark days before, and we've prevailed, and I think that I'm optimistic that we're going to prevail again. And what I mean by that is upholding core American principles and values."

The alternative is almost unthinkable. Freedoms that are lost little by little often disappear without much fanfare or protest, until it's too late and the loss cannot be reversed.

When the science fiction war film *Things to Come* came out in the late 1930s, people in London theaters laughed out loud at the scene of German bombers flying over the Channel to attack Britain. Americans now are mistaking reality for entertainment.

STATE POWER RUN AMOK

Do we live in a police state? Are we headed for one? The answers are no—and possibly. It's not difficult to understand why so many Americans are actually asking themselves such unsettling questions these days. It's difficult to turn on the news without seeing yet another story about law enforcement behaving badly—from the silly (raiding lemonade stands) to the disturbing (assaulting and arresting an ER nurse) to the lethal (a seemingly endless string of highly publicized police shootings).

But this is how police states begin. And if we are not vigilant and extremely careful about protecting *all* of our rights, we can—and probably will—degrade into one.

Previous chapters of this book mostly have dealt with violations of individual liberties that are explicitly singled out for protection under certain amendments, including freedom of religion, speech, the press, public assembly, and petitioning for redress (First Amendment); protection against unreasonable search and seizure (Fourth); due process and protection against double jeopardy and self-incrimination (Fifth); the right to a speedy trial by jury and access to counsel (Sixth); protection against excessive bail and fines and a ban on cruel and unusual punishment (Eighth); and equal protection under the law (Fifth and Fourteenth).

But what about those rights that we take for granted, yet are never mentioned in the Bill of Rights? The founding document says nothing, for example, about any explicit right to privacy. There is likewise no mention of other pressing issues confronting twenty-first-century America, including protection against police brutality and excessive, sometimes lethal force by law enforcement, the right to bodily integrity, and the legality of strip searches and stop-and-frisk programs, reproductive rights, equality based on gender and sexual orientation, and guaranteeing freedom of choice in food and health care, to name just a few.

These, I would suggest, are our "precarious rights." Because they are unnamed and only inferred, they exist at the mercy of Congress or the courts, where they have been and will continue to be relentlessly challenged by powerful political interests. Federal abortion rights and recognition of same-sex marriage, to name just two, could be eviscerated overnight at the Supreme Court, especially under the new, solid 5–4 conservative majority.

And because these fragile rights are unnamed, they are more easily violated by state power and thus more difficult to protect. But where do they come from?

That any individual rights had to be put to paper at all was hugely controversial during the framing of the Constitution. Anti-Federalists, who despised a strong central government, refused to ratify the document without a declaration of specifically protected individual liberties. But the Federalists argued that, because it was impossible to list every conceivable right, by naming only a few, all other rights not enumerated would be surrendered to the federal government.

To allay those fears, the Bill of Rights' author, James Madison, who sometimes straddled sentiments on both sides, offered an amendment that, while virtually unknown by most people today, could be our fallback protection in the years ahead as government continues to whittle away at liberties we take for granted. It is the enigmatic and still-debated Amendment IX: *The enumeration in the Constitution of certain rights shall not be construed to deny or disparage others retained by the people.*

Over time, the courts have struggled to determine, on a case-by-case basis, exactly where those rights "retained by the people" might be inferred by one or more amendments, even if they were not explicitly enumerated by the founders.

The Ninth Amendment was rarely invoked at the Supreme Court until a 1965 case, *Griswold v. Connecticut,* challenging Connecticut's ban on contraception as a violation of the right to marital privacy. While the Constitution of course makes no mention of the issue of birth control, the court, citing the Ninth Amendment in its decision, nonetheless overturned the law.[1]

Why? Because privacy is one of those values "served and protected" not only by the First Amendment's guarantee of "the right of the people peaceably to assemble" but also by the Third Amendment's protection against quartering soldiers "in any house without the consent of the owner," the Fourth Amendment's "right of the people to be secure in their persons [and] houses," and the Fifth Amendment's prohibition on compelling any person to "be a witness against himself," which in turn infers shielding the privacy of their personal information.

In *Roe v. Wade,* incidentally, the justices ruled 7–2 that the Fourteenth Amendment's Due Process Clause extended to a woman's decision to have an abortion, while still empowering states to heavily regulate the procedure.[2]

Constitutional scholars have battled for years over the ability of the Ninth Amendment to actually establish individual rights, but the broadest possible interpretation of its meaning will be critical to protect innocent Americans whose lives will increasingly be disturbed, upturned, or ended by overzealous law enforcement, while doing nothing more unremarkable than heading for work, walking their dog, or sitting quietly in their car.

It happens all the time.

PETTY CRIMES, PETTY COPS

News accounts of officers enforcing laws that, while perhaps sensible and probably constitutional, are so petty that, in many cases, prosecuting their violation seems almost laughable. But there is little humor to find here. In the next few pages, I describe incidents that, to me, raise four basic questions about modern policing in America:

- Don't officers have better things to do with their limited time and taxpayer-funded resources than pursue offenders of petty crimes?
- What is the actual harm to the state or the public here?
- Just because the police *can* enforce these laws, does that always mean that they *should*?
- And chiefly, is this really the type of country in which we want to live?

Here are just some of the ways that hyper-zealous officers have overreacted to petty "crimes" still on the books of local ordinances, some of them archaic, some of them ridiculous.

Raids on Lemonade Stands

I first heard about this phenomenon in 2015, when a high-profile case became a national story. At the time, I thought it must have been a one-off news item. After all, lemonade stands are as much a part of American childhood as miniature golf, backyard sleepovers, and trick-or-treating after dark.

The incident happened in Overton, a small town in eastern Texas where Andria Green, eight, and her sister Zoey, seven, set up a stand outside their home and stocked it with kettle corn, for a dollar per bag, and cold lemonade, at fifty cents a cup. They hoped to earn one hundred dollars to take their dad to a local water park for Father's Day. Within the first hour, the girls had already achieved one-fourth of their goal.

But then the cops showed up and shut down the enterprise. The children lacked the required $150 "peddler's permit," they informed the little girls. Their operation was illegal. "We were doing just fine until the cops came," Andria told reporters after the stand was shuttered.[3]

The young entrepreneurs were in violation of Texas's "Cottage Food Law," which specifically bans the sale of homemade lemonade or any item that could spoil without proper temperature control, though it does allow products such as baked goods, candy, nuts, fruit pie, popcorn, cereal, or pickles. There are no exceptions based on the age of the vendor.

After the raid, Police Chief Clyde Carter called the family and said the permit and fee could be waived, but the girls would still need another permit from the county health department.

After the story went viral and was widely reported on Fox News and other outlets, the Canadian site *Global News* called police to confirm the account. "'That story was made up by a local reporter,' an Overton police officer told us," the article said. Video of the raid posted by the reporter proved the officer dead wrong.[4]

Meanwhile, Carter said Overton police were just following the law: "We have to follow the state health guidelines," he said. "They have to have a permit."

This was no one-off. Lemonade stand raids are a thing. There is even a website, run by the Freedom Center of Missouri, that tracks reported cases on an interactive map.[5] And while the Green girls never got to meet their goal, at least they didn't lose any money like other child entrepreneurs did.

In June 2011, for example, six kids running a lemonade stand outside the U.S. Open at the Congressional Country Club in Montgomery County, Maryland, were slapped with a $500 fine (later rescinded when reported on the news) for not having a permit.[6]

Even celebrities are not immune. In August 2015, police raided a stand run by Jerry Seinfeld, his wife, Jessica, and their three sons outside their home in East Hampton, on Long Island, New York. The family opened the stand to raise money for Baby Buggy, a national nonprofit started by Jessica in 2001 to provide critical items to needy families.[7]

Neighbors had called police about people pulling up in cars to buy refreshments. Peddling of any kind is forbidden in the wealthy town. In typical Seinfeld fashion, the comedian and his family took a group selfie with their hands on their heads, as if under arrest, and posted it online.

Raids in New York City are not uncommon either. "You should consider getting a permit. In NYC they cost $70," *The Daily News* recommended, "so you better hope your friends and neighbors are thirsty." If cops get a complaint, the paper quoted one officer as saying, "They're not going to just say, 'Oh, they're just kids.'"[8]

There is a way around the law, however, the article added. "Give away the lemonade and ask for donations." That way, you avoiding the label of "selling" of food, and all the licenses and permits that entails.

But should little kids really have to worry about civil fines and legal loopholes? Erik Kain, a contributor to Forbes.com, lamented what he called the "inexplicable" situation in an August 2011 column.[9]

"Who stands to lose from a couple of six-year-olds selling lemonade?" Kain asked. "Who stands to gain from shutting them down? Do local governments really think parents are going to pay for $400 vendor permits, or that kids can scrape together the money for food permits? Are there any actual safety risks? Kids have been selling lemonade for decades without permits of any sort."

Maybe a few tummy aches now and then are the price we pay to preserve a beloved American tradition.

Petty New York "Crimes"

In my hometown of New York City, police harassment of citizens who break the most minor of laws is, sadly, legendary. Yes, street crime is way down, and the city is a more orderly, if still chaotic place. While the abuses got worse under the administration of Mayor Rudy Giuliani, they did not improve much with Michael Bloomberg, and by many accounts, continue under Bill de Blasio.

In February 2013, New York's local CBS news affiliate ran a special investigative piece titled "Petty Arrests Take Toll on New Yorkers, Tremendous Cost to the City." It depicted a police department and criminal justice system run amok by overzealous officers and prosecutors. "These minor offenses are taking a big toll on people's lives, prompting us to ask: Do the serious consequences really fit the petty crimes?" said coanchor Maurice DuBois. Among the cases profiled were:

- **Darren Jones.** As the fifty-year-old took the subway home from work, police arrested and jailed him for sixteen hours simply for walking between subway cars.
- **Seymour Hewitt** entered a subway station only to realize he was on the wrong side of the platform. When he entered the station for the second time without paying again, he was arrested and spent twelve hours in jail.
- **Caroline Stern.** The fifty-four-year-old and her boyfriend, George Hess, forty-four, were on a subway platform when police arrested them for something no one would ever imagine was against the law. "We were dancing. That's it," Caroline said. The couple spent the next twenty-three hours in jail.
- **Samantha Zucker.** The twenty-two-year-old was in Manhattan's Riverside Park after closing hours when police apprehended her. She spent thirty-six hours in jail before her case was dismissed. "You're locked up, you're an animal," she said.

Steven Banks, attorney in chief of the Legal Aid Society, told WCBS that jail time for petty crimes was on the rise. "It seems like they're hitting an ant with a sledgehammer," Banks said. "It's a tremendous cost to the system, and a tremendous individual cost to New Yorkers." Some experts *applauded* the aggressive use of arrests and jail time for minor offenses. Jon Shane, professor of criminal justice at John Jay College, told the news team that, while it may seem random, police have good reason for the arrests, such as the dancing couple.

Most of these charges were ultimately dismissed, as long as the defendants stayed out of trouble for six months. But the fiscal and emotional costs were real, lasting, and pointless.

School Calls Police on Eighth-Grade Girl for Two-Dollar Note

One morning in early May 2016, fourteen-year-old Danesiah Neal, an eighth-grade student at Christa McAuliffe Middle School in the Houston suburbs, went to school with a two-dollar bill her grandmother had given her for lunch. Danesiah wanted to get the chicken nuggets. But school officials accused the girl of passing counterfeit money and called in law enforcement.[10]

The police called Sharon Kay Joseph, Danesiah's grandmother, who explained that she had gotten the bill as change from a local convenience store. After confirming this at the store, the officers took the bill to a bank, which found it to be legal tender. The bill, while uncommon, has been in circulation since 1953.

Then they returned the money.

There were about forty similar reports of counterfeit currency in Houston area schools during 2013–2014, and in 2016, according to the local ABC News affiliate. All of them involved minority students.

"We see a disproportionate impact on minority youth when it comes to these charges," Houston attorney Mani Nezami told reporters.

Alec Hunter, for example, a fifteen-year-old African American student at Elkins High School, was walking to lunch with some friends one day in November 2015 when they all spotted a ten-dollar bill in the hallway and scrambled for it. Alec picked it up and brought it to the lunchroom to buy a ham sandwich and some chips. The cafeteria cashier used a counterfeit-detection pen on the bill, which failed the test. The worker turned it over to school district police, and they brought it to the DA, seeking charges of "engaging in delinquent conduct" and forgery with the "intent to defraud or harm another," a felony punishable by up to ten years in prison.[11]

Another Houston area attorney, Deron Harrington, compiled media reports on the alleged "counterfeit epidemic" in local schools. He found that, over a one-year period, there had been just six incidents, and the total money in question was $152. All the students said they had no knowledge the currency was fake. All six were African American.

Alec's parents were understandably frantic. They tried to get answers from the police and DA but got nowhere. Now frustrated, they decided to go public with their story.

Hunter said prosecutors tried to convince Alec to take a plea deal during his first hearing in juvenile court, on May 2: no jail time, but six months of probation that included a first-time offender's program for at-risk youth, and counseling. Alec rejected the offer.

One year later, in May 2016, the DA dropped all charges. But the bad taste remained; Alec had been accused of a felony offense and faced serious prison time, all for scooping up a stray bill to buy chips and a sandwich.

Feeding the Homeless Is a Crime?

What kind of government would bar its citizens from providing food to those who need it most? Do we really want to criminalize an act of charity that could save human lives? It happens all the time.

In a 2017 report, *Housing Not Handcuffs,* the National Law Center on Homelessness & Poverty surveyed 187 U.S. cities and found that 6 percent of them had enacted bans on sharing food in public places.[12] Between 2013 and 2015 alone, 26 cities passed such laws, according to the National Coalition for the Homeless (NCH).[13] Today, an estimated 70 cities have passed or proposed them in some form.[14]

The statutes are purportedly based on health concerns over handing out contaminated food, although the NCH insists there is no documented evidence of anyone getting sick from food given to homeless people in public places. Such laws routinely challenged by religious leaders and community activists, often lead to prosecution.

A case in point is El Cajon, California, just east of San Diego, which approved a temporary food-sharing ban in October 2017, citing a recent hepatitis A outbreak among the homeless. The following January, on a Sunday morning, about fifty volunteers gathered in the city's Wells Park in deliberate defiance of the ordinance and began handing out food, clothes, shoes, and toiletries to homeless people.

They called their group "Break the Ban." This was their fourth such outing. The aim was not just to feed the homeless but to trigger police into enforcing the ban so it could be challenged in court.

Those distributing food were approached by police and ordered to stop. At least twelve of them, including a fourteen-year-old girl, were placed under arrest but not handcuffed. Ultimately, they were issued summonses on misdemeanor charges and released. As planned, they said they would challenge the ordinance in court.

Scott Dreher, an attorney and member of the group who was also arrested, said the city was trying to criminalize and dehumanize the homeless. "It's discriminatory against a vulnerable class of people. Plain and simple," he told *The San Diego Union-Tribune.* Speaking at a news conference after the arrests, organizer Mark Lane quoted Dr. Martin Luther King Jr. "If a law is unjust, you're obligated to reject it," she said. "We saw an unjust law and we're rejecting it."[15]

YOUR BODY, YOUR SELF

"Don't touch my junk!"

That phrase, now part of the American vernacular, was accidentally coined in 2010 by airline passenger John Tyner, thirty-one, of Oceanside, California, as he tried to go through security at San Diego International Airport. Tyner did not want to go through the full-body scanner, out of health concerns and the invasion of privacy it entails. Instead, he asked for a physical pat-down. The TSA officer told Tyner about the agency's recently adopted "enhanced pat-down" techniques, which included using the hands and fingers to touch passengers in their groin.[16]

Tyner balked. "If you touch my junk, I'm going to have you arrested," he told the agent, who responded that a pat-down was not sexual assault. "It would be if you were not the government," Tyner replied.

A TSA supervisor appeared on the scene. By buying his ticket, "you gave up a lot of rights," the supervisor said. Tyner had seen enough. He decided not to make the trip and went to get a refund. But he wasn't in the clear. Because he had tried to go through security, the officers demanded that he submit to a search. The officer threatened Tyner with prosecution and a $10,000 fine. He left the airport anyway.

So, what right do authorities have to touch, pat, frisk, fondle, poke, prod, or strip-search members of the public? A lot depends on the circumstances. But one thing is certain: Unless you have done something wrong or want to enter a restricted area like beyond airport security, cops have no right to lay a finger on you—much less make you remove your clothes in public.

As the nineteenth-century jurist and legal scholar Thomas M. Cooley famously wrote, "The right to one's person may be said to be a right of complete immunity; to be let alone."[17] And yet, it happens all the time, with strip searches being the most common violation of what is known in legal and constitutional terms as *bodily integrity*. The tactic relies on inflicting fear and intimidation straight out of the playbook of a police state.

Many roadside police stops are simply "government-sanctioned exercises in humiliation and degradation with a complete disregard for privacy and human dignity," said John Whitehead of the libertarian legal foundation the Rutherford Institute. Motorists who committed minor infractions have been subjected to forced strip searches, outside and in public, including people who were stopped for driving with a noisy muffler, driving with an inoperable headlight, failing to use a turn signal, riding a bicycle without an audible bell, or making an improper left turn, he said.[18]

Consider the saga of Charneshia Corley, a twenty-year-old African American college student who was driving through North Houston one night in June 2015, when Harris County sheriff's deputies pulled her over at a Texaco station for allegedly rolling through a stop sign and failing to signal. Corley turned into the parking lot of a busy convenience store and began engaging the deputies.[19]

The cops said they smelled marijuana and searched Corley's car. Finding nothing, they said they wanted to search Corley herself. It took an hour and a half for a female deputy to arrive to perform a "visual strip search." When the female officer arrived, she commanded Corley to drop her pants, even though they were in clear public view.

Corley, who had no criminal record, yet was handcuffed, said she had no underwear on. "So?" responded the female cop, who yanked down Corley's pants and shined a flashlight on her genital area, even as customers walked in and out of the store.

When Corley cried out in protest, the deputies decided to conduct a "manual body cavity search." They "forcibly threw her to the ground, while she was still handcuffed, pinned her down with her legs spread apart, threatened to break her legs, and without consent penetrated her vagina in a purported search for marijuana," according to court documents. She was pinned to the ground, half-naked, for more than ten minutes.[20]

"That was extreme, to pull my clothes down, in front of people!" Corley is heard crying in a dashcam video that was released two years later.

The officers said they found a minuscule amount of marijuana—0.2 ounces, or about a half-gram—in her genitals. But their attorney later argued that Corley had not been penetrated. The cops arrested Corley on misdemeanor possession charges and resisting arrest.

"I felt like they sexually assaulted me. I really do," she told the local ABC News affiliate. "I felt disgusted, downgraded, and humiliated."[21]

The office of Harris County DA Devon Anderson eventually dismissed the charges, calling the search of Corley "offensive and shocking."[22]

The story also shocked the community and made headlines around the country, forcing Harris County sheriff Ed Gonzalez to defend his department, saying it was "fully committed to ensuring that every resident of our community is treated with dignity and respect." All deputies, he said, were prohibited from conducting strip searches without a warrant from a judge.

One year later, in June 2016, two of the three deputies involved in the search were indicted by a Harris County grand jury on charges of "official oppression." But a year after that, when a new DA presented additional evidence to the grand jury, the charges were dismissed.

Andrea J. Richie, a longtime police violence activist, told the website Splinter.com that "not only is that completely violating, degrading, and unconstitutional, but that is also a common practice in the context of the War on Drugs and how it's waged on the bodies of black women."[23]

In August 2016, Corley filed a civil right lawsuit in federal court in Houston against Harris County.

"The improper and outrageous searches were conducted in public, in a nonsterile environment and with unwarranted and unjustified physical force," the complaint alleged, calling the actions, "egregious, humiliating and traumatizing violations of Ms. Corley's rights." The search was also conducted prior to her arrest, without a warrant or probable cause, in violation of the Fourth Amendment.[24]

The illegal search of her person deprived Corley of her liberty, including her right to privacy, which in turn violated the Fourteenth Amendment's guarantee of due process under the law. The lawsuit also alleged assault and battery, "offensive physical contact," and intentional infliction of emotional distress. She sought unspecified damages.

In late January 2018, after lengthy negotiations between the county and Corley's attorney, she agreed to settle the case for $185,000. Her attorney, Samuel Cammack, called the sum "an injustice" to his client, who deserved far more for what she went through. But, he added, he felt backed into a corner by prosecutors. "We felt like it was the best thing to do for Ms. Corley. We felt we were about to end up with zero," Cammack told *The Houston Chronicle*. "We're disgusted with the process and how it all turned out."[25]

Kandice Webber, an organizer with Black Lives Matter Houston, told the paper that county officials needed to do outreach in minority communities to assure residents this would not happen again.

"No amount of money can give Charneshia Corley what those officers took from her, and that was her dignity and respect as a human being," Webber said.

According to the legal website InjusticeToday.com, Texas enacted a law in 2015 requiring all police in the state to get a search warrant before conducting roadside body cavity searches. "But critics say the practice still occurs," it said, "and police do not face any criminal penalty if they violate it."[26]

A similar but even more disturbing incident took place in December 2012, when a New Mexico woman was seized by U.S. Border Patrol agents when crossing back over from Mexico, where she was visiting a close family friend who had been deported.

When the woman, identified in court documents as "Jane Doe," a "petite" fifty-four-year-old U.S. citizen, approached the checkpoint, she was informed she would be subjected to a "random screening" with drug dogs. Although canines are notoriously inaccurate when sniffing out drugs, this dog indicated there were narcotics in her car.[27]

The agents dragged Doe out of her car and began feeling up her body, and she was then "stripped, gawked at and manually penetrated by the fingers of federal agents," according to a federal lawsuit she would later file. One agent stuck a hand in her waistband and pushed a "finger in the crevice of Ms. Doe's buttocks." She was "embarrassed and upset" by the humiliating procedure. Then she was taken to a private room.

There, they ordered Doe to pull down her pants and crouch. As one agent examined her anus with a flashlight, she was commanded to lean backward in her crouched position. "One of the agents then parted Ms. Doe's vulva with her hand, pressed her fingers into Ms. Doe's vagina and visually examined her genitalia with a flashlight."

Jane Doe had been in custody for two hours, yet the agents found nothing. But they were not giving up. She was re-dressed and taken to the University Medical Center of El Paso for more invasive examinations. When asked if they had a warrant, the officials allegedly told her, "We don't need a warrant."

Doe was forced to take a laxative and ordered to defecate in a portable toilet. No contraband was found. She was then chained to a table in a hospital room, where two staff doctors joined the agents in the search for hidden contraband. The torture, which essentially amounted to legalized medical rape, went on for more than four hours.

The doctors ordered x-rays. They revealed no drugs. Doe was shackled to the table once again and ordered to spread her legs. One doctor "inserted a speculum into Ms. Doe's vagina and observed the interior cavity," according to the complaint. He found no foreign objects. He then "stuck his fingers into Ms. Doe's vagina while palpitating her abdomen." Again, nothing abnormal. The doctor then probed her anus with his fingers while the border patrol agents watched. Doe, who was "mortified" that passersby in the hallway could see the assault, felt like "she was being treated less than human, like an animal."

And still it continued. Determined that the drug dogs had to be right, the doctors ordered a CT scan of Doe's abdomen and pelvis, exposing her to "between 150 and 1,100 times the radiation of a conventional x-ray, or around a year's worth of exposure to radiation from both natural and artificial sources in the environment," the lawsuit alleged. The scan found nothing.

Jane Doe was free to go. But there was a catch. The officials asked her to sign a medical consent form, even though she had consented to nothing, and Customs and Border Protection would cover the bill for her examinations. Otherwise, she would be billed. Doe refused to sign and left the hospital, without charges, more than six hours after she had tried to cross the border.

Soon after that, Doe was sent a bill for $5,000 from the hospital. She refused to pay it.

In December 2013, Jane Doe, represented by the ACLU of Texas, filed suit in federal court against the border patrol agents, and a separate complaint against the University Medical Center of El Paso and its board members, claiming unreasonable search and seizure, false arrest, false imprisonment, and deprivation of due process. Her pain was similar to that of a sexual-assault victim, leaving her unable "to be physically intimate with her husband." Since the incident, she tended to avoid public spaces, becoming reclusive.[28]

On July 7, 2014, the University Medical Center and emergency room physicians agreed to pay Jane Doe $1.1 million for their role in the events of that day. The hospital also agreed to meet with ACLU lawyers to review its policies on dealing with law enforcement searches.[29]

"Despite the trauma and humiliation endured by our client, she had the courage to step forward," said Rebecca L. Robertson, legal policy director for the ACLU of Texas. "Because of her, the hospital has changed its policy to prevent this from happening to others. Now we hope that CBP will also take responsibility and stop subjecting innocent people to unconstitutional and abusive searches."[30]

Back at the Airport

"Don't touch my junk," which was celebrated in at least two musical videos, raised awareness and became a battle cry among many U.S. airline passengers fed up with some of the more intrusive and invasive TSA procedures deployed in the dreaded security line. Conservative commentator Charles Krauthammer backed the San Diego passenger, John Tyner, calling his plea the "anthem of the modern man, the Tea Party patriot, the late-life libertarian, the midterm election voter." He even likened it to the iconic "Don't Tread on Me."[31] And though liberal Michael Kinsley posted a blog article called "Go Ahead, Touch My Junk," in defense of the TSA,[32] The Nation editor, Katrina vanden Heuvel, said everyone was "right to call out the TSA's invasive procedures and the threat to civil liberties . . . this issue isn't Republican and it isn't Democratic."[33]

Complaints against the TSA agents' invasive conduct have ranged from the electronic—such as agents joking with each other over the size of men's genitals captured on scanners[34]—to the psychophysical, such as poking and groping little old ladies or toddlers.

Advocacy groups such as the Electronic Privacy Information Center say the scanners are illegal and violate passenger privacy and accuse the government of not doing enough to ensure any images taken are destroyed. Ralph Nader called the technology "ineffective" because it can't detect all explosives, and also decried the lack of safety data regarding its use.[35]

No one wants to let a terrorist on a plane with a weapon or explosives. Everyone supports strict security at airports. But where do we draw the line? And where does common sense come into the equation? If it doesn't, shouldn't it? Is it really necessary, say, to intimately and repeatedly pat down down a boy traveling with his mother, just because of an oversight at the x-ray baggage screener?

That is precisely what happened in March 2017 at Dallas Fort Worth International Airport, when Jennifer Williamson was going through security to catch a flight with her thirteen-year-old special needs son, Aaron, who has a neurological condition called sensory processing disorder, which can spark severe anxiety and fear from even the gentlest touch.[36]

Aaron passed through the metal detector without incident, but a TSA agent told him that something in his carry-on had triggered an alarm—he had forgotten to remove his laptop from his bag. The mother begged the agents to find an alternative to a full-body pat-down. This went on for forty-five minutes, until finally she consented.

The creepy procedure that followed—and I do think the term is apt here—lasted two minutes. It was captured on video by Williamson, who posted the footage to Facebook. In the video, a large male TSA agent speaks to Aaron to explain what he is about to do. He then begins the pat-down from behind. He slowly rubs the boy's shoulders, then moves his hands down his flanks, rubbing his buttocks. He feels his chest and stomach. He then runs his hands up and down his legs, reaching up into his crotch each time.

The agent moves away, and one assumes the search is over. It is not. The agent moves around to Aaron's front side. He rubs his arms under the boy's armpit—and then the stomach and chest again. It is all done repeatedly and methodically. The man then feels inside Aaron's waistband before running his hands up and down the legs, touching the crotch all over again. The agent stops, walks away, pauses, and for good measure, comes back and quickly rubs the boy's legs and genital area.

"We were treated like dogs," Williamson wrote on Facebook. Several hours after the incident, she said her son was still repeating, "I don't know what I did. What did I do?"[37]

"I am livid," she added. "Please, share . . . make this viral like the other children's videos with TSA." Within two days, the post had received tens of thousands of shares and nearly 7.9 million views.[38]

It caught the attention of TSA officials, who offered a public-relations olive branch, of sorts. "We conferenced with several representatives at headquarters for over an hour," she wrote on Facebook. The officials had suggested a three-part plan for changes and also offered an apology for Aaron's treatment.[39]

The TSA formally asked Williamson to help them develop a new training manual for all agents, addressing etiquette and sensitivity and how to be more respectful toward passengers. They also invited her to review the agency's website and suggest ways to improve the way they inform passengers of TSA procedures, "especially in regards to families flying with children and those with medical challenges." Finally, they invited her to join the TSA's Disabilities and Medical Condition Coalition and encouraged her to recommend advocacy groups for specific disabilities that should also take part.

"I feel it is imperative at this time that we know we still have the ability to initiate change," she said. "Especially when we see that a government agency shows need for improvement in the way they treat us as citizens in this country. So many of us have resigned ourselves to the fact that change is not coming. This is real proof that you have the power to *be* the change."

The Constitution and "Bodily Integrity"

As explained at the beginning of this chapter, our rights to privacy, to not be unduly groped, prodded, stripped, or otherwise humiliated, are not explicitly laid out in the Constitution. Instead, they are among the "derived" rights from other amendments as stipulated in the Ninth Amendment.

In the United States, the Supreme Court set case law on invasive bodily searches and related procedures back in 1891, in a case regarding a woman who was severely injured aboard a Union Pacific railroad car when the bunk above her collapsed. The company sought and received a court order forcing the passenger to undergo a "surgical examination" to determine the extent and veracity of her alleged injuries. She refused and the case went to the court of appeals and then to the Supreme Court.

The lower court had "no legal right or power to make and enforce such an order," the High Court justices ruled. "No right is held more sacred or is more carefully guarded by the common law than the right of every individual to the possession and control of his own person, free from all restraint or interference of others unless by clear and unquestionable authority of law."[40]

Other, more recent decisions have upheld the same principle. In a 1994 case, the Supreme Court ruled that "the protections of substantive due process have for the most part been accorded to matters relating to marriage, family, and the right to bodily integrity."[41] In 2009, the justices ruled that school officials had violated the constitutional rights of a thirteen-year-old Arizona girl after strip-searching her based solely on another student's accusation that she brought Advil to school.[42]

However, the High Court has found, once someone is arrested and in custody of the state, all such protections vanish. In April 2012, it ruled 5–4 that guards may routinely strip-search even minor traffic offenders when they are arrested and detained. The case involved a New Jersey man who was arrested because of a computer error over a seven-year-old fine he had, in fact, paid. He was arrested, jailed for seven days, and strip-searched, twice. At one point, he was ordered to squat, cough, and lift up his genitals.[43]

But Justice Anthony Kennedy, writing for the majority, noted that jails are "often crowded, unsanitary, and dangerous places." The courts, he said, must defer to correctional officials when deciding whom to search to prevent the smuggling of weapons or contraband behind bars. SCOTUS did not say the searches were required but that they did not violate the Fourth Amendment as being unreasonable.

The dissenters, led by Justice Stephen Breyer, argued that corrections officers should not be able to strip-search minor offenders who have not been accused of violence or drug crimes. Some seven hundred thousand arrests for such minor offenses were made each year, he said. No one knows how many of those arrested suffered equally unneeded invasions of their privacy.

NO RAW MILK FOR YOU!

Raw milk can make you sick and, in extremely rare cases, kill you. But so can a lot of things, and not just food or alcohol. Skiing is dangerous, even deadly, yet we allow anyone with the price of a lift ticket to do it, at any time, at any resort, weather permitting. But when it comes to unpasteurized milk, people are being prosecuted or threatened with prosecution for producing, transporting, or even just bringing into their homes an ancient agricultural product that, in many instances, is still considered to be illegal contraband.

Why, in a great democratic republic, should consumers not have unfettered access to raw milk, as long as they are aware of any risks, and the dairy is operating under all state rules and regulations regarding its safe production? (Contamination typically comes from unclean udders but is sometimes the result of vaccination.) A case could be made for a federal crackdown on, say, medical marijuana, though many people would reject that. But *milk*? Don't federal agents have more important things to do with their time—and our money?

Proponents of raw milk offer several arguments, both political and medicinal, why the federal government should have no power to regulate the product. For many, barring access violates their freedom to make personal choices about their own health, as guaranteed by the U.S. Constitution's inferred right to "be left alone." They also say that buying raw milk supports small, local, family-owned farms and not distant, industrialized mega-dairies run by large corporations (although small producers can pasteurize milk, and raw milk can be transported just as far, though it seldom is). And then there are the health benefits. Proponents claim that pasteurization reduces nutrients and kills good as well as harmful bacteria. Health benefits, they say, include immune system enhancement, allergy reduction, better nerve function, and even weight loss.[44] And it tastes better. (I've tried it. It's true.)

Government researchers and food safety regulators scoff at such claims. "It is the FDA's position that raw milk should never be consumed," agency spokeswoman Tamara Ward once told *The Washington Times*.[45] The FDA says pasteurizing milk does not destroy any of its nutritive value. More importantly, "raw milk can harbor dangerous microorganisms that can pose serious health risks to you and your family," including E. coli, salmonella, and listeria, according to the FDA website. Between 1993 and 2006, more than fifteen hundred people in the United States became sick from raw dairy products, it says, adding that "unpasteurized milk is 150 times more likely to cause foodborne illness and results in 13 times more hospitalizations than illnesses involving pasteurized dairy products."[46]

In the spring of 2018, health officials urged consumers to discard raw milk from two Pennsylvania dairies that was contaminated, one batch with *Listeria monocytogenes*. No illnesses were reported, but anyone who drank the milk was told to monitor themselves for seventy days for symptoms, including fever, muscle aches, nausea, and diarrhea.[47] The bacteria, which mostly affects newborns, the elderly, those with impaired immune systems, and pregnant women, can result in miscarriage, premature delivery, or stillbirth—as well as fever, headache, confusion, loss of balance, and convulsions.

On the other hand, one study found that just 3 percent of foodborne outbreaks in 2006 were related to pasteurized or raw milk—and even the federal government admits there were only two deaths between 1998 and 2008.[48] Meanwhile, raw vegetables, sprouts, steak, eggs, oysters, and fish are freely and widely consumed around the country. They account for the majority of foodborne illnesses, yet milk and milk products are the only foods required by the FDA to be sterilized through heating.

Despite that, health officials still insist that raw milk is particularly dangerous, and it is within their purview, and power, to intervene whenever necessary to protect public health. The problem is, raw milk is now legal in some form in twenty-eight states—creating a similar state-versus-federal conflict as the medical marijuana dynamic.[49] In most states, one must obtain the milk from the farmer, either purchasing it directly on-site or joining community-supported agriculture schemes, such as buyers' clubs, organic food co-ops, and programs known as *herd sharing*, where people buy "shares" of the livestock and get milk back in return. In about eight states, raw milk is now available for sale in stores.

But it wasn't always this way. Raw milk sales were banned during the Reagan administration, but not through the regulatory process or an act of Congress. It came from a 1984 court order sought by Ralph Nader's Public Citizen consumer advocacy group and the American Public Health Association.[50] Crackdowns on producers and sellers followed, lasting well through the ensuing years. After the attacks of September 11, 2001, new bioterrorism laws granted increased powers to the FDA to keep the food supply safe from sabotage. "Mission creep" soon set in, as author David Gumpert wrote in his book

Life, Liberty, and the Pursuit of Food Rights. He uncovered evidence that the FDA secretly coordinated with state prosecutors who were going after raw milk buyers' clubs in Minnesota, Wisconsin, and Georgia.[51]

Federal harassment of legally operating dairies spiked to unprecedented levels during the Obama years, producing a number of high-profile criminal cases against the farmers. The Food Safety Modernization Act of 2010, signed by the president, bestowed vast new powers on the FDA, including the authority to confiscate any food at any farm that it deems unsafe or mislabeled. The number of raids and arrests climbed ever higher. By midyear of 2013 in California alone, for example, government agents had "conducted a sting operation on a raw milk producer in Fresno, made three raids on a boutique goat cheese maker in Ventura County and descended with guns drawn on a raw milk buying club in Venice," *The San Francisco Chronicle* reported.[52]

Sometimes, those heavy-handed tactics were headed off at the pass. David Hochstetler is a sustainable raw milk producer in the northern Indiana hamlet of Middlebury, near the Michigan border. His Forest Grove Dairy sells the product through an organic food co-op, where customers pay a monthly "fee" to help maintain the cows, in exchange for raw milk. (In this way, it is not technically a "sale," in order to comply with state law.)[53]

Between 2007 and 2011, the federal government confiscated raw milk from his dairy farm and shut his dairy farm down for several weeks on the suspicion that his products caused campylobacter illnesses, costing him thousands of dollars. Extensive testing on his products, however, revealed no pathogens in his milk.

In early 2011, agents from the DOJ and FDA showed up at Hochstetler's dairy, unannounced and without warrants, demanding to search the property. A bacterial outbreak caused by raw milk had been reported in Michigan the year before, and the feds were convinced that Hochstetler and his cows were to blame. But an investigation by the Elkhart County Sheriff's Office found no evidence to support the claims. Nevertheless, agents kept returning to the property as frequently as every two weeks, even though typical inspections take place just once a year.

Even worse, the Justice Department issued Hochstetler a subpoena to appear before a federal grand jury in Michigan, and to bring all of his production and sales records with him to court. The farmer grew tired of the feds and their warrantless, unconstitutional searches. He knew they were searching for a reason to shut him down and was terrified he would lose Forest Grove. On December 1, 2011, Hochstetler, out of sheer exasperation, called the county sheriff, Brad Rogers, for help.

Rogers is a conservative, die-hard libertarian who has threatened to ignore all gun-control executive orders and even abolish gun-free zones. He also defended his decision to visit the Bundy Ranch back during the 2014 standoff with the Bureau of Land Management. He was incensed by what Hochstetler told him.

"My research concluded that no one was getting sick from this distribution of this raw milk," Rogers wrote in a local newspaper blog, five years later, in response to a reader's question. "It appeared to be harassment by the FDA and the DOJ, and making unconstitutional searches."[54]

Rogers then fired off an email to DOJ lawyers. "This is notice that any further attempts to inspect this farm without a warrant signed by a judge, based on probable cause, will result in federal inspectors' removal or arrest for trespassing by my officers or I," he wrote. "I will expect you to forward this information to your federal associates, including the FDA."

Six days later, Hochstetler received a certified letter in the mail. It was from the Justice Department: His order to appear before the grand jury was canceled. After that, the inspectors stopped showing up. "Your local elected officials . . . can stem the tide of federal overreach if they apply just a little backbone in supporting and defending the Constitution," Rogers wrote. "Some bloggers and natural food writers have hailed me as a hero. I'm no hero. I'm just doing my job. Whether you are conservative or liberal, I will be a guardian of the Constitution for you."

Other farmers, however, were far less fortunate. Vernon Hershberger, thirty-eight, an Amish-born family farmer in Loganville, Wisconsin, was running a successful raw milk buyers' club out of his Grazin' Acres dairy without incident. But that didn't stop government agents from coming down on him with a prosecutorial sledgehammer. On June 2, 2010, officials from the Wisconsin Department of Agriculture, Trade and Consumer Protection (DATCP) raided the farm, ruining some three hundred gallons of fresh milk by pouring blue dye into the holding tank. Without any evidence, they labeled the milk "adulterated and misbranded," sealed all the coolers, and barred its sale or consumption.[55]

Upset that good food would go to waste and fearful that agents would return to destroy the remaining product, Hershberger broke the seals, posting the deed on social media, calling it an "act of civil disobedience."

Hershberger was charged with illegally producing raw milk, operating a dairy without a license, and selling food at a retail establishment without a license, as well as violating the ban on sales of his products.[56] His case quickly became a cause célèbre among proponents of the raw milk movement and garnered increasing national attention over the next three years as officials dug through every aspect of the dairy.

At his trial in May 2013, Hershberger took the stand to testify how he tried to work with state officials, to no avail, to reach a solution. The jury took four hours to reach a verdict: innocent of the first three counts, but guilty of violating the sales ban. That charge, a misdemeanor, carried maximum penalties of up to one year in jail and $10,000 in fines. Sentencing would be scheduled soon.[57]

Even so, Hershberger, his family and attorneys, and legions of supporters celebrated the acquittals, which many legal observers presumed were reached under a little-known process called *jury nullification,* which allows jurors to acquit a defendant, even if there is enough evidence to convict him—if they believe there were extenuating circumstances, or if they feel that the underlying law in the case is *unjust.* The problem is that judges and defense attorneys in all federal courts and most state courts are barred from informing jurors about their nullification options. Prosecutors, for obvious reasons, rarely if ever bring it up at trial.

As for the dairy farmer, he just wanted to go home and farm. "Now I can continue to feed my community," Hershberger told reporters.[58] His defense attorney, Glenn Reynolds, told *The Milwaukee Journal Sentinel* that the case was "one of the most incomprehensible abuses of power I have ever seen." It was a "pathetic waste of government resources" to prosecute someone who "had never been in trouble with the law in his entire life and is a hero for coming up with a new way" to connect urban dwellers to family farming.[59]

In June, Hershberger was sentenced with a $1,000 fine for violating the holding order.[60] He appealed his conviction, arguing that evidence to show that the order was improperly issued was barred at trial—a fact that deeply angered sympathetic jurors after they discovered it. The appeal was rejected.[61] But if the aim of state officials was to make an example of Hershberger and drive his raw milk enterprise out of business, it backfired. A year after his trial, raw milk sales had skyrocketed, Hershberger said, and club membership grew by 25 percent, to about 325 families.[62]

The Situation Today

In the waning years of the Obama administration, federal harassment of raw milk producers and consumers tapered off considerably. "The negative media attention on the issue was a real embarrassment to the FDA and state agencies," Liz Reitzig, founder of the Real Food Consumer Coalition, told me. But, she cautioned, "the FDA is still targeting small farms through cease-and-desist orders and other minor infractions to intimidate the people running the farms. In many cases, this tactic is working and farmers are quietly shutting down or ceasing distribution."[63]

Today, after the first two years of President Trump, the status quo—perennial friction between state law and federal regulations—has not changed much. The right to buy, sell, drink, and especially transport raw milk across state lines is still tenuous—and the animosity still comes from the top.

Today, most actions against raw milk are centered on a 1987 FDA regulation granting the agency power to ban its interstate commerce, greatly restricting the market for all producers, big and small.[64] At the same time, the FDA says on its website (though it has not committed to it in written policy) that it "has never taken, nor does it intend to take, enforcement action against" anyone who brings raw milk across state lines—but solely for their own *individual* consumption.[65] That means if you live in a state where raw milk is prohibited, the only way to obtain it is to drive to another state where it is permitted, purchase it directly from the farmer, and bring it back home yourself. But don't have it delivered to you by a third party—and don't even *think* about sharing a single glass with family, friends, or neighbors. Those are federal offenses.

It happened in New Jersey, where raw milk is strictly against the law—unless you bring it into the state yourself, again solely for personal consumption. In February 2018, the state Department of Health (NJDH) issued cease-and-desist letters to hundreds of people who were part of a large buyers' club—as well as the club operator—after a woman contracted a rare infection called brucellosis. The state enlisted two federal agencies—the CDC and the USDA—to help with the investigation.[66] Each club member was sending money to a raw milk dairy across the border in Pennsylvania, where sales by farmers are legal. The milk was then delivered to a number of drop-off points at certain members' homes, where everyone else could come and pick up their share.

The letters threatened the families operating the drop sites with fines for distributing raw milk.[67] Most of the families who received the threats were immigrants, according to Liz Reitzig. Most of them were from South Asia and Latin America. "It's their custom and culture. It's the foods they've relied on for centuries," she told me. "And there's no way they're going to find it in New Jersey, so they seek it out, and they work with these farmers." Reitzig said the harassment of immigrant families—including verbal threats from agents—was intentional, noting that drop sites run by U.S.-born residents were never targeted. Some of them were here legally; others were undocumented. "But even if they're here on a green card or a visa, or if they're here for school, they don't want to get on the wrong side of a cease-and-desist letter. It's using extreme vulnerabilities to enforce a law that literally should not exist."

So far, no one has challenged the crackdown, though Reitzig thinks it would be helpful. "It would be great to have this come up in court, because, is it really violating the law if I hold on to somebody's milk for them? Does that count as a 'distribution'?" she asked.

"We're scratching our heads over this because it's so ridiculous," Reitzig added. "We can transport guns across state lines. I can take alcohol. I can take cigarettes, and all manner of other things. And yet I cannot bring raw milk across state lines and feed it to my children legally."

In April 2017, Reitzig's group, along with Jonathan Emord, a constitutional and administrative law attorney with several victories against the FDA under his belt, filed a "citizen petition" with the agency, asking it to lift the interstate ban and instead require labeling on raw milk and raw milk products about the potential health risks, and instructions on heating milk at home to kill pathogens.[68] "We didn't want to get into the science of it," she explained. "We're not going to change the FDA's mind on raw milk, and that wasn't our intention; it's simply to remove that layer of enforcement." Under the law, the FDA had 180 days to respond. Toward the end of that period, officials requested more time. As of January 2019, nearly two years after the petition was filed, there was still no word.

The petition is aimed directly at the heart of the Trump administration's philosophy: Federal regulations hurt the economy and hurt businesses. Trump has issued at least four executive orders on lifting regulations across the board, including a rule commanding that, for every new regulation imposed, two must be rescinded.

But, I asked Emord, since lifting the interstate ban would chip away at corporate dairy profits, wouldn't it simultaneously clash with the president's staunchly pro-industry policies? "I think the president's position is clear—if a regulation is unnecessary and interferes with commerce, he's in favor of eliminating it," he told me. "And I tend to think he actually is willing to clash with those [mega-dairy] interests." And, he added, Trump has the power to "just pick up the phone, tell the dictator who runs the FDA, 'I don't want this regulation, you're sitting at my pleasure as commissioner. So, hop to it, bud, and change it.'"[69]

Milk and the Founders

How can raids and harassment of raw milk operations across state lines be constitutional? Again, we see the clash between state and federal powers. On one hand, the Commerce Clause found in Article I, Section 8, of the Constitution grants authority to Congress to "regulate *commerce* with foreign nations, and among the several states, and with the Indian tribes." In contrast, the Tenth Amendment holds that "powers not delegated to the United States by the Constitution" are reserved for the states.

In that regard, the Commerce Clause would tend to trump states' rights over raw milk. But Congress didn't regulate interstate commerce; the FDA did, but it failed to consider "obvious less restrictive means to achieve its ends . . . when it promulgated a rule," Emord said. Even then, Congress never gave specific authorization to the agency to ban interstate milk. "That is of particular concern, because the FDA appears to have used regulation to invade a province traditionally regulated by the states," he added. "And that would be a Tenth Amendment issue."

So, what would the framers of the Constitution think about all of this? "They certainly did not envision a role for the federal government in policing health and safety that is largely predicated upon consumption of traditional food sources," Emord said. "What we have here is a vast prior restraint that is imposed on parties regardless of the actual risk present."

The founders, he added, "certainly would not have been in favor of a roving federal agency that would invade states and go after specific farmers for selling what they would have understood to be a common food source, raw milk. "I mean, they *all* drank raw milk."

CAN THE GOVERNMENT FORCE YOU TO GET A SHOT?

Should vaccinations be mandatory for all children? What about adults? And if so, what should be the official state penalty for those who refuse to comply? The question of whether to vaccinate oneself or one's children is a personal one, in my opinion. But the state also has the right and the duty to prevent the spread of disease, especially among the most vulnerable populations, such as schoolchildren and the immune-compromised. So where do we draw the line, and what should that line look like?

I am not anti-vaccine; I believe they are beneficial to public health, and if I had children, I would vaccinate them, though not necessarily according to the CDC recommended schedule.

But vaccines are not without their risks. People with certain immune disorders or allergies, for example, cannot tolerate the challenge to their systems. For that exact reason, all fifty states grant medical exemptions to school-mandated shots.

Why would anyone oppose universal, state-mandated shots? Many cite religious or philosophical objections, while others view government-backed immunization programs to be overzealous control by a nanny state run amok. Among anti-vaccine parents, the majority tend to be affluent and educated. There are perhaps tens of thousands of American parents who are convinced that vaccines hurt at least one of their children.

It should be noted that childhood immunization rates are at all-time highs in the United States, and for most shots, they are generally above the 90 percent threshold considered to protect society through what is called "herd immunity." In 2016, "only 0.8% of children received no vaccinations," according to the CDC.

Meanwhile, nearly every state grants religious exemptions, and eighteen allow for "philosophical exemptions" based on personal, moral, or other beliefs.[70] But that could be changing. In 2015, California passed legislation eliminating *all* exemptions (except for medical), including religious and philosophical reasons, joining Mississippi and West Virginia as the only states in the country with such a restrictive regime.[71] Since the California bill was passed, other states have removed certain exemptions, and many lawmakers want to eliminate the provision for religious objections.

For parents in those three states who still refuse to vaccinate according to the CDC recommended schedule, their only option is homeschooling. The choice between no shots or no school may seem harsh, and homeschooling may not be feasible for many families, but it *is* an alternative. I found very few cases of children being vaccinated entirely against their parents' will, although it does happen. One study found just nine cases where a parent was brought before a judge on medical neglect charges because of vaccine refusal.[72]

Many people in the medical profession, and pediatrics in particular, have little sympathy and no patience for parents who do not want to fully vaccinate their children.

What the state can, and should, do with these refuseniks has still not been resolved. As noted previously, the Constitution makes no mention of personal health choice. It does, however, grant certain powers to the federal government when it comes to vaccinations. Under the Commerce Clause of Article I, Congress can and has required vaccines for all immigrants and for U.S. military troops. The clause also permits the secretary of health and human services to issue regulations that impede the spread of disease from foreign countries *and between the states.* There are no compulsory public vaccination regulations under federal law—and there never have been. That has been a province largely left to the states. But HHS does have the power to quarantine or isolate noncompliant individuals during health emergencies involving contagious illnesses.

At the state level, the most important challenge to mandatory vaccination came in 1905 during a smallpox epidemic in Massachusetts. Henning Jacobson, a pastor in Cambridge, refused to comply with that city's ordinance that all individuals receive the smallpox vaccine or pay a $5 fine (about $135 today). He refused to do either and instead sued the city in state court, saying the law violated his personal liberty and right to bodily integrity, as guaranteed under the Fifth and Fourteenth Amendments, which require equal protection and prohibit the deprivation of life, liberty, and property without due process under law.[73]

Jacobson lost, and he ultimately appealed the case to the U.S. Supreme

Court. "A compulsory vaccination law is unreasonable, arbitrary and oppressive, and, therefore, hostile to the inherent right of every freeman to care for his own body and health," his appeal asserted. It was the first time the High Court had heard a vaccine mandate case, and it ruled against Jacobson. His rights were not "contravened," the court said, adding that states have the right to impose "reasonable" measures to ensure public health, even if they restrict individual liberty. The court did, however, emphasize that it was not approving a blanket right of the states to enact mandatory vaccination laws *without* an imminent public-health threat, noting that "the forcible injection of medication into a nonconsenting person's body represents a substantial interference with that person's liberty."

"The Court's paradigm was clear: a mandate is permissible in 'an emergency,' when there was 'imminent danger,' when 'an epidemic of disease . . . threatens the safety of [society's] members,' or an 'epidemic that imperiled an entire population,'" wrote Mary Holland, director of the Graduate Lawyering Program at New York University School of Law, in the March 2013 issue of *The Yale Journal of Health Policy, Law, and Ethics.* Subsequent rulings in other courts, however, determined that vaccines could be required for students, even without the imminent threat of an outbreak.

Individuals do have the right to refuse medical interventions, as the Supreme Court affirmed in the 1990 *Washington v. Harper* decision by recognizing a prisoner's "significant liberty interest in avoiding the unwanted administration of antipsychotic drugs under the Due Process Clause of the Fourteenth Amendment."[74] In her concurring opinion, Justice Sandra Day O'Connor added that "the Court has often deemed state incursions into the body repugnant to the interests protected by the Due Process Clause."

Holland also raised the question of informed consent. "It is now considered in U.S. courts to be a peremptory norm—in other words, it is a fundamental human rights norm that's recognized," she said. "It comes out of World War II, out of the Nuremburg Code, and it's been reiterated in the Declaration of Helsinki and other documents."

State-mandated vaccines for kids to attend school present us with a slippery-slope scenario. Some people in government, public health, and the media want *all* children to be vaccinated, whether they attend school or not. Some even extend that argument to adults. But do states have the power to require vaccines for all adults and children outside of the school or health-care environment? And if so, how should they wield that power, and what would the punishment be for noncompliance?

According to the CDC, Americans nineteen years and older should receive about seventy-five vaccines between the ages of nineteen and eighty—mostly the annual flu shot but also tetanus-diphtheria-pertussis, measles-mumps-rubella, chicken pox, human papillomavirus, pneumococcal and shingles.[75] Are you up to date on your shots? If not, aren't you just as socially and medically irresponsible—reckless, even—as parents who do not follow the federal government schedule for their children?

The penalties for noncompliance that some medical and public health officials are calling for are beyond draconian. Which makes me wonder: Have these "experts" really thought things through?

The most common argument is that non-vaccinating parents should be charged with medical neglect of their children. "It is time to acknowledge that we do not know how to bridge the gap between doctors and vaccine-hesitant parents [and] the time has come to call vaccine refusal by another name that more accurately sums it up: medical neglect," Phoebe Day Danziger and Rebekah Diamond, pediatric residents from Ann Arbor, Michigan, wrote in a July 2016 article at *Slate*. "By continuing to allow exceptions, we are fueling the misconception that vaccinations are an option, a choice, a subjective topic about which people can have different opinions that ought to be respected, when in fact all of the data prove they are not."[76]

Other proposals include cutting off access to certain public places and services for anyone who is not fully vaccinated. "The idea of limiting access to public benefits or services can be extended beyond the school context," Dorit Rubinstein and Lois Weithorn, professors at the University of California Hastings College of the Law, opined in *The Buffalo Law Review*. "Government could condition access to a passport (which would allow the recipient to travel to areas where preventable diseases are still endemic) on vaccination status. Other possibilities include conditioning access to public pools, malls, or public transit on vaccination status." The authors also called for "publication of names of unvaccinated children," a gross violation of privacy and federal laws protecting patient records.[77]

Here we have two public-health experts calling for all Americans, one must assume, to carry around paperwork proving they are completely up to date on their immunizations. If not, under this scenario, they would be barred from shopping at Target, swimming in a public pool, leaving the country, or riding the subway to work. The authors fail to explain how much, exactly, it would cost to station an official vaccine inspector at every mall, pool, or subway entrance in a municipal system. As for buses, would drivers be expected to fulfill that role, and eject people who are not in compliance?

(In January 2019, the New York City NPR affiliate WNYC aired a sponsorship acknowledgment to the CDC in which the CDC falsely claimed that "you must be up to date on your measles vaccine" before traveling abroad.)

Some pundits go even further. Alex Berezow, founding editor of *RealClearScience* and member of *USA Today*'s Board of Contributors, wrote an opinion piece for that paper in January 2015 titled, simply enough, "Parents Who Do Not Vaccinate Their Children Should Go to Jail." Those parents, Berezow insisted, "are turning their children into little walking time bombs. They ought to be charged for endangering their children and others. It is time to end this insanity."[78]

But even some of the most ardent vaccine supporters think that jail time for incalcitrant parents is too extreme—and counterproductive. A cancer surgeon named Dr. David Gorski, also known as "Orac," author of the blog *Respectful Insolence* and managing editor of the website Science-Based Medicine, is vehemently opposed to people who question vaccine safety. But he also opposes forced vaccination. "Have they really thought about this?" he wrote of the state-enforced mandate proponents. "Are [they] willing to allow courts to order forced vaccination and have the police enforce this order?" And, he asked, would it really be better to "have the child in the crappy foster care systems in some parts of this country and vaccinated rather than unvaccinated and with their family?" When society begins to equate failure to vaccinate with medical neglect "on par with or even worse than failing to let a child with cancer be treated with chemotherapy," he said, "almost any measure is justifiable."[79]

I am not saying that state-mandated immunization for all—with or without a public-health emergency—will happen. I am saying that it *could* happen. Serious people in serious positions of influence—in politics, public health, and the media—have openly floated the idea. The question then becomes, does the right to bodily integrity, due process, and privacy under the First, Fourth, Fifth, and Fourteenth Amendments trump the duty of the government to protect public health under the Commerce Clause and other powers, or is it the other way around? I think it's a question worth asking.

OPPRESSION OF SEXUAL MINORITIES

Life in America for lesbian, gay, bisexual, and transgender people, compared to many other countries in the world at least, has been improving exponentially since a band of drag queens took on the NYPD during the Stonewall Riots of 1969, ushering in the modern LGBT movement. Tremendous victories have been achieved at the federal level, including legalizing same-sex marriage and permitting lesbian, gay, bisexual, and (until recently) transgender individuals to serve in the armed forces. At the state and local level, many governments, though still a disappointing minority, have adopted LGBT anti-discrimination measures, and judges from one-room rural courthouses to the highest court in the land have ruled and written powerfully on the need to include everyone under the federal civil rights umbrella.

Culturally, too, we have seen major—and quite sudden—shifts in public attitudes as reflected in opinion polls showing overwhelming support for LGBT rights. The hit 1990s sitcom *Will and Grace* played a major role in the increased tolerance of homosexuality in America. Now, LGBT people are represented throughout the artistic, media, literary, and political worlds. The 2017 Academy Award winner for Best Picture of the Year was *Moonlight*. That would have been unthinkable just a few years earlier, even in "liberal" Hollywood.

Under Presidents Clinton and Obama, gays and lesbians won public offices and were appointed to important positions in the government or made ambassadors to foreign countries, among other advances. Of course, threats of being fired, blatant discrimination, hate speech, police brutality, street violence, and, sometimes, even homicide remained a constant companion for many LGBT people. But most activists expected Hillary Clinton to carry the progressive civil rights mantle into the next decade and perhaps beyond.

Of course, things did not turn out that way, and, under Trump and his allies in Congress, we are actually moving backward. It is perhaps the first time in U.S. history that politicians have actively fought to take away protections against a class of citizens that have already been granted, and to codify discrimination against them into state and federal law.

Without guaranteed protections such as those provided under the Civil Rights Act of 1964, a majority of LGBT Americans are still without even the most fundamental protections when it comes to things like employment, education, health care, social services, and public accommodations, including bakeries that refuse to make cakes for same-sex marriages, in violation of their state's civil rights laws. For LGBT people of color, the situation is often exponentially worse. As long as this remains the case, stories such as the ones that follow will continue to happen, every day, in every state across the nation.

No Kissing in Aisle Three!

One balmy afternoon in Honolulu, in March 2015, Courtney Wilson and Taylor Guerrero, a female couple in their twenties from Los Angeles on a romantic getaway in purportedly progressive and tolerant Hawaii, popped into a grocery store to get some snacks. As they browsed the aisles, they held hands and at one point stopped and hugged. Wilson kissed her partner on the cheek. "We were just being goofy," Guerrero told reporters later.[80] Then they heard two men yelling. One of them was in a Honolulu Police Department uniform. "You can't do that!" he shouted. "Take that somewhere else!" The women ignored him and kept shopping. But the cop, Bobby Harrison, who was off duty, saw them holding hands and kissing again. And once again, he ordered them to stop, this time threatening to have them thrown out of the store. Still not done, he went to find the manager, asking him to issue a written trespass warning to the couple, who proceeded to checkout to pay for their food.

Harrison approached them in line. He told them the store had issued the warning, barring them from entering or remaining on the property. He ordered them out of the cashier line. Stunned at the request, the women refused. Wilson got out her cell phone and dialed 911 to report the "unlawful harassment" and then moved to go outside to get the store's address. That's when Harrison physically grabbed her, according to the lawsuit later filed by the couple, blocking her exit and ending the 911 call. Guerrero then tried to move in to get between her partner and the officer. According to the women, he shoved Guerrero toward the ground, striking Wilson in the process and slamming Guerrero's head onto the checkout counter. A "tussle" ensued, Guerrero later told CNN, adding that Harrison had punched her in the face when she tried to push him off her girlfriend.

The women fought back, they said, kicking and pushing Harrison, and hitting him in the face, breaking the cop's glasses. He handcuffed and arrested them for felony assault on a law enforcement officer. Both women spent the next two days in jail, trying to arrange bail from their vacation money.

When they got out, prosecutors told them to check in every couple of weeks with the bail bondsman until their trial. But their money was gone. They could not afford to fly back and forth to California, so they stayed in Hawaii, first sleeping at the home of a family friend and then staying with a stranger who took them in. They ended up on the streets before someone offered them shelter as they awaited trial. Meanwhile, surveillance video from the store mysteriously disappeared.

About five months later, prosecutors dropped all charges. They were, at last, free to leave "paradise."

On October 27, 2015, Wilson and Guerrero filed a civil rights lawsuit in federal district court in Honolulu against Harrison, in both his individual and official capacities, the City and County of Honolulu, and other unnamed defendants. The complaint charged that Harrison's acts were "committed with the intent to discriminate against them on the basis of their sexual preference." Harrison, it alleged, had acted "without probable, sufficient, just, or reasonable cause," in violation of the Fourth Amendment, and discriminated against them on the basis of their sexual orientation, in violation of the Equal Protection Clause of the Fourteenth Amendment.[81]

As a direct result of his illegal conduct, the suit alleged, the women had suffered physical injuries as well as "great humiliation, embarrassment, and emotional distress, anxiety, worry, and concern." The suit also alleged assault and battery, stating that the plaintiffs "at no time consented to or provoked Defendant Harrison to touch them." It asked for unspecified damages plus legal fees.

Seven months later, in May 2016, the city announced an $80,000 settlement with the women but without admitting any wrongdoing. The police department did reportedly open an investigation into Harrison, but it wasn't clear if he was disciplined. Two months after the suit was filed, he retired.[82]

"I don't really know what either of us were looking to get honestly," Wilson told *Hawaii News Now*. "It wasn't money or anything. We wanted to be compensated, but I think more or less we wanted Officer Harrison to suffer some sort of repercussions for his actions."

Denied Room at a B&B

In yet another case involving a lesbian couple from California on vacation in Hawaii, Taeko Bufford and Diane Cervelli planned a trip together in 2007 to visit a close friend in the Hawaii Kai section of Honolulu. Cervelli found a suitable place online, Aloha Bed & Breakfast, and called to inquire about room availability. When she said she was traveling with another woman and they just needed one bed, the owner, Phyllis Young, asked if the women were lesbians. Cervelli replied affirmatively.

"We're very strong Christians," Young snapped. "I'm very uncomfortable accepting this reservation from you." Then she hung up. Cervelli was badly shaken. Now in tears, she called Bufford to tell her what happened. Bufford, understandably distraught, called Young back. Again, she refused the couple accommodations.[83]

"Is this because we are lesbians?" Bufford asked. Young said that it was. The couple booked another place in Waikiki, then filed a complaint with the Hawaii Civil Rights Commission (HCRC). During the investigation, Young told commissioners that homosexuality is "detestable" and "defiles our land." The commission then found reasonable cause to believe that Young had violated the state's law against discrimination based on sexual orientation in public accommodations and issued them a "right to sue" notice.

After obtaining help from Lambda Legal, the nation's preeminent pro bono defense group for members of the LGBT community, Cervelli and Bufford filed suit in December 2011 against Young in the state's First Circuit Court in Honolulu.[84]

"I can't tell you how much it hurt to be essentially told, 'We don't do business with your kind,'" Bufford said in an interview with Lambda Legal's website. "You don't have to change your beliefs, but you do have to follow the law."[85]

Refusing to let the couple book a room "was solely based on their sexual orientation because the owner indicated that if they were married, she would not have allowed them to stay there," said the couple's lawyer, Peter Renn, of Lambda Legal's Los Angeles office. She also would have a problem if they were an unmarried heterosexual couple, he said.

Young moved to have the case dismissed, but she lost. The lawsuit, which sought a court order barring Aloha B&B from discriminating against LGBT guests, a declaration that what Young did was clearly unlawful, and unspecified monetary damages, went to trial, even though "no amount of money is going to erase the humiliation and pain," Renn said.

Young's attorney, Jim Hochberg of the Alliance Defense Fund, a religious freedom group, argued that, even though discrimination in public accommodation is "a horrible evil," Young was within her rights. Why? Because she was renting rooms out of her own private home and not operating a place of public accommodation, he argued. Therefore, forcing her to take in guests whose lives conflicted with her religious beliefs violated her First Amendment right to privacy.[86]

But as Renn argued in the complaint, "Young's religious beliefs do not compel her to operate a bed and breakfast business." If she wanted to make extra income while still adhering to her faith, he added, under a provision in Hawaii law, she could offer the rooms to tenants seeking long-term housing.

The court ruled in favor of the women, finding Young liable and granting the couple injunctive and declaratory relief. In April 2013, Young appealed the decision at the state's Intermediate Court of Appeals. It took almost five years before a ruling was finally handed down. On February 28, 2018, the appeals court affirmed the lower court ruling.[87]

"The court today affirmed that there is no excuse for discrimination," Renn said in a statement. "Hawai'i law is crystal clear: if you operate a business, you are open to all." The court, he said, "saw this case for what it was and rightly refused to allow the business owner to use religion as a fig leaf for discrimination."

Aloha B&B immediately filed an appeal at the state's supreme court. In July 2018, that court declined to hear the case—a final victory eleven years after it began.[88]

The women said they were grateful to the state courts in Hawaii. But, Bufford added, "it terrifies me to think of what might happen if the U.S. Supreme Court were to decide that businesses do have a religious license to discriminate," the issue at stake in *Masterpiece Cakeshop v. Colorado Civil Rights Commission*.

"Diane and Ty's experience shows just how pernicious and damaging a religious license to discriminate would be," Lambda Legal's then CEO Rachel B. Tiven explained. "There is no limit to the places where LGBT people would be harmed if businesses were granted the right to discriminate. It would gut antidiscrimination laws and could turn everyday, routine events into nightmares of denial, rejection, and stigmatization for LGBT people."

And remember this. Young said she would not rent to unmarried hetero-sexual couples either, because of her religious faith. But if Congress passes the First Amendment Defense Act, this sort of discrimination could occur every day in every state, even in bluest-of-blue Hawaii.

Hired, Then Unhired, for Being Gay

Mark Horton is a gay man living in Missouri with his husband, whom he mar-ried in 2014. In February 2016, Horton, a successful sales and marketing VP for Celtic Healthcare, was approached by a headhunting agency on behalf of a Celtic competitor, Midwest Geriatric Management (MGM), about a similar job available at that company. Although Horton was happy where he was, the recruitment agency convinced him to apply. In mid-April 2016, MGM's owners, Judah and Faigie (Faye) Bienstock, sent Horton a written job offer. When he accepted, the Bienstocks sent him an email saying how thrilled they were that he was coming on board.[89]

Horton gave notice at Celtic and began finalizing paperwork—including gathering all his academic records, which was taking longer than he thought—and setting the official start date with his new bosses. He continued to receive cordial emails from Faye Bienstock—that is, until May 19, when Horton wrote to Bienstock to update her on his efforts in the records search, explaining that "My partner has been on me about [my MBA] since he completed his PhD a while back."

Five days later, Bienstock wrote back to Horton. The job offer had been rescinded. Horton was shocked and devastated. He was not actively looking to leave his job; he was recruited for another job. Now he had no job at all.

Red-state Missouri does not have a law to protect LGBT rights, meaning what happened to Horton is permissible under state law. But what about fed-eral law? That question is being played out right now in several U.S. courts. Under Title VII of the Civil Rights Act, it is against federal law for employers of fifteen or more people or the government to discriminate against employees on the basis of "sex, race, color, national origin, and religion." The question is, should sexual orientation—and gender identity—be included under the pro-tected category of "sex"?

In the lawsuit filed on Horton's behalf in U.S. district court by a St. Louis firm and Lambda Legal, lawyers made three claims: First, that MGM violated

Title VII protections against discrimination based on sexual orientation. Second, the owners discriminated against Horton based on religious reasons, also a Title VII violation. "They are very open about how their Jewish faith influences how they run their business," Lambda senior attorney Omar Gonzalez-Pagan said. "And based on their disapproval of Mark's same-sex relation, they rescinded their job offer that he had already accepted." The third claim was for contract fraud.[90]

But the court summarily dismissed the case. Horton and his legal team appealed the decision before the Eighth Circuit Court on March 7, 2018, this time without the fraud claim.[91]

It was Lambda's fourth federal appeal to secure Title VII protection for LGBT employees. Just one week before, Lambda had scored a bittersweet victory in the full Second Circuit (or en banc, as opposed to the typical three-judge panel), which ruled 10–3 in favor of the estate of skydiving instructor Donald Zarda, who was fired because he was gay and had since died in a BASE jumping accident.[92]

A year earlier, in a groundbreaking 8–3 decision, the full Seventh Circuit Court made a similar en banc ruling (after the initial three-judge panel rejected the claim) extending Title VII's protections to Kimberly Hively, a community college instructor in Indiana with more than fourteen years on the job, who was denied full-time employment and ultimately fired for being a lesbian.[93] Lambda had argued that "several court rulings and a recent decision by the Equal Employment Opportunity Commission (EEOC)" supported the contention that sexual orientation is protected under the Civil Rights Act.[94]

It was now settled case law within those two circuits, which encompass six states in the upper Midwest and Northeast: No matter what those state laws say, employers can be sued for discrimination against LGBT employees.

The fourth case involved Jameka Evans, a security guard at a Savannah, Georgia, public hospital who was harassed at work and forced from her job because she is a lesbian. In April 2015, Evans filed suit against the hospital in U.S. District Court for the Southern District of Georgia, which summarily dismissed the case, ruling that Title VII does not protect gays and lesbians. That's when Lambda intervened, filing an appeal with the Eleventh Circuit the following January. But a three-judge panel ruled against Evans on March 10, 2017.[95] When attorneys asked the full court to rehear the case, they were likewise refused.[96] In September 2017, Lambda appealed the case to the U.S.

Supreme Court.[97] Attorneys general from eighteen states, more than seventy-five businesses, seventeen antidiscrimination legal scholars, and eleven LGBT organizations asked the court to review the case. The petition was denied that December.[98]

Similar corporate, legal, and civic support has been shown for Mark Horton's case, with friend-of-the-court briefs filed by forty-seven businesses, including Levi Strauss & Co., Airbnb, CBS, Microsoft, and Salesforce; fifteen state attorneys general; the nation's leading LGBT rights organizations; and several other organizations.[99] Despite Jameka Evans's defeat in the Eleventh Circuit, by far the most conservative appeals court in the county (which said it could not hear the case, citing a 1970 rule governing that particular circuit), Horton's chances look slightly better in the Eighth Circuit. After the sprawling Ninth Circuit out west, this court is the second-most liberal or, better put, the second-least conservative, in terms of its rulings.

In the meantime, Horton, who was unemployed as of mid-2018, can do little but wait on the decision about his appeal. "This should never have happened," Lambda cocounsel Mark S. Schuver said in a statement. "This has been devastating for Mark and his family, and we hope the Eighth Circuit will follow the examples of the Second and Seventh Circuits and confirm that Title VII protects you no matter whom you love or how you identify."[100]

If the Eighth Circuit sides with Horton, his case will be remanded to district court for trial on the merits. Lambda senior attorney Omar Gonzalez-Pagan told me he was optimistic about the Horton case because it hinges on the law and not partisan or moral beliefs. "This is an issue of statute interpretation—how do you read the words in a statute," he said. "And regardless of the party of the president that appointed a judge, we have had support from ideologically conservative and liberal judges in the past." He likened it to the history of mixed-race marriages in the courts, saying that issue was not settled "as a matter of partisanship or ideology."[101]

At least thirty-two states, and the federal government, have no laws to protect LGBT people *and* their families against discrimination.[102] And even in states where LGBT rights bills have been passed, they are still being challenged in Congress and the courts, including the Supreme Court decision on the bakery case, and the First Amendment Defense Act (FADA)—both of which would enshrine individuals and businesses with the right to refuse service to anybody, based on religious grounds.

Making matters worse, on January 18, 2018, Trump's Department of Health and Human Services announced a new branch of its Office for Civil Rights (OCR)—the Conscience and Religious Freedom Division—tasked with "protecting the religious and moral beliefs" of health care workers.[103] Many conservatives cheered the measure, but civil libertarians on both sides were alarmed by it, which they said gives carte blanche to doctors and nurses who don't want to treat LGBT patients and people seeking abortion care.

OCR director Roger Severino told reporters at the time that "no one should be forced to choose between helping sick people and living by one's deepest moral or religious convictions, and the new division will help guarantee that victims of unlawful discrimination find justice." But many advocacy groups scoffed at that characterization, including the ACLU, Planned Parenthood, the National Abortion Rights League (NARAL), the National Women's Law Center, and the National Center for Transgender Equality. "Despite the name, this division isn't actually here to enforce religious freedom, it's designed to protect providers who discriminate against women & LGBTQ people," NARAL said in a tweet.[104]

Transgender Student Oppressed at School

Of all the minorities in America, I can think of none more oppressed than transgender individuals. The current fight against the Trump administration to allow transgender men and women to serve bravely and honorably in the military is emblematic of how far we have to go to reverse all the stigma, ignorance, harassment, and unapologetic abuse of their constitutional rights.

Among this vulnerable population, perhaps none suffer harsher treatment than students. Many but not all of their stories pertain to letting young people use the school bathroom that corresponds to their gender identity and not their gender at birth.

That included Ashton Whitaker, a junior who was attending Tremper High School in Kenosha, Wisconsin, in 2016. A gifted honors student who was popular and active in many school activities, Whitaker was born as a girl and continued living that way until junior high. That's when he recognized that he is, in fact, a boy and "began to experience profound discomfort with being assumed to be a girl by others," according to court documents from his case.[105] At the end of eighth grade, in the spring of 2013, Whitaker told his family that he is transgender. During his freshman year in high school, he began confiding his secret to close friends and slowly began transitioning to a male identity, cutting his hair short, wearing masculine clothing, and taking on a male name and masculine pronouns.

The following year, in the fall of 2014, Whitaker informed his teachers and classmates that he is a boy, requesting that he be referred to by his male name and pronouns. He then began his gender transition under the direction of therapists and physicians. His pediatrician diagnosed him with gender dysphoria (transgender identity). "Since Whitaker's transition at school, he has been widely known and accepted as a boy by the school community," the court papers said. When he returned for his junior year, in September 2015, he used the boys' restrooms without incident or complaint for seven months. He did not discuss this decision with administrators or teachers, "because he understood it to be his legal right."

And then a teacher saw him using the boys' bathroom and reported it to two assistant principals. School officials then decreed that all students would be required to use the bathroom corresponding to their gender at birth. Whitaker, for all outward appearances now a boy, would have to use the girls' room, or a single user restroom designated solely for him, in the school office. Whitaker refused to use it, because the office was far from his classes and going there would draw questions from other students.

Despite letters from Whitaker's doctor asking for an exemption, the school said it would continue to deny him access to the boys' room because he had not completed his medical transition—a procedure for which he was still too young. Whitaker was also required to sleep either in a suite with girls, or all alone, on school trips, including an orchestra trip to Europe. He began eating and drinking less to avoid having to use female bathrooms as much as possible, often becoming weak and dizzy.

It didn't stop there. According to Whitaker's legal filings, teachers intentionally called him by his female name, using female pronouns in front of other students, despite his entreaties not to. During his junior year, school officials tried to block Whitaker from running for junior prom king, even though other students had nominated him based on his active involvement in community service. He could only run for prom queen, the school said. After protests by many of his classmates, the school relented.

And then came the wristband.

In May 2016, Whitaker's guidance counselor showed him a bright green wristband. Its purpose? Marking transgender students to monitor them and ensure they were using the correct bathroom.

Whitaker felt sickened and afraid. He knew that transgender people are at tremendous risk of violent attacks nationwide. It was an agonizing choice: refuse to wear the band and risk penalty of discipline, or don it, knowing that students he did not know would repeatedly ask why he was wearing it, causing him to explain over and over that he is transgender. Some kids would stare; others would ridicule him outright. Whitaker chose to fight.

"He felt like his safety would be even more threatened if he had to wear this visible badge of his transgender status," wrote attorneys from the Transgender Law Center, who took on Whitaker's case in a civil action filed July 19, 2016, in United States District Court for the Eastern District of Wisconsin against the school district and board of education. "Branding transgender students in this way would single them out for additional scrutiny, stigma, and potentially harassment or violence, and violate their privacy by revealing their transgender status to others," the complaint said.[106]

Educators in Kenosha had "repeatedly refused to recognize or respect Whitaker's gender identity" and had taken a series of "discriminatory and highly stigmatizing actions against him based on his sex, gender identity, and transgender status" in violation of Title IX of the Education Amendments of 1972, and the Equal Protection Clause of the Fourteenth Amendment. These actions denied Whitaker "full and equal access to KUSD's education program and activities on the basis of his sex."

Because of the stress and harm that ensued, Whitaker continued to experience lowered self-esteem, embarrassment, social isolation, stigma, depression, and anxiety. Ever since the school "singled him out as different from all other boys," the lawsuit contended, "he has felt deeply hurt, disrespected, and humiliated." Whitaker developed eating and sleeping problems and found it difficult to concentrate in class or on his homework. Although he cried very little in the past, "he frequently cries and fights back tears," and was afraid to leave the house unless with a group of friends.

In addition to "compensatory relief" and attorney fees, the suit sought an injunction ordering the school district to let Whitaker use the boys' room during his final year at school, to "otherwise to treat him as a boy in all respects," and to treat all transgender students the same way as their "similarly situated peers." It also asked the court to make the district declare that prohibiting discrimination on the basis of sex included gender identity, and to provide district-wide training to all administrators on this policy.

Oral arguments were heard in September 2016. Meanwhile, school was back in session, and Whitaker was again barred from using the boys' restroom. On the twenty-second, Judge Pamela Pepper granted Whitaker's "prayer for relief" in part. During his senior year, and pending any appeal, the school could not deny him access to the boys' room, nor could it monitor or surveil the student in any way, thus no green wristband, and no penalties could be imposed upon him for using the restroom of his gender identity. The court also denied the Kenosha Unified School District's motion to dismiss the case, and its motion to grant a stay of the temporary injunction until the appeal could be heard at the Seventh Circuit.[107]

Judge Pepper wrote that Whitaker had "shown a likelihood that his claims will succeed on the Merits." Because there was no case law defining "sex" for the purposes of Title IX education protections, "the plaintiff might succeed on his claim that that word includes transgender persons," a position, she noted, supported by the U.S. Department of Education. Whitaker likewise had enough evidence to support a claim of "gender stereotyping," and that he would "suffer irreparable injury," if the court did not block the school's actions.

Finally, the judge wrote, the decision would have no impact on anything but this one case, despite the fearmongering claims of government lawyers, who said an injunction would "force schools all over the state of Wisconsin, and perhaps farther afield," to allow transgender children to use the bathroom of their choice, the judge wrote. "The defendants accord this court's order breadth and power it does not possess," she said.

The Kenosha Unified School District promptly filed an appeal at the Seventh Circuit Court. As everyone involved braced for that hearing, the Trump administration delivered a present of sorts—politically, if not legally speaking—to the district and everyone else opposed to letting transgender students use a bathroom other than "their own." On February 22, 2017, the administration rescinded guidelines issued under Obama's Departments of Education and Justice the previous May. Those guidelines, about protecting public school students who wish to use facilities corresponding with their gender identity, were issued under Title IX of the federal education law and its ban on discrimination based on sex, which, the Obama administration said, included gender identity.[108]

Oral arguments were held in March. On May 30, 2017, a three-judge panel ruled unanimously in favor of Whitaker.[109]

The youth had scored a significant victory for transgender student rights. Ironically, if the school district had accepted defeat and not filed an appeal, the lower court ruling would have pertained only to one student at one school for one academic year. Now, it was established case law within the entire Seventh Circuit, comprising Wisconsin, Illinois, and Indiana, with a combined population of some twenty-five million people.[110]

But before Whitaker's case could be sent back to district court for adjudication of damages, the school district filed a petition, in August 2017, for the U.S. Supreme Court to review the matter. Among those submitting briefs in favor of the district were right-wing groups such as the Eagle Forum, the Family Research Council, and Concerned Women for America.

And then, in early January 2018, the defendants agreed to settle. Whitaker was awarded $800,000 in damages, although most of that, $650,000, went to his lawyers, *The Milwaukee Journal Sentinel* reported. The school district's counsel said that protracted litigation could last years and cost millions of dollars, which its insurer was not willing to pay.[111]

"I am deeply relieved that this long, traumatic part of my life is finally over and I can focus on my future," Whitaker, a freshman at the University of Wisconsin–Madison, said in a statement. "Winning this case . . . made me feel like I can actually do something to help other trans youth live authentically," he said. "If someone's telling you that you don't deserve that, prove them wrong."[112]

It was not Lambda's first victory after filing Title IX lawsuits against schools on behalf of transgender students, including successful cases in Pennsylvania, involving three high schoolers, and Ohio, in the case of an elementary school girl.

In all three cases, the government quickly settled with the plaintiffs and paid them damages. "They all set great precedents and are now having a great impact on transgender rights generally," Gonzalez-Pagan told me. "Whether we won under Title IX or Equal Protection, we educated the country about the importance of treating our kids for who they are." Two of those cases, he said, were cited in the current lawsuit seeking to overturn the Trump ban on transgender servicemembers.

The Future

If current trends continue in federal circuit courts, we could one day see a country where most, if not all, LGBT employees, students, consumers, parents, tenants, home buyers, and others are protected under court order, if not by their respective state legislatures. But that could take a long time, and it is by no means guaranteed.

What is needed in addition to court action, advocates say, is statutory federal protection achieved through passage of the Equality Act in Congress, which would define the term *sex* under Title VII of the Civil Rights Act to include "sex stereotype, sexual orientation, or gender identity." It would also vastly expand the definition of *public accommodations* to encompass things such as recreation, amusement, goods, services, or programs, including stores, online retailers, or service providers; salons, banks, funeral parlors, and health care; accounting, legal, or transportation services. There are several other related provisions. Had it passed previously, the law would have covered all the people mentioned in the above paragraphs.[113]

The act was first introduced back in 1974 by two Democratic firebrand lawmakers from New York, Representative Bella Abzug and Representative Ed Koch, but has never made it to the floor in either house. Reintroduced in 2017, the bill currently enjoys nearly two hundred House cosponsors and forty-six in the Senate, including some Republicans—almost a majority in each case. Even though it would probably survive a floor vote in both houses, the conservative Republican majority has refused to allow it.

"The Republican leadership is completely against any LGBT-inclusive protection," Lambda's Gonzalez-Pagan said. "They almost stymied the Violence Against Women Act because it included gender identity, and now they are actively trying to harm LGBT people through the First Amendment Defense Act and other policies. It's a disgrace." That could begin to change in the current Congress, now that the Democrats have taken the gavel in the House.

With so much progress, yet so much remaining uncertainty in Congress and the courts, LGBT advocates have adopted a two-pronged strategy for achieving equality. "It's called the belts-and-suspenders approach," Gonzalez-

Pagan said. "We ensure equality for people that is legally mandated [by the courts], but it's also clear that we support the Equality Act." Why? To clarify that sexual orientation and gender identity are forms of sex discrimination "consistent with the position taken in courts," he said. "We want to make sure the government explicitly states that [such] discrimination is abhorrent and not conducive to a good workplace and educational environment, nor for housing either. And we want that poster to be put up in the lunchroom to make it evidently clear to everyone."

But even if the bill sailed through Congress, it will still be opposed by President Trump, even though the former liberal billionaire playboy from Manhattan campaigned as a "new" type of Republican who would respect LGBT rights. He held up a rainbow flag at a rally and once quipped that Caitlyn Jenner could use the women's bathroom at Trump Tower. "Thank you to the LGBT community!" he tweeted from the trail. "I will fight for you while Hillary brings in more people that will threaten your freedoms and beliefs."[114]

As every LGBT person in America knows, it didn't turn out that way. "This is the most violently anti-LGBT administration ever," Gonzalez-Pagan said. "It has made it its mission to attack the civil rights of LGBT people or the civil rights of any minority that is seen as an 'other.'"

The Trump team, for example, intervened in the case of Donald Zarda, the deceased skydiving trainer who sued after being fired because he was gay. Sessions's DOJ filed a brief and sent an attorney to the courthouse to argue in *favor* of the skydiving company, even though another government lawyer, from the Equal Employment Opportunity Commission, was present to argue in favor of Zarda's estate. "The federal government actually argued against itself in court," Gonzalez-Pagan said. I asked if that was rare. "It's virtually unprecedented," he replied. "It's an example of how far this administration is willing to go to stop equality for LGBT people."

And there is more. On October 5, 2017, Jeff Sessions ended yet another Obama-era policy, this one protecting transgender employees from discrimination in the workplace. In his memo, Sessions said that Title VII only prohibits "sex discrimination between men and women" and does not "encompass discrimination based on gender identity per se, including transgender status."[115]

The next day, in a one-two punch to the LGBT community, the attorney general issued a second, far more expansive, and, advocates say, quite dangerous memo, stating that devout employers could hire only those job seekers whose faith and behavior are "consistent with the employers' religious beliefs." This protected right to discriminate, he added, extended not only to individuals "but also to organizations, associations, and at least some for-profit corporations."[116]

"No one should be forced to choose between living out his or her faith and complying with the law," Sessions wrote, in words sounding much like the HHS memo on health care workers. The religious Right roared in victory. "President Trump is demonstrating his commitment to undoing the anti-faith policies of the previous administration and restoring true religious freedom," said Tony Perkins, president of the Family Research Council.[117]

And Donald Trump, as I write this, is fighting a court challenge to his ban on transgender people enlisting in the armed forces, yet another Obama-era policy that Trump rescinded.[118] But the president's prospects here do not look rosy. So far, four U.S. district court rulings and two federal appellate court rulings have granted and preserved preliminary injunctions against enforcement of the ban.[119] On January 1, 2018, transgender servicemembers openly enlisted in the military for the first time ever.[120] It's hard to imagine that any court would agree to kicking them back out, but nothing is impossible, especially given the hard-right turn on the federal bench. In November 2018, the Justice Department asked the Supreme Court to take up three of the transgender cases. As of this writing, no decision had been made.

In October 2018, *The New York Times* published a memo from the U.S. Department of Health and Human Services that would "establish a legal definition of sex under Title IX, the federal civil rights law that bans gender discrimination in education programs that receive government financial assistance." If adopted, the measure "would define sex as either male or female, unchangeable, and determined by the genitals that a person is born with," the paper said, adding that "'transgender' could be defined out of existence."[121]

Meanwhile, should Trump ever have to leave office for any reason, his likely successor would be even worse. As governor of Indiana, Mike Pence, a famous homophobe, has been claimed to support religious-based "conversion therapy" for homosexuals ("pray away the gay," as critics derisively call it, is a fraudulent practice that so far has been outlawed in eleven states and the District of Columbia)[122] and signed a draconian religious freedom bill that sent corporations and sports teams fleeing the state and tarnishing the reputation of the future vice president and, possibly, president.[123] In January 2019, his wife,

Karen Pence, announced she would begin teaching art at a conservative Bible school in Virginia that bans LGBT employees and reserves the right, according to NBC News, to not admit or to expel any student who identifies as LGBT or comes from a home with an LGBT guardian.

"They're bringing a theocracy to America," Gonzalez-Pagan said. "It's abhorrent. They have no respect for anyone not important to them, and they have no respect for the law."

It's worth noting that President Barack Obama, in 2015, endorsed the Equality Act, as did the two candidates vying to succeed him in 2016: Hillary Clinton and Bernie Sanders. None of the seventeen Republicans who ran for their party's nomination supported the bill. President Trump is on record against it.[124]

8

COPS, COURTS, AND JAILS

We call it the "criminal justice system," but at times, the system seems more criminal than just. The rights of citizens can be—and sometimes are—abused throughout the entire law enforcement process, from surveillance, investigation, and interrogation to arrest and detention, to criminal prosecution and, in many cases, incarceration. What follows is a brief review of just a few of the ways that Americans—especially minorities and members of the working class—have been met with malevolence and lies by a wide range of authorities and had their constitutional rights shredded in the process.

It's true that much lip service is being paid in Washington right now to "prison reform," including efforts by White House aide Jared Kushner and celebrity Kim Kardashian. And there is no question that our entire criminal justice system is urgently in need of a complete overhaul—from cops to courts to prisons. Sadly, however, as the 2018 midterm election campaigns got under way, these crucial issues seemed unable to draw the attention they critically need into the national political debate, with its laser focus on the Russia probe, immigration, trade, and taxes. Why? Because few politicians want to be branded as "anti–law enforcement." It does them no good in the polls to take on police and prosecutors. And while the media do cover these cases, most reporters have failed to make criminal justice reform a standard question for any candidate running for public office. That needs to change. The public should hold mainstream media accountable for holding our politicians accountable. Criminal justice reform cannot be sidelined. It is no afterthought; it is urgent.

WRONGFUL ARRESTS?

Arrested for Depositing a Check

In early September of 2017, a Wichita State University mechanical engineering doctoral student, Sattar Ali, forty-nine, walked into the Emprise Bank in Wichita to deposit a $151,000 check he had received through the sale of a house in Dearborn, Michigan. Ali, who was born in Iraq and immigrated to the United States in 1993, had recently moved back to Wichita from Dearborn and needed the funds for the purchase of a new home.

Ali was in good standing with his Emprise account. Even so, he brought along documents relating to the sale, including the business cards of the real estate agent and title company who took part in the closing. But the banker, meeting with him in a private cubicle, said she only needed the check and the title company's card. The two engaged in casual chitchat as the bank employee walked back and forth to a private staff area. Ali didn't know it, but the employee had asked another staffer to call 911. The check, she said, was bogus. "Send someone quick," the employee told the dispatcher, who asked if any weapons were involved. "No, um, what's happening is he's trying to—he wanted me to deposit it so that he could get cash in two days, and it's not a good check," the clerk responded.

"All right, no disturbance, correct?"

"No," the clerk said. "He's being *overly* friendly." In fact, she said, his calm demeanor was cause for concern—without noting the illogic of someone willing to wait two days for a bogus check to clear.[1]

The operator asked for the customer's name. "It's, um, he's, um, I think he's, um, Pakistani," the employee replied. Two minutes into the call, the operator said she had dispatched officers to the bank. Then she tried to determine why the bank had called. The clerk said Ali was "trying to filter money" through his account and that the check lacked a phone number or watermark. The employee never attempted to contact the bank listed on the check or call the title company whose card Ali had handed over.

Several squad cars from the Wichita Police Department, Sedgwick County Sheriff's Office, and Kansas Highway Patrol pulled up outside the bank. Officers and deputies rushed in. Ali was astounded but showed them his supporting documentation. Police made no effort to follow up on his claims until after he was handcuffed, arrested, and taken away. Ali's wife and fifteen-year-old daughter, waiting outside in the family car, were arrested as well. They seized his wife's cell phone, searched their vehicle and possessions without a warrant, and searched their bodies and clothes, including beneath their headscarves. The teenage daughter was terrified and sobbing. The family was separated from each other in their own cells. Ali was kept with his hand and leg cuffed to a table. They spent four and a half hours in custody at the police station, until officers finally verified the check's authenticity.

"No one told me why I was being arrested until we were being released," Ali told *The Wichita Eagle*. "They didn't read me rights or anything. They jumped to conclusions." He claimed he was arrested because the check was made out to "someone named Sattar Ali, not James or Robert."

A few days later, the Wichita Police Department issued a formal apology, as did the bank. Ali said that was not enough. "We have the rights, we have the constitutional right, we have the freedom, we have a justice system, what happened to all of that?" he told the local CBS affiliate. "Are we guilty just because of our look and our names until we're proven innocent later on?"[2]

The Alis retained legal help from the national civil rights group Muslim Advocates, which sent a letter to the city police, county sheriff, and Kansas Highway Patrol demanding "a transparent and thorough explanation" for the arrests, any video recordings of the event, and all antibias policies implemented by their department in the past five years, among other things. The group's attorney requested the information within one week. Failing that, "they are fully prepared to pursue all legal remedies available to them," he warned.[3]

Puerto Rican Arrested, Threatened with Deportation

A Chicago man born in Puerto Rico was arrested and detained for three days in May 2010 under suspicion of being an undocumented immigrant. Chicago police arrested Eduardo Caraballo, thirty-two, for allegedly stealing a car, an accusation he denied. But whether he committed the crime or not, the treatment he received did not meet constitutional muster. When Caraballo's mother appeared to post bail for him, instead of being released, the authorities said that agents from Immigration and Customs Enforcement (ICE) were going to detain him for entering the country illegally. He told the cops several times that he was born in Puerto Rico and thus a U.S. citizen. His mother even brought his birth certificate to the station. But the cops said he would be deported.

"That's crazy. Because I was born in Puerto Rico. I never knew that Puerto Rico wasn't part of the United States," he told the Chicago NBC News affiliate. "Just because of the way I look—I have Mexican features—they pretty much assumed that my papers were fake," he said.[4]

Caraballo said the cops asked him repeated questions about the island, but he was unable to answer them because he moved to the mainland when he was just eight months old. It took nearly three days before he was released, and then only with intervention by Representative Luis Gutiérrez, also Puerto Rican. "Here we had an American citizen, that the federal government, not state authorities, but the federal government, with all their technology and all their information capacity that they have, could not determine, for more than three days, his status as an American citizen," Gutiérrez said. "It's very, very, very dangerous ground to tread."

After the arrest, ICE issued a statement saying its agents had placed a "detainer" on Caraballo "based on initially available information that he was an alien subject to deportation," CNN reported. But that defense, Jacqueline Stevens, professor of political science at Northwestern University in Evanston, Illinois, told the network, "is only valid if someone is foreign-born." What happened to Caraballo, she said, was "basically kidnapping and false imprisonment." Shockingly, such outrages are not that rare, she added. Stevens reviewed 820 deportation cases and found that 1 percent of them involved U.S. citizens. Most of them were detained for one to three months. "That would translate to four thousand of the four hundred thousand people detained last year by ICE," CNN reported. Stevens also tracked thirty cases where ICE actually *deported* U.S. citizens, including a man wrongfully expelled to Jamaica. It took him a full a decade of red tape to secure his return.[5]

False Confessions

Why would anyone plead guilty to a crime he did not commit? It is hard to fathom. Nonetheless, intentionally coerced, false confessions happen more often than you might think.

Most innocent people, when confronted by a government official asking questions, ask themselves, "'Why not talk?'" James Duane, a professor at Regent Law School in Virginia Beach and author of the book *You Have the Right to Remain Innocent,* wrote in an August 2016 opinion piece for *The Los Angeles Times.* "'I have nothing to hide.'"[6]

Why not? Because you might "end up confessing to a crime you didn't commit," Duane warned. People who are under stress or duress, under suspicion of a crime and at a police station, will sometimes say almost anything to get out of the daunting situation. Those under investigation sometimes say things to the police, hoping to be let go, because, they reckon, the truth will come out later and they will be vindicated.

"Innocent interrogation subjects confess with surprising frequency," wrote Ninth Circuit appellate judge Alex Kozinski, dissenting in a case that upheld a lower-court conviction of a nineteen-year-old California man who was not allowed access to an attorney. "This is a sad and troubling case. There can be no doubt of that," he wrote. "The Court of Appeals opinion is carefully crafted to exploit every ambiguity in the timid utterances of a scared and lonely teenager. Another uneven contest that [defendant] Sessoms was bound to lose . . . If the State of California can't convict and sentence Sessoms without sharp police tactics, it doesn't deserve to keep him behind bars for the rest of his life."[7]

Kozinski said he had witnessed "far too many cases where police extract inculpatory statements from suspects they believe to be guilty" and then halt any further investigation, because they know that judges and juries will typically convict based solely on a suspect's confession. Youth and the mentally ill are most vulnerable to false confessions, he added, citing a study of 125 such cases in which 33 percent of the suspects were under eighteen and 43 percent suffered from mental disability or illness. Another analysis of 340 exonerations showed that 13 percent of adults entered false confessions, while 42 percent of juveniles did so. "Nearly half of the exonerated children," he noted, "were put behind bars because of something they said to police without an attorney present."

As an example, Duane's op-ed described the case of a sixteen-year-old Oakland, California, boy, Felix, who was isolated and interrogated in the middle of the night without a lawyer. Finally, the exhausted youth confessed on video to a murder crime, allegedly providing details that only the killer would know. "But fortunately for young Felix," Duane wrote, "it was later revealed that he had an airtight alibi: The youth was in a juvenile detention facility at the time of the murder. He was freed from jail and his charges were dropped.

Then there was the case of twenty-two-year-old Eddie Lowery, an army soldier at Fort Riley, Kansas, who was interrogated for seven hours about a rape and murder he did not commit as he repeatedly insisted on his innocence, Duane wrote. But by the end of the grueling day, Lowery, now exhausted, provided a detailed confession. The man spent more than twenty years in prison until new evidence was uncovered to establish his innocence. Why did he do it? "I didn't know any way out of that, except to tell them what they wanted to hear, and then get a lawyer to prove my innocence," Lowery told Duane.

No matter what your age or mental faculties, the longer you spend under interrogation, the more vulnerable you are to false confession. Yet another study found that, out of forty-four proven false confessions, more than 33 percent of the interviews persisted for six to twelve hours, while others took as long as twelve and even twenty-four hours. The average interrogation was sixteen hours. Just imagine what you might say after that length of time. "The longer you speak to police officers, the more likely it is that you will confess to some crime that you did not commit," Duane warned. "Don't talk to the police—except to tell them, respectfully, that you will not answer any questions and that you would like a lawyer."

Planting Evidence

We have all seen films and TV shows about rogue cops who plant evidence in order to frame a suspect. Here, art is imitating life. In July 2017, for example, an officer in Baltimore was suspended when the suspect's defense lawyers released a body camera video which they alleged showed an officer, Richard A. Pinheiro Jr., planting heroin to incriminate the man. Police claimed there was "more to the story" than what was revealed in the ninety-second clip.

Baltimore police body cameras automatically prerecord thirty seconds of footage before they are activated, but without the audio. The officer in this case, defense lawyers said, was unaware of that fact. "What we think we see, and if you slow down the video especially in the first five seconds, [is] the officer appearing to place a red can underneath some trash, push the fence up, and hide it," Debbie Katz Levi, director of special litigation for the Maryland Office of the Public Defender in Baltimore, told the local CBS affiliate. But when the officer presses the record button and the sound comes on, "he then walks down the alley and miraculously goes to the same space where he appeared to have just planted the can with the suspected narcotics."[8]

Police offered more footage of the arrest, which also aired on the local CBS station. It showed cops finding another bag of heroin. "Police are investigating if the officer planted the second set of drugs there or if he was re-creating the discovery when his body camera was rolling," the station reported. Baltimore Police Department commissioner Kevin Davis said, "It's certainly a possibility that we're looking into, to see if the officers, in fact, replaced drugs that they had already discovered to document the discovery with their body-worn cameras on."

Prosecutors dropped the charges against the suspect because of the footage. The defendant, who had been arrested in January but could not afford his $50,000 bail, had spent more than six months behind bars before his release. Officer Pinheiro was suspended, and two others were placed on administrative duty. "This is a serious allegation of police misconduct," Davis said at a news conference. "There's nothing that deteriorates the trust of any community more than thinking for more than one second that uniformed police officers—and police officers in general—would plant evidence of crimes on citizens."[9]

The scandal, which gained national attention, came while the city was still reeling from the indictment of seven members of an elite police gun squad who were charged with robbing citizens, filing false documents in court, and claiming unearned overtime. Dozens of cases in which they were key witnesses were dropped by prosecutors.[10] But not so for Officer Pinheiro. Even after local prosecutors were made aware of the video, they allowed Pinheiro to testify in another case, even though state law barred them from informing the court about the controversial video. In fact, according to the public defender's office, Pinheiro was a witness in fifty-three other active cases. The other two cops involved in the incident were also listed as witnesses in pending cases.[11]

Ten days after the defendant's exoneration, July 27, 2017, Baltimore state's attorney Marilyn Mosby announced the dismissal of thirty-four cases involving the three officers, which relied *solely* on their credibility as witnesses. Seventy-seven other cases were still under review.[12]

David Rocah, senior staff attorney with the ACLU of Maryland, told *The Baltimore Sun* that even "a faked re-creation of officers finding the untied bag of drugs" would still be a potential crime. As such, those officers should be barred from taking the stand in court. "There is zero reason to trust any video or any statement from any of these officers," he said. And even if the cops had re-created their discovery of the drugs, they not only "destroyed their own credibility, they have single-handedly destroyed the credibility of every piece of video where BPD officers find contraband without a clear lead-in that negates the possibility of it being staged," Rocah said. "That's quite a day's work."[13]

And then it happened again. About a week later, the public defender's office released another video that appeared to depict officers planting drugs in a vehicle. The cops said they had witnessed a drug deal involving the car, which they searched thoroughly, apparently without finding any contraband. The video was switched off, and then returned to recording. Thirty seconds into that footage, one of the cops suddenly finds a bag of drugs next to the car, in an area that had already been extensively searched. The release of two damning videos in two weeks prompted prosecutors to drop dozens of cases in which the discredited officers were to testify.[14] In the end, some five hundred cases were expected to be dismissed, Baltimore public defender Debbie Katz Levi told NPR.[15]

Then, in November 2017, video of an almost identical situation, accidentally taken by the officer, surfaced in Los Angeles. It showed LAPD officers apprehending a suspect, Ronald Shields, in April 2017 for felony hit-and-run charges, as well as possession of a firearm in the trunk and possession of cocaine. The police report said the drug was found in Shields's left pocket. But in the video, one cop, identified by the local CBS affiliate as Officer Gaxiola, is seen retrieving a wallet from the ground and showing it to another cop, who then points to Shields. Gaxiola then puts the wallet back down, picks up a small bag of white powder from the street, picks up the wallet again, and inserts the bag into it. When the audio comes on, meaning that Gaxiola had activated his camera, the footage shows him "discovering" the wallet on the ground and finding the drugs inside. "Just to let you know, sir, inside his wallet, he has a little bag of narco," he says. LAPD said it would investigate the incident.[16]

Meanwhile, two months later, in January 2018, a grand jury indicted Officer Pinheiro on charges of misconduct and fabricating evidence.[17] On November 9, Baltimore circuit judge Melissa Phinn found him guilty of both, calling his actions a "willful abuse of his authority for his own personal gain."

And then he got a slap on the wrist: a three-year suspended sentence, two years' probation, and three hundred hours of community service. Meanwhile, he remained on administrative leave, with pay, pending an internal department investigation, enraging civil libertarians. "On what planet," asked Rocah, "is it not ridiculous that an officer is convicted in a court of law, beyond a reasonable doubt, of having fabricated evidence, and yet we have to continue paying him to not do his job and can't terminate him—even though his credibility is permanently destroyed?"[18]

Black Man Prosecuted After Being Beaten

Included among all the disturbing images emanating from the infamous Unite the Right rally on August 12, 2017, in Charlottesville, Virginia, was video footage of a young black man in a parking garage being pummeled repeatedly with a metal pipe and wooden boards wielded by six white men.[19]

DeAndre Harris, twenty, was a special education instructional aide at the time. He went downtown that day with friends to protest the white supremacists. Harris and his friends encountered the men, who confronted them with their weapons. When one friend was attacked, Harris tried to intervene, with a flashlight he was carrying, to defend the man. He was left bloodied on the ground, with a concussion, a broken wrist, a spinal injury, a chipped tooth, and a head wound that required ten staples.

Video of the brutal assault instantly went viral as thousands of people on social media attempted to identify the assailants. Two of them were eventually fingered: Alex Michael Ramos, thirty-three; and Daniel P. Borden, eighteen. In October 2017, they were charged with malicious wounding, a felony punishable by up to five years in prison.[20]

Then, one of the assailants, Harold Crews, a lawyer and North Carolina chairman of the League of the South, a white supremacist group, launched a campaign to discredit Harris and portray him as the actual aggressor. Bearing wounds of his own and identified by police as the "victim" in the case, he went to a local magistrate's office and asked for an arrest warrant against Harris, for the same felony crime. The judge agreed. The magistrate requested that a detective respond and verify these facts, the police said in a statement. "A Charlottesville Police Department detective did respond, verified the facts, and a warrant . . . was issued." Harris and his lawyer, S. Lee Merritt, insisted that

Harris neither instigated nor took part in any violence, adding that the man who brought the complaint had been injured in a different incident that day.[21]

"While he participated in some of the jeering of the white supremacists in his city, letting them know they were not welcome there, he did not instigate any physical assault," Merritt told *The New York Times*. "That was done by the men carrying blunt objects and weapons." It was clear from the video that Harris was "trying to get away," Merritt said. "They are surrounding him and beating him over the head with blunt objects. Their only defense is going to be self-defense, but under no one's legal standard is it self-defense to chase after someone wielding a flashlight when one of his friends is being speared with a pole, and then beating him maliciously."[22]

After the incident, Harris resigned from his job and left Charlottesville, afraid of being attacked again if he returned. But he would *have* to return to face trial for the charges against him. Although prosecutors had downgraded the assault charge to a misdemeanor, he still faced up to a year in jail and a $2,500 fine. In March 2018, Charlottesville central district judge Robert H. Downer Jr. acquitted Harris, saying it was evident from the video that he never intended to harm anyone and was acting solely in defense of his friend.[23]

Cash for Sentences

In 2002, two judges serving at the Luzerne County Court of Common Pleas in Wilkes-Barre, Pennsylvania, hatched a diabolical plot to make money by selling inmates, essentially, to new, privately owned juvenile detention facilities. At the time, Judge Michael Conahan controlled the court's budget, and Judge Mark Ciavarella had jurisdiction over the county's juvenile courts. After two private detention centers were built in the area, the judges received kickback payments from the owners in exchange for sending a steady stream of aggressively sentenced young people to fill their freshly painted cells—and their coffers. First, the two men shuttered the county-run juvenile detention center, citing its poor physical condition, and with that gone, insisted that the court had no other alternative but to ship kids off to the two private facilities. Conahan secured the contracts while Ciavarella did the actual sentencing.[24] It came to be known as the "Kids for Cash" scandal.

Complaints against Ciavarella spiked along with his sentencing of juvenile defendants—one-quarter of whom he sent to the detention centers from 2002 to 2006, even though the statewide rate for juvenile detention was just 10 percent of cases. Many of the estimated five thousand young people he sentenced were convicted for minor or even petty crimes. Kevin Mishanki of Hanover Township, a kid without a record, received a ninety-day sentence for simple assault: He'd gotten in a fight with another boy, resulting in a black eye. Hillary Transue, an accomplished Wilkes-Barre high school student, created a spoof MySpace page in which she made fun of her assistant principal. When she appeared in court with her parents, Judge Ciavarella convicted her for harassment and ordered her to spend ninety days in detention. She was handcuffed on the spot and taken away.[25]

In 2010, the two men were arraigned in federal court in Scranton, on charges of wire fraud and income tax fraud, and charged with raking in more than $2.6 million in kickbacks.[26] Eventually, Conahan pleaded guilty to one charge of racketeering conspiracy. He was given a sentence of seventeen and a half years in federal prison.[27] But Ciavarella chose to fight the charges at trial. He lost and was sentenced to twenty-eight years.[28] Meanwhile, thousands of juvenile delinquency cases in Luzerne County were dismissed.[29] Legal defense and juvenile justice advocates said the scandal exposed the need for providing all children with counsel at trial. And though the U.S. Supreme Court ruled in 1967 that minors have a constitutional right to an attorney,[30] in Pennsylvania and many other states, they can waive that right and often do. Roughly half of the juvenile defendants sentenced by Ciavarella declined such representation.

INCARCERATION

Health Care Denied

Is it cruel and unusual punishment to deny inmates adequate access to medical attention? Most people would think so. But policy makers in some states don't see it that way. Arizona is an example. In 2012, a group of inmates in the state's ten prisons sued the government over what they said was gross negligence in meeting the health care needs of some thirty-four thousand prisoners. The medical care, provided by an outside private contractor, was so shoddy, the inmates said, that some of them suffered, and some died, including a man with skin cancer whose treatment bordered on malpractice, according to several oncologists.

The 2012 lawsuit alleged that Arizona's ten state-run prisons didn't meet the basic requirements for providing adequate medical and mental health care. It said some prisoners complained that their cancer went undetected or they were denied other potentially lifesaving diagnostic tests. Some prisoners, after begging for treatment, were allegedly told to pray for a cure. In one case, doctors failed to diagnose a man with metastasized cancer, which caused his liver to enlarge, swelling his stomach to the size of a fully pregnant woman. Another inmate with prostate cancer waited more than two years for a biopsy.[31]

The inmates were represented by attorneys from the ACLU, the ACLU of Arizona, and the Prison Law Office, a prisoner-advocacy group. In October 2014, just before the case went to trial in federal district court, they reached a settlement with the State Department of Corrections. Under the terms, the state, without admitting wrongdoing, was ordered to enact a battery of reforms, such as meeting more than one hundred health-care performance measures, monitoring inmates with diabetes, high blood pressure, and other chronic conditions, offering free flu shots to all prisoners, and other vaccines to those with chronic diseases, providing annual colorectal and breast cancer screening for older inmates, and allowing at least six to ten hours of outside-the-cell exercise per week for maximum-security inmates. The settlement did not include inmates in the state's private-prison system.[32]

The state also agreed to spend $8 million more per year on prison health care and to cover the plaintiffs' legal fees, which, combined with the government's own expenditures in fighting the suit, now totaled more than $10 million in taxpayer money. Still, three years went by with little improvement. In February 2018, the plaintiffs were back in court, demanding enforcement of the settlement. One physician who had worked at the Florence prison for six months in 2017 gave damning testimony that the private health care company, Corizon, was still failing to uphold the state's end of the settlement. Dr. Jan Watson felt compelled to speak out, she said, after one of her patients suffered a heart attack. She was told by another doctor that surgery would not save the man and to make him comfortable and let him die. "I couldn't get that out of my mind," she said on the stand. In the end, she defied orders and brought in a specialist for a consultation.

Watson said there was rarely enough time to give proper routine treatment to patients because she often had to respond to emergency situations. Her superiors chastised her for spending too much time speaking with patients, claiming she prescribed too many narcotics and ordered too much medical equipment. She added that medications were often not given on time. One nurse, she alleged, had refused to give someone insulin because the inmate had failed to take it on schedule. "What you're doing is dangerous," she said she told the nurse. Watson also made a series of requests for patients to see specialists like neurologists or cardiologists. Many were canceled, or redirected to an "alternative treatment plan," including a patient who was having seizures.

U.S. magistrate David Duncan made his displeasure known, decrying what he called the state's "abject failure" to enact the improvements it was obligated to adopt. He had already threatened to hold corrections director Charles Ryan and another official in contempt of court, with a $1,000 fine to the state for each instance of noncompliance in December 2017 and January 2018. The state had admitted to more than 1,900 such cases during that period, raising its monetary liability to nearly $2 million just for those two months.[33]

In May 2018, Duncan announced that he would issue a judgment and fines against the state, though he was still completing an order to show cause why contempt charges were not warranted.[34] Ryan then appealed that decision at the Ninth Circuit, which rejected the case in late May. Denying medical care to the incarcerated clearly is a violation of all civil, constitutional, and human-rights norms.[35]

"Sheriff Joe"

Arizona seems to have more than its share of controversies over treatment of prisoners. On August 25, 2017, President Trump issued a pardon for Sheriff Joseph Arpaio, who was convicted in July 2017 of criminal contempt of court for refusing to carry out mandated changes to his patently racist and unconstitutional behavior—especially in regard to Latinos.[36] According to the DOJ, his record was "the worst pattern" of racial profiling in American history. His office paid out nearly $150 million in lawsuits and settlements over accusations of racism.[37]

Trump's defenders nonetheless sang Arpaio's praises as a "great public servant," saying that his only crime was contempt, a "simple" misdemeanor. In fact, much of his career as sheriff was a crime, spent trampling on the constitutional rights of thousands of people, and not only undocumented immigrants—who are protected by the same equal-protection and due-process rights as everyone else—but hapless U.S. citizens who were detained because they could not produce papers on demand. Arpaio's heavy-handed sweeps through Latino districts in the county as cops hunted down the "illegals" were not only illegal acts of racial profiling, they violated the Fourth, Fifth, Eighth, and Fourteenth Amendments—which prohibit unreasonable search and seizure and cruel and unusual punishment, and guarantee equal protection under the law and the right to due process before being deprived of life, liberty, or property.

Arpaio was caught boasting on tape that he once rounded up five hundred Latinos "out of spite." When confronted with it, he bragged to the Associated Press that the number had actually been in the thousands.[38] A top aide, meanwhile, was also caught on tape, bragging that sweeps were done for favorable publicity.[39] This was not just a simple case of contempt of court. Arpaio was committing criminal acts that resulted in physically harming human beings.

Thousands of people who were rounded up by Arpaio's deputies, under suspicion of having entered the country illegally, were warehoused in giant desert tents, where interior temperatures reached 145 degrees, with no fans and limited access to water.[40] That would seem to violate the Eight Amendment. One woman under Arpaio's "care" said she was forced to give birth in shackles.[41]

"Constitutional policing is an essential element of effective law enforcement," the original federal criminal complaint against the former sheriff said. "Arpaio's conduct is neither constitutional nor effective law enforcement."[42] Obama's DOJ tried to settle the case out of court, but Arpaio would not agree to the claim of racial profiling on his part. Federal attorneys then filed suit against Arpaio and Maricopa County in May 2012. The court granted summary judgment—against Arpaio. After that, a partial settlement was reached to rein in work-site raids, retaliation against inmates, and language requirements for Spanish speakers.[43]

Sobering Statistics

Whether, or for how long, someone may go to jail may well depend on his or her race and gender. A number of recent studies have examined how these factors affect conviction rates and lengths of sentencing. A March 2017 study conducted by the National Registry of Exonerations, at the University of California–Irvine, found that while African Americans make up just 13 percent of the U.S. population, they comprise more than 50 percent of innocent people who were wrongly convicted of crimes and later exonerated. That means that innocent black people are about seven times more likely to be sentenced to jail and exonerated than white people. In murder cases of black defendants, the race of the victim plays a significant role as well. While just 15 percent of murders by African Americans involve white victims, nearly a third of blacks exonerated of murder had been convicted of killing white people. Misconduct by police in these cases was found to be 22 percent higher than in homicide cases with white defendants. Results for sexual assault were similar.[44]

"Judging from exonerations, a black prisoner serving time for sexual assault is three and a half times more likely to be innocent than a white sexual assault convict," the authors wrote. "The major cause for this huge racial disparity appears to be the high danger of mistaken eyewitness identification by white victims in violent crimes with black assailants." Blacks who are eventually exonerated for sexual assault spent, on average, nearly four and a half years more time behind bars than white convicts who were exonerated. As for drug crimes, innocent African Americans are twelve times more likely to be convicted than innocent white people.

Another study, from October 2017, conducted by the Prison Policy Initiative, found that women are far more likely to spend time in jail, even before they are convicted of any crime. The study said that 219,000 women were incarcerated in the United States at the time. Sixty percent of them had still not been convicted of any crime, and one-fourth did not even have a trial set. The likely reason? Women typically make lower incomes and find it more difficult to meet bail than men. The average black female inmate, for example, had an income that was just 20 percent of the average white non-incarcerated male. Even after a conviction, women were 2.5 times more likely to face a jail sentence than the population as a whole.[45] That would explain why, between 1970 and 2015, the female inmate population increased fourteenfold, from 8,000 to nearly 110,000, according to a 2016 study by the Vera Institute of Justice.[46]

Finally, a recent study on sentencing published in late May 2018 by researchers at the Harvard Law School found that the political affiliation of federal judges had a significant impact on who was sentenced, and for how long. Judges appointed by Republican presidents handed down sentences that were six to seven months longer for black defendants than white ones. Judges put on the bench by Democrats were still more likely to sentence African Americans to longer terms than whites, although the discrepancy was about half that of the GOP judges.[47]

POLICE OVERKILL

Of all the constitutional abuses discussed in this book, none are more serious, or alarming, than cases of police officers killing or wounding American citizens who neither threatened nor assaulted them. When a cop shoots a suspect without probable cause and not in self-defense, that is a violation of the Due Process Clause of the Fifth Amendment, which stipulates that no person may be deprived of "*life*, liberty, or property" by the state without a fair hearing and, if needed, a jury trial.

African American men often fall victim to such acts. What now appears to be a trend of high-profile police killings of mostly unarmed black men began under the Obama administration when, on a muggy day in late July 2017, in a working-class section of Staten Island, New York, NYPD officers confronted Eric Garner, whom they suspected of vending "loosie" cigarettes out of a pack, without paying the required sales tax. The cops tackled the "suspect" and hurled him onto the ground. "I can't breathe!" Garner gasped repeatedly as one officer, Daniel Pantaleo, put him in a choke hold until he died. The killing sparked months of massive protests in New York City and around the country, where the refrain "I can't breathe!" became a battle cry for civil rights activists. Although the medical examiner ruled Garner's death as a homicide, a jury refused to indict Pantaleo. However, Garner's family sued the city and was awarded a settlement of $5.9 million.[48]

Just two weeks later, on August 9 in Ferguson, Missouri, Officer Darren Wilson, who is white, shot eighteen-year-old Michael Brown six times, killing him instantly. While some witnesses said Brown had raised his hands and pleaded, "Don't shoot!" a subsequent FBI investigation concluded there was no evidence to support that. Police alleged that Brown, who carried no weapon, had engaged in a scuffle inside of Wilson's squad car and had lunged for his gun. The killing sparked a week of protests, including violence, vandalism, and the torching of local businesses. It also helped launch the Black Lives Matter movement and the protest chant "Hands Up! Don't Shoot!" Obama's Justice Department declined to file charges against Wilson, saying he had acted in self-defense.

In an October 20, 2014, Chicago police dashcam video that shocked the world, seventeen-year-old Laquan McDonald can be seen running away from cops. Officer Jason Van Dyke, who is white, jumps from his car and begins firing sixteen bullets in rapid succession at the youth, killing him instantly. They found a small knife in his pocket. A year later, when the video was finally released, Van Dyke was charged with murder. The City of Chicago braced itself for a tumultuous, emotional trial, which was scheduled for summer 2018. At trial, he was convicted of second-degree murder and later sentenced to six years and nine months in jail.

On November 22, 2014, twelve-year-old Tamir Rice wielded a BB gun outside a park in Cleveland, Ohio, and, apparently without warning, was shot and killed by a white officer in training, Timothy Loehmann. A grand jury failed to indict the cop, although he was later fired by the city, which also reached a $6 million settlement with the family without admitting responsibility.

The killings, as we know, continue.

The murder of unarmed black men, especially by white officers, would seem to be epidemic in the United States, though the official numbers, at least, do not support that. A *Washington Post* analysis found that 987 people in the United States were killed by police in 2017, about 3 per day and more than double the number killed in mass shootings the same year. Of those, 19 victims, or about 2 percent, were black males, who make up 6 percent of the total population. Perhaps surprisingly to most people, the number of unarmed black men killed by police actually declined by half since 2015, when there were 36 killed, compared with 2016, with 17 deaths, and 2017, with 19 deaths, according to *The Post*.[49]

But that was just about the only good news the paper reported. "While the number of black males—armed and unarmed—who have been killed has fallen, black males continue to be shot at disproportionately high rates," it said. Of *all* people shot and killed by police in 2017, black males comprised more than 1 in 5 victims. Hispanic males, at less than 9 percent of the total population, accounted for 18 percent of such deaths—an unacceptably high ratio, by any standards.

A similar analysis completed by *The Guardian* at the end of 2015 found that during the year, young black men—between the ages of fifteen and thirty-four—were nine times more likely than the average American to be killed by police. They comprised 15 percent of all such deaths, despite making up just 2 percent of the population, a rate that was five times higher than for white men in the same age group. "This new finding indicates that about one in every sixty-five deaths of a young African American man in the U.S. is a killing by police," the newspaper determined.[50]

OTHER CASES

Despite these findings, people of all races and ages are killed by police every year in the United States. It is a problem that affects us all. What follows is a brief description of just some of the ways that cops kill Americans (not to mention their pets: about 25 dogs are killed by U.S. cops each day, or more than 9,100 a year, according to the DOJ)[51] and a look at what might be done to address the unwarranted use of deadly force against citizens who are, generally speaking, doing nothing more than going about their daily lives.

Consider the case of Bobby Dean Canipe, a white, seventy-year-old disabled Vietnam veteran from North Carolina.[52] He was driving his pickup in Clover, South Carolina, one night in February 2014 when York County Police deputy Terrance Knox pulled him over for an expired license plate. On the dashcam video, Canipe can be seen stepping down from the truck and moving toward the bed as Knox, shouting, "Sir! Sir! Whoa, whoa!" tries to persuade him not to do so. Canipe reaches the bed and pulls out a long object. Knox fires six shots—one of which hits Canipe in the stomach—only to realize the object was a cane, which Canipe uses to break his fall to the ground. Knox rushes to Canipe's side and apologizes. Canipe says he will "be okay." Other deputies arrive shortly after that, and one of them tries to console Knox, who is now sobbing. "You did what you had to do," he tells Knox. "Calm down, calm down."

Canipe recovered from the gunshot. Knox was placed on administrative leave, pending a police investigation. York County sheriff Bruce Bryant called the shooting "very unfortunate," in a written statement issued the next day. "It does appear, at this time, that Deputy Knox's actions were an appropriate response to what he reasonably believed to be an imminent threat to his life."[53] Later, at a news conference, Bryant said, "I stand behind this officer," and announced he would lobby for new state and federal laws mandating drivers' education programs on how to respond when pulled over by police. "You do not exit your vehicle and go meet the police officer," he said. "You do not do that. There's no law against it—you can—but the police officer is going to give you some strict orders."[54] In August 2014, prosecutors announced they would not indict Knox on any charges. "In the split seconds he had to assess the situation in the darkness," solicitor Kevin Brackett wrote in a letter to the State Law Enforcement Division, "his fear was entirely reasonable."[55]

Then there was Dustin Pigeon. On November 15, 2017, the twenty-nine-year-old called 911 in Oklahoma City and said he was going to kill himself. When police arrived at the home of Pigeon (whose race was not described in media accounts, though he looks white or Hispanic in photos), he was brandishing a lighter and lighter fluid. Officers ordered him to drop both, which he refused to do and instead doused himself with the fluid and set himself ablaze. Sergeant Keith Sweeney then shot him five times and killed him. The police said Sweeney acted in self-defense. "It would be unknown if he was going to run at somebody and douse them with the fluid and light it," police department spokesman Captain Bo Mathews told reporters. Prosecutors, who determined that Pigeon posed no threat to Sweeney, scoffed, and charged Sweeney with second-degree murder.[56] As of this writing, he was still awaiting trial.

Even naked people have been shot and killed by law enforcement. At about 1:30 a.m. on October 6, 2012, Gilbert Collar, a white eighteen-year-old freshman at the University of South Alabama, died after a bizarre encounter with campus police. Collar had traveled with friends from Birmingham to Mobile that night, the cops alleged, to attend the BayFest music festival. There, according to police reports, he ingested 25-I, a synthetic drug similar to LSD—one that was so new, it was still legal in Alabama.

The lawyer for Collar's family, Ben Locklar, said it was not clear whether Gilbert ever attended the festival, adding that the youth may not have taken the drug on purpose. He also said that at around midnight that night, Collar, who had no criminal record, was in his dorm with a number of other students, along with "two kids from Birmingham" who were not students. At that point,

Locklar said, "Gil seemed to start going out of his head, took off his clothes and he ran."[57] He headed for the campus police station and, according to eye-witnesses, tried to break into two cars and attempted to bite a woman, even though nobody called the police. Collar approached the station, banged on the windows, and walked away. Campus police surveillance video—with no audio—shows him returning to the police building, at which point Officer Trevis Austin, who is black, emerges with his gun drawn. As Collar advances, Austin retreats from the naked student, who suddenly buckles to the ground on his knees. Suddenly, Collar gets back up and approaches Austin. The two men circle each other before Austin fires his weapon into the chest of the young man, who was five feet seven and weighed just 135 pounds. Collar tumbles to the ground, gets up once more, and says, "Shoot me" (captured on microphones from other officers arriving on the scene), and then collapses before dying.

The student may have been running *to* the police not to threaten or harm them, however, but to seek help. At his campus orientation, university police spoke with new arrivals and handed them fridge magnets listing their contact information. Collar's mom told him to go to the police if he ever had a problem. "They'll help you," she told him, according to attorney Locklar, saying the unexpected disorientation from the drug panicked the youth. Meanwhile, county sheriff Sam Cochran offered up an excuse for Austin. "Had the officer had a Taser or some other less lethal instrument, I don't know if that officer would have had an opportunity to shoulder his pistol and to use something else because the events were evolving so rapidly and he was approaching so close," he told reporters.[58]

After killing Collar, Officer Austin was put on administrative leave. When a local grand jury cleared him of any criminal liability in 2014, he was rein-stated. Collar's parents, Bonnie and Reed, then sued the university and campus police chief in federal court, promising that any damages received would fund a scholarship in their son's name. But the case was dismissed by U.S. district court judge William Steele.[59]

A DAUNTING CHALLENGE

The use of deadly force against citizens by an increasingly militarized law enforcement apparatus might seem an intractable problem. Civil rights activists have for decades struggled to bring about reform, with a mixed record, at best. But it doesn't have to be that way. The police, like everyone else, are human. Despite the horrors described above, few want to shoot someone unnecessarily. Yet still it happens. How to combat this chronic situation? Here are some proposed ideas:

Body Cams

Community activists and police reform advocates insist that body cameras can reduce warrantless violence by the cops. After all, we all behave differently when we know a lens is focused on us. But, as discussed in this book, video can't always help resolve issues of "how people interpret facts," according to Floyd Abrams. "If existing incidents caught on tape are any indication, video won't be a saving grace for police reform," he told me. Civil rights attorney Norman Siegel said he is likewise "wary" of body cams but still called them "a step in the right direction," even though it can be difficult, and expensive, to extract footage from a recalcitrant police department.

Body cam skeptics—from both a law enforcement and, to a certain extent, a civil libertarian point of view—also worry about invasion of personal privacy when innocent people are captured on police video. But that concern is largely "nonsense," Siegel told me. "You can just block out the faces of people," he said.

Siegel has another concern. When camera-bearing police approach, say, a group of young people hanging out on the street, "my fear is . . . they will create a database of all the kids, and then they have this computer-generated database of troublemakers. If an incident occurs in that community, they go to that database to start questioning people about crime, or even political activity that's going on." He said any officer that used cameras in such an unauthorized manner should face criminal penalties. "We'll have to wait and see," Siegel said. "It's not the end-all and be-all of this issue; it's one step that I think is helpful and positive."

Improved Training

It is possible to train officers not to be trigger-happy, according to Chuck Wexler, executive director of the Police Executive Research Forum. His group developed a curriculum for cops aimed at de-escalating encounters with civilians, thus reducing the number of shootings. Already, it has been taught to dozens of police departments. "We are giving officers more options," he said, "like slowing the situation down and using time and distance to gain a tactical advantage."[60]

Like most reform advocates, Normal Siegel is supportive of intensified training, but also skeptical, because most departments resist the idea. "It takes me three years to go to law school, but training for a police officer is just five, six months," he said. Siegel has for years lobbied to increase police academy training to a full year—and has been consistently rebuffed with arguments that the cost would be prohibitive. After NYPD officers arrested Haitian immigrant Abner Louima in 1997, when he was raped with a toilet plunger, then mayor Rudy Giuliani approached Siegel to serve on a commission he was forming to investigate the issue. He accepted. "And the more I looked at the training at the police academy, it actually reinforced the stereotypes." For example, dealing with the relatively tiny Hasidic Jewish population in the city was given about four pages in the training manual, "while the quickest-growing immigrant community in the city, the Dominican community, got about two paragraphs. So, anyone who reads it realizes suddenly they're talking about who's important—the Hasidic community, not the Dominicans. Meaning you can violate the rights of the Dominican community; don't do it in the Hasidic community, because they've got power."

Mental Health Screening and Time Out

More than a decade ago, at least in New York City, potential officers were randomly chosen for mental health screenings. But that precaution is no longer deployed. Today, "you could potentially have people who've been there ten, twelve years, with all the anger of what they see, the shit that's out on the street," Siegel told me. "And so they're walking time bombs. Why don't we randomly test them every so often?" Nobody in the top brass, he said, is interested in doing that. Nor were they receptive to his idea of offering sabbaticals to overstressed cops with dubious records. "We could recognize this, and present it not like we're going to punish people, but if they're stressed out, we should be able to be supportive of their mental health. Why not give them time off with pay?" The city's police commissioner at the time, William Bratton, told Siegel the idea was too costly. "And I said, 'Think of all the millions and millions of dollars we would save in lawsuits each year." The wise counsel fell on deaf ears.

Reward Cops for Not Shooting?

It is a sad state of affairs when police departments must remind officers that not killing suspects is a top priority, but such is twenty-first-century America. In Los Angeles in 2014, for example, the LAPD began awarding a "preservation-of-life medal" to cops who go to great lengths to avoid a deadly shooting.[61] Police unions balked at the idea, but top brass at the LAPD later reported a modest improvement: In 2015, officers fatally shot twenty-one people. That number dropped to eighteen the following year and to fifteen in 2017. So-called de-escalation incentives work, First Assistant Chief Michel Moore said. "Our officers are in 1.5 million volatile encounters a year, so shooting someone is an incredibly rare event," he added, "yet we pull each instance apart and see what factors might have played a role and train our officers to make that rare event even more rare." Unfortunately, the new system will still grossly undercount fatal shootings by police because, "as before, data submissions under the new program will be voluntary."[62]

Fighting Undue Influence

Most cops who shoot civilians are not indicted, and most of those who are get acquitted. One reason, critics say, is a cozy relationship between police and prosecutors. After all, prosecutors at the local, state, and federal levels work routinely with police agencies to investigate, solve, and adjudicate crimes. They not only depend on a thriving working relationship with officers to act as witnesses for the state and gather solid evidence, they are often on intimate terms with cops, both personally and professionally. In some—though not all—cases, the urge not to pursue criminal charges against an officer is strong.

But even in the minority of cases where officers are prosecuted for shooting a civilian, most of them are acquitted at trial. One main reason is because in many jurisdictions, cops routinely attend trials where one of their own is accused of murder, Norman Siegel told me. "The PBA [Police Benevolent Association, as it is known in New York City] usually fills the courtroom with officers in uniform, or in civvies," he said. "And the subliminal message, either to the judge or the jury, especially to the jury, goes something like, 'We protect you, and we support you. And we in return need you to protect and support us.' And so it's extremely difficult to get a conviction of an officer on duty."

If that is the case in enormous, anonymous New York, imagine a small rural county, where many people know each other, and officers are staring directly into the eyes of jurors. The potential for influencing the verdict is easy to understand. How to rein in this practice without violating First Amendment rights is much more difficult. On the other hand, if people wearing political buttons or bringing literature into the courtroom can be prosecuted for attempted jury tampering, should police be allowed to wear their uniforms while observing a trial?

Before we give up the fight to rein in the police, I offer this thought from Norman Siegel: He notes that the Preamble to the U.S. Constitution—"We, the people of the United States, in order to form a more perfect union"—lists the very first goal as establishing justice, "even before ensuring domestic tranquility, providing for the common defense, or promoting the general welfare," he told me. "You have to believe that they put certain concepts and values in order of importance."

Even in the Preamble, he said, "justice comes before order."

AFTERWORD

The threat is real. The future is unsettled. The question is: Where will we the people carry this vast experiment in democratic republicanism next? The answer remains to be seen. I am hopeful that we will survive these mounting aggressive assaults on our constitutional rights. But I am not entirely convinced.

When it comes to protecting our constitutional rights, two types of courts have been remarkably effective: courts of law and the court of public opinion. That latter has recently evolved into a hyper-amplified bullhorn, thanks to social media, paired with an increasingly aggressive traditional press, led by an extraordinary cadre of Upton Sinclair–worthy muckrakers. Without investigative reporters, our besieged nation would be utterly lost.

But what of our courts of justice? In many of the cases profiled in this book, local, state, and federal judges often—though not always—fulfilled their traditional constitutional role: They served as a strict buffer against state officials chipping away at our constitutional rights and in support of the rule of law. If they come for you, the courts are your most promising refuge—for now. And remember, there are literally thousands of very fine civil rights lawyers at foundations and pro bono law firms across the country ready to help you seek redress, with little or no out-of-pocket costs.

But in the Trump era, it is the role of the judiciary that worries me the most. In his first twenty-two months in office, the president won Senate confirmation on eighty-four judicial appointments, nearly all of them white and very conservative, and most of them male, to serve on the federal bench for life.[1] These mostly young district and circuit court judges—abetted by a right-wing Supreme Court that will dominate federal jurisprudence over the next decades—likely will not manifest the sympathy toward oppressed citizens as do many of the federal judges profiled in this book. It is enough to keep a civil libertarian up at night; even if Trump is not reelected in 2020, his anti-liberty legacy will live on long after he has left the national stage.

As I write this, Justice Brett Kavanaugh has just been seated on the High Court. I do not expect him to be a jurist with tremendous zeal for protecting the constitutional rights of all of us, and I am hardly alone. "Kavanaugh's troubling record on civil rights includes rulings denying employees protection against discrimination, and upholding a South Carolina voter photo ID law that disproportionately disadvantaged people of color," according to the progressive group Alliance for Justice.[2] The new justice's views "undermine the core civil rights principles for which we have long advocated," said Kristen Clarke, president and executive director of the Lawyers' Committee for Civil Rights Under Law, which completed an extensive analysis of Kavanaugh's record, on and off the bench, prior to his confirmation. "He is someone who, if confirmed, would dramatically alter the balance of the Court in ways that will prove harmful for African Americans and minority communities for generations to come."[3]

And, as *New York Times* columnist Charles Blow asserted on October 7, 2018, "Kavanaugh is just one part of a much larger plan by conservatives to fundamentally change the American political structure so that it enshrines and protects white male power even after America's changing demographics and mores move away from that power."[4]

Stacking the courts with conservative zealots who are appointed for life becomes even more ominous when you consider this analysis offered by New York attorney Elmer Robert Keach III: "We still have our rights, but we are losing our remedies." I believe he is right. Throughout this book, I have profiled people who sought remedies—typically through the court system—when their rights were threatened or abridged. Most of these efforts enjoyed some degree of success, but not all. Keach himself represented John Swartz and Judy-Mayton Swartz, the couple who sued the police after they arrested John for flipping off a cop and who lost their case after several extremely costly years of fighting. John Swartz had the right to display his middle finger to law enforcement, without question, but when that right was violated (by his wrongful arrest) no remedy, ultimately, was available to him.

The same is true for Brandon Raub, the former Marine who was detained against his will for his unsettling Facebook posts calling for a revolution: He had the First Amendment right to make those posts but no remedy after that right was eviscerated when he was confined to a psych hospital for more than thirty days.

Likewise, under the Fourth Amendment, citizens have the right to be "secure in their persons, houses, papers, and effects, against unreasonable searches and seizures," but when the police seize cash they suspect is connected to criminal activity, the remedy, a return of the full amount, is difficult if not impossible to procure. Some victims of warrantless, SWAT-style home raids have sued the police and lost.

The Fifth Amendment, as we have seen, is violated routinely, sometimes without remedy. For example, despite the right it grants against being "compelled in any criminal case to be a witness against himself," we see an unacceptably high rate of false confessions among innocent suspects. And in many cases throughout this book, we saw the deprivation of "life, liberty, or property, without due process of law."

The Sixth Amendment, in kind, guarantees "the right to a speedy and public trial," yet we have seen that is not always the case. It also grants the right of a defendant "to be confronted with the witnesses against him," yet many parents have their children removed by CPS following a report from a source who will remain anonymous; and the accused have a right to "the Assistance of Counsel," even though defendants in court-fee cases and civil asset forfeiture proceedings, for example, do not always receive such a remedy.

As for the Eighth Amendment's protections against "cruel and unusual punishments," for the thousands of undocumented workers packed into Sheriff Joe Arpaio's 145-degree tents in the Arizona desert, no remedy was made available to them. Meanwhile, many criminal justice reform advocates allege that solitary confinement for juvenile offenders violates the amendment, yet it still goes on—not to mention other patently inhumane conditions in our most notorious, violent jails and prisons.

Under the Tenth Amendment, "the powers not delegated to the United States . . . are reserved to the States respectively." But that hasn't stopped the feds, for example, from interfering in legal, state-run medical cannabis programs, or going after dairy farmers who legally produce raw milk, under state statute, for local consumption.

Remedies are also not always available when Fourteenth Amendment rights are violated. This critical addition to the Constitution not only guarantees the right to due process at the state level but also grants "equal protections of the laws." Given the disproportional number of poor people and minorities who fall victim to rights violations, it is reasonable to surmise that no remedy was extended to many of them. The amendment also declares that "all persons born or naturalized in the United States" are citizens and that "no state shall make or enforce any law which shall abridge the privileges or immunities of citizens." But as we saw in North Dakota in the 2018 election, the voting rights of thousands of Native American citizens were threatened because their addresses were post office boxes and not street numbers as required under a new state law. Six tribal members sued the state in federal court, citing "violations of the Equal Protection Clause of the Fourteenth Amendment and section 2 of the Voting Rights Act."[5] They lost.[6] The Supreme Court then refused to hear the case.[7] Equal protection denied.

In the end, the tribes scrambled to issue thousands of free qualifying IDs to their members and get them to the polls. Most of those who wanted to vote were able to do so. But it had nothing to do with (purported) Fourteenth Amendment protections. "Hard work ahead of time paid off pretty well," observed Bret Healy, a consultant for the Indian voting rights nonprofit Four Directions. But, he added, "you shouldn't have to move heaven and earth just to be able to cast a ballot."[8]

Meanwhile, President Trump thinks he can unilaterally rewrite the Fourteenth Amendment with the stroke of a presidential pen to remove its guaranteed right of citizenship through birth.[9] He can't. But such reckless ambition is nonetheless extraordinarily perilous to our democracy.

One final, deeply troubling issue is the notion of the states calling for the nation's second-ever Constitutional Convention. This favored right-wing project would allow delegates to change, delete, or add new sections to the U.S. Constitution, without having to submit the question for approval by Congress and three-fourths of the state legislatures and their governors.

Under Article V, it would take two-thirds of the states, or thirty-four in total, to convene a convention. "Congress may face this issue very soon," the right-wing Federalist Society predicted in May 2018. "At least 27 state legislatures have valid applications outstanding for a convention to propose a balanced budget amendment (BBA)," said the group, which supplies lists of candidates for federal judgeships to the Trump White House. "At least six states without BBA applications have outstanding applications calling for a plenary convention. Thus, if aggregation is called for, 33 of the 34 applications needed for Congress to call a convention likely exist."[10]

Critics say that the goals listed in some state petitions differ widely from and even conflict with other petitions, making it impossible for Congress to aggregate them as required. What's more, the push for a Constitutional Convention was dealt a setback in the 2018 midterm elections, when Democrats gained complete control of six statehouses and the GOP surrendered full control of four,[11] while seven governorships flipped from red to blue.[12]

But convention proponents are not going away. They are part of a brilliant scheme launched by the Koch brothers and other conservative power brokers who have not only bought and paid for a number of statehouses but have also bankrolled an influential national group called the American Legislative Exchange Council (ALEC). ALEC's members literally draft new state laws to gut regulation, boost corporate profits, and trample civil liberties.

The current urgency for a second Constitutional Convention is fueled by an ideological yearning for three new amendments: one to mandate a balanced federal budget; one to limit the federal government's power; and a third to set term limits for Congress. But once that process is commenced, literally anything could happen. Amendments could be put forth by states to permanently curtail many of the liberties we currently take for granted: reproductive rights; same-sex marriage; limits on police powers over citizens; restrictions on certain forms of protest; the gutting of the Freedom of Information Act (FOIA); weakening of due process and equal protection; establishing harsh and exclusionary federal voting requirements; permitting politically motivated gerrymandering; and, conceivably, even establishing an official national religion. Convention delegates might also empower themselves to, say, eliminate the EPA or rewrite the Tenth Amendment to permit states to select which federal laws and regulations they want to follow. This is an alarming prospect.

"Calling an Article V convention is reckless, especially at this divisive moment in our nation's political history," said David A. Super, a professor of law at Georgetown Law. "Nothing these groups propose does anything even to mitigate the risks that a convention would bring. State legislatures should not delude themselves that the dangers of an Article V convention can somehow be contained."[13]

Or, as the late Supreme Court justice Antonin Scalia once quipped in his usual blunt style, "I certainly would not want a constitutional convention. Whoa! Who knows what would come out of it?"[14]

Constitutional scholar Floyd Abrams agrees that a convention would "put us all at risk as citizens." The original convention in 1787, he said, eradicated the Articles of Confederation in favor of the Constitution. "That was all good," Abrams said. "But it was not purportedly what they were about to meet about." A constitutional convention, Abrams warned, "is sort of an open invitation to the most egregious overstepping of limitations on individual rights. And it would be a matter of great national peril if we really started down that road." The result could be "fraught with enormous risk to individual liberties," Abrams predicted. It could conceivably produce extreme measures, even the establishment of a king to rule the country.

Kings, of course, are autocrats, the precise opposite of what the framers envisioned for our republic. What American wants to be ruled by a monarch? As veteran constitutional lawyer Norman Siegel said, "When you look at autocratic and demagogic figures in history, what do they do? They go after the press, they go after the right to protest, and they go after the court system." Consolidating centers of state power would "undermine the institutions that give us the information we need to make our judgments about what's true and who's abusing power," Siegel said. "And on those institutions and structures, the Trump people have got a pretty ugly record."

Things could get even uglier. It depends on whether—and how strenuously—citizens fight back. The stakes are at their highest: to protect the astonishing liberties granted to us by those remarkable American visionaries who crafted the Bill of Rights more than two centuries ago.

Everything—including our very way of life—now hangs in the balance. Let's rise to the challenge.

ACKNOWLEDGMENTS

To me, real journalism is about real people, and not just facts and figures, rules and regulations. More than two dozen "ordinary" Americans who fell victim to official corruption, abuse, and/or abridgement of their rights (and who are actually quite extraordinary for fighting back) agreed to open their lives, and often their hearts, to tell me their harrowing stories. For many, the scars linger. For some, their battles drag on. Although I was not able to use everyone's story, I sincerely want to thank Sharyl Attkisson, Shahid Buttar (who also was invaluable as a constitutional attorney), Russ Caswell, Chad Chadwick, George Christian, Angel Cook, Larry Curtis, Rinaldo del Gallo, William Elliott, Raymond Farzan, Nathan Fort, David Heleniak, Stephen Hitner, Shay Horse, Karen Hudson, Sunny Kelley, Jay Korff, Elizabeth Lagesse, Dick Lindsay, George Magas, Brandon Raub, Jeremy Rothe-Kushel, Kevin Thompson, Angela Warner, and John Waldorf.

It goes without saying that this book never would have been written—and indeed, these legal cases never would have happened—without lawyers. No fewer than forty-five brilliant civil rights and defense attorneys—some working for marquee national organizations, some for pro bono law firms, others in private practice—generously agreed to speak with me and tutor me in the challenging school of constitutional theory and law. They also supplied me with reams of court and other legal documents, graciously gave me access to clients, and, in some cases, helped me fact-check certain sections. It shouldn't be surprising that many of these dedicated attorneys work for the American Civil Liberties Union and several of its state chapters, and I give a very special thanks to Nusrat Jahan Choudhury, Scott Michelman, Lee Rowland, Chris Calabrese, Cade Crawford, and Ezekiel Edwards. At the Institute for Justice,

Scott Bullock, Darpana M. Sheth, Wesley Hottot, and especially Lee McGrath
went beyond the call of duty to help me. I also deeply thank attorneys Nick
Allen and Merf Ehman of Columbia Legal Services, Mary Holland and Helen
Hershkoff of the NYU School of Law, Omar Gonzalez-Pagan of Lambda Legal,
Danielle Diamond of the Socially Responsible Agricultural Project, Andrew
Crocker and Jennifer Lynch of the Electronic Frontier Foundation, John White-
head of the Rutherford Foundation, Glenn Katon of Muslim Advocates, John
Wesley Hall of FourthAmendment.com, and Urszula Masny-Latos of the Mas-
sachusetts Chapter of the National Lawyers Guild. Among the many skilled at-
torneys in private practice who helped me, perhaps Norman Siegel and Floyd
Abrams, two lions of constitutional law, should be thanked first, but it is with
no less enthusiastic gratitude that I acknowledge the invaluable help of Joshua
Covert, Donnie Cox, Benjamin Durham, Blaine H. Elliot, Jonathan Emord,
Michael Haddad, Gregory Hession, Elmer Robert Keach III, Joshua Koltun,
David Lane, Jason Leventhal, Ben Locklar, Alan Maestas, John T. Martin, Trey
Martinez, Robert Powell, Michael Reiter, Renee Sandler, and Joe Weinberger.

Meanwhile, a wide range of experts, activists, opinion leaders, nonprofit
executives, academics, journalists, and other talented individuals contributed
to the depth and breadth of this endeavor. Whether agreeing to be interviewed;
providing other people to interview; furnishing me with reports, studies, court
papers, and other critical documents; providing guidance and support; reviewing certain sections of the manuscript; or all of the above, they generously
offered their deep knowledge, precious time, and expansive expertise. Among
those that I thank are policy and communications staff at the ACLU National
Office, New York Chapter, D.C. Chapter, and several others, including Jay
Stanley, Suzanne Ito, Inga Sarda-Sorensen, Tom Hargis, Christopher Ott, and
Mike Pinto. I am likewise deeply indebted to *Miami Herald* columnist Leonard
Pitts Jr.; Shira Rawlinson of the Institute for Justice; Amina Rubin of the Coun-
cil on American-Islamic Relations; Liz Reitzig of the Real Food Consumer
Coalition; Nisha Whitehead of the Rutherford Institute; Paul Armentano of
NORML; author and former CPS social worker Melinda Murphy; historian
and Cato Institute scholar Jeffrey Rogers Hummel; Kris Hermes, formerly of
Americans for Safe Access; Mandela Jones of Communities United for Police
Reform; Charla Bansley of Liberty Counsel; Chris Holbrook of the Minnesota
Libertarian Party; Fatima Khan of Muslim Advocates; Harley Geiger of the
Center for Democracy & Technology; Brian Burghart of FatalEncounters.com;

Elizabeth Nash of the Guttmacher Institute; Amanda Harrington of the Planned Parenthood Federation of America; Coy Barefoot of the University of Virginia; Elvin T. Lim, professor of government at Wesleyan University; Bruce Dain, University of Utah history professor; Ken Ward Jr., reporter for *The Charleston Gazette;* Arnie Robbins of the American Society of News Editors; Katherine McFate of the Center for Effective Government; David Cuillier of the Society of Professional Journalists; Ashley Nerz of Fox News Channel; Adam Marshall of the Reporters Committee for Freedom of the Press; Meghann Farnsworth of the Center for Investigative Reporting; Lauren Grandestaff of Investigative Reporters and Editors; and Andrea Blanford, reporter at ABC11 Eyewitness News.

The professional team behind this volume have now helped me publish four books: my spectacular agent, Todd Shuster of Aevitas Creative Management; my sage editor at St. Martin's Press, George Witte, and his able assistant, Sara Thwaite; my indefatigable transcriber, Nancy Hokkanen; and my dear friend Jay Blotcher, who pre-edited the book, honing and polishing it along the way— like the pro he truly is.

Finally, I offer my most heartfelt gratitude to other friends who tendered moral support and listened to me complain over a grueling five-year process that sometimes seemed interminable. Many of them kindly read various chapters and gave me feedback. That list begins with my partner of twelve years, Carlos Arturo Jimeno Gallad, who was the rather insistent but genius inspiration for this book and who pushed me up the hill when I needed it. I also thank Mark and Cindy Sichel, Alex Lewis, my dear sister Nancy Bue, Rob Arnold, Gabriel Rotello, Laura Perry, Sasha Silverstein and Len Heisler, Matthew Singer, Shimon Attie, Lou Pansulla, Doug Fredman, Jane Bayer Goodman, Steve Goodman, and Ginger Taylor. And, as per usual, I thank my terrier mutt, Wilson, for sticking by me, often literally, during this exceedingly trying undertaking.

NOTES

Author's Note

1. Danielle Root and Aadam Barclay, "Voter Suppression During the 2018 Midterm Elections," Center for American Progress, November 20, 2018, https://www.americanprogress .org/issues/democracy/reports/2018/11/20/461296/voter-suppression-2018-midterm -elections/.

Preface

1. *West Virginia State Board of Education v. Barnette,* 319 U.S. 624 (1943).

Chapter 1: When Cops Burst Through Your Door: Warrantless Home Raids

1. District Court of Maryland for Montgomery County, Rockville, *Statement of Probable Cause,* Local Incident #14000624, January 5, 2014.
2. Phone interview with George Magas, July 26, 2015.
3. District Court of Maryland, *Statement of Probable Cause,* Local Incident #14000624.
4. Rebecca Guteman, "State Drops Damascus Underage Drinking Party Case," *Montgomery County Sentinel,* November 17, 2014.
5. Mila Mimica, "Md. Cops Assaulted at Underage Drinking Party," NBC4 Washington, January 6, 2014.
6. Phone interview with Rene Sandler, August 16, 2015.
7. *Oliver v. United States,* 466 U.S. 170 (1984).
8. *United States v. Dunn,* 480 U.S. 294 (1987).
9. *Alvarez v. Montgomery County,* United States Court of Appeals, Fourth Circuit, No. 97-1648, decided June 22, 1998.
10. Judge's Ruling, *State of Maryland v. George Magas,* Circuit Court for Montgomery County, Maryland, Judge Steven G. Salant presiding, Rockville, MD, November 10, 2014.
11. Rebecca Guteman, "Judge Rules Against Police in Civil Rights Case," *Montgomery County Sentinel,* November 13, 2014.
12. Guteman, "State Drops Damascus."
13. Phone interview with John Wesley Hall, November 17, 2015.
14. *Ortega et al. v. City of New York et al.,* U.S. District Court for the Eastern District, Case No. 1:13-cv-06646, originally filed November 29, 2013.

15. John Marzulli, "NYPD Cops Beat Up My Loved Ones, Killed My Parakeet: Staten Island Mom," *New York Daily News,* December 8, 2013.

16. Megan Gallegos, "Police Tell a Different Tale of Tense Incident," *Courthouse News,* July 12, 2013.

17. *Anthony Mitchell, Linda Mitchell, and Michael Mitchell v. City of Henderson, Nevada, et al.,* U.S. District Court, District of Nevada, Case 2:13-cv-01154-APG-CWH, filed July 1, 2013.

18. Ilya Somin, "Federal Court Rejects Third Amendment Claim Against Police Officers," *Washington Post,* March 23, 2015.

19. Phone interview with Benjamin Durham, August 2018.

20. Phone interview with Hall.

Chapter 2: L'Enfant C'est Moi—Child Protective Services and State-Sponsored Kidnapping

1. Phone interview with Nathan Fort, January 2015.

2. *Molly A. Fort, Nathan M. Fort, and Madison Mewborn v. County of San Benito, Donna Elmhurst et al.,* U.S. District Court for the Northern District of California, San Jose Division, Case No. C03-03587-RMW, 2003.

3. Phone interview with Robert Powell, April 6, 2015.

4. Videotaped deposition of Paul Peterlin in the matter of *Fort et al. v. San Benito County et al.,* U.S. District Court for the Northern District of California, San Jose Division, volume 1, November 4, 2004.

5. "The Two Faces of CPS," *San Benito Pinnacle,* December 11, 2005.

6. In-person interview with Gregory Hession, October 2014.

7. Phone interview with Joshua Covert, September 30, 2014.

8. *Wallis et al. v. Spencer et al.,* U.S. Court of Appeals for the Ninth Circuit, No. 97-55579, argued and submitted November 6, 1998, filed September 14, 1999, amended February 7, 2000.

9. Information on this case comes from the *Washington Post,* the *Louisville Courier Journal,* and other media sources.

10. Deborah Yetter, "E'town Couple Shaken by False Child-Abuse Calls," *Louisville Courier Journal,* August 14, 2015.

11. *Swartwood v. San Diego County et al.,* U.S. District Court for the Southern District of California, case No. 3:12-cv-01665-W-BGS, filed July 3, 2012.

12. Greg Moran, "County to Pay $1.1M for Invasive Exams," *San Diego Union-Tribune,* February 12, 2015.

13. Email from Donnie Cox, July 7, 2018.

14. Neil Swidey, "Judge Approves Shifting of Teen's Care to Tufts-Led Team," *Boston Globe,* March 4, 2014.

15. Liz Klimas, "'Irresponsible' and 'Wrong': Lawyer Hits Back at Judge's Leaked Ruling That Includes Accusations Against Justina Pelletier's Parents," *Blaze,* March 26, 2014.

16. "Parents of Justina Pelletier Sue Boston Children's Hospital," *Boston Globe,* February 25, 2016.

17. Julian J. Dominguez and Melinda Murphy, *A Culture of Fear: An Inside Look at Los Angeles County's Department of Children & Family Services* (Houston, TX: Strategic Book Publishing & Rights Agency, 2013).

18. Phone interview with Melinda Murphy, August 31, 2016.

19. *Doe v. Kearney,* No. 8:00-cv-184-T-26B (M.D. Fla. 2000) (deposition of Beth Pasek at 12–13).

20. Mark R. Brown, "Rescuing Children from Abusive Parents: The Constitutional Value of Pre-Deprivation Process," *Ohio State Law Journal* 65 (2004): 913.

21. United States Code, Sec. 473A. 673b of the Social Security Laws: "Adoption and Legal Guardianship Incentive Payments."

22. *Kids Count 2014 Data Book* (Baltimore: Annie E. Casey Foundation, 2014).

23. *Memo to State and Tribal Agencies Administering or Supervising Administration of IV-E of the Social Security Act,* U.S. Department of Health and Human Services, Administration on Children, Youth and Families, Log No. ACYF-CB-IM-12-05, May 14, 2012.

24. *Lauren Wallis et al. v. Mary Spencer, M.D., et al.,* United States Court of Appeals, Ninth Circuit, No. 97-55579, decided September 14, 1999.

Chapter 3: Your Money or Your Freedom

1. Tina Rosenberg, "Out of Debtors' Prison, with Law as the Key," *New York Times,* March 27, 2015.

2. Phone interview with Kevin Thompson, February 2016.

3. "Decatur, GA," DataUSA, https://datausa.io/profile/geo/decatur-ga/.

4. Complaint, *Kevin Thompson v. DeKalb County et al.,* United States District Court, Northern District of Georgia, Atlanta Division, Case 1:15-mi-99999-UNA, filed January 29, 2015.

5. Human Rights Watch, *Profiting from Probation: America's "Offender-Funded" Probation Industry,* February 5, 2014, https://www.hrw.org/report/2014/02/05/profiting-probation/americas-offender-funded-probation-industry.

6. Kevin Thompson, "For-Profit Companies Are Helping to Put People in Jail for Being Poor. I Should Know, I Was One of Them," ACLU, January 29, 2015, https://www.aclu.org/blog/speakeasy/profit-companies-are-helping-put-people-jail-being-poor-i-should-know-i-was-one-them?page=3.

7. Complaint, *Kevin Thompson v. DeKalb County et. al.*

8. "Thompson v. DeKalb County," ACLU, updated March 19, 2015, https://www.aclu.org/cases/thompson-v-dekalb-county.

9. Phone interview with Nusrat Choudhury, January 24, 2016.

10. Mark Niesse, "DeKalb Traffic Fines Decline After Court Abolished," *Atlanta Journal-Constitution,* January 15, 2016, https://politics.myajc.com/news/local-govt—politics/dekalb-traffic-fines-decline-after-court-abolished/RcRiS6uY6euGn0mWUuZncN/.

11. *Williams v. Illinois,* United States Supreme Court, Case No. 399 U.S. 235 (1970), argued April 22, 1970, decided June 29, 1970, https://www.oyez.org/cases/1969/1089.

12. *Tate v. Short,* United States Supreme Court, Case No. 401 U.S. 395 (1971), argued January 14, 1971, decided March 2, 1971, https://supreme.justia.com/cases/federal/us/401/395/.

13. *Bearden v. Georgia,* United States Supreme Court, Case No. 81–6633 (1983), argued January 11, 1983, decided May 24, 1983, https://caselaw.findlaw.com/us-supreme-court/461/660.html.

14. Joseph Shapiro, "As Court Fees Rise, the Poor Are Paying the Price," *All Things Considered,* NPR, May 19, 2014.

15. Phone interview with Nick Allen, January 8, 2016.

16. Samantha Sunne, "Why Your Right to a Public Defender May Come with a Fee," *Special Series: Guilty and Charged,* NPR, May 29, 2014.

17. Human Rights Watch, *Profiting from Probation: America's "Offender-Funded" Probation Industry.*

18. Katherine A. Beckett, Alexes M. Harris, and Heather Evans, *The Assessment and*

Consequences of Legal Financial Obligations in Washington State (Olympia: Washington State Minority and Justice Commission, 2008), http://www.courts.wa.gov/committee /pdf/2008LFO_report.pdf.

19. *Modern-Day Debtors' Prison—The Ways Court-Imposed Debt Punishes People for Being Poor,* ACLU of Washington and Columbia Legal Services, February 2014, https://www .aclu-wa.org/docs/modern-day-debtors-prisons-washington.

20. Carl Takei, "WTF? Our Tax Dollars Are Being Spent to Jail a Vet for Being Poor," ACLU, May 28, 2014, https://www.aclu.org/blog/smart-justice/wtf-our-tax-dollars-are-being -spent-jail-vet-being-poor.

21. Ibid.

22. "Thompson v. DeKalb County," ACLU.

23. *Investigation of the Ferguson Police Department* (Washington, DC: United States Department of Justice, Civil Rights Division, 2015), https://www.justice.gov/sites/default/files /opa/press-releases/attachments/2015/03/04/ferguson_police_department_report .pdf.

24. Bret Crow, "Bench Card Offers Guidance on Collection of Court Fines, Costs," *Court News Ohio,* February 4, 2014.

25. Rosenberg, "Out of Debtors' Prison."

26. Jocelyn Rosnick and Mike Brickner, "The Ohio Model for Combatting Debtors' Prisons," *Michigan Journal of Race & Law* 21, no. 2 (2016).

27. Erin Edgemon, "Montgomery Will No Longer Jail Those Who Can't Afford to Pay Fines for Minor Traffic Offenses Under Settlement with SPLC," *Advance Local,* August 27, 2014, https://www.al.com/news/montgomery/index.ssf/2014/08/montgomery_will_no _longer_jail.html.

Chapter 4: When Policing Pays for Itself

1. Phone interview with Lee McGrath, January 2014.

2. Michael Sallah, Robert O'Harrow Jr., Steven Rich, and Gabe Silverman, "Stop and Seize—Aggressive Police Take Hundreds of Millions of Dollars from Motorists Not Charged with Crimes," *Washington Post,* September 6, 2014.

3. Daniel Jennings, "Tennessee Police Under Investigation for Taking Cash from Citizens," *Off the Grid News,* December 26, 2013.

4. Phone interview with Scott Bullock, October 1, 2014.

5. *Review of the Department's Oversight of Cash Seizure and Forfeiture Activities* (Washington, DC: Office of the Inspector General, United States Department of Justice, Evaluation and Inspections Division, 2017), https://oig.justice.gov/reports/2017/e1702 .pdf.

6. C. J. Ciaramella, "Poor Neighborhoods Hit Hardest by Asset Forfeiture in Chicago, Data Shows," *Reason,* June 13, 2017, https://reason.com/blog/2017/06/13/poor-neighborhoods -hit-hardest-by-asset.

7. *Criminal Forfeitures in Minnesota* (St. Paul: State of Minnesota, 2017), http://www.osa .state.mn.us/reports/gid/2017/forfeiture/forfeiture_17_report.pdf.

8. Phone interview with Russ Caswell, December 2016.

9. *United States of America v. 434 Main Street, Tewksbury, Massachusetts,* Civil Action No. 09-11635-JGD, Findings of Fact and Rulings of Law, DEIN, USMJ, United States District Court, District of Massachusetts, January 24, 2013.

10. Dick M. Carpenter II, Lisa Knepper, Angela C. Erickson, and Jennifer McDonald, with Wesley Hottot and Keith Diggs, *Policing for Profit—The Abuse of Civil Asset Forfeiture,* 2nd ed. (Arlington, VA: Institute for Justice, 2015), http://ij.org/report/policing-for-profit/.

11. Information on this case came from the Institute for Justice, the *Washington Post,* and other news sources.
12. "Policing for Profit: Oklahoma," Institute for Justice, 2015, http://ij.org/pfp-state-pages /pfp-oklahoma/.
13. Ibid.
14. Christopher Ingraham, "How Police Took $53,000 from a Christian Band, an Orphanage and a Church," *Washington Post,* April 25, 2016.
15. *The State of Oklahoma v. Eh Wah,* in the District Court of the Fifteenth Judicial District of the State of Oklahoma Sitting in and for Muskogee County. Case No. CF-2016-354, filed April 5, 2016.
16. Matthew Slaughter, "Supreme Court's Treatment of Drug Detection Dogs Doesn't Pass the Sniff Test," *International and Interdisciplinary Journal* 19, no. 2 (2016): 279–311, doi:10.1525/nclr.2016.19.2.279.
17. "Highway Robbery in Muskogee," Institute for Justice, http://ij.org/case/muskogee-civil -forfeiture/.
18. Phone interview with Ezekiel Edwards, January 2015.
19. 372 U.S. 335 (1963). In *Gideon,* the Supreme Court unanimously held that in criminal cases states are required under the Sixth Amendment to the U.S. Constitution to provide an attorney to defendants who are unable to afford their own attorneys.
20. *Review of the Department's Oversight of Cash.*
21. Ibid.
22. Jefferson E. Holcomb, Tomislav V. Kovandzic, Marian R. Williams, "Civil Asset Forfeiture, Equitable Sharing, and Policing for Profit in the United States," *Journal of Criminal Justice* 39 (2011): 273–285.
23. "Attorney General Prohibits Federal Agency Adoptions of Assets Seized by State and Local Law Enforcement Agencies Except Where Needed to Protect Public Safety," U.S. Department of Justice, January 16, 2015, https://www.justice.gov/opa/pr/attorney-general -prohibits-federal-agency-adoptions-assets-seized-state-and-local-law.
24. Ilya Somin, "Justice Department Suspends Abusive Asset Forfeiture Program—for Now," *Washington Post,* December 24, 2015.
25. "Resumption of Equitable Sharing Payments," *Equitable Sharing Wire,* U.S. Department of Justice, March 28, 2016, https://www.justice.gov/criminal-afmls/file/835661 /download.
26. "Policy Directive 17-1," U.S. Department of Justice, Criminal Division, July 19, 2017, https://www.justice.gov/criminal-mlars/file/985636/download.
27. Fox News Channel, July 18, 2017.
28. *Review of the Department's Oversight of Cash.*
29. Information on this story was collected from the Institute for Justice, civil court case filings, CNN, and other national and local news organizations.
30. Pamela Brown, "Parents' House Seized After Son's Drug Bust," CNN, September 8, 2014.
31. "Civil Forfeiture Laws Examined," *The Lead with Jake Tapper,* transcript, September 1, 2014.
32. Cherri Gregg, "Suit Claims Philadelphia's Seizure Practices Are Unconstitutional," 3 CBS Philly, August 13, 2014.
33. *Christos Sourvelis et al. v. City of Philadelphia,* United States District Court for the Eastern District of Pennsylvania, Case No. 103 F. Supp. 3d 694, filed August 11, 2014, https://www.leagle.com/decision/infdco20150513b75.
34. C. J. Ciaramella, "Philadelphia Drops Asset Forfeiture Cases That Drew National Attention," *Washington Free Beacon,* December 18, 2014.

35. Jeremy Roebuck, "Negotiations to Settle City's Forfeiture Suit Fail," *Philadelphia Inquirer,* March 2, 2015.

36. Jeremy Roebuck, "D.A.'s Office Reaches Partial Settlement in Forfeiture Suit," *Philadelphia Inquirer,* updated June 25, 2015.

37. Information on this case collected from court documents, the *Philadelphia Inquirer, Forbes,* and other news outlets.

38. *Commonwealth of Pennsylvania v. 1997 Chevrolet and Contents Seized from James Young,* appeal of Elizabeth Young. *Commonwealth of Pennsylvania v. The Real Property and Improvements known as 416 S. 62nd Street, Philadelphia, PA 19143,* appeal of Elizabeth Young. Nos. 1990 CD 2012, 1995 CD 2012, Commonwealth Court of Pennsylvania, decided December 17, 2014.

39. Appeal from the Order of the Commonwealth Court dated December 17, 2014, at Nos. 1990 CD 2012, 1995 CD 2012, reversing the Order of the Court of Common Pleas of Philadelphia County, Criminal Division, dated May 1, 2012 at No. CP-51-MD-0013471-2010, CP-51-MD-002972-2010. *Commonwealth of Pennsylvania v. 1997 Chevrolet and Contents Seized from James Young,* appeal of Elizabeth Young. *Commonwealth of Pennsylvania v. The Real Property and Improvements known as 416 S. 62nd Street, Philadelphia, PA 19143,* appeal of Elizabeth Young. Nos. 1990 CD 2012, 1995 CD 2012.

40. George Leef, "Four States Advance Against the Evils of Civil Asset Forfeiture, but the Feds Do Nothing," *Forbes,* June 26, 2017.

41. Joanna H. Kunz, "Pennsylvania Supreme Court Strengthens Protections for Property Owners in Landmark Civil Forfeiture Decision," *Money Laundering Watch,* June 1, 2017, https://www.moneylaunderingwatchblog.com/2017/06/pennsylvania-supreme-court-strengthens-protections-for-property-owners-in-landmark-civil-forfeiture-decision/.

42. "Civil Asset Forfeiture Reform Act of 2000," *Public Law 106–185* (Washington, DC: United States Government Printing Office, 2000), https://www.congress.gov/106/plaws/publ185/PLAW-106publ185.pdf.

43. Dick M. Carpenter II and Larry Salzman, *Seize First, Question Later—The IRS and Civil Forfeiture* (Arlington, VA: Institute for Justice, 2015), https://ij.org/report/seize-first-question-later/.

44. *Financial Management: Audit of the Department of the Treasury's Consolidated Financial Statements for Fiscal Years 2017 and 2016,* OIG-18-015 (Washington, DC: Office of the Inspector General, United States Department of the Treasury, 2017), https://www.oversight.gov/sites/default/files/oig-reports/OIG-18-015_1.pdf.

45. Much of the information on the Hinders case came from "Iowa Forfeiture," Institute for Justice, https://ij.org/case/iowa-forfeiture/.

46. Daniel P. Finney, "Forfeiture Target Calls It 'a Violation of Civil Rights,'" *Des Moines Register,* November 1, 2014.

47. "Statement of Richard Weber, Chief of I.R.S. Criminal Investigation," *New York Times,* October 25, 2014.

48. *United States v. Carole Hinders,* 15–2622, U.S. Court of Appeals for the Eighth Circuit, filed September 30, 2016.

49. Charles P. Pierce, "President Trump Has the Power to Destroy Whatever the Hell He Wants," *Esquire,* February 7, 2017.

50. Jeffrey St. Clair, "Roaming Charges: Big Boss Man," *CounterPunch,* February 10, 2017.

51. Jennifer G. Hickey, "Libertarians Split with Trump over Controversial Police Tactic," Fox News, February 13, 2017.

52. Ibid.

53. Eric Boehm, "Here Are All the Things Idaho's Governor Got Wrong About Asset For-feiture in His Veto Statement," *Reason*, April 13, 2017.

Chapter 5: Free Speech and the Individual American

1. Alix Bryan, "Full Text, Brandon Raub's Proclamation: Take Our Republic Back," CBS 6 WTVR-TV, August 21, 2012.
2. Phone interview with Brandon Raub, May 2015.
3. SYWTSAR, "Who Is Brandon Raub and Why Maybe It Matters to the Rest of Us [Up-date: Raub Has Been Released]," *Daily Kos*, August 20, 2012.
4. *Brandon Raub v. Michael Campbell et al.*, U.S. Court of Appeals, Fourth Circuit, No. 14–1277, decided April 29, 2015.
5. *Brandon Raub v. Michael Campbell et al.*, appeal from the United States District Court for the Eastern District of Virginia, at Richmond, Henry E. Hudson, district judge (3:13-cv-00328-HEH-MHL), U.S. Court of Appeals for the Fourth Circuit, No. 14–1277, decided April 29, 2015.
6. Many of the law-enforcement actions against Raub described here are taken from Raub's allegations in a civil lawsuit filed in 2013. *Brandon Raub v. Daniel Lee Bowen et al.*, U.S. District Court for the Eastern District of Virginia, Richmond Division, filed May 22, 2013.
7. *Raub v. Campbell et al.*, U.S. Court of Appeals.
8. Mark Holmberg, "Mother of Detained Marine Vet Says He's a Patriot, Not a Threat," CBS 6 WTVR-TV, August 21, 2012.
9. "Rutherford Institute Defends Marine Arrested, Incarcerated in Psych Ward & Detained Indefinitely for Posting Political Views, Song Lyrics to Facebook," Rutherford Institute, August 20, 2012.
10. Michael B. Kelly, "Marine Veteran Brandon Raub Sentenced up to 30 Days in Psych Ward over Facebook Posts," *Business Insider*, August 20, 2012.
11. Statement to the media, Colonel Thierry Dupuis, Chesterfield (VA) Police Department, August 20, 2012.
12. Jason Howerton, "Attorney of Former Marine Detained for Facebook Posts Tells Beck: Psychiatrist Threatened to 'Brainwash' My Client with Meds," *Blaze*, August 23, 2012.
13. SYWTSAR, "Who Is Brandon Raub."
14. Kelly, "Marine Veteran Brandon Raub Sentenced."
15. *In re: Brandon J. Raub*, Motion to Suspend and/or Modify Involuntary Admission Or-der Pending Appeal Under § 37.2-821, in the Circuit Court of the City of Hopewell, Virginia, August 22, 2012.
16. Lawrence Hunter, "Arrest of Ex-Marine Points to Virginia's Casual Disregard for the Constitution," *Forbes*, August 26, 2012.
17. *60 Minutes*, CBS, December 23, 1984.
18. *Raub v. Bowen et al.*, U.S. District Court for the Eastern District of Virginia.
19. Cam Simpson and Gary Fields, "Veterans a Focus of FBI Extremist Probe," *Wall Street Journal*, April 17, 2012.
20. "Rutherford Institute Counters Government Attempt to Dismiss Lawsuit over Wrong-ful Arrest, Psych Ward Detention of Marine Because of Facebook Posts," Rutherford Institute, July 17, 2013.
21. Memorandum opinion (motion to dismiss), *Brandon Raub v. Daniel Lee Bowen et al.*, U.S. District Court for the Eastern District of Virginia, Richmond Division, Civil Ac-tion No. 3:13CV328-HEH, January 28, 2015.

22. *Brandon Raub v. Michael Campbell,* U.S. District Court for the Eastern Division of Virginia, Richmond Division, Civil Action No. 3:13CV328-HEH. Signed February 28, 2014.

23. *Raub v. Campbell et al.,* United States Court of Appeals.

24. "U.S. Supreme Court Refuses to Hear Case of Marine Brandon Raub Who Was Arrested & Locked Up in a Mental Hospital for Criticizing the Gov't on Facebook," Rutherford Institute, November 17, 2015.

25. "Professor Taken to Hospital over Alleged Violent Threats," Associated Press, November 16, 2016.

26. Rocco Parascandola and Larry McShane, "EXCLUSIVE: Rutgers University Professor Taken for Psych Evaluation After 'Threatening' Gun Control, Flag Burning Tweets," *New York Daily News,* November 16, 2016.

27. Scott Jaschik, "Professor's Incendiary Rhetoric in the Age of Donald Trump," *Inside Higher Ed,* November 21, 2016.

28. "ACLU Briefing Paper Number 10—Freedom of Expression," American Civil Liberties Union, http://www.mit.edu/activities/safe/writings/aclu/freedom-of-expression.aclu.

29. Felisa Cardona, "The F-Bomb Isn't Polite or Illegal," *Denver Post,* June 13, 2011.

30. Evann Gastaldo, "Mom Arrested for Swearing in Front of Kids," *USA Today,* August 15, 2014.

31. Jim Totten, "Cursed? Teen Gets $200 Ticket for Playground Profanity," *Daily Press & Argus* (Livingston County, MI), May 19, 2014.

32. "Michigan Teen Fined $200 After Using Naughty Words in Public Park," *Police State USA,* May 23, 2014.

33. "ACLU: First Amendment Protects Cursing Brighton Teen from Fine," *Daily Press & Argus* (Livingston County, MI), May 22, 2014.

34. Most information for this section is from *John Swartz, Judy Mayton Swartz v. Richard Insogna, Kevin Colling,* U.S. Court of Appeals, Second Circuit, Docket No. 11-2846-cv, decided January 3, 2013.

35. *John Swartz, Judy Mayton-Swartz v. Richard Insogna, Kevin Colling,* U.S. Court of Appeals, Second Circuit, Docket No. 11-2846-cv, decided January 3, 2013.

36. Phone interview with Elmer Robert Keach III, August 2018.

37. Benjamin Weiser, "Middle Finger Flashed in '06 Lives On in Suit," *New York Times,* January 3, 2013.

38. Bill Chappell, "Georgia Woman Gets $100K over Her Arrest for Cursing at Police," NPR, December 12, 2014.

39. Steve Visser, "Cobb County to Pay $100K to Woman Arrested for 'F-Bombing' Cops," *Atlanta Journal-Constitution,* December 11, 2014.

40. Ibid.

41. Lisa George, "Cobb County Woman Jailed for Cursing at Cops Wins $100K Settlement Against County," WABE-FM Atlanta, December 12, 2014.

42. Phone interview with George Christian, March 18, 2015.

43. National security letter, sent to Kenneth Sutton, systems and telecommunication manager, Library Connection Inc., from Michael J. Wolf, special agent in charge, U.S. Department of Justice, Federal Bureau of Investigation, New Haven Division, May 19, 2005, File No. NH-43906.

44. *Doe v. Gonzales,* U.S. District Court for the Southern District of New York, September 6, 2007, 500 F. Supp. 2d 379.

45. Ruling on Plaintiffs' Motion for Preliminary Injunction (Dkt. No. 33), *John Doe et al. v. Alberto Gonzales et al.,* U.S. District Court for the District of Connecticut, September 9, 2005, 386 F. Supp. 2d 66 (2005).

46. Alison Leigh Cowan, "Four Librarians Finally Break Silence in Records Case," *New York Times,* May 31, 2006.

47. *John Doe, John Doe II, American Civil Liberties Union, ACLU Foundation v. Alberto Gonzales et al.,* U.S. Court of Appeals for the Second Circuit, argued November 2, 2005, decided May 23, 2006, Docket Nos. 05-0570-cv(L), 05-4896-cv(CON).

48. On Emergency Application to Vacate Stay Entered by the United States Court of Appeals for the Second Circuit, *John Doe et al., American Civil Liberties Union, and American Civil Liberties Foundation v. Alberto Gonzales et al.,* Supreme Court of the United States, filed under seal October 3, 2005.

49. On Application to Vacate Stay, *John Doe et al. v. Alberto R Gonzales et al.,* Supreme Court of the United States, Justice Ginsburg, Circuit Justice, October 7, 2005, No. 05A295.

50. U.S. Code, Title 18, Part II, Chapter 223, § 3511—"Judicial Review of Requests for Information."

51. "National Security Letters: FAQ," ACLU.

52. Brian Ross, "President Obama's Own Experts Recommend End to NSA Phone Data Spying," ABC News, December 18, 2013.

53. Jeff Carlson, "Bypassing the Inspector General—Sally Yates and the DOJ's National Security Letter Carve-Out," themarketswork, May 28, 2018.

54. Phone interview with Jeremy Rothe-Kushel, October 2018.

55. From video footage of the incident shot by Greg McCarron.

56. Brent Parsons's LinkedIn page, https://www.linkedin.com/in/brent-parsons-30386313/.

57. George M. Eberhart, "Kansas City Public Library Embroiled in Free-Speech Case," *American Libraries,* October 3, 2016.

58. Ian Cummings, "KC Library Gets 2 Awards for Free Speech Defense; Librarian Charged with 2 More Offenses," *Kansas City Star,* April 21, 2017.

59. Ian Cummings and Tony Rizzo, "Man Arrested at Kansas City Library Event Sues KCPD, Jewish Community Foundation," *Kansas City Star,* April 26, 2018.

60. Mark Hicks, "Woman Sues Dearborn Heights for Forced Hijab Removal," *Detroit News,* January 22, 2015.

61. *Kazan v. City of Dearborn Heights et al.,* U.S. District Court for the Eastern District of Michigan, January 22, 2015, case #: 2:15-cv-10250.

62. "Lawsuit Filed Against Dearborn Heights Police for Forcing Woman to Remove Hijab," Fox News 2 Detroit, January 22, 2015.

63. Samer Hijazi, "Woman Files Lawsuit Against Dearborn Heights Police for Forcing Her to Remove Hijab," *Arab American News,* January 23, 2015.

64. Niraj Warikoo, "Muslim Women Fight for Right to Wear Islamic Headscarf," *Detroit Free Press,* July 1, 2015.

65. Niral Warikoo, "Dearborn Heights Police to Allow Muslim Women to Wear Hijab After Arrests," *Detroit Free Press,* July 10, 2015.

66. "Muslim Woman Drops Lawsuit Against Detroit Suburb over Scarf," Associated Press, March 16, 2016.

67. *Burwell v. Hobby Lobby,* 573 U.S. (2014)

68. "Trump Administration Issues Rules Protecting the Conscience Rights of All Americans," U.S. Department of Health and Human Services Press Office, October 6, 2017.

69. *Masterpiece Cakeshop Ltd. et al. v. Colorado Civil Rights Commission et al.,* United States Supreme Court, No. 16–111, argued December 5, 2017, decided June 4, 2018.

70. Many of the facts of this case were derived from *Hazle v. Crofoot,* U.S. District Court for the Eastern District of California, No. 2:08-cv-02295-GEB-EFB, 2014, and related media accounts.

71. Bob Egelko, "Atheist Inmate Settles for $1.95 Million over 12-Step Drug Rehab," *San Francisco Chronicle,* October 15, 2014.

72. Denny Walsh, "Shasta Atheist Wins $2 Million Settlement over Drug Program," *Sacramento Bee,* October 14, 2014.

73. *Barry A. Hazle Jr. v. Mitch Crofoot et al.,* U.S. Court of Appeals for the Ninth Circuit, No. 11-15354 D.C. No. 2:08-cv-02295GEB-EFB.

74. Walsh, "Shasta Atheist Wins $2 Million."

75. Phone interview with Karen Hudson, September 7, 2017.

76. *In re: The Matter of the Criminal Contempt of Susan Turner & Karen L. Hudson,* appeal from Circuit Court of Scott County, Appellate Court of Illinois, Fourth District, No. 14CC2, December 28, 2016.

77. Ibid.

78. *West Virginia State Board of Education v. Barnette,* 319 U.S. 624 (1943).

79. *Texas v. Johnson,* 491 U.S. 397 (1989).

80. Philip Bump, "Donald Trump v. the First Amendment, Part 5," *Washington Post,* November 29, 2016.

81. John Wagner, "Trump Suggests Loss of Citizenship or Jail for Those Who Burn U.S. Flags," *Washington Post,* November 29, 2016.

82. *Trop v. Dulles,* 356 U.S. 86 (1958).

83. Facts in this case derived from *Snider v. City of Cape Giradeau,* United States District Court for the Eastern District of Missouri, Southeastern Division, Case No. 1:10-CV-100 (CEJ), March 20, 2012.

84. *Snider v. City of Cape Giradeau,* United States District Court for the Eastern District of Missouri.

85. "*Snider v. City of Cape Girardeau* (Flag Desecration)," ACLU Missouri, https://www.aclu-mo.org/en/node/166.

86. *Frank L. Snider v. City of Cape Girardeau,* United States Court of Appeals for the Eighth District, No. 13–1072, filed May 3, 2014.

87. Katie Mettler, "On July 4, This Man Exercised His Right to Burn the American Flag. Then He Was Arrested," *Washington Post,* July 6, 2016.

88. Fernando Alfonso III, "Illinois Man Charged with Desecrating American Flag After Posting Photos on Facebook," *Forbes,* July 4, 2016.

89. 2016 Iowa Code, Title XVI—Desecration of flag or insignia, IA Code § 718A.1A (2016).

90. Transcript of Senator Bernie Sanders on *Face the Nation,* CBS, June 18, 2017.

91. *Shelton v. Tucker,* 364 U.S. 479 (1960).

92. Joshua Gill, "Students Score Victory for Free Speech at Dixie State University," *Daily Signal,* October 5, 2015.

93. "NEW SURVEY: Majority of College Students Self-Censor, Support Disinvitations, Don't Know Hate Speech Is Protected by First Amendment," Foundation for Individual Rights in Education, October 11, 2017, https://www.thefire.org/new-survey-majority-of-college-students-self-censor-support-disinvitations-dont-know-hate-speech-is-protected-by-first-amendment/.

94. Andrew Desiderio, "Students Told They Cannot Lampoon U.S. Presidents Because Campus Forbids 'Mocking,'" Society for Academic Freedom and Scholarship, April 2015, http://www.safs.ca/newsletters/article.php?article=875.

95. Complaint for Injunctive and Declaratory Relief and Damages, *William Jergins, Joey Gillespie, and Forrest Gee v. Richard B. Williams et al.,* U.S. District Court, District of Utah, Central Division, No. 2:15-cv-00144-PMW, filed March 4, 2015.

96. "Dixie State University—Stand Up for Speech Lawsuit," Foundation for Individual Rights in Education, https://www.thefire.org/cases/dixie-state-university-stand-speech/.

97. Elissa Masatani, "Citrus College to Pay $110,000 to Settle Student's First Amendment Lawsuit," *San Gabriel Valley Tribune,* December 3, 2014.

98. Tal Kopan, "Student Stopped from Handing Out Constitutions on Constitution Day Sues," *Politico,* October 10, 2013.

99. Information of this case derived from *Joseph Frederick, Plaintiff Appellant v. Deborah Morse; Juneau School Board, Defendants-Appellees,* U.S. Court of Appeals for the Ninth Circuit, 439 F. 3d 1114 (9th Cir. 2006), argued and submitted July 8, 2004, filed March 10, 2006.

100. Andrew Trotter, "Supreme Court Weighs 'Bong Hits' Speech Case," *Education Week,* March 19, 2007.

101. *Morse v. Frederick,* 551 U.S. 393 (2007).

102. "Morse v. Frederick," ACLU, updated June 25, 2007, https://www.aclu.org/cases/morse-v-frederick.

103. Facts of this case derived from *Kizzy Landry and Next Friend of I.L., a Minor, v. Cypress Fairbanks ISD and Principal Martha Strother,* U.S. District Court for the Southern District of Texas, Houston Division, filed October 7, 2017.

104. David Boroff, "Houston Student Kicked Out of Her High School for Sitting During Pledge of Allegiance," *New York Daily News,* October 7, 2017.

105. *Landry v. Cypress Fairbanks,* U.S. District Court for the Southern District of Texas.

106. Boroff, "Houston Student Kicked Out."

107. "AG Paxton Intervenes into Lawsuit to Defend Texas Pledge of Allegiance Statute and Parental Rights," Texas Attorney General's Office, September 28, 2017.

108. Jake Offenhartz, "NJ High School Teacher Suspended After Pro-Trump References Disappeared from Yearbook," *Gothamist,* June 13, 2017.

109. Ibid.

110. Donald J. Trump's Facebook page, June 19, 2017, https://www.facebook.com/Donald Trump/posts/thank-you-wyatt-and-montana-two-young-americans-who-arent-afraid-to-stand-up-for/10159334593870725/.

111. Shaun King, "KING: School's Natural Hairstyle Ban Condemns Black Culture," *New York Daily News,* July 28, 2016.

112. "School District OKs Sharing Bible Verses," CBN News, August 16, 2016, https://www1.cbn.com/cbnnews/us/2016/august/school-district-oks-sharing-bible-verses.

113. Todd Starnes, "School Sends Sheriff to Order Child to Stop Sharing Bible Verses," Fox News, June 3, 2016.

114. Letter to Palmdale School District Superintendent Raul Maldonado from Richard L. Mast Jr. and Mary E. McAlister, Liberty Counsel Attorneys, "Re: Unconstitutional Suppression and Censorship of Student Religious Speech," May 24, 2016.

115. "School District OKs Sharing Bible Verses," CBN News.

Chapter 6: Protestors, the Press, and an Embattled First Amendment

1. Corey Brettschneider, "Trump vs. the Constitution: A Guide," *Politico,* August 4, 2016.

2. Orin Kerr, "Trump Wants to Protect Article XII of the Constitution," *Washington Post,* July 7, 2016.

3. Naomi Wolf, "Revealed: How the FBI Coordinated the Crackdown on Occupy," *Guardian,* August 5, 2018.

4. Sam Levin, "Dakota Access Pipeline Protests: UN Group Investigates Human Rights Abuses," *Guardian,* October 31, 2016.
5. Donald Trump (@realdonaldtrump), Twitter, August 5, 2018, 8:27 a.m., https://twitter.com/realdonaldtrump/status/1026069857589227520?lang=en.
6. "Statement of Elaine Frisbee-Fulton," ACLU-D.C., https://www.acludc.org/en/statement-gwen-frisbie-fulton.
7. Information on these events gathered from multiple news reports, civil complaints, and eyewitness interviews.
8. Sarah Lazare, "Law Enforcement Using Facebook and Apple to Data-Mine Accounts of Trump Protest Arrestees," *AlterNet,* February 22, 2017.
9. Phone interview with Elizabeth Lagesse, November 2017.
10. Kelly Weill, "ACLU Sues D.C. Police over Journalist's Inauguration Arrest," *Daily Beast,* June 23, 2017.
11. From *Shay Horse, Judah Ariel, Elizabeth Lagesse, and Milo Gonzalez v. District of Columbia et al.,* U.S. District Court for the District of Columbia, Case No. 1:17-cv-01216-ABJ, filed June 21, 2017.
12. Phone interview with Shay Horse, November 2017.
13. Weill, "ACLU Sues D.C. Police."
14. "Journalists Charged with Rioting in Washington," Committee to Protect Journalists, January 24, 2017, https://cpj.org/2017/01/journalists-charged-with-rioting-in-washington.php.
15. Mark Hand, "Felony Charges Against Inauguration Protesters Represent 'Historic Crossroads,'" *ThinkProgress,* May 19, 2017, https://thinkprogress.org/felony-charges-mark-historic-crossroads-a6c7c4cb06bd/.
16. "Grand Jury Returns Superseding Indictment in Inauguration Day Felony Rioting Case," WJAL TV, April 27, 2017.
17. Keith L. Alexander, "Prosecutors File Additional Charges Against Inauguration Protesters," *Washington Post,* April 28, 2017.
18. Defendants' Motion to Dismiss the Indictment, *The United States of America v. (Redacted),* Superior Court of the District of Columbia, Criminal Division—Felony Branch, filed May 26, 2017.
19. Matt Grubs, "SFR Writer Indicted Following Inaugural Protest Coverage," *Santa Fe Reporter,* June 6, 2017.
20. Emily Miller, "One Reporter Still Faces Inauguration Charges in D.C.," Reporters Committee for Freedom of the Press, July 24, 2017, https://www.rcfp.org/browse-media-law-resources/news/one-reporter-still-faces-inauguration-charges-dc.
21. *Horse, Ariel, Lagesse, and Gonzalez v. District of Columbia et al.,* U.S. District Court for the District of Columbia.
22. Miller, "One Reporter."
23. "ACLU of D.C. Sues D.C. Police for False Arrests, Free Speech Violations, Police Abuse at Inauguration Day Protests," ACLU-D.C., June 21, 2017, https://www.aclu.org/news/aclu-dc-sues-dc-police-false-arrests-free-speech-violations-police-abuse-inauguration-day.
24. Phone interview with Shahid Buttar, August 2016.
25. *Branzburg v. Hayes,* 408 U.S. 665 (1971).
26. Martin Matishak and Bryan Bender, "National Intelligence Chief Clapper Resigns," *Politico,* November 17, 2016.
27. "Shahid Buttar of BORDC Arrested Confronting James Clapper," YouTube video, 1:30, February 26, 2015, posted by "CODEPINK," https://www.youtube.com/watch?v=JN2973g0QUw.

28. Shahid Buttar, "Arrested for Asking Questions About Corruption," Center for Advanced Medicine and Clinical Research, April 22, 2015.
29. John Raby, "Reporter Arrested While Trying to Question Cabinet Member," Associated Press, May 10, 2017.
30. Ed Mazza, "Journalist Arrested for 'Yelling Questions' at HHS Secretary Tom Price, Kellyanne Conway," *Huffington Post,* May 10, 2017.
31. Joe Pompeo with Cristiano Lima, "Asking Qs 'Not in a Press Conference' Now a Crime?—Murdochs Avoid Elephant in Room—Lucky Lester," *Politico,* May 11, 2017.
32. Doug Stanglin, "W. Va. Reporter Arrested for 'Yelling Questions' at HHS Secretary," *USA Today,* May 10, 2017.
33. "CEO Defends Journalist Arrested for Yelling Questions at Tom Price," Associated Press, May 11, 2017.
34. "Reporters Committee for Freedom of the Press Announces $1 Million Gift from Jeff Bezos; New Partnership with First Look Media," Reporters Committee for Freedom of the Press, May 23, 2017.
35. Jennifer Gould Keil, "Donations for Press Freedom Group Spike in Trump Era," *New York Post,* May 24, 2017.
36. Keith Coffman, "Prosecutors Drop Charges Against Reporter Who Questioned U.S. Health Secretary," Reuters, September 6, 2017.
37. "CEO Defends Journalist," Associated Press.
38. Kalhan Rosenblatt, "Activist Faces New Trial for Laughing During Jeff Sessions Hearing," NBC News, July 14, 2017.
39. "Charges Dropped Against Woman Who Laughed at Jeff Sessions," YouTube video, 0:50, November 7, 2017, posted by "Wochit News," https://www.youtube.com/watch?time_continue=2&v=1XrTzF_zZ_U.
40. Desiree Fairooz, "I'm Facing Jail Time After Laughing at Jeff Sessions. I Regret Nothing," *Vox,* May 8, 2017.
41. Laurel Wamsley, "DOJ Drops Case Against Woman Who Laughed During Sessions Hearing," NPR, November 8, 2017.
42. "Woman Who Laughed at Sessions' Confirmation Hearing Convicted of a Crime," *Huffington Post* video, 1:56, https://www.huffingtonpost.com/entry/jeff-sessions-congressional-hearing_us_590a772ce4b05c3976861d12.
43. Ryan J. Reilly, "Jury Convicts Woman Who Laughed at Jeff Sessions During Senate Hearing," *Huffington Post,* May 3, 2017.
44. Aida Chavez, "Judge Tosses Conviction of Woman Who Laughed During Sessions Hearing," *Hill,* July 14, 2017.
45. Ibid.
46. David Boroff, "Woman Who Laughed During Jeff Sessions Confirmation Hearing Turns Down Plea Deal, Gets Second Trial," *New York Daily News,* September 1, 2017.
47. Maureen Dowd, "Where's the Justice at Justice?," *New York Times,* August 16, 2014.
48. "Pulitzer Prize Winners' Statements in Support of James Risen," RootsAction, August 11, 2014, https://rootsaction.org/statements-for-risen.
49. Guy Taylor, "Armed Agents Seize Records of Reporter, Washington Times Prepares Legal Action," *Washington Times,* October 23, 2013.
50. Kellan Howell, "Washington Times Sues Homeland over Seizure of Reporter's Notes," *Washington Times,* November 21, 2013.
51. Rob Bluey, "Government Agrees to Settlement for Raiding Reporter's Home, Seizing Confidential Files," *Daily Signal,* October 2, 2014.

52. "Gov't Obtains Wide AP Phone Records in Probe," Associated Press, May 13, 2013.

53. "Government Seizes AP Phone Records," Associated Press, May 13, 2013.

54. "Ann E. Marimow, "A Rare Peek into a Justice Department Leak Probe," *Washington Post,* May 19, 2013.

55. Justin Sink, "Report: Holder Signed Warrant to Seize Fox Reporter's Private Email," *Hill,* May 23, 2013.

56. Dana Milbank, "In AP, Rosen Investigations, Government Makes Criminals of Reporters," *Washington Post,* May 21, 2013.

57. Josh Gerstein, "Justice Department Defends Actions in James Rosen Case," *Politico,* May 24, 2013.

58. Information from this section comes from multiple interviews with Attkisson, from her book *Stonewalled: My Fight for Truth Against the Forces of Obstruction, Intimidation, and Harassment in Obama's Washington* (New York: Harper, 2014), and from *Sharyl Thompson Attkisson et al. v. Eric H. Holder et al.,* District of Columbia Superior Court, January 5, 2015.

59. Brandi Buchman, "Judge Tosses Reporter's Claim of Obama-Era Wiretaps," *Courthouse News,* November 3, 2017.

60. *Sharyl Thompson Attkisson et al. v. Eric H. Holder et al.,* United States Court of Appeals for the Fourth Circuit, No. 18–1677.

61. Colin Campbell, "Donald Trump on Reporters: 'I Would Never Kill Them, but I Do Hate Them,'" *Business Insider,* December 21, 2015.

62. Donald Trump (@realDonaldTrump), Twitter, February 17, 2017, 4:48 p.m., https://twitter.com/realDonaldTrump/status/832708293516632065.

63. David Jackson, "Trump Again Calls Media 'Enemy of the People,'" *USA Today,* February 24, 2017.

64. Transcript, press briefing by Press Secretary Sarah Sanders, White House, October 20, 2017.

65. Dan Merica, "Sanders: It Is 'Highly Inappropriate' to Debate Kelly," CNN, updated October 20, 2017.

66. Michael M. Grynbaum and Emily Baumgaertner, "White House Must Restore Press Credentials for CNN's Jim Acosta, Judge Rules," *New York Times,* November 16, 2018.

67. Ibid.

68. Phone interview with Floyd Abrams, October 30, 2017.

69. Phone interview with Norman Siegel, November 5, 2017.

70. Eric Levitz, "White House Bars *New York Times,* CNN, and *Politico* from Press Briefing," *New York Magazine,* February 24, 2017.

71. Christianna Silva, "The ~20 Times Trump Has Threatened to Sue Someone During This Campaign," FiveThirtyEight, October 24, 2016.

72. Ed Payne, "Trump Sues Maher for $5 Million for Orangutan Sex Joke," CNN, February 6, 2013.

73. Trevor Timm, "Trump's Many, Many Threats to Sue the Press Since Launching His Campaign," *Columbia Journalism Review,* October 3, 2016.

74. Phone interview with Lee Rowland, October 26, 2017.

75. Taylor Lorenz, "Trump Threatens to 'Change Libel Laws' to Go After NY Times," *Hill,* March 30, 2017.

76. *New York Times Co. v. Sullivan,* 376 U.S. 254 (1964).

77. Peter Baker, "Trump Demands That Publisher Halt Release of Critical Book," *New York Times,* January 4, 2018.

78. Jim Milliot, "Letter from the Editor: Macmillan Stands Up to President Trump," *Publishers Weekly,* January 12, 2018.

79. Andrew Blake, "Prosecutors Extracting Data from Cellphones of Dozens of Inauguration Day Arrestees: Court Filing," *Washington Times,* March 23, 2017.

80. Kelly Weill, "Feds Crack Trump Protesters' Phones to Charge Them with Felony Rioting," *Daily Beast,* July 26, 2017.

81. Ibid.

82. Thomas Brewster, "Feds Demand '1.3 Million IP Addresses' of Visitors to Trump Protest Website," *Forbes,* August 14, 2017.

83. Order, *In the matter of the search of* www.disruptj20.org *that is stored at premises owned, maintained, controlled, or operated by DreamHost,* Superior Court of the District of Columbia, Special Proceedings No. 17 CSW 3438, Chief Judge Robert E. Morin, October 10, 2017.

84. Matt Apuzzo and Adam Goldman, "NYPD Infiltrated Liberal Political Groups, According to New Documents," Associated Press, updated May 23, 2012.

85. Ibid.

86. George Joseph, "NYPD Sent Undercover Officers to Black Lives Matter Protest, Records Reveal," *Guardian,* September 29, 2016.

87. Ibid.

88. Janet Winter and Sharon Weinberger, "The FBI's New U.S. Terrorist Threat: 'Black Identity Extremists,'" *Foreign Policy,* October 6, 2017.

89. "Fatal Force: 987 People Have Been Shot and Killed by Police in 2017," *Washington Post,* https://www.washingtonpost.com/graphics/national/police-shootings-2017/.

90. "Factsheet: The NYPD Muslim Surveillance Program," ACLU, https://www.aclu.org/other/factsheet-nypd-muslim-surveillance-program.

91. *Hamid Hassan Raza et al. v. City of New York et al.,* U.S. District Court for the Eastern District of New York, No. CV13 3448, filed July 18, 2013.

92. "Factsheet: The NYPD Muslim Surveillance Program."

93. "Landmark Settlement Protects American Muslims from Discriminatory NYPD Surveillance," ACLU-NY, January 7, 2016, https://www.nyclu.org/en/press-releases/landmark-settlement-protects-american-muslims-discriminatory-nypd-surveillance.

94. Christopher Ingraham, "Republican Lawmakers Introduce Bills to Curb Protesting in at Least 18 States," *Washington Post,* February 24, 2017.

95. "Anti-Protest Bills Around the Country," ACLU, updated June 23, 2017, https://www.aclu.org/issues/free-speech/rights-protesters/anti-protest-bills-around-country.

96. Colin Campbell, "Drivers Who Hit Protesters Blocking Roads Could Be Protected Under NC House Bill," *Charlotte News & Observer,* April 26, 2017.

97. Steven Nelson, "N.C. House Votes to Protect Drivers Who Hit Protesters," *US News and World Report,* April 28, 2017.

98. "North Dakota Lawmaker's Bill Protects Drivers Who Negligently Hit Someone Obstructing Traffic," Fox News, January 17, 2017.

99. "An Act Relating to Prohibiting the Use of a Mask, Hood, or Device Under Certain Conditions," Senate Bill 5941, State of Washington, 65th Legislature, 2017 1st Special Section.

100. David Colon, "Schumer, Gillibrand Cosponsor Senate Bill That Would Make Boycotting Israel a Felony," *Gothamist,* July 19, 2017.

101. Madina Toure, "Gillibrand Now Says She Won't Support Israel Boycott Bill 'in Its Current Form,'" *Observer,* July 31, 2017.

102. Phone interview with Scott Michelman, November 2017.

103. Laurel Wamsley, "First Trials Begin for Those Charged over Inauguration Day Rioting," NPR, November 15, 2017.

104. Alan Pyke, "Judge: No, Wearing All Black Isn't 'Inciting a Riot,'" *ThinkProgress,* December 14, 2017.

105. Keith L. Alexander and Ellie Silverman, "Not-Guilty Verdicts for First Six People on Trial in Violent Inauguration Day Protests," *Washington Post,* December 21, 2017.

106. Sean Rossman, "6 Trump Inauguration Protesters Found Not Guilty," *USA Today,* December 21, 2017.

107. Amanda Iacone and Megan Cloherty, "6 Protesters Acquitted of Rioting, Related Charges Stemming from Inauguration Day," WTOP, December 21, 2017.

108. "ACLU-D.C. Applauds Jury Verdict in Inauguration Day Protestor Criminal Trials," ACLU-D.C., December 21, 2017, https://www.aclu.org/news/aclu-dc-applauds-jury-verdict-inauguration-day-protestor-criminal-trials.

109. Camilla Domonoske, "Jury Finds First Batch of Inauguration Protesters Not Guilty of Riot Charges," NPR, December 21, 2017.

110. Tim Ryan, "Riot Charges Dropped Against 129 Inauguration Day Protesters," *Courthouse News,* January 19, 2018.

111. Government's Notice of Intent to Proceed, *The United States of America v. Christopher Akerich et al.,* Superior Court of the District of Columbia, Criminal Division—Felony Branch, Criminal Nos. 2017cf2001160–2017cf2007213, January 18, 2018.

112. "ACLU-D.C. Names 27 D.C. Police Officers and Adds 10-Year-Old Boy as Plaintiff in Inauguration Day Lawsuit," ACLU-D.C., January 3, 2018, https://www.aclu.org/news/aclu-dc-names-27-dc-police-officers-and-adds-10-year-old-boy-plaintiff-inauguration-day-lawsuit.

113. *Horse, Ariel, Lagesse, and Gonzalez v. District of Columbia et al.,* U.S. District Court for the District of Columbia.

114. *Brady v. Maryland,* 373 U.S. 83 (1963).

115. Sam Adler-Bell, "Prosecutors Withheld Evidence That Could Exonerate J20 Inauguration Protesters, Judge Rules," *Intercept,* May 23, 2018.

116. Justin Wise, "Charges Dismissed for More Trump Inauguration Protesters After Prosecutors Found to Have Withheld Evidence," *Hill,* May 31, 2018.

117. "Federal Prosecutor Dismisses 8 More Inauguration Day Protest Cases in Advance of Upcoming Trial," *DefendJ20Resistance.org,* June 14, 2018, http://defendj20resistance.org/press/.

118. Ryan J. Reilly, "Justice Department Drops More Charges Against Trump Inauguration Defendants," *Huffington Post,* June 13, 2018.

119. Matthew Stabley, "Charges Against 39 Remaining Inauguration Riot Defendants Dismissed," NBC4 Washington, July 6, 2018.

120. Order, *United States of America v. Daniel Meltzer et al.,* Superior Court for the District of Columbia, Criminal Division—Felony Branch, November 9, 2018.

Chapter 7: State Power Run Amok

1. *Griswold v. Connecticut,* 381 U.S. 479 (1965).

2. "Roe v. Wade—Law Case," *Encyclopaedia Britannica,* updated September 27, 2018, https://www.britannica.com/event/Roe-v-Wade.

3. Destiny McKeiver, "ETX Girls Upset After Lemonade Stand Is Shut Down by Police," CBS19-KYTX, June 10, 2015.

4. Ashley Terry, "A Lemonade Raid, a Racist Reminder, and Other Things That Were Real and Fake Online This Week," *Global News*, June 12, 2015.
5. Dave, "The Government War on Kid-Run Concession Stands," Freedom Center of Missouri, July 26, 2011, http://www.mofreedom.org/2011/07/the-government-war-on-kid-run-concession-stands/.
6. "Montco Allows Kids' Lemonade Stand to Stay Open," NBC4 Washington, June 17, 2011.
7. "Police Shut Down Jerry Seinfeld's Lemonade Stand: Report," NBC4 New York, August 28, 2015.
8. Joe Dziemianowicz, "Your Kid's Lemonade Stand May Be Illegal, Here Are the Rules," *New York Daily News,* July 13, 2017.
9. Erik Kain, "The Inexplicable War on Lemonade Stands," *Forbes,* August 3, 2011.
10. Ted Oberg and Trent Seibert, "Lunchroom Lunacy: ISD Cops Investigate $2 Bill Spent on School Lunch," ABC13 Houston, April 28, 2016.
11. Effrey L. Boney, "Counterfeit Conspiracy," *Houston Forward Times,* May 11, 2016.
12. *Housing Not Handcuffs, Ending the Criminalization of Homelessness in U.S. Cities,* National Law Center on Homelessness & Poverty, https://www.nlchp.org/documents/Housing-Not-Handcuffs.
13. "Illegal to Be a Good Samaritan," National Coalition for the Homeless, July 17, 2015, https://nationalhomeless.org/good-samaritan/.
14. John Wilkens, "Food for Thought: Do Free Meals Help the Homeless?," *San Diego Union-Tribune,* November 5, 2018.
15. Lauryn Schroeder and Karen Pearlman, "Homeless Activists Say El Cajon Law Is Unconstitutional," *San Diego Union-Tribune,* January 15, 2018.
16. Peter Rowe, "'Junk' Catchphrase Rockets into Pop Culture Lexicon," *San Diego Union-Tribune,* November 17, 2010.
17. *Union Pacific Railway Company v. Botsford,* 141 U.S. 250 (1891).
18. John W. Whitehead, "What Country Is This? Forced Blood Draws, Cavity Searches and Colonoscopies," Rutherford Institute, September 5, 2017, https://www.rutherford.org/publications_resources/john_whiteheads_commentary/what_country_is_this_forced_blood_draws_cavity_searches_and_colonoscopies.
19. Some information for this case taken from *Charnesia Corley v. Harris County, Texas,* U.S. District Court for the Southern District of Texas, Houston Division, Case No. 4:16-cv-00382, filed August 5, 2016.
20. Tom Dart, "Dashcam Video Shows Police Sexually Assaulted Texas Woman, Lawyer Says," *Guardian,* August 16, 2017.
21. Jessica Willey, "Charges Dropped Against Deputies Accused of Controversial Strip Search," ABC13 Houston, August 10, 2017.
22. Pooja Lodhia, "HCSO, DA's Office in Heated Debate over Indictments Against Deputies," ABC13 Houston, July 1, 2016.
23. Britni Danielle, "Reminder: Police Violence Is So Much More Than Cops Shooting Black Men," *Splinter News,* September 8, 2017.
24. *Corley v. Harris County, Texas,* U.S. District Court for the Southern District of Texas.
25. Jay R. Jordan and St. John Barned-Smith, "Harris County Settles Lawsuit with Woman in Roadside Cavity Search," *Houston Chronicle,* January 24, 2018.
26. Larry Hannan, "Houston Police Officers Will Not Be Tried over Invasive Body Cavity Search of Black Woman," *Appeal,* August 24, 2017.
27. Information on this case is from *Jane Doe v. The El Paso County Hospital District et al.,* U.S. District Court for the Western District of Texas, El Paso Division, Civil Action No. 3:13-cv-00406, filed December 18, 2013.

28. Ibid.

29. Julian Aguilar, "Woman Settles Cavity Search Lawsuit for $1.1 Million," *Texas Tribune,* July 7, 2014.

30. "El Paso Hospital and Doctors Compensate New Mexico Woman for Their Role in an Illegal Body Cavity Search Performed at the Border," ACLU Texas, July 7, 2014.

31. Charles Krauthammer, "Don't Touch My Junk," *Washington Post,* November 19, 2010.

32. Michael Kinsley, "Go Ahead, Touch My Junk," *Politico,* November 23, 2010.

33. Katrina vanden Heuvel, "An Apology to John Tyner," *Nation,* November 28, 2010.

34. Andy Greenberg, "TSA Genitalia Jokes Bode Badly for Full-Body Airport Scans," *Forbes,* May 7, 2010.

35. Ralph Nader, "TSA Is Delivering Naked Insecurity," *USA Today,* November 18, 2010.

36. Kalhan Rosenblatt, "TSA Pat-Down of Son at DFW Airport Leaves Mother 'Livid,'" NBC News, March 28, 2017.

37. Joshua Rhett Miller, "Mom Says Family Missed Flight After TSA Treated Them 'Like Dogs,'" *New York Post,* March 28, 2017.

38. Monica Garske, "'My Son Felt Extremely Violated': Mom of Teen Troubled by TSA Pat-Down," NBC5 Dallas–Fort Worth, March 28, 2017.

39. Jennifer Williamson's Facebook page, March 30, 2017.

40. *Union Pacific Railway Company v. Botsford,* 141 U.S. 250 (1891).

41. *Albright v. Oliver,* 114 U.S. 807 (1994).

42. *Safford Unified School District v. Redding,* 557 U.S. 364 (2009).

43. *Florence v. Board of Chosen Freeholders,* 566 U.S. 318 (2012).

44. "The Many Benefits of Raw Milk," A Campaign for Real Milk, https://www.realmilk .com/many-benefits-raw-milk/.

45. Stephan Dinan, "Feds Sting Amish Farmer Selling Raw Milk Locally," *Washington Times,* April 28, 2011.

46. "The Dangers of Raw Milk: Unpasteurized Milk Can Pose a Serious Health Risk," U.S. Food and Drug Administration, https://www.fda.gov/Food/ResourcesForYou/consumers /ucm079516.htm.

47. Linda Larsen, "Consumers Warned to Discard Raw Milk from Pool Forge Dairy in Harrisburg, PA for Possible Listeria Contamination," *Food Poisoning Bulletin,* May 8, 2018.

48. "Outbreak Studies," U.S. Centers for Disease Control and Prevention, https://www.cdc .gov/foodsafety/rawmilk/rawmilk-outbreaks.html.

49. "Raw Milk Laws State-by-State," ProCon.org, updated February 2, 2018, https://milk .procon.org/view.resource.php?resourceID=005192.

50. Patricia Picone Mitchell, "Raw Milk: Ripe for Regulation?," *Washington Post,* February 24, 1985.

51. David E. Gumpert, *Life, Liberty, and the Pursuit of Food Rights: The Escalating Battle over Who Decides What We Eat* (White River Junction, VT: Chelsea Green, 2013).

52. Carolyn Lochead, "Dan Allgyer Latest Target in FDA War on Raw Milk," *San Francisco Chronicle,* May 22, 2011.

53. David Gumpert, "Have the Feds Finally Found Food Producers They Can Throw the Book At?," *Food Safety News,* November 30, 2011.

54. Sheriff Brad Rogers, "ASK THE SHERIFF: Sheriff Revisits Defending Raw Milk Provider," *Goshen News,* February 5, 2016.

55. Pete Kennedy, "Wisconsin: DATCP Raids Hershberger Farm," Farm-to-Consumer Legal Defense Fund, June 7, 2010, https://www.farmtoconsumer.org/blog/2010/06 /07/wisconsin-datcp-raids-hershberger-farm/.

56. "Prosecution: Wisconsin Trial Is Not About Raw Milk," Associated Press, May 21, 2013.

57. Tim Damos, "Hershberger Acquitted on 3 of 4 Charges in Raw Milk Trial," *Baraboo News Republic,* May 27, 2013.
58. "State Seeks to Jail Hershberger After Comments Made to Newspaper," *Baraboo News Republic,* May 31, 2013.
59. Rick Barrett, "Dairy Farmer Acquitted on Three of Four Charges in Raw Milk Trial," *Milwaukee Journal Sentinel,* May 25, 2013.
60. Rick Barrett, "Dairy Farmer Vernon Hershberger Receives $1,000 Fine in Raw Milk Case," *Milwaukee Journal Sentinel,* June 13, 2013.
61. "Hershberger Denied Raw Milk Supreme Court Hearing," Wisconsin Ag Connection, December 15, 2014.
62. "UPDATE: Wisconsin Raw Milk Farmer Loses Appeal," Associated Press, July 17, 2014.
63. Phone interview with Liz Reitzig, February 2018.
64. Daniel P. Puzo, "FDA to Ban Interstate Raw Milk Sales," *Los Angeles Times,* August 12, 1987.
65. "Food Safety and Raw Milk," U.S. Food & Drug Administration, https://www.fda.gov/food/foodborneillnesscontaminants/buystoreservesafefood/ucm277854.htm.
66. "DOH Issues Cease-and-Desist Orders to Company That Illegally Sold Raw Milk in NJ," State of New Jersey Department of Health, November 13, 2017, https://www.nj.gov/health/news/2017/approved/20171113c.shtml.
67. "'Raw Milk Moms' Are Targets of NJ Enforcement Action Against Food Clubs," *Food Safety News,* January 5, 2018.
68. *Citizen Petition to Except from 21 C.F.R. 1240.61(a) Certain Unpasteurized Milk and Milk Products If Properly Labeled,* delivered via electronic submission to Division of Dockets Management, Department of Health and Human Services, Food and Drug Administration, from Jonathan W. Emord, Esq., and Bethany R. Kennedy, Esq., Emord & Associates, PC, April 26, 2017.
69. Phone interview with Jonathan Emord, February 2017.
70. "States with Religious and Philosophical Exemptions from School Immunization Requirements," National Conference of State Legislators, December 20, 2017, http://www.ncsl.org/research/health/school-immunization-exemption-state-laws.aspx.
71. Senate Bill 277, California State Legislature, introduced February 19, 2015, signed into law June 30, 2015.
72. Efthimios Parasidis and Douglas J. Opel, "Parental Refusal of Childhood Vaccines and Medical Neglect Laws," *American Journal of Public Health,* December 7, 2016.
73. *Jacobson v. Massachusetts,* 197 U.S. 11 (1905).
74. *Washington v. Harper,* 494 U.S. 210 (1990).
75. "Recommended Immunization Schedule for Adults Aged 19 Years or Older, United States, 2018," U.S. Centers for Disease Control and Prevention, https://www.cdc.gov/vaccines/schedules/downloads/adult/adult-combined-schedule.pdf.
76. Phoebe Day Danziger and Rebekah Diamond, "The Vaccination Double Standard," *Slate,* July 25, 2016.
77. Dorit Reiss Rubinstein and Lois A. Weithorn, "Responding to the Childhood Vaccination Crisis: Legal Frameworks and Tools in the Context of Parental Vaccine Refusal," *Buffalo Law Review* 63, no. 881 (2015).
78. Alex Berezow, "Parents Who Do Not Vaccinate Their Children Should Go to Jail (COMMENTARY)," *USA Today,* January 28, 2015.
79. Oracknows, "Should Vaccines Be Compulsory?," *ScienceBlogs,* July 25, 2016.
80. Sara Sidner, "Kiss on the Cheek Triggers Trouble for Same Sex Couple on Hawaiian Vacation," CNN, October 31, 2015.

81. Joe Wojtas, "Groton Woman and Girlfriend Sue Honolulu Police After Supermarket Kissing Incident," *Day,* November 1, 2015.

82. "Gay Couple Arrested After Kissing in Grocery Store Gets $80K Settlement," *Hawaii News Now,* May 20, 2016.

83. Information on this case derived from various news accounts and *Cervelli v. Aloha Bed & Breakfast,* Intermediate Court of Appeals of Hawai'i, decided February 23, 2018, 415 P.3d 919 (Haw. Ct. App. 2018).

84. *Diane Cervelli and Taeko Bufford v. Aloha Bed & Breakfast,* Complaint for Injunctive Relief, Declaratory Relief, & Damages, Circuit Court of the First Circuit State of Hawaii.

85. "Lambda Legal Files Lawsuit on Behalf of Lesbian Couple Rejected by Hawaii Bed & Breakfast," Lambda Legal, December 19, 2011, https://www.lambdalegal.org/news/hi _20111219_lambda-legal-files.

86. *Cervelli v. Aloha Bed & Breakfast,* Intermediate Court of Appeals of Hawai'i.

87. "Hawai'i Appeals Court Rejects Religious Justification for B&B That Refused Room to Lesbian Couple," Lambda Legal, February 23, 2018, https://www.lambdalegal.org/news /hi_20180223_appeals-court-rejects-religious-discrimination.

88. Order Rejecting Application for Writ of Certiorari, *Diane Cervelli and Taeko Bufford v. Aloha Bed & Breakfast,* in the Supreme Court of the State of Hawai'i, SCWC-13-0000806, July 10, 2018.

89. Information on this case derived from *Mark Horton v. Midwest Geriatric Management,* U.S. District Court for the Eastern District of Missouri, Case No. 4:17-cv-02324-JCH, filed August 28, 2017, and "Horton v. Midwest Geriatric Management," Lambda Legal, https://www.lambdalegal.org/in-court/cases/horton-v-midwest-geriatric-management.

90. *Horton v. Midwest Geriatric Management,* U.S. District Court for the Eastern District of Missouri.

91. *Horton v. Midwest Geriatric Management,* U.S. Court of Appeals for the Eighth Circuit, Case No. 18–1104, filed March 7, 2018.

92. *Zarda v. Altitude Express, Inc.,* U.S Court of Appeals for the Second Circuit, 15–3775 (en banc), argued September 26, 2017, decided February 26, 2018.

93. *Kimberly Hively, Plaintiff-Appellant v. Ivy Tech Community College of Indiana, Defendant-Appellee,* U.S. Court of Appeals for the Seventh Circuit, No. 15–1720 (en banc), argued November 30, 2016, decided April 4, 2017.

94. "Lambda Legal Urges Full Eleventh Circuit to Rehear Georgia Employment Discrimination Case," Lambda Legal, March 31, 2017, https://www.lambdalegal.org/news/ga _20170331_ll-urges-11th-circuit-rehear-evans.

95. Decision, *Jameka K. Evans, Plaintiff-Appellant v. Georgia Regional Hospital, Charles Moss et al., Defendants-Appellees,* U.S. Court of Appeals for the Eleventh Circuit, Case No. 15–15234, filed March 10, 2017.

96. Order on Petition(s) for Rehearing and Petition(s) for Rehearing En Banc, *Jameka K. Evans, Plaintiff-Appellant v. Georgia Regional Hospital, Charles Moss et al., Defendants-Appellees,* U.S. Court of Appeals for the Eleventh Circuit, Case No. 15-15234-BB, filed July 6, 2017.

97. On Petition for a Writ of Certiorari to the United States Court of Appeals for the Eleventh Circuit, *Jameka K. Evans, Petitioner v. Georgia Regional Hospital, et al., Respondents,* in the Supreme Court of the United States, No. 17–370, filed September 7, 2017.

98. "Evans v. Georgia Regional Hospital," Lambda Legal, https://www.lambdalegal.org/in -court/cases/ga_evans-v-ga-regional-hospital.

99. "Horton v. Midwest Geriatric Management," Lambda Legal, https://www.lambdalegal
.org/in-court/cases/horton-v-midwest-geriatric-management.

100. "Lambda Legal Presses Fight for Federal LGBT Employment Discrimination Protection
in New Appeals Court Case," Lambda Legal, March 7, 2018, https://www.lambdalegal
.org/news/mo_20180307_lgbt-employment-discrimination-appeal.

101. Phone interview with Omar Gonzalez-Pagan, November 2017.

102. "Map: How Many States Still Lack Clear Non-Discrimination," Human Rights Campaign, July 10, 2015.

103. "HHS Announces New Conscience and Religious Freedom Division," U.S. Department
of Health and Human Services, Office for Civil Rights, January 18, 2018.

104. Kimberley Lawson, "Doctors Who Oppose Abortion and LGBT Rights Get New Government Protections," *Broadly,* January 18, 2018.

105. Information for this case derived from various news accounts and *Ashton Whitaker, a
Minor, by His Mother and Next Friend, Melissa Whitaker v. Kenosha Unified School District No. 1 Board of Education and Sue Savaglio-Jarvis, in Her Official Capacity as Superintendent of the Kenosha Unified School District No. 1,* Amended Complaint, U.S. District
Court for the Eastern District of Wisconsin, Civil Action No. 2:16-cv-00943, filed August 15, 2016.

106. *Whitaker v. Kenosha Unified School District No. 1 Board of Education and Sue Savaglio-
Jarvis,* Amended Complaint, U.S. District Court for the Eastern District of Wisconsin.

107. Order Denying Defendants' Civil L.R. 7(H) Expedited, Nondispositive Motion to Stay
Preliminary Injunction (Dkt. No. 33) Pending Appeal (Dkt. No. 44), *Ashton Whitaker
v. Kenosha Unified School District No. 1 Board of Education and Sue Savaglio-Jarvis,* U.S.
District Court for the Eastern District of Wisconsin, Case No. 16-Cv-943-PP, filed October 3, 2016.

108. "Dear Colleague Letter," Sandra Battle, acting assistant secretary for civil rights, U.S.
Department of Education, and T. E. Wheeler II, acting assistant attorney general for
civil rights, U.S. Department of Justice, February 22, 2017.

109. *Ashton Whitaker Plaintiff-Appellee v. Kenosha Unified School District No. 1 Board of Education et al., Defendants-Appellants,* U.S. Court of Appeals for the Seventh Circuit,
No. 16-3522, decided May 30, 2017.

110. "Federal Court Management Statistics: Statistics and Reports," United States Courts,
USCourts.gov, September 2018.

111. Annysa Johnson, "Kenosha Schools Settle Transgender Discrimination Suit for
$800,000," *Milwaukee Journal Sentinel,* January 12, 2018.

112. Christianna Silva, "School District Pays Transgender Student $800,000 After Banning
Him from the Boys Bathroom," *Newsweek,* January 10, 2018.

113. H.R.2282-Equality Act, 115th Congress (2017–2018), introduced May 2, 2017.

114. Donald Trump (@RealDonaldJTrump), Twitter, June 14, 2016, 10:31 a.m., https://
twitter.com/realdonaldtrump/status/742771576039460864?lang=en.

115. Memorandum from Jefferson Sessions, U.S. Attorney General, to U.S. Attorneys &
Heads of Department Components 1, October 4, 2017.

116. Memorandum for All Executive Departments and Agencies, from: The Attorney General, subject: Federal Law Protections for Religious Liberty, Office of the Attorney General, U.S. Department of Justice, October 6, 2017.

117. David Crary and Ricardo Alonso-Zaldivar, "Religious Conservatives Cheer Trump's
One-Two Punch Against Birth Control, LGBT Rights," Associated Press, October 6, 2017.

118. "Judge Rejects Trump's Attempts to Quash Trans Military Ban Lawsuit and to Dissolve
Preliminary Injunction," GLBTQ Legal Advocates & Defenders, August 6, 2018.

119. Chris Johnson, "Latest Ruling Could Give Supreme Court Crack at Trans Military Ban," *Washington Blade,* July 18, 2018.

120. Tara Copp, "Transgender Recruits Can Now Enlist, as Pentagon and White House Weigh Overall Policy," *Military Times,* December 30, 2017.

121. Erica L. Green, Katie Benner, and Robert Pear, "'Transgender' Could Be Defined Out of Existence Under Trump Administration," *New York Times,* October 21, 2018.

122. Maureen Groppe, "After Rippon: Searching for Clarity on Mike Pence's Stance on Gay Conversion Therapy," *USA Today,* February 16, 2018.

123. Indiana Senate Bill 101, the Religious Freedom Restoration Act (RFRA), approved March 26, 2015; Amanda Terkel, "Mike Pence's Religious Freedom Law Continues to Hang over Indiana," *Huffington Post,* September 1, 2016.

124. "2016 Presidential Candidates on LGBTQ Issues," Ballotpedia, https://ballotpedia.org/2016_presidential_candidates_on_LGBTQ_issues.

Chapter 8: Cops, Courts, and Jails

1. Amy Renee Leiker, "911 Call Sheds Light on Iraqi-American Handcuffed at Wichita Bank," *Wichita Eagle,* September 15, 2017.

2. "Wichita Police Apologize for Detaining Man, Family over Large Check," KWCH-12 CBS, September 13, 2013.

3. Letter to Chief Gordon Ramsay, Wichita Police Department, Sheriff Jeff Easter, Sedgwick County Sheriff's Office, and Colonel Mark Bruce, Kansas Highway Patrol, from Juvaria Khan, staff attorney, Muslim Advocates, September 20, 2017.

4. Alex Perez and B. J. Lutz, "American Citizen Faced Deportation," NBC-5 Chicago, May 24, 2010.

5. Tom Watkins, "Chicago Man Accuses Feds of Racial Profiling," CNN, May 28, 2010.

6. James Duane, "Innocent? Don't Talk to the Police," *Los Angeles Times,* August 26, 2016.

7. Order and Amended Opinion, Dissent by Chief Judge Kozinski, *Utio Dinero Sessoms, Petitioner-Appellant v. Randy Grounds, Warden, Respondent-Appellee,* on Remand from the United States Supreme Court, U.S. Court of Appeals for the Ninth Circuit, No. 08–17790 D.C. No. 2:05-cv-01221-JAM-GGH, argued and submitted en banc, March 18, 2014.

8. Kimberly Eiten, "Public Defenders: Body Cam Footage Shows Officer Planting Drugs," WJZ-13 CBS, July 19, 2017.

9. Justin Carissimo, "34 Baltimore Cases Dismissed After Video Appears to Show Officer Planting Drugs," CBS News, July 27, 2017.

10. Justin Fenton, "Baltimore Police Officers Found Guilty of Racketeering, Robbery in Gun Trace Task Force Corruption Case," *Baltimore Sun,* February 12, 2018.

11. Paul DeWolfe, "Blog—Public Defender Discloses Video Evidence of Officers Planting Drugs; Demands Swift Action by Prosecutors and Thorough Review by Police," National Association for Public Defense, July 19, 2017, https://www.publicdefenders.us/blog_home.asp?display=594.

12. Carissimo, "34 Baltimore Cases Dismissed."

13. Justin Fenton and Kevin Rector, "Body Camera Footage Shows Officer Planting Drugs, Public Defender Says," *Baltimore Sun,* July 19, 2017.

14. Phil McCausland, "Another Baltimore Police Body-Cam Video Shows Officers 'Plant' Drugs," NBC News, August 3, 2017.

15. James Doubek, "Baltimore Police Officer Indicted on Charges of Misconduct, Fabricating Evidence," NPR, January 25, 2018.

16. "Only on 2: LAPD Bodycam Video Appears to Contradict Officer Testimony, Investigation Discovers," KCAL-9 CBS, November 9, 2017.

17. Doubek, "Baltimore Police Officer Indicted."

18. Kevin Rector, "Baltimore Police Officer Found Guilty of Fabricating Evidence in Case Where His Own Body Camera Captured the Act," *Baltimore Sun,* November 9, 2018.

19. "Victim of Charlottesville Beating Wanted for Arrest," *The Young Turks,* YouTube video, posted October 11, 2017, https://www.youtube.com/watch?v=k24ayPWaH-c&t=105s.

20. Frances Robles, "Three Charged After Violence in Charlottesville," *New York Times,* August 27, 2017.

21. "Arrest Warrant Obtained for DeAndre Harris," WVIR-NBC29, October 9, 2017.

22. Daniel Victor, "Black Man Beaten During Charlottesville Rally Charged with Felony," *New York Times,* October 10, 2017.

23. "Update: DeAndre Harris Found Not Guilty in Connection to Aug. 12 Rally," WVIR-NBC29, March 16, 2018.

24. Opinion of the Court, *United States of America v. Mark Ciavarella, Jr., Appellant,* United States Court of Appeals for the Third Circuit, No. 11–3277, decided May 24, 2013.

25. Matthew Lippman, *Criminal Procedure,* 2nd ed. (Thousand Oaks, CA: SAGE Publications, 2013).

26. "Federal Officials Announce the Filing of Federal Fraud and Tax Charges Against Two Luzerne County Common Pleas Court Judges in an On-Going Public Corruption Probe," U.S. Department of Justice, Middle District of Pennsylvania, January 26, 2009.

27. "Former Luzerne Judge Conahan Sentenced to 17.5 Years," *Times Tribune* (Scranton, PA), September 23, 2011.

28. "Pennsylvania Judge Gets 28 Years in 'Kids for Cash' Case," NBC News, August 11, 2011.

29. Frank Mastropolo, Lauren Pearle, and Glenn Ruppel, "Pa. Supreme Court Throws Out Thousands of Juvenile Delinquency Cases," ABC News, October 29, 2009.

30. *In re: Gault,* 387 U.S. 1 (1967).

31. Jacques Billeaud, "Arizona Could Face Fines over Failures in Prison Health Care," Associated Press, February 12, 2018.

32. "Parsons v. Ryan," ACLU of Arizona, https://www.acluaz.org/en/cases/parsons-v-ryan.

33. "Judge Won't Remove Himself from Prison Health Care Case," Associated Press, May 3, 2018.

34. Michael Kiefer, "Judge: Contempt Ruling, Fines Ahead for State in Prison Health-Care Case," *Arizona Republic,* May 9, 2018.

35. Opinion, *Victor Antonio Parsons et al., Plaintiffs-Appellees v. Charles L. Ryan, Richard Pratt, Defendants-Appellants,* United States Court of Appeals for the Ninth Circuit, No. 13–16396, D.C. No. 2:12-cv-00601NVW, argued and submitted November 6, 2013, filed June 5, 2014.

36. "President Trump Pardons Sheriff Joe Arpaio," White House, August 25, 2017, https://www.whitehouse.gov/briefings-statements/president-trump-pardons-sheriff-joe-arpaio/.

37. Jacques Billeaud, "AZ Sheriff's Officers Turn in Federal Credentials," Associated Press, December 15, 2011.

38. Ruben Navarrette, "Immigration Officials Taking Full Advantage of Sheriff Arpaio's Rights Abuses," *Dallas Morning News,* April 2012.

39. Jana Bommersbach, "Will Sheriff Joe Stop at Nothing?," *Phoenix Magazine,* February 2005.

40. Eugene Scott, "Temperatures Rise to 145 Inside Tent City," *Arizona Republic,* July 3, 2011.

41. Valeria Fernandez, "Pregnant Latina Says She Was Forced to Give Birth in Shackles After One of Arpaio's Deputies Racially Profiled Her," *Phoenix New Times,* October 22, 2009.

42. *United States of America v. Maricopa County, Arizona; Maricopa County Sheriff's Office; and Joseph M. Arpaio,* U.S. District Court for the District of Arizona, Case No. 2:10-cv-01878-LOA, filed September 2, 2010.

43. Matt Pierce, "Timeline: The Rise and Fall of Arizona Sheriff Joe Arpaio," *Los Angeles Times,* August 1, 2017.

44. Samuel R. Gross, Maurice Possley, and Klara Stephens, *Race and Wrongful Convictions in the United States* (Irvine: University of California–Irvine, 2017).

45. Aleks Kaistura, "Women's Mass Incarceration: The Whole Pie 2017," Prison Policy Project, October 19, 2017, https://www.prisonpolicy.org/reports/pie2017women.html.

46. Elizabeth Swavola, Kristine Riley, and Ram Subramanian, "Overlooked: Women and Jails in an Era of Reform," Vera Institute of Justice, 2016.

47. Alma Cohen and Crystal S. Yang, "Judicial Politics and Sentencing Decisions" (working paper no. 24615, NBER, Cambridge, MA, May 7, 2018).

48. Elisha Fieldstadt, "New York City Reaches $5.9 Million Settlement with Family of Eric Garner," MSNBC, July 15, 2015.

49. John Sullivan, Zane Anthony, Julie Tate, and Jennifer Jenkins, "Nationwide, Police Shot and Killed Nearly 1,000 People in 2017," *Washington Post,* January 6, 2018.

50. Jon Swaine, Oliver Laughland, Jamiles Lartey, and Ciara McCarthy, "Young Black Men Killed by US Police at Highest Rate in Year of 1,134 deaths," *Guardian,* December 31, 2015.

51. Andrea B. Scott, "Police Kill Nearly 25 Dogs Each Day," *Nation,* July 5, 2016.

52. Paresh Dave, "Deputy Heard Crying After Shooting Man, 70, Who Was Grabbing Cane," *Los Angeles Times,* March 12, 2014.

53. Sara Morrison, "Cop's Shooting of Unarmed 70-Year-Old Man Deemed 'Appropriate Response,'" *Atlantic,* February 26, 2014.

54. Kashmira Gander, "US Police Officer Shot Old Man Because He Thought His Walking Stick Was a Gun," *Independent,* March 14, 2014.

55. "No Charges for S.C. Cop Who Shot 70-Year-Old Man," *Savannah Morning News,* August 15, 2014.

56. Josh Wallace and Robert Medley, "OKC Officer Kills Man Who Threatened Suicide," *Oklahoman,* November 16, 2017.

57. Cassie Fambro, "Two Years Later, the Death of Gil Collar Still Haunts the University of South Alabama in Mobile," *Advance Local,* October 6, 2014.

58. "Police: Student Took LSD Before Campus Shooting," Associated Press, October 9, 2012.

59. Alyssa Newton, "South Alabama Officer Cleared in 2012 Shooting of Collar," *Vanguard USA,* September 21, 2015.

60. Sullivan, Anthony, Tate, and Jenkins, "Nationwide, Police Shot and Killed Nearly 1,000 People."

61. Cindy Chang, "LAPD Hands Out Annual Awards for Bravery and 'Preservation of Life,'" *Los Angeles Times,* September 27, 2018.

62. Sullivan, Anthony, Tate, and Jenkins, "Nationwide, Police Shot and Killed Nearly 1,000 People."

Afterword

1. "List of Donald Trump's Federal Judicial Nominees," Ballotpedia, https://ballotpedia .org/List_of_Donald_Trump%27s_federal_judicial_nominees.

2. "AFJ Review of Kavanaugh Record Highlights Extreme Views," Alliance for Justice, July 24, 2018, https://www.afj.org/press-room/press-releases/afj-review-of-kavanaugh -record-highlights-extreme-views.

3. "Racial Justice Organizations Oppose Judge Brett Kavanaugh's Confirmation to U.S. Supreme Court," Lawyers' Committee for Civil Rights Under Law, August 30, 2018, https://lawyerscommittee.org/press-release/racial-justice-organizations-oppose-judge -brett-kavanaughs-confirmation-to-u-s-supreme-court/.

4. Charles M. Blow, "Opinion: Liberals, This Is War," *New York Times,* October 7, 2018.

5. On Renewed Motion for Stay Pending Appeal, *Richard Brakebill et al., Plaintiffs-Appellees v. Alvin Jaeger, North Dakota Secretary of State, Defendant-Appellant,* United States Court of Appeals for the Eighth Circuit, No. 18–1725, submitted September 10, 2018, filed September 24, 2018.

6. Ruben Kimmelman, "Judge Rules Native Americans in North Dakota Must Comply with Voter ID Law," NPR, November 2, 2012.

7. On Application to Vacate Stay, *Richard Brakebill et al. v. Alvin Jaeger, North Dakota Secretary of State,* Supreme Court of the United States, 586 U.S. No. 18A335 (2018), Ginsburg, J., Dissenting, No. 18A335, October 9, 2018.

8. Blake Nicholson, "Few Native American Voters Had ID Issues in North Dakota," Associated Press, November 7, 2018.

9. Jonathan Swan and Stef W. Kight, "Exclusive: Trump Targeting Birthright Citizenship with Executive Order," *Axios,* October 30, 2018.

10. "Counting to Two Thirds: How Close Are We to a Convention for Proposing Amendments to the Constitution?," *Federalist Society Review* 19 (2018).

11. John W. Schoen and Emma Newburger, "Democrats' Expanded Control of State Governments Could Change the 2020 Political Landscape," CNBC, November 7, 2018.

12. "2018 Election: Governors," RealClearPolitics, https://www.realclearpolitics.com/epolls /2018/governor/2018_elections_governor_map.html.

13. David A. Super, "Opinion: A 'Convention of States' Is the Last Thing America Needs Right Now," *Hill,* March 27, 2018.

14. Fred Wertheimer, "The Battle to preserve the Constitution," *Huffington Post,* April 13, 2017.

INDEX

abortion rights, 262–63, 299
Abrams, Floyd, 232–35, 328, 338
Abundiz, Jennifer, 42
Acosta, Jim, 232
Adams, John, 17–18
African Americans, ix, 98, 334
  criminal justice system abuses and,
    316–17, 322–25
  embattled First Amendment and, 206,
    217, 239, 241–43, 246–47
  free speech and, 155, 187, 196–98, 200
  prison system and, 74–85, 90–92, 94,
    322–23
  state power run amok and, 267–68,
    270–72, 292
  surveillance of, 241–43
  violence against, 316, 323–25
Aldhalimi, Maha, 171
Ali, Sattar, 309–10
Allen, Nick, 84, 86–89, 94
Allred, Kevin, 145–48
Aloha Bed & Breakfast, 294–96
Alvarez v. Montgomery County, 13–14
American Civil Liberties Union (ACLU):
  civil asset forfeitures and, 108, 110–11,
    127
  criminal justice system abuses and,
    314–15, 319
  embattled First Amendment and, 207,
    213–14, 220, 233–34, 243–45,
    248–51, 253–55
  free speech and, 149–50, 152, 159–62,
    186

  LFOs and, 89–90
  prison system and, 79–84, 89–91,
    93–95, 319
  state power run amok and, 274, 299
Andersen, Colin, 151
Anderson, Devon, 271
Animal Factory (Kirby), 175
Applegate, Joseph, Jr., 59
Ariel, Judah, 213–14
Armento, Jennifer, 253
Arpaio, Joseph, 320–21, 335
Assets Forfeiture Fund, 104
Associated Press (AP), 204, 207, 220–21,
  227, 239–4–41, 321
Attkisson, Jim and Sarah Judith Starr,
  229
Attkisson, Sharyl, 204, 228–30
attorneys, 35, 89, 261, 333–35, 338
  civil asset forfeitures and, 98, 100–102,
    108–9, 115–16, 118, 120, 122–24,
    126, 129
  CPS and, 33, 42–43, 45–47, 49–50,
    52–57, 60, 63–70
  criminal justice system abuses and, 310,
    312–18, 321, 326–28
  embattled First Amendment and,
    211–12, 214, 220, 223–24, 234–35,
    237, 250–59
  free speech and, 136, 138, 140, 143–44,
    150, 155–57, 159–60, 162, 167, 170–71,
    174, 176, 178–82, 186, 188–89, 191–92,
    195, 198, 201
  Magas case and, 9–16, 18, 30

attorneys (*continued*)
   Mitchell case and, 27, 29
   prison system and, 76–84, 90, 93–94,
      321
   state power run amok and, 266–69,
      271–72, 274, 281–82, 284, 294,
      296–98, 301–5
Austin, Trevis, 327
Avellanet, Edwin, 19–21

balanced budget amendment (BBA),
   336–37
bank accounts, bank deposits, 99, 157, 258
   civil asset forfeitures and, 122–24,
      128–29
   federal law on, 121–22, 128–29
Banks, Steven, 266–67
Barnes, Amy, 155–56
Barr, William, 132, 205
Barstow, David, 225
Bearden v. Georgia, 83
Beck, Glenn, 139
Berardo, Grant and Joseph, 199
Berezow, Alex, 290
Bible verses, 184, 200–201
Bienstock, Judah and Roigin (Fnyo), 306
Bill of Rights Defense Committee, 216–17
birth control, 171, 262
Blow, Charles, 334
Bogash, Sam, 223
Bollen, Howard, 134
Bond, Beth, 59
BONG HiTS 4 JESUS case, 193–96
Border Patrol, U.S., 272–74
Brackett, Kevin, 326
Bradley, Ed, 141
Brady Rule, 257, 259
Branzburg v. Hayes, 215
Bratton, William, 329–30
Breen, Thomas, 45–50
Breyer, Stephen, 277
Brown, Angela, 77–79
Brown, Mark R., 67
Brown, Michael, 91, 323–24
Bryant, Bruce, 325–26
Bufford, Taeko, 294–95
Bullock, Scott, 97–98, 103–4, 107–8, 111,
   126–27, 130

Burrell, Garland E., Jr., 173–74
Bush, George W., 141, 163, 190–91, 225,
   228, 240
Butler, Smedley, 133
Buttar, Shahid, 215–19

Cammack, Samuel, 272
Campbell, Michael, 135–36, 138, 142–45
Canipe, Bobby Dean, 325–26
Cantú, Aaron, 208, 212–13, 254–55
Caraballo, Eduardo, 310–11
Carroll, Kathleen, 220
Carter, Clyde, 264
Caswell Motel, 100–104, 111, 119
CBS, CBS News, 141, 189, 204, 228–30,
   266–67, 298, 310, 313–15
censoring, censorship, 65, 244
   free speech and, 132, 148–50, 156, 161,
      166, 190, 194, 199, 201
Centers for Disease Control (CDC), 283,
   286–87, 289–90
Central Intelligence Agency (CIA), 141,
   225, 227–28, 240
Cervelli, Diane, 294–95
Chaney, Corey and Summer, 58–59
Charles, Andrew, 107
Chase, Peter, 158, 161
Cherry, David, 176–82
Child Protective Services (CPS):
   abuses of, 55–72
   and alleged child abuse or neglect,
      32–34, 36–48, 50–51, 53–61,
      63–64, 68–72
   case studies on, 57–63
   children removed from homes by, 33–34,
      40–43, 45–47, 51–53, 56–58, 60–69,
      335
   Fort case and, 37–55, 67
   lawsuits against, 37–38, 41, 43–45, 47,
      50–55, 71, 66
   Peterlin's deposition and, 52–54
   reforms and, 69–71
children, ix, 1, 18, 20, 23, 29
   criminal justice system abuses and,
      312–13, 317–18, 324–25, 328
   embattled First Amendment and, 206–7
   free speech and, 151–52
   prison system and, 74–85, 90, 94

removed from their homes, 33–34, 40–49, 51–54, 56–58, 60–69, 335
  state power run amok and, 264–65, 267–69, 275–76, 284, 286–90
  see also Child Protective Services
Choudhury, Nusrat, 80–82, 84–85, 93–95
Christian, George, 157–61
Christians, 35, 62, 105, 169, 201, 240, 294
Ciavarella, Mark, 317–18
City of Houston v. Hill, 152–53
civil asset forfeitures, xiv, 96–130
  abuse and corruption in, 107–8, 127
  cash and, 96–99, 105–6, 109–10, 112, 116, 122–25, 127–29, 335
  Caswell Motel case and, 100–104, 111, 119
  Constitution and, 102, 109–10, 115–21, 124–25, 127–28
  criminal vs., 105, 108–9, 127
  Eh Wah case and, 105–7
  equitable sharing and, 97, 102, 110–12, 125, 128–30
  hearings, lawsuits, and trials in, 101–5, 107, 113, 115–19, 124–25, 127–28
  Hinders case and, 122–25
  history of, 96–97
  homes and, 96, 112–21, 127, 130
  reforms and, 105, 117, 125–30
  Sourovelis case and, 112–17
  structuring laws and, 122, 124, 128–29
  targets of, 99–104
  Young case and, 118–20, 130
Civil Rights Act, 291–92, 296–98, 301–4, 306
Clapper, James, 216–18
Clarke, Kristen, 334
Clayton, Melodie, 155–56
Cleveland, Harriet, 94
Clinton, Bill, 137, 291
Clinton, Hillary, 199, 291, 307
CNN, 113, 205, 228, 230–33, 292, 311
Coast Guard, U.S., 226–27
Cochran, Sam, 327
Code Pink, 221, 224
Collar, Gilbert, 326–27
Collins, Lee, 42–44
Comey, James, 219, 231
Comstock Act, 149

Conahan, Michael, 317–18
concentrated animal feeding operations (CAFOs), 175–82
Congress, U.S., 219, 221–25, 262, 333
  civil asset forfeitures and, 97, 102, 123–24, 126, 129
  embattled First Amendment and, 205, 216–17, 222–25, 234–35, 248
  free speech and, 148, 152, 160–64, 168–69, 172
  new Constitutional Convention and, 336–37
  state power run amok and, 279, 285, 287, 291, 296, 298, 304
Connecticut Four, 160–62
Connolly, Allison, 199
Constitution, U.S., ix, xiii, xv, 30, 34, 51, 54, 262, 333–38
  Article I of, 120, 203, 285, 287, 290
  Article V of, 336–37
  bodily integrity and, 276–77, 287–88, 290
  civil asset forfeitures and, 102, 109–10, 115–21, 124–25, 127–28
  CPS abuses and, 61–63, 68–70, 72
  criminal justice system abuses and, 308, 310, 318, 320–21, 323, 331
  embattled First Amendment and, 203, 205–6, 211–12, 214–15, 218, 223, 226, 229–35, 238–39, 244–45, 248, 250–51, 253, 259
  Ferguson case and, 91–92
  free speech and, 131–32, 137–41, 143–54, 156–62, 165, 167–75, 180, 183–89, 192–96, 198, 200–201
  Magas case and, 9–11, 13, 15–16, 19
  Mitchell case and, 27–28
  prison system and, 73, 80–83, 86, 91–92, 95, 321
  searches and, 1–2, 10–11, 15, 18–19, 21–22, 280–81
  state power run amok and, 263, 270, 272, 274, 276–78, 280–81, 284–85, 287–88, 290, 293, 295–96, 299, 301, 304
Constitution, U.S., amendments to, 21–23, 203–63
  First, 27, 51, 61–62, 69, 131–32, 137–38,

Constitution (*continued*)
 140, 143–45, 147–53, 157–58, 160,
 162, 165, 167–74, 183–89, 192,
 194–96, 198, 200–261, 263, 290,
 295–96, 298, 304, 331, 335
 Second, ix–x, 145–46, 148
 Third, 23, 27–29, 148, 263
 Fourth, 1–2, 10–11, 13, 16–19, 21–22,
 27–28, 30, 51, 68–69, 83, 92,
 143–44, 157–58, 170, 214, 230, 238,
 261, 263, 272, 277, 290, 293, 321, 335
 Fifth, 51, 68–69, 83, 117, 121, 128–29,
 157–58, 183, 198, 214, 232, 261, 263,
 287, 290, 321, 323, 335
 Sixth, 55, 83, 121, 261, 335
 Eighth, 27, 115, 119–21, 124, 185, 214,
 321, 335
 Ninth, 262–63, 276
 Tenth, 285, 335, 337
 Fourteenth, 51, 68–69, 81, 117, 121,
 128, 170, 183, 192, 198, 244, 261,
 263, 272, 287–88, 290, 293, 301,
 321, 335–36
Constitutional Conventions, 336–38
Conway, Kellyanne, 219–20
Conyers, John, 224
Coogan, Carrie, 166
Cooley, Thomas M., 270
Corbeil, Lark, 220
Corley, Charneshia, 270–72
Corn–Revere, Robert, 189, 191–92
Coulter, Ann, 188–89
Counts, Cynthia, 155
Covert, Joshua, 56–57, 69
Cowan, Peggy, 194
Cox, Donnie, 50, 52, 55, 60
Crews, Harold, 316
criminal asset forfeitures, 96–97, 108–10,
 119
 civil vs., 105, 108–9, 127
criminal justice system abuses, 308–31
 evidence planting and, 313–16
 false confessions and, 311–13
 incarcerations and, 318–23
 reforms and, 308, 327–31, 335
 alleged wrongful arrests and, 309–18
Cruz, Crystal, 20–21
Cuevas, Alba, 20–22

Culture of Fear, A (Dominguez and
 Murphy), 64–65
curtilage, 10–13

Dakota Access Pipeline, 204, 247
Danziger, Phoebe Day, 289
Davis, Kevin, 314
de Blasio, Bill, 200, 266
Dein, Judith, 102–3
DeVenecia, Robert, 45, 47–50, 54
DeVille, Keith, 255
Diamond, Rebekah, 289
DiPiero, Tim, 220
DisruptJ20, 237–38, 252, 255, 258
Dixie State University, 190–92
Dobrovish–Fago, Wyatt and Montana,
 199
Dominguez, Julian, 64–65
Douglas, William O., 149
Dowd, Maureen, 225
DreamHost, 237–38
Dreher, Scott, 269
Drug Enforcement Agency (DEA), 97,
 100–102, 110, 112
drugs, ix, xiv, 9, 219–20, 225
 civil asset forfeitures and, 96–106, 108,
 111–13, 115–16, 118–20, 125, 130
 CPS and, 32, 34, 58
 criminal asset forfeitures and, 108–9
 criminal justice system abuses and,
 313–15, 320, 322, 326–27
 Fort case and, 46–47
 free speech and, 172, 174, 191–95
 Magas case and, 4, 7, 14
 prison system and, 320, 322
 state power run amok and, 270–73,
 277–79, 288
Duane, James, 312–13
DuBois, Maurice, 266
Duncan, David, 320
Durham, Benjamin, 29
Durham, John, 3–7, 12, 14

Eavenson, Harold, 125
Edwards, Ezekiel, 108, 110
Eh Wah, 105–7
Electronic Frontier Foundation (EFF), 163,
 215, 217

Elmhurst, Donna, 37–39, 43–44, 46, 48, 52–54
Elmir, Rana, 152
Emord, Jonathan, 284–86
English common law, 17, 31, 277
Equal Employment Opportunity Commission (EEOC), 297, 305
Equality Act, 304–5, 307
equitable sharing, 97, 102, 110–12
    reform or ending of, 125, 128–30
Evans, Jameka, 297–98

Facebook, 163, 334–35
    embattled First Amendment and, 205–6, 239, 250
    free speech and, 131–45, 149, 187–88, 199
    state power run amok and, 275–76
Fairooz, Desiree, 221–25
Fast and Furious gunrunning fiasco, 228–29
Federal Bureau of Investigation (FBI), 219, 323
    embattled First Amendment and, 204, 229, 231, 238–39, 241–43
    free speech and, 134, 136, 138, 142, 157–60
Federal Reserve, 133, 136, 139, 141
Felix (as described by James Duane), 312–13
Ferguson, Mo., 91–92, 323
Fifth Amendment Integrity Restoration (FAIR) Act, 129
Fire and Fury (Wolff), 235
First Amendment Defense Act (FADA), 169, 296, 298, 304
flag desecration, 131, 146, 184–88, 205
Flaherty, Jordan, 240–41
Flake, Jeff, 231
Flanagan, Paul, 226
Flores–Williams, Jason, 211–12
Food and Drug Administration (FDA), 278–81, 283–85
Forcum, Karen, 47
Foreign Policy, 242–43
Forest Grove Dairy, 280–81
Fort, Esther, 35, 38, 40–44, 47, 49
Fort, Madison, 35–54
    alleged abuse of, 36–48, 50–51, 53–54

CPS interview with, 38–41, 46, 51
    damage done to, 49–50
    Peterlin's deposition and, 52–53
    police interview with, 41, 45–48, 51–52
    psychological evaluations of, 47, 49
    removed from her home, 40–45, 47–49, 51–54
Fort, Molly, 35–54
    and daughter removed from her home, 40–45, 47–49, 51–54
Fort, Nathan, 34–55
    and daughter removed from her home, 40–42, 44–45, 47–49, 52–54
    Peterlin's deposition and, 52–53
Fort case, 34–55
    arrests in, 37, 42
    child abuse allegations in, 36–48, 50–51, 53–54
    hearings, lawsuits, and trials in, 37–38, 41–55, 67
foster care, 67–68, 70, 290
Foundation for Individual Rights in Education (FIRE), 147, 189
Fox News, 62, 71, 126, 170, 201, 204, 227–28, 232–33, 264
Frederick, Joseph, 193–96
free speech, 51, 131–202, 211, 215, 220, 233, 245, 248, 250
    Allred case and, 145–48
    and arrests, imprisonments, and detentions, 147, 151–56, 166–69, 173, 177, 185–88
    Barnes case and, 155–56
    BONG HiTS 4 JESUS case and, 193–96
    censorship and, 132, 148–50, 156, 161, 166, 190, 194, 199, 201
    Dixie State case and, 190–92
    finances and, 131, 151, 153, 155–56, 174, 179, 183, 186, 192–95, 198
    flag desecration and, 131, 184–88
    in future, 259–60
    Hazle case and, 172–74
    and hearings, trials, and lawsuits, 131, 136–37, 142–45, 151–52, 154–57, 159–63, 166–68, 170–84, 186, 188–89, 191–96, 198
    history of, 148–49
    Hudson case and, 175–83

free speech (*continued*)
  Kazan case and, 169–71
  legislation and, 160–64, 188, 190
  Library Connection case and, 157–63
  media and, 131, 137–42, 147, 150–51,
    155–56, 161–62, 166–67, 170, 172,
    174, 187, 189, 193, 197–201
  Mellott case and, 186–88
  paroles and, 172–73
  and Pledge of Allegiance, xv, 184,
    196–98
  prior restraint and, 156–57, 161–62, 175,
    191–92, 201, 235, 285
  protests and, 131–32, 152, 183, 187–89,
    196, 199
  Raub case and, 132–45, 149, 334–35
  Rothe–Kushel case and, 164–68
  schools and, 132, 145–47, 174, 183–84,
    188–202
  Snider case and, 185–86
  social media and, 132–49, 181–82
  Swartzes case and, 153–55, 334
  swearing and, 26–27, 131, 150–56, 186
  Turner case and, 175, 177–82
  Wolf case and, 150–51
Frisbie–Fulton, Gwen and A. S., 207, 255

Gard, Lowell, 167
Garner, Eric, 217, 241, 323
Gaxiola, Officer, 315
Gillibrand, Kirsten, 248
Ginsburg, Ruth Bader, 162, 196
Giuliani, Rudy, 266, 329
Goldstone, Mark, 237
Gonzales, Alberto, 159–60
Gonzalez, Ed, 271
Gonzalez, Milo, 210, 213–14, 254–55
Gonzalez–Pagan, Omar, 297–98, 303–5,
  307
Gordon, Andrew P., 27–29
Gorski, David "Orac," 290
Graham, Donald, 118–19, 130
Grazin' Acres, 281–82
Great Britain, 16–17, 31, 148, 165, 188–89,
  260, 277
Green, Andria and Zoey, 264–65
Gregorio, Ana, 20–21
Grimm, Julie Ann, 213

Griswold v. Connecticut, 262
Guerrero, Taylor, 292–93
Guevara, Che, 190–91
Gumpert, David, 279–80
Gutiérrez, Luis, 311

hairstyles, 200
Hall, John Wesley, 18–19, 30–31
Hamilton, Karen, 45–47
Harder, Charles, 235
Harrington, Deron, 267–68
Harris, DeAndre, 316–17
Harris, Oliver, 253
Harrison, Bobby, 292–93
Hazle, Barry, Jr., 172–74
Health and Human Services Department,
  U.S. (HHS), 219, 287, 299, 306
Healy, Bret, 336
Heller, John, 174
Heller v. District of Columbia, x
Henry, Patrick, xi, 133, 138–39
Hershberger, Vernon, 281–83
Hess, George, 266
Hession, Gregory, 55–56, 60, 68–70
Hewitt, Seymour, 266
Heyman, Daniel Ralph, 219–21
Hinders, Carole, 122–25
Hively, Kimberly, 297
Hobby Lobby, 171
Hochstetler, David, 280–81
Holder, Eric:
  embattled First Amendment and, 225,
    227–29
  equitable sharing and, 111–12, 125
Holland, Mary, 288
Homeland Security Department, U.S.
  (DHS), 121, 204, 226–27, 229,
  243
homeless people, 92, 114, 268–69
Horse, Shay, 207–8, 210–11, 213–14
Horton, Mark, 296–98
Hudson, Audrey, 226–27
Hudson, Henry, 143
Hudson, Karen, 175–83
Hudson, Rocky, 175–77, 179, 181
Huizar, Laura, 79–80
Human Rights Watch, 78–79, 83, 86
Hunter, Alec, 267–68

immigrants, immigration, 132, 240, 284
    civil asset forfeitures and, 99, 105–7
    criminal justice system abuses and,
        308–11, 321, 329
    undocumented, ix, 99, 284, 310, 321, 335
Insogna, Richard, 153–54
Institute for Justice (IJ), 96–97, 102–4,
    106–9, 111, 114, 116–18, 120–23, 127
Internal Revenue Service (IRS), 121–25,
    128–29
Israel, 164–65, 240, 248

Jackson, Robert H., xv, 184
Jacobson, Henning, 287–88
Jehovah's Witnesses, 184, 198
Jergins, William, 191
Jews, 149, 164–69, 297, 329
Johnston, Joseph, 62
Jones, Darren, 266
judges, justices, xiii, xv, 333–34
    civil asset forfeitures and, 102–3, 109,
        113–14, 117–18, 121, 123, 127
    CPS and, 33, 45, 61–63, 67, 70–72
    criminal justice system abuses and, 312,
        315–18, 323, 327
    embattled First Amendment and, 215,
        223–24, 228, 230, 232, 234, 238,
        252–53, 256–57, 259
    Fort case and, 42–43, 45–50
    free speech and, 136–37, 140, 143–44,
        150, 152–56, 160–62, 167–68, 173–84,
        186, 188, 194–96
    Kids for Cash scandal and, 317–18
    LFOs and, 89–90
    Magas case and, 7, 12–16
    Mitchell case and, 27–29
    prison system and, 76–79, 81–84, 90,
        92–93, 323
    searches and, 1, 7, 12, 14–16
    state power run amok and, 271, 277,
        281–82, 287, 291, 297, 302–3
Judicial Correction Services Inc. (JCS),
    75–81, 86, 94
Justice Department, U. S. (DOJ), 121
    civil asset forfeitures and, 97–99, 110–12,
        123–24
    criminal justice system abuses and,
        320–21, 324–25

embattled First Amendment and,
    204–6, 212, 224–25, 227–29, 233,
    235–38, 242, 250–51, 255–59
Ferguson case and, 91–92
free speech and, 132, 163
prison system and, 91–92, 94, 320–21
state power run amok and, 280–81, 302,
    305–6

Kain, Erik, 265
Kavanaugh, Brett, 188, 334
Kazan, Malak, 169–71
Keach, Elmer Robert, III, 155, 334
Keller, Jack, 208
Kelly, John, 231–32
Kempenich, Keith, 247
Kemper, R. Crosby, III, 166–67
Kennedy, Anthony, 277
Kids for Cash scandal, 317–18
King, Shaun, 200
Kinsley, Michael, 274
Kleinfeld, Judge, 194
Knox, Terrance, 325–26
Koehler, Judy, 175, 178
Korionoff, Ramon, 15
Korson, Mark, 60–61
Kozinski, Alex, 312
Kroger, 150–51
Krauthammer, Charles, 274
Kunz, Joanna, 120

Lagesse, Elizabeth, 209–11, 213–14, 236,
    249–51, 253–59
Lambda Legal, 294–98, 303–4
Landry, India, 196–98
Landry, Kizzy, 197–98
Latinos, 21, 234, 247, 310–11, 320–21,
    324–26
Lauría, Carlos, 211
Lawson, Brittne, 253
Leary, Brian, 138
legal financial obligations (LFOs), 84–90, 94
Leibovitz, Lynn, 252–53
lemonade stand raids, 261, 264–65
lesbian, gay, bisexual, and transgender
    (LGBT) people, 187, 222
    denied room at bed and breakfast,
        294–96

lesbian (*continued*)
  and employment, 296–98, 304–6
  in future, 304–7
  kissing, 292–93
  oppressed at school, 299–304
  and state power run amok, 291–307
Leslie, Gregg, 212
Leventhal, Jason, 22
Levi, Debbie Katz, 313, 315
libel, 156, 201, 205, 234–35
Liberty Counsel, 62, 196, 201
Library Connection, Inc., 157–63
Lincoln, Abraham, xi
Locklar, Ben, 326–27
Louima, Abner, 329
Lowery, Eddie, 313
Lugo, Evelyn, 19–21
Lugo, George, 20–22

McCarron, Greg, 164, 166, 168
McDonald, Laquan, 324
McGrath, Lee, 96, 108, 120–21
Madison, James, 148, 262
Magas, Cathy, 2–6, 8, 10, 14
Magas, Eric, 6, 8
Magas, George, 2–10, 13–14, 16, 19
Magas, Marc, 5–6
Magas, Nicholas, 3–4, 6–8
Magas case, 2–16, 18–19, 30
  alcohol in, 2–4, 6–9, 12–13, 16, 18–19
  assaults and arrests in, 5–7, 9, 19
  charges in, 6–10, 14–15
  damages to home in, 7–8
  and hearings, trials, and lawsuits, 10–16
Maher, Bill, 234
Makled, Amir, 170
Maldonado, Raul, 201
Martin, John T., 63
Mason, George, 120–21, 133, 138–39
Masterpiece Cakeshop v. Colorado Civil
  Rights Commission, 295, 298
Mathews, Bo, 326
Mayton–Swartz, Judy, 153–55, 334
media, x, xiv–xv, , 28, 333–34
  chilling effects on, 215, 220–21, 225,
    227, 230, 234
  civil asset forfeitures and, 97–99, 105–7,
    111, 113–14, 116–18, 124–26, 129–30

CPS abuses and, 59, 62–63, 66, 70–71
criminal justice system abuses and, 308,
  310–15, 317, 321, 324–26
embattled First Amendment and,
  203–35, 237, 240–43, 245–47,
  253–55, 259–60
Fort case and, 34–35, 54–55
free speech and, 131, 137–42, 147,
  150–51, 155–56, 161–62, 166–67, 170,
  172, 174, 187, 189, 193, 197–201
Lugo case and, 19–20, 22
Magas case and, 7–10, 15–16
Mitchell case and, 23–24, 27
prison system and, 73, 80, 82, 85–86,
  93–94, 321
questioning public officials and, 216–21
and spying on reporters, 225–30
state power run amok and, 261, 263–69,
  271–72, 274, 278, 281–83, 288–93,
  303, 306–7
Trump's assault on, 230–31
Mellott, Bryton, 186–88
Merritt, S. Lee, 316–17
Mertz, Douglas, 195
Mewborn, Michael:
  child abuse allegations made by, 36–38,
    40, 42–43, 45–46, 54
  Fort case and, 35–38, 40, 42–49, 52–54
Mewborn, Pamela, 35–36, 48–49, 53
Michaux, Henry, 246–47
Michelman, Scott, 214, 250, 253–55
middle finger, 26–27, 152–56
Middleton, Richard, 176
Mihet, Horatio, 201
Milbank, Dana, 228
military, military veterans, 52, 90, 325
  distinction between police and, 28–29
  embattled First Amendment and,
    226–27, 231–32
  free speech and, 132–35, 139–40, 142–44,
    149, 153, 174, 185, 188, 334–35
Miller, Emily, 213
minorities, 126, 187, 308, 336
  embattled First Amendment and, 209,
    216
  prison system and, 90–92
  state power run amok and, 267, 272,
    291–307

Mishanki, Kevin, 318
Mitchell, Anthony, 23–28
Mitchell, Linda, 23–26, 28
Mitchell, Michael, 23, 25–27
Mitchell case, 23–29
  arrests in, 25–29
  charges in, 25–27
  home commandeered in, 23–27
  lawsuit in, 23–24, 26–29
  violence in, 23–26, 28
MK–Ultra, 141
Modesto Community College, 192–93
Mohamed, Ahmed, 18
money laundering, 98, 111, 122
Moore, Michel, 330
Morin, Robert E., 223–24, 238, 257,
  259
Morse, Deborah, 193–94
Mrs. Lady's Mexican Food, 122–25
Mueller, Robert, III, 158, 160
Murphy, Melinda, 64–66, 68
Muslims, ix, 202, 309–10
  embattled First Amendment and, 217,
    239, 241, 243–45
  free speech and, 169–72
  surveillance of, 241, 243–44

NAACP v. Claiborne Hardware, 250
Nader, Ralph, 275, 279
Napolitano, Andrew, 228
national anthem, 183, 197–98, 205
National Football League (NFL), 183,
  197–98, 205
National Security Agency (NSA), 216–17
national security letters (NSLs), 157–64
Native Americans, ix, 204, 285, 336
NBC, NBC News, 8, 205, 216–17,
  230–31, 307, 311
Neal, Danesiah, 267
Newton, Alice, 63
New York Daily News, The, 265
  free speech and, 147, 197–98, 200
  Lugo case and, 20, 22
New York Times, The, 124, 306, 317, 334
  embattled First Amendment and, 225,
    230, 232–35
  free speech and, 155, 161–62
  prison system and, 73, 93

9/11, 133, 135–36, 139, 141, 144, 157,
  164–65, 226
Nixon, Richard, xiv, 228, 232
NPR, 83, 85–86, 222, 290, 315

Obama, Barack, ix, xiii–xiv, 126, 164,
  219
  criminal justice system and, 321,
    323–24
  embattled First Amendment and,
    203–4, 211, 216, 218, 225, 227–28,
    233–34
  free speech and, 131, 148, 163, 184–85,
    190–91
  state power run amok and, 280, 283,
    291, 302–3, 305–7
Occupy Wall Street, 139, 204, 239
Ochoa–Perez, Rebecca, 38, 40–44
O'Connor, Maureen, 93
O'Connor, Sandra Day, 288
Ortega, Luis, 20–22
Ortiz, Carmen, 102
Orwell, George, 187, 215–16, 227
Otis, James, 17–18
Otter, Butch, 130

Palestine, Palestinians, 165, 240–41
Pantaleo, Daniel, 323
Papa, Stephan, 90
Paris, Michael, 135
Paschall, Kimberly, 223
Paul, Rand, 129
Paxton, Ken, 198
Pelletier, Justina, 60–63
Pelletier, Lou and Linda, 61–62
Pence, Karen, 307
Pence, Mike, 306–7
Pepper, Pamela, 302
Perez, Lucy, 38–42, 45–48, 52–53
Perkins, Tony, 306
Peterlin, Paul, 43, 52–54
Peters, Matthew, 186
Phillips, Jack, 171
Phinn, Melissa, 315
Pigeon, Dustin, 326
Pinheiro, Richard A., Jr., 313–16
Pitt, William, 16
Pledge of Allegiance, xv, 184, 196–98

police, xiii, 308–16, 334–35, 337
  body cams and, 313–14, 328
  brutality and overkill of, 1, 5–6, 9, 19–22,
     24, 26–31, 91, 107–8, 110–11, 217, 241,
     261–77, 291, 313, 323–27, 329
  civil asset forfeitures and, 96–97, 99–101,
     103–7, 109–11, 113, 116–18, 120,
     125–30
  CPS and, 32, 57, 70
  criminal asset forfeitures and, 108–9
  defending yourself against, 30–31
  distinction between military and, 28–29
  embattled First Amendment and,
     206–14, 217, 219–20, 222–23, 226,
     236–37, 239–45, 247–50, 255–56, 258
  equitable sharing and, 102, 110–12, 128
  Fort case and, 36–37, 40–42, 44–48,
     51–52
  free speech and, 131, 134–36, 138, 144,
     146–47, 150–56, 164–68, 170, 178,
     183, 186–88, 191, 196–97, 201
  lemonade stand raids of, 261, 264–65
  Lugo case and, 19–22
  Magas case and, 2–3, 16, 18–19, 30
  militarization of, 29–30
  Mitchell case and, 71–72
  pepper spray used by, 20–21, 24–26,
     206–10, 213–14, 255
  prison system and, 320–22
  reforms and, 327–31
  searches and, 1–2, 4–15, 18–22, 261–62,
     269–75, 280–81
  state power run amok and, 261–77,
     280–81, 290–93
  alleged wrongful arrests and, 19, 21–22,
     309–13
Politico, 203
Posse Comitatus Act, 28
poverty, 16, 63–64, 187, 336
  civil asset forfeitures and, 98, 126, 129
  LFOs and, 88, 90
  prison system and, 73–86, 88, 93–95
  state power run amok and, 265, 268–69
Powell, Robert, 50, 52–54, 57, 63, 66–67
Price, Tom, 219–20
prisons, prison system, 8, 10, 21, 26, 29, 39,
     51, 55, 73–95, 105, 311–23, 335
  debtors', 73, 82, 84, 89–90, 92–93

  denial of health care in, 318–20
  embattled First Amendment and, 204,
     206, 212, 219, 222, 231, 247, 249, 252,
     258
  free speech and, 132, 135, 141, 144,
     151–53, 155, 166–67, 172–75, 177–79,
     185–87, 190
  lawsuits and, 78–84, 95, 319–21
  LFOs and, 84–90, 94
  minorities and, 90–92
  probations and, 75–79, 81–83, 85–86, 90
  reforms and, 81–82, 87, 92–95, 308, 319
  sentencings and, 75, 77–78, 82–83, 85
  sobering statistics on, 321–23
  state power run amok and, 266–67, 277,
     290
  for unpaid traffic and criminal fines,
     74–85, 88, 90–94
  alleged wrongful arrests and, 311–18
privacy, 51, 132, 261
  embattled First Amendment and, 239,
     243
  Magas case and, 10–15
  searches and, 1–2, 10–11, 13–14, 228
  state power run amok and, 263, 269–70,
     272, 282, 284, 285
Profiting from Probation, 78–79
Project Veritas, 251, 256–57
prosecutors, xiii–xiv, 33, 85, 109
  civil asset forfeitures and, 96–97, 102–7,
     110, 114–18, 120–21, 126–28, 130
  corruption of, 107–8
  criminal justice system abuses and, 308,
     314, 317, 326, 330
  embattled First Amendment and,
     211–12, 220–21, 224, 236–37, 251,
     254–55, 257–59
  equitable sharing and, 110, 112, 128
  Fort case and, 46–47, 49, 52
  free speech and, 132, 135, 152, 166–67
  Magas case and, 10, 12–15
  state power run amok and, 266, 268,
     280, 282, 292
protests, 261, 337
  chilling effects on, 214–15, 224–25, 245,
     250, 253
  criminal justice abuses system and,
     316–17, 324

embattled First Amendment and,
204–16, 221–25, 236–42, 245–58
free speech and, 131–32, 152, 183,
187–89, 196, 199
outlawing of, 245–48
spying on, 236–39
Pruitt, Gary, 227

race, racism, 21, 91, 296, 298
criminal justice system abuses and,
320–22, 325–26
embattled First Amendment and, 234,
240, 242, 244–45
free speech and, 132, 145–48, 183,
190–91
prison system and, 320–21
Ramirez, David, 89–90
Raub, Brandon, 132–45, 334–35
background of, 133–37, 140, 142–44,
149
detention of, 135–42
interrogations of, 134–36, 144
litigations and, 136–37, 142–45
psychological evaluations of, 135–45
raw milk, 278–86, 335
FDA and, 278–81, 283–85
founders and, 285–86
Hershberger case and, 281–83
Hochstetler case and, 280–81
situation today and, 283–85
Reilly, Ryan, 223
Reinhardt, Stephen Roy, 71–72
Reitzig, Liz, 283–84
religions, religion, xv, 35, 261, 337
First Amendment and, 148–49, 168–74,
184, 187, 200–202, 241, 243–45
state power run amok and, 268, 286–87,
294–99, 306
Renn, Peter, 294–95
Reporters Committee for Freedom of the
Press (RCFP), 212, 220
Reynolds, Glenn, 282
Rice, Tamir, 324
Richie, Andrea J., 271
Rietz, Julia, 188
Risen, James, 225
Robbins, Ira, 153
Roberts, Charlie, 12–13

Roberts, John, 195
Robertson, Rebecca L., 274
Rocah, David, 314–16
Rodgers, April, 58–59
Rogers, Brad, 281
Rosen, James, 204, 227–28
Rosenberg, Tina, 73
Ross, Dennis, 164–66
Rothe–Kushel, Jeremy, 164–68
Rowland, Lee, 234, 245, 250–51
Rubinstein, Dorit, 289–90
Russia, 101, 141–42, 158, 163, 184, 208,
221, 231, 308
Rutgers University, 145–47, 244
Rutherford Institute, 132, 137, 140,
142–44, 270
Ryan, Charles, 320

Salant, Steven G., 12–14
same–sex couples and marriages, 262, 337
and free speech, 169, 171
and state power run amok, 291–96
Sanders, Bernie, 189, 307
Sanders, Sarah Huckabee, 205, 231–32
Sandler, Rene, 9–11, 13, 15–16, 30
Sargent, John, 235
Sarwark, Nicholas, 126
Scalia, Antonin, x, 185, 188, 338
schools, xiv–xv, 3, 8, 18, 56–57, 74, 105
criminal justice system abuses and,
326–27
embattled First Amendment and, 244,
248, 259
free speech and, 132, 145–47, 174,
183–84, 188–202
state power run amok and, 267–68, 277,
284, 286–89, 291–92, 297, 299–304,
306–7
Schuver, Mark S., 298
searches, 1–31, 71, 310
civil asset forfeitures and, 97, 105–7,
118–19
embattled First Amendment and, 204,
226–28, 236–38, 250
exigent circumstances and, 1–2, 7, 9–10,
12, 22, 51
Fort case and, 36, 42, 51
in history, 16–17

searches (*continued*)
Lugo case and, 19–22
Magas case and, 4–16, 18–19, 30
Mitchell case and, 23–29
probable cause in, 1, 4, 10, 12, 17,
21–22, 30
seizures and, 1, 11, 17–18, 28, 51, 83,
105–7, 157, 226–27, 261, 335
state power run amok and, 261–62,
269–77, 280–81
unreasonable, 1, 11, 51, 68, 83, 51
warrantless, 2–3, 15, 18–28, 30–31, 42,
97, 271–73, 280–81, 335
Secret Service, 134, 138, 143, 219, 221
Seinfeld, Jerry and Jessica, 265
Sessions, Jeff, 132, 221–24
civil asset forfeitures and, 112, 126
embattled First Amendment and, 205–6,
212, 222–24, 236–38
state power run amok and, 305–6
Sessoms (defendant), 312
Severino, Roger, 299
sex, 137, 234, 277, 322
abuse and, 34, 37–39, 41, 44–45, 58, 63,
71, 135
free speech and, 190–91, 194
same, 169, 171, 262, 291–307, 337
state power run amok and, 269, 271,
273–76
Sharrett, Allan, 140
Shelby, Richard, 221–22
Shelton v. Tucker, 189
Sheth, Darpana, 118
Shibley, Robert L., 147
Shields, Ronald, 315
Siegel, Norman, 233, 239, 259–60, 338
police reform and, 328–31
Smalley, Jeremy, 3–5, 12, 14
Snider, Frank, 185–86
Snowden, Edward, 216
Socially Responsible Agricultural Project
(SRAP), 175, 181
social media, 282, 316, 333
embattled First Amendment and,
236–37, 251, 255
free speech and, 132–49, 181–82
Solomon, John, 226
Somin, Ilya, 28–29

Sourovelis, Christos, 112–17
Sourovelis, Markela, 113–17
Sourovelis, Yanni, 112–13, 115–16
Souter, David, 195–96
Speciale, Michael, 246
speech codes, 189–90
Stack, Tom, 3, 13–14
Starks, Paul, 16
Starr, Kenneth, 194–95
Staver, Mat, 62
Stern, Caroline, 266
Stevens, Jacqueline, 311
Stevens, John Paul, 196
Strother, Martha, 197–98
structuring, 122, 124, 128–29
Sullivan, Kevin, 181–82
Super, David A., 337
Supreme Court, U.S., xv, 262, 318,
333–34, 336, 338
civil asset forfeitures and, 119–20
curtilage and, 10–11, 13
embattled First Amendment and, 215,
235, 245, 250–51, 257
free speech and, 144–45, 149, 152–53,
159, 162, 171, 184–85, 188–89,
194–96, 198
prison system and, 82–84, 91, 93
state power run amok and, 276–77,
287–88, 291, 295, 298, 303
Swartwood, Joanna, 59–60
Swartz, John, 153–55, 334
swearing, 26–27, 131, 150–56, 186
Sweeney, Keith, 326

Takei, Carl, 90
Terminiello v. Chicago, 149
Thomas, Clarence, 195–96
Thomas, Shanekia, 76–77
Thompson, Kevin, 74–86, 90, 94
Tiven, Rachel B., 295
Tobias, Harry, 49–50
Transportation Security Administration
(TSA), 226, 269–70, 274–76
Transue, Hillary, 318
Trop v. Dulles, 185
Truman, Harry, 164–65, 168
Trump, Donald J., xiii, 29, 71, 218–22,
333–34, 336

civil asset forfeitures and, 99, 104, 112, 125–26
criminal justice system abuses and, 320–21
embattled First Amendment and, 203–7, 209–10, 212, 218–21, 224, 228, 230–39, 242, 245, 249, 259–60
free speech and, 131–32, 145–46, 148, 169, 171, 183, 185, 196, 199
and Russian interference in U.S. elections, 158, 163
state power run amok and, 283–85, 291, 298–99, 302, 304–6
Turner, Susan, 175, 177–82
Tyner, John, 269–70, 274

USA Patriot Act, 157–64
USA Today, 221, 253, 290

vaccinations, 32, 278, 286–90, 319
vanden Heuvel, Katrina, 274
Van Dyke, Jason, 324

Waite, Daren, 114–15
Waithe, Elsa, 242
Ward, Tamara, 278
Washington, George, 139
Washington Post, The, 28, 324
   civil asset forfeitures and, 97, 106–7
   embattled First Amendment and, 212, 216, 220, 228, 242, 245
Washington Times, The, 226–27, 278

Washington v. Harper, 288
Watson, Jan, 319–20
Webber, Kandice, 272
Webermann, Michael, 209, 236, 249–50, 254, 258
Weeks, James, II, 152
Weithorn, Lois, 289–90
West Virginia v. Barnette, xv, 184
Wexler, Chuck, 328–29
Whitaker, Ashton, 299–303
White, Phillip, 23, 25–26, 29
Whitehead, John W., 137–40, 143, 270
Wightman, Tom, 151
Williams, Seth, 116–17
Williamson, Jennifer and Aaron, 275–76
Wilson, Courtney, 292–93
Wilson, Darren, 323–24
Wilson, Frederica, 231–32
Wilson, John K., 147–48
Wolf, Danielle, 150–51
Wolff, Michael, 235
Wood, Alexei, 208, 212–13, 251
Woolfolk, Steve, 166–67
Wyden, Ron, 216–17

Yiannopoulos, Milo, 188–89
Young, Elizabeth, 118–20, 130
Young, Phyllis, 294–96

Zarda, Donald, 297, 305
Zavala, Christina, 200–201
Zucker, Samantha, 266

civil asset forfeitures and, 99, 104, 112,
   125–26
criminal justice system abuses and,
   320–21
embattled First Amendment and, 203–7,
   209–10, 212, 218–21, 224, 228,
   230–39, 242, 245, 249, 259–60
free speech and, 131–32, 145–46, 148,
   169, 171, 183, 185, 196, 199
and Russian interference in U.S.
   elections, 158, 163
state power run amok and, 283–85, 291,
   298–99, 302, 304–6
Turner, Susan, 175, 177–82
Tyner, John, 269–70, 274

USA Patriot Act, 157–64
USA Today, 221, 253, 290

vaccinations, 32, 278, 286–90, 319
vanden Heuvel, Katrina, 274
Van Dyke, Jason, 324

Waite, Daren, 114–15
Waithe, Elsa, 242
Ward, Tamara, 278
Washington, George, 139
Washington Post, The, 28, 324
   civil asset forfeitures and, 97, 106–7
   embattled First Amendment and, 212,
      216, 220, 228, 242, 245
Washington Times, The, 226–27, 278

Washington v. Harper, 288
Watson, Jan, 319–20
Webber, Kandice, 272
Webermann, Michael, 209, 236, 249–50,
   254, 258
Weeks, James, II, 152
Weithorn, Lois, 289–90
West Virginia v. Barnette, xv, 184
Wexler, Chuck, 328–29
Whitaker, Ashton, 299–303
White, Phillip, 23, 25–26, 29
Whitehead, John W., 137–40, 143, 270
Wightman, Tom, 151
Williams, Seth, 116–17
Williamson, Jennifer and Aaron, 275–76
Wilson, Courtney, 292–93
Wilson, Darren, 323–24
Wilson, Frederica, 231–32
Wilson, John K., 147–48
Wolf, Danielle, 150–51
Wolff, Michael, 235
Wood, Alexei, 208, 212–13, 251
Woolfolk, Steve, 166–67
Wyden, Ron, 216–17

Yiannopoulos, Milo, 188–89
Young, Elizabeth, 118–20, 130
Young, Phyllis, 294–96

Zarda, Donald, 297, 305
Zavala, Christina, 200–201
Zucker, Samantha, 266